THE
BEST OF
FOOD & WINE
1985 COLLECTION

THE BEST OF FOOD&WINE
1985 COLLECTION

American Express
Publishing Corporation
New York

Kentucky Burgoo (p. 87) reprinted from *Honest American Fare*, © 1981 by Bert Greene, with permission of Contemporary Books, Inc., Chicago.

Chicken in Beer with Leeks (p. 94) reprinted from *Cuisine of Olympe* by Dominique Nahmias, original © 1982 by Editions Menges; American © 1983 by New Century Publishers, Inc., Piscataway, New Jersey 08854.

Fromage Blanc (p. 117) from *Michel Guérard's Cuisine Minceur*. English translation © 1976 by William Morrow and Company, Inc. Originally published in French under the title *La Grande Cuisine Minceur* © 1976 by Editions Robert Laffont, S.A. By permission of William Morrow.

Simone Beck's Le Diabolo (p. 170) from *Simca's Cuisine*, by Simone Beck, in collaboration with Patricia Simon. Copyright © 1972 by Simone Beck and Patricia Simon. Reprinted by permission of Alfred A. Knopf, Inc.

Curried Pear Butter (p. 221) from *Another Blue Strawbery: More Brilliant Cooking Without Recipes*, © 1983 by James Haller. Published by The Harvard Common Press, 535 Albany St., Boston, MA 02118.

The Best of Food & Wine/1985 Collection
Editor: Kate Slate
Art Director: Bette Duke
Designers: René-Julien Aussoleil, Loretta Sala
Copy Editor: Lilyan Glusker
Editorial Assistants: Martha Crow, Melinda Roberts

© 1985 American Express Publishing Corporation

Published by American Express Publishing Corporation
1120 Avenue of the Americas, New York, New York 10036

Manufactured in the United States of America

Library of Congress Cataloging in Publication Data

Main entry under title:

The Best of Food & Wine

Includes index.
1. Cookery, International. I American Express Publishing Corporation II. Food & Wine (New York, NY) III. Title: Best of Food & Wine
TX725.A1B4823 1985   641.5'14   84-24565
ISBN 0-916103-01-3

10 9 8 7 6 5 4 3 2 1
First Edition

TABLE OF CONTENTS

FOREWORD

Welcome to *The Best of Food & Wine/1985 Collection,* more than 490 recipes and 32 pages of glorious color photographs from issues of our magazine that appeared during the past year. This volume is the successor to our very well received inaugural *Best of Food & Wine* cookbook.

Those of you who know our magazine realize how highly we prize the food we present in each issue. Those who do not can rest assured that every recipe in *Food & Wine,* and therefore every recipe in this volume, has been tested and, where necessary, adapted or adjusted for use by home cooks. Two major responsibilities of our Test Kitchen cooks are to create workable recipes filled with flavor, and to simplify food preparation without robbing dishes of their fundamental integrity.

Where do these recipes come from? Some, a higher percentage than in any other American epicurean magazine, are developed by the Test Kitchen staff itself. During the period of time spanned by the contents of this book, our kitchen was directed by Diana Sturgis. Her principal assistants are John Robert Massie and Anne Disrude. Other recipes are sent to us by readers for inclusion in our monthly "Simply Splendid" column. Most of the remainder are created by contributors to the magazine. You will find a list crediting these talented cooks and writers on pages 239-240.

The recipes that we have gathered together represent a balance of foods and of the various courses that make a meal. They also represent what we feel to be a superb sampling of the best of contemporary cooking, delicious and beautiful food equally suitable for your family or for entertaining the best of friends.

—William Rice
Editor-in-Chief

FOOD & WINE'S VINTAGE RATINGS
1973-1983

COMPILED BY ELIN McCOY & JOHN FREDERICK WALKER

	1973	1974	1975	1976	1977
Red Bordeaux	5 Light, fruity, soft. Most past it.	4 No charm. Hard & lightweight. Drink now.	9 Classic, concentrated. Start drinking. Will last.	7 Soft, full, attractive. Drink now.	4 Lightweight, lacks fruit. Best now.
Sauternes	4 Lightweight & little character. Drink up.	3 Very poor. Avoid.	9 Deep, rich; some classics. Start drinking.	9 Elegant & luscious. Start drinking.	3 Very weak. Avoid.
Red Burgundy	6 Light & pleasant; fading fast. Don't wait.	4 Light & lean; no depth. Now or never.	3 Thin, weak; most are poor. Avoid.	7 Deep, full, tannic. Drink now.	4 Light, thin, uneven. Drink now.
White Burgundy	6 Attractive, fruity. Most past best.	4 Thin & fading. Most past best.	4 Very light wines. Drink up.	7 Big, soft, rich wines. Drink now.	5 Light, lean, acidic. Drink now.
Napa/Sonoma Cabernet Sauvignon	7 Very good, well-balanced year. Drink up.	8 Fat, rich, tannic; some overripe. Drink now.	7 Lacks power, but best have elegance. Drink now.	7 Variable. Many heavy and tannic. Drink now.	7½ Variable. Some well-balanced wines. Drink now.
Napa/Sonoma Chardonnay	7 Fragrant, fruity, fading. Most past it.	6 Full-bodied, fast-maturing. Most past it.	8 Intense, well-balanced. Drink now.	6 Big, ripe; some too powerful. Drink up.	7 Uneven. Some attractive. Drink now.
Piedmont Barolo & Barbaresco	5 Light & fragrant. Drink now.	8 Excellent, full & round. Drink now.	5 Light & attractive. Drink now.	6 Light, well-balanced. Drink now.	4 Light, thin wines. Drink now.
Chianti	5 Variable: fair to very good. Fading. Drink up.	6 Light, pleasant, fading. Drink up.	9 Exceptional. Well-balanced wines. Now ready.	3 Lightweight, disappointing. Now or never.	7 Good to very good; firm, stylish. Drink now.
Germany	6 Appealing, soft wines; most past best. Drink up.	5 Uneven & fading. Drink up.	8 Excellent balance, stylish. Drink now.	9½ Super-rich wines. Enjoy; best balanced will keep.	6 Lightweight, crisp. Drink up.
Vintage Porto	No vintage declared.	No vintage declared.	6½ Light & stylish. Try in 2-4 years. Some wines fast-maturing.	No vintage declared.	9½ Superlative; ripe & dense. Wait 8-10 years.

The following ratings and comments reflect a variety of opinions, including our own, on the quality and character of various categories of wines from recent vintages. The ratings—0 for the worst, 10 for the best—are averages, and better or worse wine than indicated can be found in each vintage. Assessments of the most current vintages are more predictive and hence less exact than those of older vintages.

Scores are based on a wine's quality at maturity. A lower-rated but mature wine will often be superior to a higher-rated but immature wine. When-to-drink advice is based on how such wines seemed to be developing in mid-1984, and presumes good storage. The earliest date suggested for consumption applies to the lesser wines of the vintage, which will mature faster than the finest examples of that year.

1978	1979	1980	1981	1982	1983
8½ Rich, full, good depth. Wait 2-5 years.	8 Fruity & delicious. Start drinking.	5 Small-scale, lightweight, pleasant. Not for keeping.	7½ Well-balanced wines. Wait 3 years.	10 Fabulous. Try in 4-8 years.	8 Firm, powerful. Try in 5 years.
5 Big, but lacks typical richness. Drink now.	6 Light but has character. Now.	7 Attractive, small-scale. Now.	7½ Well-balanced wines. Start drinking.	7 Variable. Best are big, powerful wines. Sample now.	9 Very promising, rich, classic wines.
8 Outstanding; excellent balance. Drink now.	6 Soft, supple, appealing. Drink now.	7 Mostly light wines for early drinking.	6 Variable vintage. Most early maturing.	7 Big, soft wines. Drink now.	9 Very good, powerful wines. Start sampling.
9 Superb; well-balanced. Wonderful now.	7 Attractive, fruity wines. Most best now.	5 Variable; the best are attractive.	8 Attractive wines for early drinking.	9 Excellent. Big, rich wines. Start drinking.	8 Good, promising wines.
8½ Full, rich, balanced. Start drinking; best will keep.	7 Uneven quality; some very good. Start drinking.	9 Excellent, well-balanced. Will keep.	7 Variable. Early maturing; try now.	7 Lighter style; some attractive. Try now.	7 Good, but not particularly promising.
8 Powerful, ripe wines. Drink now.	8 Rich, intense, impressive. Drink now.	9 Many have superb balance. Drink now.	7 Soft, ripe wines. Drink now.	7 Many light, some excellent. Start drinking.	7 Good moderate year.
9 Classic, concentrated & tannic. Wait 2-4 years; will last.	8 Elegant, well-balanced wines. Start drinking; will hold.	6 Uneven. Best are well-balanced, attractive. Start drinking.	7 Firm, solid wines. Start sampling.	8½ Big, powerful wines; very promising. Wait 2-5 years.	7½ Promising vintage.
9 Exceptional; big, solid, tannic. Start drinking; will hold.	7 Attractive, ripe wines. Drink now.	6 Uneven; best are small-scale.	7 Good, firm wines.	8 Attractive but early maturing.	8 Attractive, early maturing.
6 Lightweight, crisp. Drink up.	7 Good quality & balance. Drink now.	5 Light & lean. Drink now.	8 Well-balanced, attractive. Drink now.	7 Soft, fruity. Drink now.	9 Excellent year. Marvelous late-harvest wines. Start tasting.
5 Not generally declared. Rich, soft. Try in 3-4 years.	No vintage declared.	7 Light but promising. Sample in 5-8 years.	No vintage declared.	8 Firm, well-balanced.	———

BEVERAGES

Rye-Rum Eggnog

Rich and creamy, eggnog is a festive holiday drink. This recipe, from *Food & Wine*'s test kitchen director, Diana Sturgis, makes a large batch suitable for a party or for bottling to give to friends. Eggnog will keep, refrigerated, for up to one week.

MAKES ABOUT 5 QUARTS

18 eggs, separated
2 cups confectioners' sugar
2 quarts milk
1 bottle (1 liter) rye whiskey
1½ cups dark rum
3 cups heavy cream
Freshly grated nutmeg

1. In a large mixer bowl, beat the egg yolks and sugar until thick and pale, about 3 minutes. Scrape into a punch bowl or a large pot. Stir in the milk, rye and rum.

2. In a medium bowl, beat the cream until soft peaks form. Fold into the milk mixture until well blended.

3. Beat the egg whites until stiff but not dry. Fold into the eggnog until blended. Sprinkle a generous amount of nutmeg over the eggnog, and stir until the spice is evenly distributed. Refrigerate, covered, until serving time.

Hot French Cocktail

4 SERVINGS

1⅔ cups milk
¼ cup (2 ounces) orange liqueur, such as Grand Marnier
2 tablespoons (1 ounce) Cognac

1. Fill a blender with hot water and set aside to warm.

2. In a medium saucepan, warm the milk over moderately high heat, whisk-ing vigorously to create a foamy layer of bubbles. Pour the water out of the blender. Pour in the hot milk.

3. Blend at medium speed until very foamy and frothy, about 30 seconds. Add the orange liqueur and Cognac and blend for 30 seconds longer. Pour into four 8-ounce wine glasses and serve hot.

Prince of Wales Cocktail

This festive cocktail, created especially for Prince Charles's investiture, may be served by itself or with desserts.

2 SERVINGS

1 ounce (2 tablespoons) fresh lemon juice
½ ounce (1 tablespoon) cherry-flavored brandy
1½ teaspoons superfine sugar
8 ounces (1 cup) chilled Champagne
2 whole strawberries, for garnish

Shake the lemon juice, brandy and sugar with ice until the sugar is dissolved. Strain into two tall stemmed glasses. Fill with Champagne and stir briefly to mix. Garnish each with a strawberry.

La Côte St-Jacques Dans Un Verre

A full-bodied orange cocktail served at La Côte St-Jacques restaurant in Burgundy. If you like, the rim of the glass may be moistened and then dipped in sugar.

1 SERVING

1 ounce (2 tablespoons) fresh orange juice, chilled
½ teaspoon Campari, chilled
½ ounce (1 tablespoon) Grand Marnier, chilled
4 ounces (½ cup) Champagne or sparkling wine, chilled

In a 6-ounce Champagne flute, combine the orange juice, Campari and Grand Marnier. Gently pour in the Champagne and serve at once.

Cocktail Michel Pasquet

Michel Pasquet, at the Paris restaurant bearing his name, macerates his own bitter cherries to garnish this cocktail.

1 SERVING

½ ounce (1 tablespoon Cherry Marnier or other cherry liqueur, chilled
½ teaspoon gin, chilled
4 ounces (½ cup) Champagne or sparkling wine, chilled
1 bitter cherry macerated in eau-de-vie (optional)

In a 6-ounce tulip-shaped glass, combine the Cherry Marnier and the gin. Gently pour in the Champagne. Garnish with the cherry and serve at once.

Taillevent's Cocktail aux Framboises

Taillevent restaurant in Paris serves this cocktail only during fresh raspberry season. We found, however, that frozen raspberries work well.

4 SERVINGS

½ pint (1 cup) fresh raspberries or 1 package (10 ounces) frozen raspberries, thawed and drained
2 teaspoons blue Curaçao, chilled
1 pint (2 cups) Champagne or sparkling wine, chilled
4 thin wedges of fresh pear and 4 fresh raspberries, for garnish

1. In a blender or food processor, puree the raspberries. Pass through a fine-mesh sieve to remove the seeds.

2. Squeeze the puree through a triple layer of dampened cheesecloth to extract a clear juice; there will be about ½ cup.

3. In each of four 6-ounce tulip-shaped glasses, combine 1 ounce (2 tablespoons) of the raspberry juice with ½ teaspoon of the blue Curaçao. Gently pour ½ cup of Champagne into each glass.

4. Spear a pear slice and a fresh raspberry, if available, on a pick to garnish each cocktail. Serve at once.

Yan-Toit de Passy's Optimiste

1 SERVING

½ ounce (1 tablespoon) pear eau-de-vie, chilled
½ ounce (1 tablespoon) blue Curaçao, chilled
1 teaspoon Pimm's No. 1, chilled
4 ounces (½ cup) Champagne or sparkling wine, chilled
A thin wedge of fresh pear, a small sprig of mint and a green maraschino cherry, for garnish

1. In a 6-ounce brandy snifter, combine the eau-de-vie, Curaçao and Pimm's.
2. Gently pour in the Champagne down the side of the snifter. The mixture will foam and you may need to add the Champagne in 2 or 3 parts. Stir gently.
3. Spear the pear, mint and the cherry on a pick and set on the rim of the glass. Serve at once.

Apple Sour

This is a refreshing variation on the classic whiskey sour.

1 SERVING

1 teaspoon superfine sugar
1 tablespoon fresh lemon juice
3 tablespoons (1½ ounces) apple brandy, such as applejack or Calvados

In a container with a tight-fitting lid, combine the sugar, lemon juice and apple brandy. Shake vigorously to dissolve the sugar and serve over ice.

Ramos Gin Fizz

This traditional cocktail offers a sprightly beginning to any brunch.

4 SERVINGS

¼ cup fresh lemon juice
¼ cup fresh lime juice
¼ cup superfine sugar
4 egg whites
¾ cup (6 ounces) gin
¼ cup heavy cream
¾ teaspoon vanilla extract
¾ teaspoon orange flower water
2 cups ice cubes
Seltzer water, chilled

1. Place all the ingredients except the seltzer water into the container of a blender. Puree until thick and foamy, about 30 seconds.
2. Strain the mixture into a pitcher and pour into chilled 8- to 10-ounce glasses. Top with a dash of seltzer water.

Planter's Punch

There are as many rum punches as there are islands in the Caribbean. This version comes from the Royal Caribbean Hotel in Montego Bay, Jamaica.

1 SERVING

1½ ounces (3 tablespoons) gold or dark rum
1 ounce (2 tablespoons) fresh lime juice
1½ ounces (3 tablespoons) plain sugar syrup or 1½ tablespoons sugar dissolved into 1½ tablespoons water
3 ounces (6 tablespoons) unsweetened pineapple juice
Dash of Angostura bitters
Pineapple and orange slices, for garnish

Stir together the rum, lime juice, sugar syrup, pineapple juice and bitters. Pour into a 12-ounce highball glass, half-filled with cracked ice. Garnish with pineapple and/or orange slices. Serve with a straw.

Piña Colada

This especially rich and creamy version is served at the Caribe Hilton in San Juan, Puerto Rico.

1 SERVING

2 ounces (4 tablespoons) white rum
1½ ounces (3 tablespoons) coconut cream
3 ounces (6 tablespoons) unsweetened pineapple juice
1 ounce (2 tablespoons) half-and-half or 1 tablespoon heavy cream mixed with 1 tablespoon milk
Pineapple slice, for garnish

Combine the rum, coconut cream, pineapple juice and half-and-half with 3 to 4 cracked ice cubes in a blender. Starting on low speed and gradually increasing to high, blend until slushy, about 1 minute. Pour into a 12- to 14-ounce glass. Garnish with a slice of pineapple.

Margaritas

Traditionally served in salt-rimmed glasses as presented below, margaritas are being ordered more and more frequently without salt. If you prefer yours salt free, omit the wedge of lime and salt and skip to Step 2.

1 SERVING

Wedge of lime
Coarse (kosher) salt
1 tablespoon fresh lime juice
½ ounce Triple Sec or Cointreau
1½ ounces tequila
Ice

1. Moisten the rim of the glass by rubbing a cut lime around it. Invert the glass onto a dish of coarse salt to coat the surface. Let the salt dry to form a crust.
2. Pour the lime juice, Triple Sec and tequila over ice and stir well to serve the drink "on the rocks." For a frozen margarita, whirl the ingredients in a blender with ice until slushy.

Lemonade Concentrate

Refreshing and bursting with vitamin C, this concentrated drink base is ideal as a mixer with vodka, gin or light rum, or as a sauce for vanilla ice cream. To make lemonade, combine ¼ to ⅓ cup of the concentrate with ½ cup water or seltzer over ice. It keeps, refrigerated, for several weeks.

MAKES ABOUT 2 CUPS/ENOUGH FOR 8 SERVINGS

12 large lemons
About 2 cups sugar

1. Wash the lemons and scrape off any colored stamp marks.

2. With a very sharp knife, slice one of the lemons as thin as possible and remove the seeds. Spread the slices in one layer on the bottom of a large noncorrodible bowl and sprinkle with 2 rounded tablespoons of sugar.

3. Continue slicing and layering the remaining lemons and sugar until all the ingredients are used up. Cover the bowl and refrigerate overnight.

4. The next day, set a nonaluminum colander or strainer over a bowl and pour in the lemons and their juice. Let drain for about 10 minutes, pressing firmly with a small plate to extract as much juice as possible. Strain the syrup and refrigerate, covered, in a bottle or jar until serving time.

NOTE: To extract another ⅔ cup of lemonade concentrate, do not discard the lemon slices and repeat the layering process using all of the slices in four layers with a total of ½ cup of sugar. Cover and refrigerate overnight. Drain off the juice the following day.

Limeade

This tart, thirst-quenching drink is best served soon after making it, when the lime's perfume is most aromatic.

MAKES 5 TO 6 CUPS

1 cup fresh lime juice (from about 8 limes)
¾ cup sugar
Lime slices, for garnish

Combine the lime juice and sugar in a pitcher; stir briskly until the sugar dissolves. Add 4 cups of cold water. Taste for tartness and acidity. If desired, add up to 1 cup additional cold water. Serve over ice with a slice of lime to garnish each glass.

Banana and Orange Breakfast Drink

This tart and frothy fruit drink is inspired by the classic Indian yogurt beverage, *lassi*. Filling and nutritious, it's a fast, refreshing breakfast for people on the run.

1 SERVING

1 very ripe banana, cut into large chunks
2 tablespoons frozen orange juice concentrate
½ cup milk
½ cup plain yogurt

In a blender, combine the banana, orange juice concentrate, milk and yogurt. Blend until smooth and frothy, about 30 seconds. Pour into a large glass.

Creamy Hot Chocolate

This is one of the nicest hot chocolate drinks we've come across. It's a smooth, comforting beverage for a morning meal, mid-afternoon tea or a late-night snack.

6 SERVINGS

3 ounces (3 squares) semisweet chocolate
Grated zest of 1 large orange
1 cup heavy cream
6 cups milk

1. In a small heavy saucepan, melt the chocolate with ½ cup of water over moderate heat. Stir in the orange zest. Pour the sauce into a shallow dish and place in the freezer until cool, about 10 minutes.

2. Meanwhile, in a medium mixer bowl, whip the cream until stiff peaks form.

3. Stir about one-third of the whipped cream into the cooled chocolate sauce to lighten it. Fold in the remaining cream; place in the freezer to firm slightly, about 10 minutes. (If you are making the chocolate cream several hours ahead of time, then place it, covered with plastic wrap, in the refrigerator.)

4. In a large saucepan, warm the milk over moderate heat until hot. Divide the milk among 6 large mugs and top each with generous spoonfuls of the cold chocolate cream. Serve hot.

Café de Olla

The following recipe is traditional. It can also be made a quick way in an automatic drip coffeemaker. Add the brown sugar and ground cinnamon to the pot, drip the coffee into it and let it stand for 1 minute before serving.

MAKES 8 CUPS

1½ cups dark-roasted, coarsely ground coffee
3 cinnamon sticks (3 to 4 inches each) or 2 teaspoons ground cinnamon
2 tablespoons plus 2 teaspoons brown sugar

In a large flameproof earthenware pot or a saucepan, bring 8 cups of water to a boil. Add the coffee, cinnamon and brown sugar. Remove from the heat. Bring to a boil and remove from the heat two more times. Strain and serve.

APPETIZERS

Tortilla Chips

MAKES ABOUT 10 CUPS

3 dozen corn tortillas
About 1 quart corn oil
Salt (optional)

1. Cut each tortilla into sixths to form wedges.

2. In a deep-fat fryer or a large saucepan, heat about 2 inches of oil to 375°, or until hot enough to brown a chip immediately. Fry the tortillas in batches without crowding until brown, about 30 seconds. Remove with a slotted spoon and drain on paper towels. Season lightly with salt if desired. **(These can be prepared several hours ahead of time.)**

Bacon Bread Cubes

8 TO 10 SERVINGS

1 pound lean slab bacon, rind removed, cut into ¼-inch cubes
1 unsliced loaf (about 1½ pounds) of firm-textured white bread, cut into ¾-inch cubes
½ cup minced fresh parsley
2 tablespoons grated lemon zest
½ cup finely diced red onion

1. Bring a medium saucepan of water to a boil. Add the bacon cubes, reduce the heat to moderate and simmer until the fat is translucent, about 25 minutes. Drain and rinse the bacon under cold water; pat dry with paper towels.

2. In a large skillet, sauté the bacon over moderately low heat until the cubes render most of their fat and turn a pale golden color, 15 to 20 minutes. Remove with a slotted spoon and drain on paper towels.

3. In the fat that remains in the skillet, sauté the bread cubes, tossing all the time, over moderately high heat until they turn pale gold, about 7 minutes. Drain on paper towels.

4. In a decorative bowl, combine the bacon and bread cubes. Set aside, covered; do not refrigerate. To serve, toss the bacon and bread with the parsley, grated lemon zest and onion.

Nachos San Diego Style

12 TO 20 SERVINGS

½ pound lean ground beef
½ pound chorizo (Mexican sausage) or hot Italian sausage
1 large onion, finely chopped
½ teaspoon hot pepper sauce
Salt
2 cans (1 pound each) refried beans
1 can (4 ounces) whole California green chilies—rinsed, seeded, deveined and chopped, or 6 ounces of fresh Anaheim or *poblano* chilies—roasted, peeled, seeded, deveined and chopped
6 ounces Monterey Jack cheese, shredded (about 1½ cups)
6 ounces sharp Cheddar cheese, shredded (about 1½ cups)
¾ cup mild green taco sauce
¾ cup mild red taco sauce
½ cup chopped scallions
¾ cup sliced pitted ripe olives
2 cups Guacamole (p. 18)
1 cup sour cream
8 sprigs of fresh coriander (cilantro)
1 radish rose, for garnish
Tortilla chips, preferably homemade (at left)

1. Preheat a large skillet over moderately high heat. Crumble the ground beef and sausage into the pan.

2. Add the onion and cook, stirring, until the meat is lightly browned and the onion softened, about 5 minutes. Pour off any fat and season with the hot pepper sauce and salt to taste. Set aside to cool.

3. In a large (4-quart), shallow, oven-proof dish, spread the refried beans over the bottom. Spread the cooked meat

evenly over the beans. Sprinkle the chopped chilies over the meat.

4. Toss together the Jack and Cheddar cheeses and arrange on top. Drizzle the two taco sauces over all in a decorative pattern. (**The recipe may be made ahead to this point.** Cover and refrigerate for up to 24 hours. Let return to room temperature before baking.)

5. Preheat the oven to 350°. Bake for 20 to 30 minutes, or until hot and bubbly.

6. Remove from the oven and immediately sprinkle on the chopped scallions and sliced olives. Mound the guacamole in the center. Top with the sour cream, leaving some guacamole showing around the edges. Garnish with coriander sprigs and a radish rose. Serve with a basket of tortilla chips for dipping.

Shrimp Toast

MAKES 32 PIECES

½ pound medium shrimp, shelled and deveined
1 tablespoon water chestnut powder* or cornstarch
½ tablespoon dark soy sauce*
2 teaspoons medium-dry sherry
¼ cup minced white icicle radish or water chestnuts, preferably fresh*
1 egg, lightly beaten
2 teaspoons minced fresh ginger
¼ cup thinly sliced scallions
1 teaspoon Oriental sesame oil
½ teaspoon sugar
½ teaspoon salt
¼ teaspoon white pepper
8 slices of stale firm-textured white bread
4 teaspoons sesame seeds
1 quart peanut oil, for frying
*Available at Oriental groceries

1. Using a Chinese cleaver or a chef's knife, mince the shrimp and put them in a medium bowl.

2. In a small bowl, dissolve the water chestnut powder in the soy sauce and the sherry. Add to the shrimp. Add the radish, egg, ginger, scallions, sesame oil, sugar, salt and pepper to the minced shrimp. Stir until blended. Cover and refrigerate for at least 1 hour and up to 24 hours.

3. Spread about 2 tablespoons of the shrimp mixture on each slice of bread. Sprinkle ½ teaspoon sesame seeds over each piece. Cut each slice into 4 triangles. (**The recipe may be made up to 4 hours ahead to this point.** Refrigerate wrapped in waxed paper; remove from the refrigerator 30 minutes before frying.)

4. Place a large wok over high heat for about 1½ minutes. Pour in the oil, reduce the heat to moderate and bring the oil to 350°. Frying 8 to 12 at a time (depending on the size of your wok), gently lower the triangles, shrimp-side down, into the oil. Fry for about 2 minutes, until the sesame seeds are golden brown. Turn the toasts over and fry until the toast is golden brown, about 30 seconds longer. Remove from the hot fat and drain on paper towels. Serve hot or warm.

Tsaziki (Cucumber Yogurt Dip)

A thick, flavorful dip, *tsaziki* is traditionally served with warm triangles of pita bread. It is also good with raw, blanched or deep-fried vegetables.

MAKES ABOUT 3 CUPS

1 large cucumber—peeled, halved lengthwise and seeded
1 teaspoon coarse (kosher) salt
2 cups plain yogurt
2 tablespoons fresh lemon juice
4 garlic cloves, minced
2 tablespoons minced parsley
¼ cup olive oil

1. Place the cucumber halves, seeded-side up, on a plate and sprinkle with the salt. Let stand for 10 minutes. Pat dry.

2. Shred the cucumber into a large bowl. Add the yogurt, lemon juice, garlic and parsley. Stir until blended. Gradually whisk in the olive oil in a thin stream. Cover and refrigerate until serving time.

Caviar Mosaic

Presentation is everything with this striking, simple dish. To duplicate it as shown on page 17, you will need a 14-inch and an 8-inch round platter, preferably glass. Though the pattern looks difficult to execute, it really isn't. In fact, you can choose any design that suits your fancy—geometric, floral or whatever comes to mind.

🍷 **F&W Beverage Suggestion:**
French Champagne, such as Moët & Chandon Brut

12 SERVINGS

6 Belgian endives
1 pint sour cream
3 ounces golden caviar
2 ounces imported black caviar, or ½ cup minced chives or scallion greens

1. Trim the bottom 1 inch off the root end of the endives. Separate the heads into two piles of leaves, one with the large outside leaves, the other the small inner leaves.

2. Spread the sour cream evenly over an 8-inch round platter. Cut out strips of waxed paper and arrange in the desired design over the sour cream. Spoon the golden caviar over all the exposed areas and smooth it gently. Remove the waxed paper cut-outs and carefully top the exposed sour cream with the black caviar to create a contrasting design.

3. Place the small platter in the middle of a 14-inch round platter. Arrange the Belgian endive around the large platter like the petals of a flower, with the larger leaves underneath.

Le Cirque's Mousse of Smoked Salmon in Terrine

10 SERVINGS

1 tablespoon olive oil
½ pound fresh salmon fillet— skinned, sliced ¼ inch thick and cut into strips 1 by ¼ inch
1 tablespoon Cognac
½ pound smoked Norwegian salmon, sliced and cut into small pieces
1½ cups heavy cream
Pinch of freshly ground black pepper
1 tablespoon green peppercorns, rinsed and drained

1. In a large skillet, preferably nonstick, warm the olive oil over moderately low heat. Add the fresh salmon strips and sauté, stirring, until the salmon is opaque and begins to break up, about 3 minutes.

2. Add the Cognac and ignite.

3. When the flames subside, transfer the salmon and any pan juices to a plate. Cover loosely and refrigerate until just chilled, about 10 minutes.

4. In a food processor, puree the smoked salmon, 1 cup of the cream and the black pepper until smooth, 5 to 10 seconds.

5. Transfer the smoked salmon puree to a large bowl. Stir in the fresh salmon and the green peppercorns.

6. In a medium mixer bowl, beat the remaining ½ cup of cream until soft peaks form. Gently stir half of the whipped cream into the salmon mixture until thoroughly incorporated. Fold in the remaining whipped cream.

7. Transfer the mousse to a terrine and refrigerate overnight. Serve accompanied with toast points.

The Four Seasons' Rillettes of Salmon

8 TO 10 SERVINGS

¾ pound fresh salmon steak, 1¼ inches thick
Quick Court Bouillon (p. 220)
¾ pound Scotch smoked salmon, diced
1 cup (2 sticks) unsalted butter
Pinch of cayenne pepper
1 jar (4 ounces) salmon caviar

1. In a skillet that will hold the salmon steak snugly, bring the court bouillon to a boil over moderately high heat.

2. Lower the heat to a simmer and add the salmon steak; cover and poach until just slightly translucent in the center, about 5 minutes, turning once. Remove the salmon to a bowl and let cool until it can be handled. Using your hands, flake the salmon steak, discarding the skin and bones.

3. In a food processor, blend the diced smoked salmon with the butter and cayenne until smooth, about 1 minute.

4. Add the flaked fresh salmon and turn the machine on and off quickly 2 or 3 times until the mixture is blended but still has a coarse texture.

5. Transfer to a medium bowl and fold in the salmon caviar. Serve at room temperature accompanied with toast points or crusty French bread.

Cheddar and Jalapeño Dip

Piquant and extremely popular, this is a wonderful dip for crudités or tortilla chips. It will keep covered in the refrigerator for at least five days.

MAKES ABOUT 4½ CUPS

1¼ pounds cream cheese
6 ounces sharp Cheddar cheese, grated
6 ounces fresh semi-hot green chilies—stemmed, seeded, deribbed and minced
1 jalapeño pepper (fresh or canned), seeded and minced
2 dashes of Worcestershire sauce
2 dashes of Tabasco sauce

1 dash of cayenne pepper
3 scallions, finely chopped
Salt and freshly ground black pepper, to taste
Milk (optional)

In a food processor, whip all the ingredients together until smooth and light. If too thick, thin with a little milk. Cover and refrigerate for at least 30 minutes before serving.

Buttery Salmon Spread

Accompany this creamy spread with crisp crackers, sliced French bread or raw vegetables.

MAKES ABOUT 1 CUP

1 can (7 ounces) red salmon, picked over to remove skin and bones
1 tablespoon plus 1 teaspoon fresh lemon juice
½ teaspoon Dijon-style mustard
¼ teaspoon hot pepper sauce
4 tablespoons melted unsalted butter, at room temperature
½ cup sour cream
Minced fresh chives, for garnish

1. In a blender or food processor, puree the salmon, lemon juice, mustard and hot pepper sauce. Pour in the butter and puree until incorporated.

2. Scrape into a small serving dish and stir in the sour cream. Refrigerate, covered, for at least 1 hour. Sprinkle with the chives before serving.

Cashew Cream Pesto Dip

This thick, rich green dip, perfumed with fresh basil, is perfect when tossed with pasta or served with a platter of crisp raw or blanched vegetables. The dip will keep for about a week, refrigerated.

MAKES ABOUT 1 CUP

½ cup dry-roasted unsalted cashews
2 tablespoons light vegetable oil
¾ cup chopped fresh basil
2 garlic cloves, minced
1 tablespoon olive oil
⅓ cup freshly grated Parmesan cheese
Salt and freshly ground pepper

In a food processor or blender, grind the cashews with the vegetable oil until smooth. Add the basil, garlic, olive oil and ¼ cup of hot water; blend until smooth. Add the Parmesan and blend until mixed. (If the dip seems too thick, add 1 tablespoon of water.) Season with salt and pepper to taste. Scrape into a small bowl and cover tightly with plastic wrap until ready to serve.

Guacamole

As part of Nachos San Diego Style (p. 16), this guacamole needs no additional seasoning. If served by itself, however, as a salad or dip, season with salt and pepper to taste.

MAKES ABOUT 2 CUPS

2 ripe avocados, coarsely mashed
1 medium tomato—peeled, seeded and coarsely chopped
1 tablespoon finely chopped onion
1 *serrano* chili, seeded and minced, or 3 tablespoons chopped canned California chilies—rinsed, seeded and deveined
1 teaspoon chopped fresh coriander (cilantro)

Combine all the ingredients in a bowl. Stir to blend well.

Tyropita (Feta Cheese Triangles)

These flaky, buttery phyllo triangles have a tart feta cheese filling. They can be completely prepared ahead and frozen. Keep the phyllo dough covered with a damp kitchen towel to prevent drying out while you are working with it.

MAKES 24 TRIANGLES

1 stick plus 3 tablespoons unsalted butter
¼ cup all-purpose flour
1 cup milk, at room temperature
1 pound feta cheese, crumbled
1 egg yolk
3 tablespoons minced chives
¼ teaspoon freshly ground pepper
12 sheets of phyllo dough

1. In a heavy medium saucepan, melt 3 tablespoons of the butter over moderately low heat. Whisk in the flour and cook, stirring, for 2 minutes without coloring to make a roux. Slowly whisk in the milk until smooth. Bring to a boil, reduce the heat slightly and cook, whisking frequently, until the sauce is thick, about 2 minutes.

2. Add the feta cheese and cook, stirring, until smooth. Whisk in the egg yolk, chives and pepper and cook over low heat, stirring, for 3 minutes. Remove from the heat and scrape into a bowl. Let cool to room temperature, then cover and chill until firm, about 45 minutes. **(The filling may be prepared a day ahead to this point.)**

3. Preheat the oven to 375°. In a small heavy saucepan, melt the remaining stick of butter over low heat. Brush a baking sheet with about 2 teaspoons of the butter and set aside.

4. Lay 1 sheet of dough on a flat surface. Lightly brush with about 1 teaspoon butter. Cut the sheet lengthwise in half; fold each strip in half lengthwise again. Brush the tops of each lightly with butter.

5. Mound 1 rounded teaspoon of cheese on the bottom left-hand corner of both phyllo strips. (Too much filling will cause the pastries to leak when baking.) Loosely fold up each strip, using the classic flag-folding technique, to make a tri-angular pastry. Transfer to the baking sheet and lightly brush with butter. Make the remaining pastries in the same way. **(The recipe may be made ahead to this point.** Wrap and freeze the pastries. Allow an additional 5 to 7 minutes baking time.)

6. Bake for 12 to 15 minutes, until crisp and golden. Serve warm.

Délices de Gruyère

Here is a warm, crusty cheese hors d'oeuvre complemented by a lightly seasoned tomato sauce.

8 TO 10 HORS-D'OEUVRE SERVINGS

1½ cups milk
12 tablespoons (1½ sticks) unsalted butter, cut into tablespoons
½ teaspoon salt
¼ teaspoon white pepper
1 cup plus 2 tablespoons all-purpose flour
¼ pound Gruyère cheese, grated
¼ pound Emmenthaler cheese, grated
3 egg yolks, beaten
1 small onion, finely chopped
1 cup Italian peeled tomatoes, drained and crushed
2 tablespoons finely chopped parsley
½ teaspoon thyme
2 whole eggs, beaten
1½ cups fine dry bread crumbs

1. In a large heavy saucepan, combine the milk, 4 tablespoons of the butter and the salt and pepper. Bring to a boil over moderately high heat. Remove from the heat and stir in the flour all at once; the mixture will gather quickly into a smooth ball. Add the cheeses and beat until incorporated. Add the egg yolks and beat again until smooth. Scrape the dough into a shallow container, cover and chill in the refrigerator until several hours before serving.

2. In a medium saucepan, melt 2 tablespoons of the butter over moderately low heat. Add the onion and sauté until softened and translucent, about 2 minutes. Add the tomatoes, parsley and thyme and simmer for 3 minutes. Let cool, then refrigerate until serving time. **(The recipe may be prepared a day ahead to this point.)**

3. Several hours before serving time, divide the chilled dough into sixths. Using your hands, roll each piece into a cylinder ¾ inch in circumference. Cut into 3-inch lengths.

4. Dip the sticks of dough into the beaten eggs and roll in the bread crumbs. Place on a tray, cover loosely and refrigerate until serving time.

5. To assemble the dish, rewarm the tomato sauce over moderately low heat until bubbling.

6. Meanwhile, in a large heavy skillet, melt 3 tablespoons of the butter over moderate heat until sizzling. Add half of the sticks and sauté, turning frequently, until golden brown, about 4 minutes. Remove to a large round serving platter and cover to keep warm. Add the remaining 3 tablespoons butter to the skillet and sauté the remaining pieces. Arrange them on the platter and spoon the tomato sauce into the center; serve warm.

Walnut-Cheddar Triangles

These bite-size cheese- and nut-flavored pastries are a nice hors d'oeuvre to serve at a cocktail party or before dinner.

MAKES ABOUT 40

6 tablespoons unsalted butter
1 cup all-purpose flour
1 cup grated Cheddar cheese
¼ teaspoon salt
¼ teaspoon freshly ground black pepper
⅛ teaspoon cayenne pepper
1 egg, beaten
1 cup chopped walnuts, lightly toasted

1. Preheat the oven to 350°. Line 2 baking sheets with foil. In a medium bowl, cut the butter into the flour until the mixture resembles coarse meal. Add the grated cheese, salt, black pepper and cayenne and mix until blended; shape into a ball. (If the dough is very soft, wrap in plastic wrap and place in the freezer for about 10 minutes, until firm.)

2. On a lightly floured board, roll out the dough into a ⅛-inch-thick rectangle. Cut into 2-inch strips; cut the strips into bite-size triangles. Place on the baking sheets and brush with the beaten egg. Sprinkle the walnuts on top and gently press the nuts onto the dough.

3. Bake for 15 to 18 minutes, until golden. Transfer to a rack and let cool before serving.

Keftedes (Sautéed Lamb Meatballs)

🍷 **F&W Beverage Suggestion:** Dry red Greek wine, such as Castel Danielis, or California Petite Sirah, such as Fetzer

MAKES ABOUT 50 SMALL MEATBALLS

4 slices of French bread, cut 1 inch thick and crusts removed
¼ cup milk
1 pound lean ground lamb (preferably shoulder)
1 egg, beaten
1 small onion, finely chopped
¼ cup finely chopped parsley
1 teaspoon salt
1 garlic clove, minced
1 tablespoon chopped fresh mint or 1 teaspoon dried
½ cup all-purpose flour
½ cup olive oil
Lemon wedges, for garnish

1. Soak the bread slices in the milk for about 5 minutes. Squeeze out the milk and crumble the bread into a large bowl. Add the lamb, egg, onion, parsley, salt, garlic and mint. Mix to blend well.

2. Form the meat by rounded teaspoonfuls into small balls about 1 inch in diameter. Dredge the meatballs lightly in the flour; shake off any excess. (**The recipe may be prepared up to 4 hours ahead to this point.** Refrigerate until ready to cook.)

3. In a large heavy skillet, heat the oil until shimmering. Add as many meatballs as will fit loosely in a single layer and cook over moderately high heat, turning, until well browned all over, 4 to 5 minutes. Remove with a slotted spoon and drain on paper towels. Transfer to a serving platter and cover loosely with foil to keep warm. (The meatballs may also be kept warm or reheated, covered, in a 300° oven.) Repeat with the remaining meatballs in several batches. Garnish with lemon wedges and serve with toothpicks.

Scallion and Potato Omelet Squares

6 SERVINGS

12 eggs
1 teaspoon salt
Dash of hot pepper sauce
2 tablespoons vegetable oil
1 tablespoon Oriental sesame oil
½ cup minced scallions (the white and 2 inches of the green)
1 medium potato, cooked and cut into ¼-inch dice
3 anchovy fillets, minced
½ cup minced fresh coriander (cilantro) leaves

1. Preheat the oven to 375°. In a large bowl, lightly beat the eggs with the salt and hot sauce.

2. Brush the bottom of a 12-by-9-inch ovenproof baking dish with some of the vegetable oil. Line the pan with a sheet of waxed paper and brush it with more oil. Pour half of the egg mixture into the baking dish and bake until almost set, about 15 minutes.

3. Meanwhile, in a small skillet, warm the remaining vegetable oil and the sesame oil over moderate heat. Sauté the scallions until softened, about 2 minutes. Off heat, add the diced potato and anchovies and mix well.

4. Remove the dish from the oven and spread the scallion-potato mixture evenly over the egg layer. Pour on the remaining egg mixture and bake until set, about 15 minutes.

5. When the baking dish is cool enough to handle, invert it onto a cutting board and carefully remove the waxed paper. (**The recipe can be made several hours ahead to this point.** Wrap airtight and refrigerate.)

6. Trim away ¼ inch of the browned edges and cut the omelet into diamond shapes, about 2 inches from point to point. Sprinkle with the minced coriander and serve at room temperature.

Kotletki with Horseradish Cream Sauce

6 TO 8 SERVINGS

⅔ pound ground beef, put through a meat grinder twice
⅔ pound ground pork, put through a meat grinder twice
⅔ pound ground veal, put through a meat grinder twice
4 slices of white bread
1 cup chicken stock or canned broth
6 tablespoons unsalted butter
2 tablespoons vegetable oil
1 medium onion, minced
1 egg
1 teaspoon salt
1 teaspoon freshly ground pepper
2 tablespoons dried dillweed
1 cup all-purpose flour
½ cup sour cream
¼ cup heavy cream
¼ cup prepared red horseradish, drained

1. In a large bowl, combine the beef, pork and veal.

2. Soak the bread in the stock. Squeeze to remove the liquid, reserving the stock. Combine the bread with the meat.

3. In a heavy skillet, melt 2 tablespoons of the butter with 1 tablespoon of the oil over moderate heat. Add the onion and sauté until soft, about 10 minutes. Combine the onion with the meat mixture and add the egg, salt, pepper and dill. Mix thoroughly.

4. Form the meat mixture into 1½-inch balls and use the back of a spoon to flatten each into a ¾-inch-thick patty.

5. Dredge each patty lightly in the flour. In a large heavy skillet, melt the remaining 4 tablespoons butter with the remaining 1 tablespoon oil over moderate heat. Sauté the patties, turning once, until lightly browned, about 2 minutes on each side. Remove the skillet from the heat; spoon off as much fat as possible.

6. Meanwhile, in a saucepan, bring the reserved chicken stock to a simmer over moderately low heat. Pour the stock over the patties, cover tightly and simmer over moderately low heat until the meat is cooked through, about 10 minutes. Remove from the heat and let cool.

7. Gently remove the patties and discard the stock. Refrigerate in a covered dish until 1 hour before serving (**The patties can be made several days ahead.**)

8. In a small bowl, combine the sour cream, heavy cream and horseradish. Season with salt and pepper to taste. Pour the sauce over the patties and serve at room temperature.

Cold Ham, Cheese and Asparagus Rolls

This pretty antipasto is perfect for serving at a small summer party.

MAKES 8 SMALL ROLLS

8 asparagus tips, 4 inches long
8 very thin slices of ham (about ½ pound), preferably Black Forest
3 ounces Swiss cheese, sliced ¼ inch thick
6 tablespoons mayonnaise
Grated zest of ½ navel orange
½ teaspoon fresh orange juice
Grated zest of ½ lime
1 teaspoon fresh lime juice
1 teaspoon minced fresh ginger
¼ teaspoon freshly ground pepper
3 large leaves of romaine lettuce, cut into 4-inch julienne strips

1. In a medium saucepan of boiling water, cook the asparagus until crisp-

tender, 2 to 3 minutes. Drain and rinse under cold running water; drain and pat dry. Halve the asparagus lengthwise.

2. Cut the ham slices into 3-inch circles. Cut the cheese into 3-by-¼-inch sticks.

3. In a small bowl, combine the mayonnaise, orange zest and juice, lime zest and juice, ginger and pepper and whisk until blended.

4. Spread a thin layer of the seasoned mayonnaise on each circle of ham. Lay 2 asparagus halves and 2 cheese sticks down the center. Lay a few strips of lettuce on top and roll into a cone; glue the ham shut with a small dab of mayonnaise. (If necessary, secure with a toothpick.) Arrange on a platter and chill until ready to serve.

Saganaki (Fried Feta Cheese Cubes)

MAKES ABOUT 40

1 pound feta cheese, cut into 1-inch cubes
½ cup all-purpose flour
1 egg, beaten
⅔ cup fine dry bread crumbs
½ cup olive or corn oil
Lemon wedges, for garnish

1. Pat the cheese cubes dry with paper towels. To bread them, dredge lightly in the flour, shake off any excess, dip in the beaten egg and roll in the bread crumbs until well coated.

2. In a large deep skillet, heat the oil to 350°. Fry the cubes in batches in a single layer without crowding until golden brown, 30 seconds to 1 minute. Drain on paper towels and serve garnished with lemon wedges.

Oriental-Style Chicken Lollipops

8 SERVINGS

24 chicken wings (about 4 pounds)
1¼ cups soy sauce
½ cup honey
¼ cup vegetable oil
2 star anise pods, broken apart
2 tablespoons grated fresh ginger
3 medium garlic cloves, crushed
    through a press
20 black peppercorns, crushed
½ teaspoon salt

1. Using a boning knife, cut through the upper joint of each wing, separating the large top section from the rest of the wing; reserve the lower section and the tips for making stock. Cut through the tendons at the base of the narrower end and, using the knife, gently scrape the meat from the bone, pushing it toward the large end. Pull the loosened meat around the top of the bone to form a ball or lollipop shape. Place the lollipops in a dish just large enough to hold them in a single layer.

2. In a medium bowl, combine the soy sauce, honey, oil, star anise, ginger, garlic, peppercorns and salt. Pour over the lollipops and marinate in the refrigerator, turning once or twice, for at least 4 hours or overnight.

3. Preheat the oven to 400°. Let the lollipops come to room temperature; then remove from the marinade and place them in a shallow roasting pan or baking dish. Pour ½ cup of the marinade over the lollipops and bake for 20 minutes, or until golden.

4. Meanwhile, place the remaining marinade in a small saucepan and bring to a boil over high heat. Boil for about 3 minutes, until slightly thickened. Let cool to room temperature and serve as a dipping sauce with the lollipops.

Rosemary Chicken Lollipops

8 SERVINGS

24 chicken wings (about 4 pounds)
½ cup olive oil, preferably extra-
    virgin
1 tablespoon dried rosemary,
    crumbled
½ teaspoon salt
¼ teaspoon freshly ground pepper
Spicy Tomato Dipping Sauce
    (p. 223)

1. Prepare the chicken wings as in Step 1 of Oriental-Style Chicken Lollipops (at left).

2. Preheat the oven to 400°. In a medium bowl, combine the olive oil, rosemary, salt and pepper. Add the wings a few at a time and toss to coat.

3. Transfer the wings to a shallow roasting pan or large baking dish. Bake for 20 minutes, or until golden and lightly crisped. Serve with Spicy Tomato Dipping Sauce.

Kentucky-Style Potted Shrimp

Here is a buttery spread to serve with thin, plain, crisp crackers.

MAKES ABOUT 1½ CUPS

1 pound shrimp, shelled and
    deveined
1 stick (¼ pound) unsalted butter,
    cut into cubes
2½ teaspoons fresh lemon juice
1 teaspoon minced onion
¾ teaspoon salt
½ teaspoon Worcestershire sauce
½ teaspoon hot pepper sauce
½ teaspoon anchovy paste
¼ teaspoon freshly ground black
    pepper
Salt

1. In a medium saucepan of boiling water, cook the shrimp until pink and opaque throughout, 2 to 3 minutes. Drain and rinse briefly under cold water; drain well.

2. Place the shrimp and butter in a food processor and blend until smooth, about

1 minute. Add the lemon juice, onion, salt, Worcestershire and hot pepper sauces, anchovy paste and black pepper and blend until smooth and well mixed, 1 to 2 minutes. Season with salt to taste. Scrape into a small serving bowl and smooth the top. Serve immediately, or cover and refrigerate. Bring to room temperature before serving.

Cold Poached Shrimp and Fennel in Pernod

6 SERVINGS

4 tablespoons unsalted butter
¼ cup Pernod
1 head of fennel—stalks removed,
    bulb trimmed and cut into
    matchsticks
1 pound medium shrimp, shelled
    and deveined
1 tablespoon fresh lemon juice
1 tablespoon minced fresh parsley
Salt and freshly ground pepper

1. In a noncorrodible medium saucepan or deep skillet, melt the butter over moderate heat. Add the Pernod and cook for 2 minutes. Add the fennel, cover and poach until slightly softened, about 2 minutes.

2. Add the shrimp and cook, tossing until just opaque outside and still slightly translucent inside, about 3 minutes.

3. Sprinkle the shrimp with the lemon juice, parsley and salt and pepper to taste. Refrigerate, covered, until 1 hour before serving. Serve at room temperature.

The Four Seasons' Smoked Salmon Cornets with Horseradish Cream

MAKES 36 HORS D'OEUVRE

10 ounces thinly sliced Scotch or other good-quality smoked salmon
6 thin slices of square pumpernickel bread
½ cup heavy cream
2 tablespoons well-drained prepared white horseradish

1. Cut the salmon slices into 2-inch squares, reserving the scraps for another use, and refrigerate between sheets of waxed paper.

2. Trim off the crusts of the bread and cut each into 6 small triangles. Wrap in plastic wrap to prevent drying out.

3. Beat the cream until stiff peaks form. Fold in the horseradish.

4. To assemble, roll the squares of salmon into small cornets. Place one on each bread triangle. Using a small pastry bag with a star tip, pipe the horseradish cream into the cornets. Refrigerate, covered, for up to 3 hours before serving.

Pickled Cauliflower and Broccoli with Lime

The vegetables marinate overnight, so plan accordingly.

6 SERVINGS

2 cups dry white wine
½ cup sugar
1 tablespoon coarse (kosher) salt
1 tablespoon oregano
2 large bay leaves
1 small head of cauliflower (about 1 pound), cut into 1½-inch florets
1 bunch of broccoli (about 1 pound), cut into 1½-inch florets
¼ cup olive oil

2 tablespoons fresh lime juice
Salt and freshly ground pepper
6 thin slices of lime

1. In a large noncorrodible pot, combine the wine, sugar, salt, oregano and bay leaves with 2 cups of water. Simmer over low heat for 20 minutes.

2. Add the cauliflower and broccoli florets and bring to a boil. Reduce the heat to moderately low and simmer slowly until the vegetables are tender but still slightly firm, 8 to 10 minutes. Remove from the heat and let cool overnight in the liquid. (**The recipe can be made to this point 2 or 3 days ahead.** Keep the vegetables refrigerated and tightly covered.)

3. Before serving, remove the vegetables and discard the marinade. Let the vegetables come to room temperature. Just before serving, toss the vegetables in the olive oil and lime juice. Season with salt and pepper to taste and garnish with the lime slices.

Deep Dish Spinach Pie

When cut into small squares this wonderful pie makes a great hors d'oeuvre. Serve warm or chilled.

8 SERVINGS

Flaky Pastry (p. 199)
1 egg yolk
2 pounds fresh spinach
½ teaspoon tarragon
¼ cup fresh lemon juice
1 cup (about 4 ounces) crumbled feta cheese or coarsely shredded sharp Cheddar cheese
4 whole eggs, at room temperature
2 cups heavy cream
½ teaspoon salt
¼ teaspoon freshly grated nutmeg

1. Preheat the oven to 400°. On a lightly floured surface, roll out the pastry to a 13-inch square. Loosely drape into an 8-inch square baking pan; press the dough to conform to the pan. Roll the overhanging pastry all around to make a raised edge and crimp decoratively. Place a sheet of aluminum foil slightly larger than the pan over the dough and press to conform to the pastry. Fill with pie weights. Bake until the crimped edge is set, about 10 minutes. Carefully remove the foil and pie weights, return the shell to the oven and bake, tapping the bottom with a wooden spoon if it bubbles up, for about 8 minutes, until the bottom is dry and firm.

2. Beat the egg yolk in a small bowl with a fork. Generously paint enough of the yolk over the bottom of the shell to coat. Return the shell to the oven until set, about 2 minutes. Let cool on a wire rack. Reduce the oven temperature to 350°.

3. Meanwhile, stem the spinach and rinse the leaves well. Place the leaves, with just the water clinging to them, in a large pot. Cook, covered, over moderately high heat, stirring once or twice, until wilted and greatly reduced in bulk, about 3 minutes. Drain the spinach into a colander; press with the back of a spoon to extract the excess liquid. Coarsely chop the spinach; there will be 1½ to 2 cups.

4. In a large bowl, combine the spinach with the tarragon, lemon juice and cheese. Toss the mixture to blend.

5. In another bowl, whisk together the eggs, cream, salt and nutmeg.

6. Arrange the spinach mixture in the partially baked pastry shell and pour the egg mixture over the top. Place the pie on a cookie sheet and bake until puffed all over and lightly speckled with golden brown, about 50 minutes. Cool on a rack for 1 hour, or refrigerate until chilled, before cutting.

Sherried Olives

The olives need to marinate for three to four days, so plan accordingly.

6 SERVINGS

1 can (7½ ounces) pitted medium
  black olives
1 can (7½ ounces) pitted medium
  green olives
3 cups olive oil
1 cup dry sherry
1 cup sherry vinegar
1 small garlic clove, smashed
1 small red onion, cut into thin
  rings
1 tablespoon thyme

1. Drain the olives and discard the brine.

2. In a large jar with a tight lid, combine the olives with the remaining ingredients. Refrigerate, covered, for 3 or 4 days, shaking the jar from time to time.

3. To serve, drain the olives and onions and discard the garlic. Reserve the marinade for another batch if desired. Serve in a decorative bowl.

Toasted Almonds

6 TO 8 SERVINGS

½ cup coarse (kosher) salt
4 cups whole unblanched almonds

1. Preheat the oven to 325°. In a large bowl, dissolve the salt in 2 cups of hot water and add the almonds. Set aside to soak for 30 minutes; drain well.

2. Scatter the almonds over a baking sheet and bake, stirring occasionally, until golden in color, about 20 minutes.

3. Remove the baking sheet from the oven and allow to cool for 20 minutes. Place the baking sheet in the still-warm oven and leave there overnight. Serve in decorative bowls. Store any remaining nuts tightly covered in the refrigerator.

NOTE: If a garlic taste is desired, rub the baking sheet with a mixture of 2 crushed garlic cloves and 2 teaspoons vegetable oil before roasting the almonds.

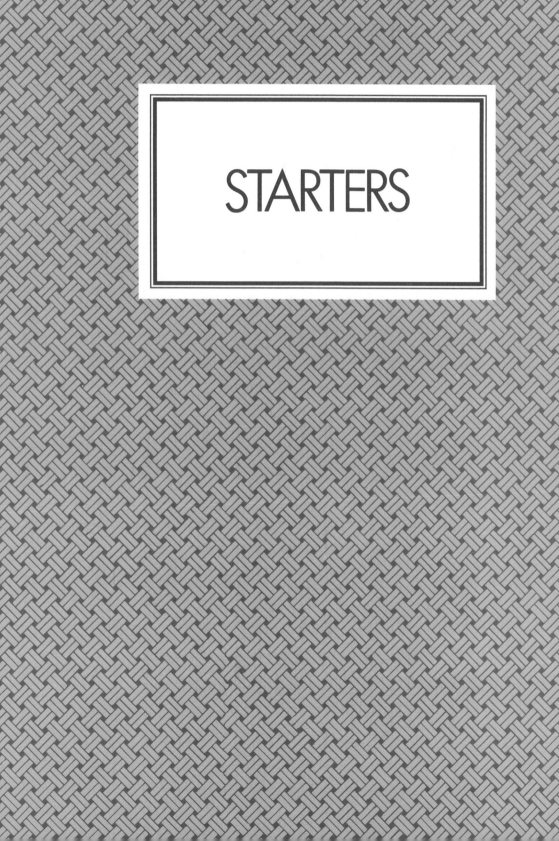

STARTERS

Stuffed Mushroom Caps Monégasque

4 SERVINGS

Garlic Butter:

1 tablespoon unsalted corn oil margarine, at room temperature
¼ teaspoon minced garlic
½ teaspoon finely chopped shallot
2 teaspoons chopped fresh parsley

Mushrooms:

1 teaspoon unsalted corn oil margarine
1½ teaspoons finely chopped shallot
½ teaspoon minced garlic
2 teaspoons finely chopped onion
1 pound ripe tomatoes—peeled, seeded and finely chopped, or 1½ cups drained, seeded and finely chopped canned tomatoes
½ teaspoon freshly ground pepper
1 imported bay leaf
½ teaspoon basil
½ teaspoon oregano
⅛ teaspoon thyme
1¼ pounds mushrooms (24 small or 16 large), stemmed
1 tablespoon fresh lemon juice
1 cup dry white wine

1. Make the garlic butter: In a small bowl, blend the margarine, garlic, shallot and parsley. Refrigerate, covered, until needed.

2. Prepare the mushrooms: In a small saucepan, melt the margarine. Add the shallot, garlic and onion and cook over moderate heat for 1 minute, until fragrant. Add the tomatoes, pepper, bay leaf, basil, oregano and thyme. Simmer, uncovered, stirring occasionally, until the liquid from the tomatoes has evaporated, about 20 minutes. Remove from the heat and let cool.

3. Rinse the mushrooms briefly and drain in a colander. Toss with ½ tablespoon of the lemon juice.

4. In a medium noncorrodible saucepan, combine the remaining ½ tablespoon lemon juice and the wine. Bring to a boil, add the mushroom caps, reduce the heat to moderately low and simmer, covered, until just tender, 2 to 4 minutes, depending upon the size of the mushrooms. Drain and place, stemmed-side up, on a baking sheet.

5. Preheat the broiler. Divide the tomato filling among the mushroom caps. Top each with a dab of the garlic butter.

6. Broil the mushrooms about 4 inches from the heat for 2 to 3 minutes, until heated through and the tops are lightly browned. Serve hot.

Avocado Tartare

Raw minced beef is "cooked" here in lime juice, as in ceviche, and is served with avocado. The addicting combination can be made from any cut of beef you choose, as long as it is fat free. The beef stuffing must marinate twice, so plan your time accordingly by starting a day ahead.

4 SERVINGS

½ pound very lean beef (without streaks or marbling), such as sirloin, flank or fillet
⅓ cup plus 2 tablespoons fresh lime juice (from about 3 limes)
¼ cup olive oil
2 large red ripe tomatoes—peeled, seeded and chopped or 1 can (16 ounces) Italian peeled tomatoes—seeded, drained and coarsely chopped
½ cup finely chopped red onion
2 tablespoons minced fresh coriander (cilantro)
½ teaspoon salt
¼ teaspoon freshly ground pepper
2 ripe, but firm, avocados
¼ cup thinly sliced scallions

1. Cut the meat into small dice and then mince on a cutting board with one or two sharp knives until the texture is slightly coarser than ground beef. Place the beef in a medium bowl, add ⅓ cup plus 1 tablespoon of the lime juice and toss well. Cover and refrigerate for at least 8 hours or overnight.

2. Stir in the olive oil, tomatoes, onion, coriander and salt and pepper. Cover and refrigerate for at least 2 hours. **(The recipe can be prepared a day ahead to this point.)**

3. Taste for seasoning and add more salt to taste if desired. Halve and peel the avocados lengthwise; remove the pits. Slice each half lengthwise into 6 or 7 slices and fan them out on one side of each of four plates. Drizzle with the remaining 1 tablespoon lime juice. Divide the beef filling into four equal mounds and place one on each of the four plates. Garnish with the scallions and serve chilled.

Chicken Medallions with Roasted Red Pepper Sauce

F&W Beverage Suggestion: Spanish red, such as Torres Coronas

12 TO 18 SERVINGS

12 skinless, boneless chicken breast halves
6 tablespoons unsalted butter
4 medium shallots, minced
2 large carrots, finely chopped
¾ pound mushrooms, stemmed and finely chopped
¾ teaspoon salt
¾ teaspoon freshly ground pepper
24 large spinach leaves
12 thin slices of prosciutto, cut crosswise in half
2 cups all-purpose flour
3 tablespoons olive oil
Roasted Red Pepper Sauce (recipe follows)

1. Pound each chicken breast between sheets of plastic wrap or two large heavy plastic bags until evenly ⅜ inch thick and rectangular in shape.

2. In a large skillet, melt the butter. Add the shallots and sauté over moderately high heat until translucent, about 1 minute. Add the carrots and mushrooms and sauté until most of the moisture from the mushrooms has evaporated, about 2 minutes. Season with ¼ teaspoon each of the salt and pepper.

3. Dip the spinach leaves in boiling water for about 10 seconds, until just limp but still bright green. Drain on paper towels and press out as much moisture as possible without tearing the leaves.

4. To assemble, place each chicken breast smooth-side down on the work surface. Cover with a piece of prosciutto and 1 or 2 spinach leaves. Spread about 2 tablespoons of the mushroom-carrot mixture on top in a thin even layer. Starting at one of the long sides, roll up. **(The recipe can be prepared ahead to this point.** Wrap well and refrigerate. Remove from the refrigerator about 30 minutes before proceeding.)

5. Season the flour with the remaining ½ teaspoon salt and ½ teaspoon pepper. Dredge the rolled chicken breasts in the seasoned flour and set on a rack for about 10 minutes to dry.

6. In a large heavy skillet, warm 1½ tablespoons of the oil over moderately high heat until shimmering. Add half the rolls seam-side down in a single layer and brown briefly on all sides; remove and set aside. Add the remaining 1½ tablespoons oil to the skillet and repeat with the remaining chicken.

7. Preheat the oven to 375°. Transfer the chicken to a baking sheet and roast for 8 to 10 minutes, until just cooked through. When cool enough to handle, slice crosswise into ¾-inch-thick medallions. Serve warm or at room temperature with Roasted Red Pepper Sauce as a condiment on the side.

Roasted Red Pepper Sauce

This sauce can be made a day or two ahead and refrigerated. Let return to room temperature before serving.

MAKES ABOUT 2½ CUPS

12 large red bell peppers
1 medium red onion, minced
2 garlic cloves, minced
Pinch of sugar
Pinch of salt
2 tablespoons vegetable oil

1. Preheat the oven to 500°. Place the peppers on a baking sheet and roast, turning frequently, until the skin is black and blistered all over, about 15 minutes. Seal the charred peppers in a plastic bag and let sit for at least 10 minutes.

2. Rub the skin off the peppers. Remove the stems, seeds and ribs. In a food processor, puree the peppers with the onion, garlic, sugar and salt.

3. In a large heavy skillet, heat the oil. Add the pepper puree and cook over moderate heat, stirring frequently, until slightly thicker than ketchup, about 15 minutes.

Asparagus with Oysters

F&W Beverage Suggestion: California Cabernet Sauvignon, such as Grand Cru Vineyards

2 SERVINGS

½ small onion
1 cup heavy cream
3 thin slices Smithfield ham, chopped
8 fresh oysters, shucked, with their liquor
10 large asparagus spears, trimmed and peeled
Salt and freshly ground pepper
1 tablespoon minced fresh chives

1. In a heavy medium saucepan over moderate heat, bring the onion, cream and ham to a boil. Cook, stirring occasionally, until the cream is reduced by half, about 15 minutes. Add the oyster

liquor and cook until the sauce thickly coats the back of a spoon, 10 to 15 minutes. Strain into a medium saucepan, cover and keep warm over low heat.

2. In a large pot of boiling salted water, cook the asparagus until tender but still bright green, about 3 minutes. Drain and rinse under cold running water; drain well and pat dry.

3. Divide the asparagus spears between 2 heated plates. Bring the sauce back to a boil, add the oysters and cook until they are barely warm, about 10 seconds, or until just firm, about 30 seconds, if you prefer oysters fully cooked. Season with salt and pepper to taste. Place 4 oysters on each plate, pour the sauce over all and garnish with the chives.

Broiled Crumbed Oysters and Shallots

If you half fill a baking pan with rock salt, you'll find it easy to anchor the oysters on the half shell so that they will not tip as they broil.

6 TO 8 SERVINGS

5 tablespoons unsalted butter
½ cup finely diced shallots (about 5 large)
¾ cup fine dry bread crumbs
¼ cup fresh lemon juice
½ teaspoon Pernod (optional)
¼ cup finely chopped parsley
¼ cup freshly grated Parmesan cheese
2 dozen oysters, on the half shell
Rock salt

1. Preheat the broiler. In a heavy medium skillet, melt the butter; add the shallots and sauté until golden, 4 to 5 minutes. Add the crumbs and cook, tossing, until the crumbs have absorbed all the butter, about 1 minute. Off heat, mix in the lemon juice, Pernod, parsley and Parmesan.

2. Arrange the oysters in a large shallow baking pan filled with rock salt (or crumpled aluminum foil); top each with about 1 tablespoon of the shallot-crumb mixture. Broil the oysters 4 inches from the heat until bubbly and lightly browned, about 3 minutes. Serve at once.

Mussels in Saffron Cream Sauce (Mouclade)

F&W Beverage Suggestion:
Sancerre or California Fumé Blanc

4 SERVINGS

3 pounds fresh mussels
1 cup dry white wine
3 medium shallots, minced
2 small garlic cloves, minced
⅛ teaspoon saffron threads, crumbled
1 cup crème fraîche or heavy cream
2½ teaspoons cornstarch

1. Scrub the mussels under cold water; trim off the beards. Discard any mussels that are open.

2. In a large noncorrodible pot, bring the wine, shallots and garlic to a boil over high heat. Add the mussels, cover and steam, shaking the pan once or twice, until the shells are open, 3 to 4 minutes. Remove from the heat. Divide the mussels among 4 large soup plates, discarding any that have not opened. Cover with aluminum foil to keep warm.

3. Pour the cooking liquid through a strainer lined with a double thickness of dampened cheesecloth into a medium saucepan. Return the liquid to a boil over high heat. Add the saffron and boil until the liquid is reduced by one-quarter, about 3 minutes.

4. Whisk the crème fraîche into the reduced liquid until blended. Warm the sauce over moderate heat until simmering. Place the cornstarch in a small bowl. Whisk in ½ cup of the hot sauce until blended. Scrape into the saucepan and whisk until blended. Simmer, stirring, until thick enough to coat the back of a spoon, 1 to 2 minutes. Spoon the sauce over the mussels.

Marinated Shrimp with Shrimp Mousse

12 SERVINGS

½ lemon, thinly sliced
1 small red onion, thinly sliced
½ cup Calamata olives, quartered and pitted
1 tablespoon chopped pimiento
2 tablespoons vegetable oil
1 garlic clove, crushed
1½ teaspoons powdered mustard
1¼ teaspoons salt
¼ cup plus 1 tablespoon fresh lemon juice
1½ teaspoons red wine vinegar
2 bay leaves
2 to 3 drops hot pepper sauce
12 large shrimp in the shell (about 1 pound)
½ pound medium shrimp in the shell
2 teaspoons olive oil
¼ cup dry white wine
1 large shallot, sliced
⅛ teaspoon ground coriander
1 tablespoon unflavored gelatin
½ cup mayonnaise
½ teaspoon paprika
1 cup heavy cream
Pinch of white pepper
1 tablespoon chopped parsley

1. In a large bowl, make a marinade by combining the lemon slices, red onion, olives, pimiento, vegetable oil, garlic, mustard, 1 teaspoon of the salt, ¼ cup of the lemon juice, the vinegar, 1 bay leaf, crumbled, and the hot pepper sauce.

2. Shell the large shrimp leaving the tails connected; reserve the shells. Cook the shrimp in a large saucepan of boiling salted water until faintly translucent in the thick part of the shrimp, about 1 minute. Drain and add the shrimp to the marinade. Let cool in the marinade; then refrigerate, tossing occasionally, for at least 2 hours, or overnight.

3. Meanwhile, peel the medium shrimp, reserving the shells. In a small skillet with a cover, warm the olive oil over moderate heat. Add all the reserved shrimp shells and sauté, stirring occasionally, until pink and highly aromatic, 3 to 4 minutes.

4. Add the wine, ¾ cup of water, the shallot, remaining bay leaf and the coriander. Bring to a boil, cover and simmer over low heat for 10 minutes.

5. Add the medium shrimp and cook, uncovered, until they just begin to lose their translucency, about 3 minutes.

6. Strain through a sieve into a bowl. Remove the shrimp and set aside to cool; discard the other solids. There will be about ½ cup of liquid. If there is less, add water to equal ½ cup; if there is more, boil to reduce it to ½ cup.

7. Sprinkle the gelatin into a food processor and pour the remaining 1 tablespoon lemon juice over it. Bring the reserved ½ cup liquid to a boil and add it to the bowl. Process until all of the gelatin is dissolved, about 2 minutes. Add the mayonnaise, paprika and medium shrimp and puree until smooth. With the machine on, add the cream. Pass the mixture through a sieve for finer texture. Taste and season with the remaining ¼ teaspoon salt, the white pepper and more lemon juice if desired.

8. Line a 9-inch square pan with 2 long sheets of waxed paper or plastic wrap in perpendicular directions. Pour in the mousse; it will be about ⅜ inch thick. Cover and refrigerate until set, about 1 hour. **(The recipe can be prepared a day ahead to this point.)**

9. To assemble, remove the large shrimp from the marinade. Strain the marinade and pick out the quartered olives. Chop the olives and toss with the parsley.

10. Lift the sheets of waxed paper to remove the mousse from the pan. Cut into twelve 1½-by-2-inch ovals or rectangles and arrange on a chilled platter. Make a slit along the back of each shrimp, cutting about three-quarters of the way through. Spoon a little of the olive and parsley mixture onto the cut shrimp and place on the mousse. Serve chilled.

Shrimp and Vegetable Timbales with Watercress Sauce

10 SERVINGS

1 quart half-and-half
Bouquet garni: ½ onion, 1 bay leaf, 10 peppercorns, 6 parsley stems and 1 strip of lemon zest tied in a double thickness of cheesecloth
Pinch of nutmeg
Pinch of cayenne pepper
½ teaspoon salt
Pinch of white pepper
8 ounces Gruyère cheese, finely grated
5 whole eggs
4 egg yolks
1 medium carrot, peeled and cut into fine 2-inch julienne strips
1 medium leek (white and tender green), cut into 2-inch julienne strips
¼ pound fresh spinach, cleaned and stemmed
¼ pound cooked small shrimp, shelled and quartered
Watercress Sauce (recipe follows)

1. In a medium saucepan, scald the half-and-half, bouquet garni, nutmeg, cayenne, salt and white pepper over moderate heat. Remove from the heat, cover and let stand for 10 minutes.

2. Strain the mixture. Stir in the grated cheese. Reheat briefly over moderate heat to melt the cheese.

3. Preheat the oven to 350°. In a medi-

um bowl, beat the whole eggs and egg yolks together. Gradually whisk 1 cup of the hot cream mixture into the beaten eggs to warm them. Stir this mixture into the pan with the remaining cream.

4. In a small pan of boiling salted water, cook the carrots until crisp-tender, about 3 minutes. Drain, rinse under cold running water and drain well; pat dry.

5. In another saucepan of boiling water, cook the leek until just tender, about 1 minute. Remove with a slotted spoon and rinse briefly under cold running water. Drain well and pat dry.

6. In the same water, blanch the spinach leaves for 30 seconds. Drain and rinse under cold running water. Drain well and pat dry. Cut into thin strips.

7. Butter ten ¾-cup ramekins and line the bottoms with a circle of parchment or waxed paper. Combine the vegetables and distribute half evenly among the ramekins. Place a few pieces of shrimp in each (using only half the shrimp). Pour in the custard mixture. Top with the remaining vegetables and a few more pieces of shrimp.

8. Place the ramekins in a baking dish set in the middle of the oven. Pour enough hot water into the baking dish to reach halfway up the sides of the ramekins. Bake for 30 minutes, or until the custard is set.

9. Remove the ramekins from the water bath. To serve, unmold onto individual plates and surround with several spoonfuls of Watercress Sauce. Pass the remaining sauce separately.

Watercress Sauce

MAKES ABOUT 1¾ CUPS

½ cup dry white wine
½ cup chicken stock or canned broth
1 cup heavy cream
2 cups firmly packed, coarsely chopped watercress, stems removed
Salt and white pepper
1 egg yolk, lightly beaten

1. In a medium noncorrodible saucepan, boil the white wine and stock over high heat until reduced to ¼ cup. Stir in the heavy cream and set aside.

2. In a large pot of boiling salted water, blanch the watercress for 1 minute. Drain, rinse under cold running water and squeeze out the excess liquid.

3. In a blender or food processor, puree the watercress with the cream mixture. Season with salt and white pepper to taste. **(The sauce may be made ahead to this point.)**

4. Just before serving, add the lightly beaten egg yolk to the watercress cream. Place over moderately low heat, stirring, until hot; do not let boil.

Timbales of Smoked Salmon with Tomato-Basil Sauce

🍷 **F&W Beverage Suggestion:** Dry Creek Chardonnay

12 SERVINGS

1½ to 2 pounds thinly sliced smoked salmon
4 cups crème fraîche
½ cup fresh lemon juice
¼ cup chopped fresh basil
Salt and freshly ground pepper
Tomato-Basil Sauce (recipe follows)
Chopped fresh basil and whole mint leaves, for garnish

1. Line the bottom and sides of each of 12 half-cup (4-ounce) timbales, muffin tins or foil cups with about 1½ ounces of the smoked salmon. Patch to fill any holes or empty spots. Trim off any excess and reserve. Coarsely chop the remaining salmon and trimmings.

2. In a bowl, combine the crème fraîche, lemon juice, basil, chopped smoked salmon and salt and pepper to taste. Stir well to blend; the cream will tighten and thicken. Pack this mixture into each of the lined timbales. Cover and refrigerate for at least 4 hours, or overnight.

3. To serve, run a small knife around the inside edge of each timbale and gently pry loose to unmold. Arrange the timbales on plates or a platter. Spoon 2 to 3 tablespoons of the Tomato-Basil Sauce in a ribbon around each timbale, or cover the platter with a thin coating of sauce. Garnish the tops of the timbales with a pinch of chopped basil and 1 mint leaf.

Tomato-Basil Sauce

MAKES ABOUT 2 CUPS

4 medium tomatoes
4 large basil leaves
½ cup dry white wine
1 tablespoon tomato paste
¼ teaspoon Worcestershire sauce
Salt and freshly ground pepper

1. In a large saucepan of boiling water, cook the tomatoes for 5 minutes. Remove and rinse under cold running water until cool enough to handle. Core and peel the tomatoes.

2. In a blender or food processor, combine the tomatoes, basil, wine, tomato paste and Worcestershire sauce. Puree until smooth. Season with salt and pepper to taste. Strain to remove the seeds; the sauce will be thin. Cover and refrigerate until serving time.

Russian Tea Room's Blini with Smoked Salmon and Sour Cream

🍷 **F&W Beverage Suggestion:** Dry, nonvintage French Champagne, such as Perrier-Jouët Grand Brut or Moët et Chandon Brut Imperial

8 TO 10 SERVINGS

1⅓ cups sifted all-purpose flour
1⅓ cups sifted buckwheat flour
4 teaspoons active dry yeast
¼ cup sugar
½ teaspoon salt
2⅔ cups milk
2 cups (1 pound) unsalted butter, melted
4 eggs, lightly beaten
12 ounces Scotch or Irish smoked salmon, sliced
2 pints sour cream

1. In a large bowl, combine the all-purpose flour, buckwheat flour, yeast, sugar and salt.

2. In a small heavy saucepan, combine the milk and ½ cup of the butter over low heat. Heat, stirring frequently, until the milk is lukewarm (105° to 115°).

3. Stir the milk mixture into the flour mixture and mix well. Add the eggs. Beat with an electric mixer at low speed until smooth, about 1 minute, scraping the sides of the bowl occasionally. Or beat vigorously by hand for 3 to 5 minutes.

4. Cover and let rise in a warm place for 1 to 1½ hours, or until doubled in volume and light and bubbly.

5. Preheat a griddle or large heavy skillet, preferably nonstick, over moderately high heat. Lightly brush the griddle with a thin film of melted butter.

6. Stir down the batter. Ladle about 3 tablespoons of batter onto the griddle. Cook for 40 to 60 seconds, or until the top is bubbly and the bottom is browned. Turn over with a large flat spatula and cook until browned on the other side, about 30 seconds. Transfer to a warm platter and keep hot in a warm oven while making the remaining blini.

7. To serve, brush melted butter on the blini; top with sliced smoked salmon and a spoonful of sour cream and roll up.

Wildflowers' Bay Scallops "Cloud Nine"

🍷 **F&W Beverage Suggestion:** California Chardonnay, such as Beringer Private Reserve

4 SERVINGS

6 ounces prepared puff pastry, such as Pepperidge Farm
1 egg yolk
2 tablespoons unsalted butter
1 large leek (white plus tender green), cut into 6-inch-long julienne strips
¾ cup dry vermouth
¾ pound bay scallops
1½ cups heavy cream
2 tablespoons chopped fresh parsley
¼ teaspoon salt
⅛ teaspoon freshly ground white pepper
2 to 3 teaspoons fresh lemon juice

1. Roll out the puff pastry ⅛ inch thick. Using a very sharp knife or a pastry cutter, cut into four 3-by-5-inch rectangles or ovals. Place on an ungreased cookie sheet and refrigerate for ½ hour. Preheat the oven to 425°.

2. Beat the egg yolk with 1 tablespoon of water to make a glaze. Lightly brush the tops of the pastry with the egg glaze; do not let it run over the sides of the pastry or it will inhibit rising.

3. Bake for 10 minutes, or until the pastry is light brown and puffed. Reduce the heat to 300° and bake for 15 minutes to cook the inside of the pastry. (If the pastry is browning too much, cover lightly with foil.) Remove from the oven and let cool on a rack.

4. Using a serrated knife, halve each pastry puff horizontally. Remove and discard any uncooked pastry in the center.

5. In a large saucepan, melt the butter over moderate heat. Add the leeks, cover and cook until softened, about 3 minutes. Add the vermouth and bring to a simmer. Add the scallops and cook until firm but only slightly opaque, about 2 minutes. Strain the scallops and leeks into a sieve set over a bowl. Return the cooking liquid to the saucepan. Put the scallops and leeks in the bowl; cover loosely and set aside.

6. Boil the cooking liquid until reduced to ¼ cup, about 10 minutes. Add any additional juices that collect in the bowl of scallops and leeks and continue boiling until reduced to ¼ cup. Add the heavy cream and boil until reduced by nearly half to yield 1 cup of sauce, about 15 minutes. Add the parsley, salt and pepper. Season with the lemon juice to taste. **(The recipe may be prepared up to this point up to 1½ hours ahead.)**

7. Shortly before serving, return the scallops and leeks to the sauce and cook briefly over moderate heat until just warmed through, about 30 seconds.

8. To serve, place the bottom of a pastry puff on each of 4 plates. Spoon the scallops and leeks on and around the pastry. Add the tops and spoon the remaining sauce over all.

Spago's Pizza with Smoked Salmon and Golden Caviar

♀ F&W Beverage Suggestion: California Fumé Blanc, such as Parducci

4 INDIVIDUAL 8-INCH PIZZAS

3 cups all-purpose flour
1 envelope (¼ ounce) active dry yeast
1 teaspoon salt
1 tablespoon honey, preferably clover
6 tablespoons olive oil, preferably extra-virgin
2 teaspoons minced chives
6 tablespoons sour cream
8 large thin slices of smoked salmon (about 4 ounces)
2 ounces golden caviar

1. In a food processor, briefly mix the flour and the yeast.

2. In a small bowl, mix the salt, honey, 2 tablespoons of the olive oil and ¾ cup of water. With the motor running, slowly pour the liquid into the processor. Process until the dough masses together on the blade, using up to an additional ¼ cup of water if necessary. (The yeast will not be fully incorporated at this point but will be after rising.)

3. Transfer the dough to a lightly floured surface. Knead 1 teaspoon of the chives into the dough. Continue kneading, adding additional flour if necessary to prevent sticking, until smooth and satiny, about 5 minutes. Place the dough in a lightly oiled bowl, turn once to oil the surface, then cover with a damp kitchen towel and let rise until doubled in size, about 30 minutes.

4. Turn the dough out onto a lightly floured surface. Cut into quarters and roll each quarter into a tight smooth ball. Place them on a baking sheet, cover with a damp kitchen towel and refrigerate until baking time. **(The recipe may be prepared up to this point 3 hours in advance.)**

5. One hour before baking time, remove the dough from the refrigerator and let it return to room temperature. Preheat the oven to 500°.

6. On a lightly floured surface, flatten one of the balls of dough into a 6-inch circle leaving the outer edge thicker than the center. Gently stretch the edges to form an 8-inch circle. Crimp the outer edges to form a small lip. Place the circle of dough on a heavy baking sheet and brush with 1 tablespoon of olive oil. Repeat with the remaining dough and oil.

7. Bake the dough in the lower third of the oven about 10 minutes, until golden brown.

8. Spread each hot crust with 1½ tablespoons of the sour cream and top with a slice of the smoked salmon. Place a spoonful of the caviar in the center of each pizza. Sprinkle with ¼ teaspoon of the remaining chives and serve warm.

Olive and Roasted Red Pepper Pizza

MAKES 3 SMALL FLAT PIZZAS

3 flat anchovy fillets, rinsed and patted dry
1 large garlic clove, crushed through a press
¼ teaspoon freshly ground black pepper
¼ cup olive oil
1 can (6 ounces) pitted black olives, rinsed and drained
12 ounces (3 balls) Basic Pizza Dough (p. 38)
Cornmeal
4 ounces mozzarella cheese, cut into 9 thin slices
1 red bell pepper—roasted, peeled, seeded and finely chopped

1. Preheat the oven and a pizza stone or tiles (see Note, below) to 500° 1 hour before use. Place the anchovies, garlic, black pepper and 2 tablespoons of the oil in a processor or blender and puree until almost liquefied. Add the olives and process until chopped but not pureed.

2. On a lightly floured surface, roll out each ball of dough into a round 7 inches in diameter and ¼ inch thick. For each pizza, dust a pizza peel or a baking sheet with some cornmeal and lay the dough on top. Lightly brush each pizza crust with about 1 teaspoon of olive oil. Spread ⅓ cup of the olive mixture evenly on each crust. Drizzle the remaining tablespoon of oil over all.

3. Slide the pizza onto the hot pizza stone. Bake for 6 to 8 minutes, or until the bottom of the crust is lightly browned. Remove from the oven and place 3 slices of the mozzarella on each crust. Sprinkle with the red pepper and return to the oven and bake for about 5 minutes, or until the cheese is melted.

NOTE: For a crisp crust, we recommend using a pizza stone (available in specialty cookware stores for about $20) or unglazed stone tiles (available from floor covering stores for $2 to $6 apiece). Of course, it's perfectly possible to make a pizza on a baking sheet, preferably a heavy one.

Duck Pizza with Leeks and Garlic

MAKES 2 SMALL FLAT PIZZAS

1 head of garlic, separated into cloves
¼ cup plus 1 tablespoon olive oil
1 boneless whole duck breast, cut in half and trimmed of excess fat
Salt and coarsely cracked pepper
2 medium leeks (white and tender green), cut into 2-inch long julienne strips
8 ounces (2 balls) Basic Pizza Dough (p. 38)
Cornmeal

1. Preheat the oven and a pizza stone or tiles (see Note, p. 31) to 500° 1 hour before use. Combine the garlic cloves and ¼ cup of the olive oil in a small saucepan. Cover and cook over moderate heat until the garlic is soft, 20 to 30 minutes. Pass through a food mill or fine-mesh sieve. Discard the skins; reserve the puree.

2. In a medium skillet, sauté the duck breasts, skin-side down, over moderately high heat until the skin is browned, about 8 minutes. Pour off the excess fat. Turn the breasts and sauté until lightly browned on the other side, about 3 minutes.

3. Remove the duck from the skillet and, when cool enough to handle, remove the skin. Slice the duck breasts into thin strips. Season lightly with salt and pepper. Cover loosely and set aside. Cut the skin into thin strips and return to the skillet. Cook over moderate heat until the fat is rendered and the skin is crisp, about 20 minutes. Drain the cracklings on paper towels.

4. Toss the leeks with the remaining 1 tablespoon olive oil; season lightly with salt and pepper.

5. On a lightly floured surface, roll out each ball of dough into a round 7 inches in diameter and ¼ inch thick. For each pizza, dust a pizza peel or a baking sheet with some cornmeal and lay the dough on top. Spread half of the garlic puree over each pizza crust.

6. Reserve 2 tablespoons of the cracklings for garnish; sprinkle the remainder over the garlic puree. Reserve 2 tablespoons of the leeks for garnish; divide the remainder between the pizzas.

7. Slide the pizza onto the hot pizza stone. Bake in the oven for 5 to 7 minutes. Remove from the oven and arrange the duck slices on top. Continue baking for about 3 minutes, until the duck is warmed through and the bottom of the crust is browned. Garnish with the reserved cracklings and leeks.

Caramelized Onion and Bacon Pizza

MAKES 2 SMALL FLAT PIZZAS

¼ cup plus 2 tablespoons olive oil
3 Spanish onions (about 2 pounds), thinly sliced
¾ teaspoon thyme
2 imported bay leaves
½ cup dry red wine
2 tablespoons red wine vinegar
½ teaspoon salt
¼ teaspoon coarsely cracked pepper
¼ pound thickly sliced slab bacon, cut crosswise into ¼-inch strips
8 ounces (2 balls) Basic Pizza Dough (p. 38)
Cornmeal
Chopped parsley, for garnish

1. Preheat the oven and a pizza stone or tiles (see Note, p. 31) to 500° 1 hour before use. In a large heavy noncorrodible skillet, heat ¼ cup of the olive oil until shimmering. Add the onion, thyme and bay leaves and stir to coat well. Cover and cook over low heat until the onions are soft and translucent, about 10 minutes. Uncover and cook, stirring occasionally, until the onions are golden, 30 to 40 minutes.

2. Stir in the wine and vinegar. Cook until the liquid evaporates, about 10 minutes. Season with the salt and pepper. Remove from the heat and and set aside.

3. In a medium skillet, fry the bacon until lightly browned. Drain on paper towels.

4. On a lightly floured surface, roll out each ball of pizza dough into a round 7 inches in diameter and ¼ inch thick. Dust a pizza peel or a baking sheet with some cornmeal and place the dough on top. Lightly brush the pizza crusts with about 2 teaspoons of olive oil. Spread the onions on top and sprinkle with the bacon. Drizzle the remaining oil over all.

5. Slide the pizza onto the hot pizza stone. Bake for 8 to 10 minutes, or until the bottom of the crust is browned. Sprinkle with the parsley before serving.

Fresh Tomato and Basil Pizza

MAKES 1 SMALL FLAT PIZZA

4 ounces (1 ball) Basic Pizza Dough (p. 38)
Cornmeal
3 tablespoons olive oil
1 small tomato, sliced ¼ inch thick
⅛ teaspoon salt
Pinch of freshly ground pepper
8 large basil leaves

1. Preheat the oven and a pizza stone or tiles (see Note, p. 31) to 500° 1 hour before use. On a lightly floured surface, roll out the dough into a round 7 inches in diameter and ¼ inch thick. Dust a pizza peel or a baking sheet with cornmeal and lay the dough on top.

2. Generously brush the crust with about 1½ tablespoons of the olive oil. Arrange the tomato slices on top and sprinkle with the salt and pepper. Place the basil leaves on top. Drizzle the remaining olive oil over all. Slide the pizza onto the hot pizza stone. Bake for 8 to 10 minutes, or until the bottom of the crust is browned.

Morel and Fontina Pizza (p. 37).

33

Above, Eggplant and Goat Cheese Pizza (p. 37) and Zucchini and
Sausage Pizza (p. 38). Left, Champagne cocktails from top-rated
restaurants in France (left to right): Cocktail aux Framboises (p. 12),
Optimiste (p. 13), Cocktail Michel Pasquet (p. 12) and La Côte St-Jacques
Dans Un Verre (p. 12).

Top, Caviar Mosaic (p. 17). Bottom, Timbales of Smoked
Salmon with Tomato-Basil Sauce (p. 29).

Seafood Pizza

<u>MAKES 1 SMALL FLAT PIZZA</u>

**1 pound mussels, scrubbed and
  debearded**
¼ cup dry white wine
1 large shallot, coarsely chopped
2 tablespoons olive oil
1 tablespoon minced fresh basil
Salt and freshly ground pepper
**8 medium shrimp, shelled and
  deveined**
1 large garlic clove, minced
½ to 1 teaspoon Chinese chili paste
**6 ounces (1½ balls) Basic Pizza
  Dough (p. 38)**
Cornmeal
Sprigs of parsley, for garnish

1. Preheat the oven and a pizza stone or
tiles (see Note, p. 31) to 500° 1 hour
before use. In a large noncorrodible
saucepan, combine the mussels, wine
and shallot. Bring to a boil over high
heat and cook, covered, tossing occasionally, until the mussels open, about 5
minutes; discard any mussels that have
not opened. Drain and remove from the
shells. Toss with 2 teaspoons of the olive
oil and the basil and season with salt and
pepper to taste. (**This can be done a
day ahead.** Cover and refrigerate. Let
the mussels return to room temperature
before continuing.)

2. In a small skillet, heat 2 teaspoons of
the oil. Add the shrimp and cook over
high heat, tossing, for 1 minute. Add the
garlic and chili paste and toss to coat.
Cook, until the shrimp start to lose their
translucency, 1 to 2 more minutes. Remove from the heat.

3. On a lightly floured surface, roll out
the whole ball of dough to a round 7
inches in diameter and ¼ inch thick.
Divide the remaining half ball of dough
in two; roll each half into a rope 12

inches long. Fold the rope in half and
twist together. Lay the twists on top of
the pizza to divide it into quadrants;
moisten the ends of the twists and press
to seal.

4. Dust a pizza peel or a baking sheet
with some cornmeal and lay the dough
on top. Brush with the remaining 2 teaspoons of oil. Prick the surface to prevent the dough from bubbling.

5. Slide the pizza onto the hot pizza
stone. Bake for 8 to 10 minutes, until the
top of the crust is golden. Remove from
the oven and arrange the mussels and
shrimp on alternating quadrants. Garnish with the parsley sprigs in the center.

Eggplant and Goat Cheese Pizza

<u>1 DEEP-DISH PIZZA 9 INCHES IN DIAMETER</u>

**3 small eggplants (about 2½
  pounds)**
⅓ cup coarse (kosher) salt
½ cup olive oil
**½ teaspoon finely chopped fresh
  rosemary or ½ teaspoon dried**
Salt and freshly ground pepper
**14 ounces (½ recipe) Basic Pizza
  Dough (p. 38)**
**5 to 6 ounces (about ½ large log)
  Montrachet goat cheese**

1. Cut 1 eggplant lengthwise into ¼-
inch slices and trim to 4½ inches. Peel
the 2 remaining eggplants and cut into
½-inch cubes.

2. Sprinkle both sides of the eggplant
slices with half of the coarse salt and
place on a rack to drain. Toss the cubed
eggplant with the remaining coarse salt
and place in a large colander to drain.
Let stand for about 30 minutes.

3. Rinse the eggplant slices and cubes;
drain well and press dry between towels.
Wrap in kitchen towels, place in a colander or on a rack and weight down to force
out more liquid. Let stand for 1 hour.

4. Preheat the oven to 450°. Warm a
large, heavy, well-seasoned skillet over
high heat. In batches, lightly brush the

eggplant slices with olive oil. Place in the
skillet and cook until lightly browned,
about 2 minutes on each side. Remove to
a plate.

5. Add ¼ cup of oil to the skillet. When
almost smoking, add the eggplant cubes
and toss in the oil. Add the rosemary and
cook, tossing occasionally, until the eggplant is translucent and browned around
the edges, about 10 minutes. Season with
salt and pepper to taste.

6. On a lightly floured surface, roll out
the dough and place a deep-dish pan
(see Note, below) in the center. Cut out
a round of dough that will comfortably
line the pan with an additional 1 inch for
overlap. Coat the deep-dish pan with a
heavy film of olive oil to ensure a crisp
crust. Drape the dough loosely over the
pan and ease it in and against the bottom
and sides of the pan.

7. Brush the dough with about 1 tablespoon of the oil. Crumble the goat
cheese over the dough. Cover with the
cubed eggplant. Arrange the eggplant
slices in an overlapping pinwheel pattern on top. Drizzle any remaining oil on
top and sprinkle lightly with salt and
pepper.

8. Bake for 20 minutes, or until the crust
is golden. Remove from the pan and let
stand on a rack for 10 minutes before
slicing, to allow the filling to set.

NOTE: To make this deep-dish pizza you
will need a pan 9 inches in diameter and
about 2 inches deep. For the best results,
use one made of black carbon steel.

Morel and Fontina Pizza

<u>MAKES 1 SMALL FLAT PIZZA</u>

1 ounce dried morel mushrooms
2 tablespoons olive oil
⅛ teaspoon salt
**⅛ teaspoon coarsely cracked
  pepper**
**4 ounces (1 ball) Basic Pizza
  Dough (p. 38)**
Cornmeal
**3 ounces Italian Fontina cheese,
  shredded**
Freshly minced chives, for garnish

1. Preheat the oven and a pizza stone or
tiles (see Note, p. 31) to 500° 1 hour
before use. Soak the morels in 2 cups of

warm water until soft, about 15 minutes. Scoop them out, reserving the soaking liquid, and let drain on paper towels. Trim off the sandy bottoms. Taste a morel to see if the sand is all gone; if not, soak again, discarding the liquid from the second soaking.

2. Strain the soaking liquid through several layers of dampened cheesecloth into a saucepan. Boil over high heat until reduced to ¼ cup, about 20 minutes.

3. In a medium skillet, heat 1 tablespoon of the oil. Add the morels and sauté over moderate heat, stirring, until softened, about 3 minutes. Add the reduced soaking liquid and cook, uncovered, until the liquid is absorbed. Season with the salt and pepper.

4. On a lightly floured surface, roll out the pizza dough into a round 7 inches in diameter and ¼ inch thick. Dust a pizza peel or a baking sheet with some cornmeal and lay the dough on top. Lightly brush the pizza crust with about 1 teaspoon of the oil, then prick all over with a fork.

5. Slide the pizza onto the hot pizza stone. Bake for 5 minutes until a light crust has formed. Remove from the oven and sprinkle with the cheese. Place the morels on top and drizzle with the remaining 2 teaspoons oil. Return to the oven and bake for 5 more minutes, or until the cheese is melted and the bottom of the crust is browned. Garnish with the chives before serving.

Zucchini and Sausage Pizza

1 DEEP-DISH PIZZA 9 INCHES IN DIAMETER

½ **pound sweet Italian sausage**
6 **tablespoons olive oil**
2 **medium zucchini, cut lengthwise into ¼-inch slices and trimmed to 4½ inches**
14 **ounces (½ recipe) Basic Pizza Dough (p. 38)**

¼ **cup freshly grated Parmesan cheese**
6 **ounces Monterey Jack cheese, shredded (1¼ cups)**
½ **cup Chunky Tomato Sauce (p. 222)**
¼ **teaspoon salt**
⅛ **teaspoon freshly ground pepper**

1. Preheat the oven to 450°. Remove the sausage from its casing and crumble into a medium skillet. Fry over moderate heat until browned. Drain on paper towels.

2. Lightly brush the bottom of a large, heavy, well-seasoned skillet with olive oil and warm over moderate heat until the oil is hot enough to evaporate a drop of water upon contact. Working in batches, lay as many zucchini strips into the skillet as will easily fit in a single layer. Lightly brush the tops of the strips with oil and cook, turning once, until lightly browned, about 2 minutes on each side. Remove to a plate. Lightly oil the skillet and repeat with the remaining slices.

3. On a lightly floured surface, roll out the dough and place a deep-dish pan (see Note, p. 37) in the center. Cut out a round of dough that will comfortably line the pan with an additional 1 inch for overlap. Coat the deep-dish pan with a heavy film of olive oil to ensure a crisp crust. Drape the dough loosely over the pan and ease it in and against the bottom and sides of the pan.

4. Brush the dough with about 1 tablespoon of oil. Sprinkle with the Parmesan and 1 cup of the Monterey Jack. Dot with the sausage, then spoon the tomato sauce on top. Lay the zucchini slices on top in an overlapping pinwheel pattern. Drizzle with the remaining oil and sprinkle with the salt and pepper.

5. Bake for 25 minutes, or until the crust is golden. Remove from the oven and sprinkle the remaining ¼ cup of Monterey Jack over the pizza. Bake for 5 minutes until melted.

6. Remove the pizza from the pan. Let stand on a rack for 10 minutes before slicing, to allow the filling to set.

Basic Pizza Dough

MAKES 1¾ POUNDS

1 **envelope (¼ ounce) active dry yeast**
1 **tablespoon sugar**
1½ **cups warm water (110° to 115°)**
3¼ **cups unbleached flour, preferably bread flour**
½ **teaspoon salt**
¼ **cup olive oil, preferably extra-virgin**

1. In a small bowl, combine the yeast and sugar. Add the water and stir to mix. If the yeast is not active and bubbling within 5 minutes, discard it and repeat the procedure with a new envelope of yeast.

2. Measure 3 cups of flour by spooning into a one-cup measure and leveling off with a knife, and place in a large bowl. Stir in the salt, then form a well in the center of the flour.

3. Pour the yeast mixture into the well and add the oil. Stir in the flour, beginning in the center and working toward the sides of the bowl. When all the flour is incorporated and the dough is still soft but begins to mass together, turn out onto a lightly floured work surface.

4. Using a dough scraper to lift any fragments that cling to the work surface, knead the dough, adding just enough of the remaining ¼ cup flour until the dough is no longer sticky. (It is better that the dough be too soft than too stiff.) Continue to knead until smooth, shiny and elastic, 10 to 15 minutes.

5. Shape the dough into a ball and place it in a large, oiled bowl; turn the dough over to coat with the oil. Cover with plastic wrap, set in a warm draft-free place and let rise until doubled in bulk, 1 to 1½ hours. Punch the dough down and reshape into a ball. Cover and refrigerate until doubled in bulk, 20 minutes to 1 hour.

6. If making deep-dish pizza, divide the dough in half. If making flat pizza, divide the dough into 7 balls of equal weight (4 ounces) and use one for each flat pizza. To freeze, wrap each ball well in plastic; let thaw before proceeding.

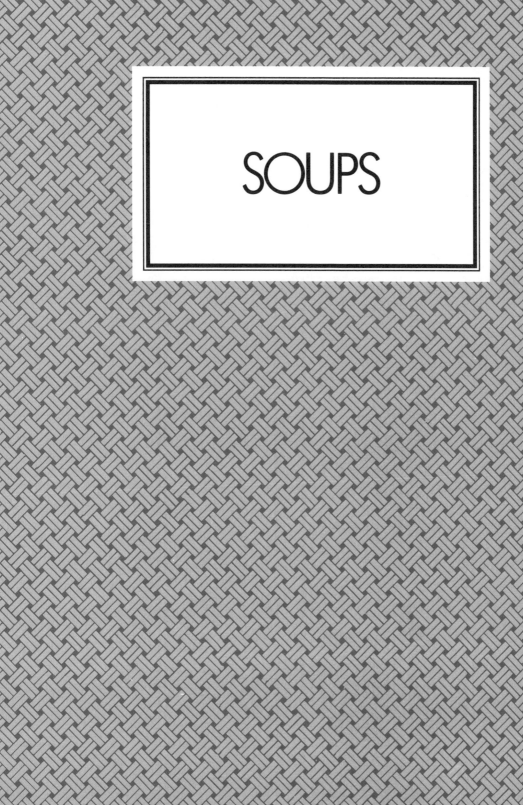

SOUPS

Smoky Onion Broth

To turn this basic broth into a hearty entrée soup, add ¼ cup meat, poultry or fish; ⅓ cup of a starch, and 1 cup of vegetables for every 1 cup of broth. Smoky Onion Broth works particularly well with one of the following combinations: 1) strips of chicken thigh, cubed slab bacon, black-eyed peas, tomato, green peppers and leeks; 2) mussels (8 per person), sweet potato, lettuce and leeks.

MAKES ABOUT 2½ QUARTS

4 tablespoons unsalted butter
4 large Spanish onions (4 pounds), coarsely chopped
6 unpeeled garlic cloves
10 peppercorns
3 imported bay leaves
6 cups canned chicken broth
2 smoked ham hocks (1 pound)
2 cups dry white wine

1. In a large noncorrodible stockpot, melt the butter over moderate heat and add the onions, garlic, peppercorns and bay leaves. Cook, uncovered, until the onions are golden, 15 to 20 minutes.

2. Add the chicken broth, 1 quart of water and the ham hocks. Bring to a boil, reduce the heat and simmer, partially covered, for 45 minutes to extract the flavors.

3. Add the wine. Bring to a boil again, then reduce the heat to low and simmer, uncovered, for 3 minutes. Strain the broth through a sieve lined with several layers of dampened cheesecloth, pressing down on the solids to extract as much liquid as possible; let cool. If desired, refrigerate up to a week before using, or freeze.

Mushroom Broth

To turn this basic broth into a hearty entrée soup, add ¼ cup meat, poultry or fish; ⅓ cup of a starch, and 1 cup of vegetables for every 1 cup of broth. Mushroom Broth works particularly well with one of the following combinations: 1) sliced Polish sausage, pinto beans, cabbage, carrots and onions; 2) bluefish or mackerel, small pasta shells, celery, mushrooms and red peppers.

MAKES ABOUT 2½ QUARTS

1 tablespoon unsalted butter
6 unpeeled onions (¾ pound), chopped
3 unpeeled garlic cloves, coarsely chopped
1 pound plum tomatoes, quartered, or 1 cup crushed canned plum tomatoes
2½ pounds opened (see Note) mushrooms, finely chopped
6 cups canned chicken broth
10 peppercorns
3 imported bay leaves

1. In a large stockpot, melt the butter over moderate heat. Add the onions and cook, covered, until translucent, about 5 minutes.

2. Add the garlic, tomatoes, mushrooms, broth, peppercorns, bay leaves and 6 cups of water. Bring to a boil, reduce the heat to low and simmer, partially covered, for 1 hour, skimming occasionally.

3. Strain the broth through a sieve lined with several layers of dampened cheesecloth, pressing down on the solids to extract as much liquid as possible; let cool. If desired, refrigerate up to a week before using, or freeze.

NOTE: We recommend using slightly older mushrooms with opened caps and exposed dark gills for this recipe. They will contribute a fuller mushroom flavor to the soup. Avoid packaged mushrooms with chemical preservatives.

Fennel Broth

To turn this basic broth into a hearty entrée soup, add ¼ cup meat, poultry or fish; ⅓ cup of a starch, and 1 cup of vegetables for every 1 cup of broth. Fennel Broth works particularly well with one of the following combinations: 1) shrimp and/or bay scallops, red potato cut into matchsticks, red pepper, spinach and fennel; 2) (no meat—increase the quantity of vegetables), barley, whole shallots, green beans, carrots, red pepper, zucchini and mushrooms.

MAKES ABOUT 2½ QUARTS

2 tablespoons olive oil
3 large fennel bulbs, including stalks and leaves, coarsely chopped (about 12 cups)
2 medium leeks (white and tender green parts), coarsely chopped
6 unpeeled garlic cloves
2 sprigs of fresh thyme or ½ teaspoon dried
3 imported bay leaves
10 peppercorns
6 cups canned chicken broth

1. In a large noncorrodible stockpot, heat the oil. Add the fennel, leeks, garlic, thyme, bay leaves and peppercorns. Stir to coat with the oil. Cover and cook the vegetables over low heat, stirring occasionally, until softened but not browned, about 10 minutes.

2. Add the chicken broth and 6 cups of water. Simmer, partially covered, for 1 hour.

3. Strain the broth through a sieve lined with several layers of dampened cheesecloth, pressing down on the solids to extract as much liquid as possible; let cool. If desired, refrigerate up to a week before using, or freeze.

Celery-Leek Broth

To turn this basic broth into a hearty entrée soup, add ¼ cup meat, poultry or fish; ⅓ cup of a starch, and 1 cup of vegetables for every 1 cup of broth. Celery-Leek Broth works particularly well with one of the following combinations: 1) diced smoked ham, wild and white rice, yellow squash and collard greens; 2) strips of chicken breast, pastina, sliced red potatoes, celery strips and diced cucumber.

MAKES ABOUT 2½ QUARTS

2 tablespoons olive oil
1½ bunches of celery, finely chopped (about 10 cups)
4 medium leeks (white and tender green parts), finely chopped (about 5 cups)
3 unpeeled garlic cloves, lightly crushed
2 quarts canned chicken broth
1 imported bay leaf
1 teaspoon thyme
12 peppercorns

1. In a large stockpot, heat the oil. Add the celery and leeks, cover and cook over moderate heat until the vegetables are softened and translucent, about 5 minutes. Add the garlic, broth, bay leaf, thyme, peppercorns and 1 quart water.

2. Bring to a boil, then reduce the heat to low and simmer, partially covered, for 1 hour, skimming occasionally.

3. Strain the broth through a sieve lined with several layers of dampened cheesecloth, pressing down on the solids to extract as much liquid as possible; let cool. If desired, refrigerate up to a week before using, or freeze.

Lisa's Green Chili Soup

8 SERVINGS

2 tablespoons vegetable oil
1 pound *poblano* or Anaheim chilies—roasted, peeled and seeded—or 2 cans (7 ounces each) roasted peeled California chilies, drained
1 small onion, chopped
2 quarts chicken stock or canned broth
4 skinless, boneless chicken breast halves
1 sprig (4 or 5 leaves) of fresh *epazote*, minced, or ¼ teaspoon dried (see Note; optional)
½ teaspoon salt
¼ teaspoon freshly ground pepper
4 corn tortillas, cut into ¼-inch squares
4 cups corn kernels (from 6 to 8 ears of corn) or 3 packages (10 ounces each) frozen, thawed
1 pound Monterey Jack cheese, cut into ¼-inch dice
Sour cream

1. Preheat the oven to 300°. In a medium skillet, heat the oil. Add the chilies and the onion and sauté over moderately high heat until tender, about 5 minutes. Scrape the mixture into a food processor or a blender and puree. Set aside.

2. In a large saucepan, bring the stock to a boil over high heat. Reduce the heat to a simmer and add the chicken. Poach until tender and no longer pink in the center, about 15 minutes. Remove the chicken and let stand until cool enough to handle. Shred the chicken and return it to the stock. Add the pureed chilies, the *epazote*, salt and pepper and simmer gently for 30 minutes.

3. Meanwhile, spread out the tortilla squares on a large baking sheet. Bake for about 15 minutes, until brown. (These crunchy garnishes are called *totopos*.)

4. In a blender or food processor, puree 2 cups of the corn with 2 cups of the soup stock. Add to the soup along with the remaining 2 cups corn kernels. Simmer until tender, about 5 minutes.

5. To serve, put about ¼ cup of the diced Monterey Jack into each bowl. Ladle in the hot chili soup. Top with a spoonful of sour cream and a sprinkling of *totopos*.

NOTE: A mild Mexican herb available at Latin American groceries and some spice shops.

Lemon-Orange Broth with Scallions and Dill

Here is a refreshing citrus-flavored cold soup that can be made a day ahead of serving. The taste of fresh orange juice is particularly light and delicate, but reconstituted orange juice is a satisfactory substitute.

4 SERVINGS

2 cans (13¾ ounces each) low-sodium chicken broth or unsalted stock, degreased
2 medium carrots, coarsely chopped
1 celery rib, coarsely chopped
3 sprigs of parsley
½ small onion, quartered
1 bay leaf
½ cup orange juice, preferably fresh
3 tablespoons fresh lemon juice
4 eggs, at room temperature, well beaten
Freshly ground pepper
2 scallions (green part only), thinly sliced on the diagonal
2 tablespoons chopped fresh dill

1. In a large heavy saucepan, combine the broth, carrots, celery, parsley, onion and bay leaf. Bring to a boil over high heat. Reduce the heat and simmer for 20 minutes. Strain the hot broth through a sieve into a medium bowl, pressing down on the solids to extract as much liquid as possible.

2. Stir in the orange and lemon juices. Whisk ½ cup of the broth into the beaten eggs; then whisk the eggs in a thin stream into the remaining broth. Refrigerate, covered, until chilled, 4 hours or overnight.

3. Season with pepper to taste. Divide the broth among 4 soup bowls and garnish with the scallions and dill. Serve cold.

Two-Mushroom Consommé

8 SERVINGS

2 pounds opened (see Note) button mushrooms, finely chopped
1½ ounces dried *porcini* mushrooms
1½ pounds unpeeled onions, cut into eighths
5 medium carrots, cut into 1-inch pieces
1 can (14 ounces) Italian peeled tomatoes, drained and coarsely chopped
12 to 15 parsley stems
3 unpeeled garlic cloves, lightly crushed
3 cups chicken stock or canned broth
¼ teaspoon thyme
¼ teaspoon freshly ground pepper
Salt
Fresh *enoki* mushrooms or thinly sliced button mushrooms, for garnish

1. In a large heavy saucepan, place the button mushrooms, *porcini*, onions, carrots, tomatoes, parsley, garlic, stock, thyme and pepper. Add 2 quarts of cold water and slowly bring to a boil over moderate heat. Immediately reduce the heat to low, cover and simmer, skimming occasionally, for 1 hour.

2. Pour the soup through a fine sieve lined with several layers of dampened cheesecloth; discard the solids. Return the liquid to the saucepan, increase the heat to high and boil, uncovered, until the consommé is reduced by about one-fourth. Season with salt to taste. Serve hot, garnished with fresh mushrooms.

NOTE: We recommend using slightly older button mushrooms, with opened caps and exposed dark gills for this recipe. They will contribute a fuller mushroom flavor to the soup. Avoid packaged mushrooms with chemical preservatives.

Pork, Turnip and Cellophane Noodle Soup

The pungent flavor of turnips mingles with the sweetness of pork in a meal-in-broth reminiscent of Japanese *nabe mono* (one-pot meals). The dish, which can be assembled in minutes, is unusually flavorful for a soup that is quickly prepared, with no mellowing time allotted.

2 SERVINGS

4 scallions
6 ounces trimmed lean pork, cut into 1-inch pieces
2 teaspoons cornstarch
2 teaspoons sake or dry sherry
1 teaspoon soy sauce
⅛ teaspoon ground nutmeg
2 ounces cellophane noodles*
4 cups degreased pork, chicken, veal, light beef stock or canned chicken broth
¾ pound turnips or rutabaga, cut into very fine julienne strips or coarsely grated
1 medium carrot, cut into paper-thin rounds
About ¼ teaspoon pepper
*Available in Oriental groceries

1. In a food processor, mince 2 of the scallions. Add the pork and chop coarsely. Add the cornstarch, sake, soy sauce and nutmeg and chop to a medium-fine texture. Let stand until needed.

2. Place the noodles in a bowl and add boiling water to cover; let stand. Form the meat mixture into balls about ¾ inch in diameter (there should be 25 or more).

3. In a large saucepan, combine the stock and turnips, cover and bring to a simmer; if you prefer a mild turnip flavor, do not cover the pan. Add the meatballs and cook, uncovered, at a slow simmer for 2 minutes.

4. Drain the noodles. With scissors, cut them into 4- to 5-inch lengths and add to the soup, along with the carrot and ¼ teaspoon pepper or more to taste. Simmer until the carrots are barely tender, about 3 minutes. Slice the 2 remaining scallions, using the green part only; sprinkle over the top and serve at once.

Smoked Pork and Cabbage Soup

The smoky flavors of this soup blend and intensify when heated, so prepare ahead for optimum results. The salty, assertive savor of the hock (knuckle) is most worthwhile, although the cut yields a good deal of fat when simmered. This is easily skimmed, and should be.

4 SERVINGS

2 small (1½ pounds) meaty smoked pork hocks (knuckles, ham hocks), split
1 large onion, chopped
2 medium green bell peppers, chopped
1 large garlic clove, minced
1½ pounds firm green cabbage, very thinly sliced
1 can (16 ounces) tomatoes, with their liquid
2 tablespoons barley
¾ teaspoon marjoram
¼ teaspoon cayenne pepper, or less to taste
Salt and freshly ground black pepper

1. In a large pot, combine the pork with 2 quarts of water. Simmer, covered, until tender, about 1 hour. Remove the hocks and set aside to cool a bit. Skim off 1 tablespoon fat from the stock and place this fat in a large flameproof casserole. Skim off and discard all the remaining fat (or if you have time, cool and chill the stock and scrape off the hardened fat).

2. Heat the fat in the casserole. Stir in the onion and green peppers and cook, stirring occasionally, over moderate heat until lightly browned, about 10 minutes. Add the garlic and stir for 1 minute. Add the cabbage, increase the heat to high and cook, stirring, for a few minutes, until wilted slightly.

3. With kitchen scissors, snip the tomatoes in the can into small pieces and add to the soup along with the liquid. Add

the stock, barley, marjoram and cayenne and bring to a simmer.

4. Meanwhile, remove and discard the skin and fat from the hocks. Cut the meat into small dice and add to the soup. Simmer, until the cabbage is tender, about 1 hour. Season with salt and black pepper to taste and serve at once. Or let cool, refrigerate and reheat the soup at serving time.

Butternut Squash Soup au Gratin

The temptation in making a winter squash soup is to cream it and spice it in the manner of pumpkin soup. This one couldn't be more different. It's garlicky and gratinéed in the manner of French onion soup, and nourishing enough to serve as a main dish. You'll find that this soup will have richer flavor if you make it a day or two before you serve it.

8 TO 10 SERVINGS

¼ cup olive oil
1 large onion, chopped
2 small garlic cloves, minced
¼ teaspoon thyme
¼ teaspon crumbled rosemary
2 pounds butternut or other winter squash—peeled, seeded and coarsely shredded (to yield about 5½ cups)
7 cups chicken stock or canned broth
2 cups beef stock or canned broth
1¼ cups fresh whole wheat bread crumbs (from about 4 slices)
Salt and freshly ground pepper
1 thin loaf of French bread, sliced 1-inch thick
4 tablespoons unsalted butter, at room temperature
½ cup freshly grated Parmesan cheese

1. In a large heavy saucepan, heat 2 tablespoons of the oil. Add the onion and half of the garlic and sauté over moderately low heat, stirring often, until softened and translucent but not browned, about 10 minutes. Reduce the heat to low, blend in the thyme and rosemary and cook for 5 minutes.

2. Add the shredded squash and sauté, stirring frequently, until slightly translu-

cent, about 5 minutes. Add the chicken and beef stocks. Cover and simmer gently for 1 hour.

3. Strain the soup, reserving the solids and liquid. In a blender or food processor, puree the soup solids in batches with ½ cup of the liquid until silky smooth. Return the remaining liquid and the puree to the saucepan and set over low heat.

4. In a heavy medium skillet, heat the remaining 2 tablespoons oil. Add the remaining garlic and sauté over low heat until softened but not browned, about 2 minutes. Add the bread crumbs and cook, tossing, until all of the oil is absorbed and the bread is lightly browned, 1 to 2 minutes. Stir the crumb mixture into the soup, then season to taste with salt and pepper. **(The soup can be made ahead to this point and either refrigerated or frozen. Reheat before proceeding.)**

5. To gratinée the soup, preheat the oven to 350°. Lightly spread the slices of French bread with the butter on one side only. Place on a baking sheet, buttered-side up, and bake for 8 to 10 minutes, until lightly toasted. Preheat the broiler with the rack set 6 inches from the heat.

6. For each serving, place 2 slices of toast in the bottom of a flameproof soup plate. Ladle the steaming hot squash soup over the toast and sprinkle with about 1 tablespoon Parmesan cheese. Set the soup plates on a sturdy metal tray or baking sheet. Slide the tray under the broiler and broil just until the cheese is bubbly and lightly browned, 2 to 3 minutes.

Onion-Squash Soup

6 SERVINGS

½ cup (1 stick) unsalted butter
3 tablespoons vegetable oil
6 large onions, coarsely chopped (about 10 cups)
4 large garlic cloves, smashed with a knife
2½ quarts beef stock or canned broth
2 cups dry white wine
3 large acorn squashes
¼ cup Cognac or brandy
2 tablespoons red wine vinegar
Salt and freshly ground pepper
6 eggs
Sour cream and minced fresh chives, for garnish

1. In a stockpot, melt the butter in the oil over moderately low heat. Add the onions and garlic, cover and cook, stirring occasionally, until soft, about 20 minutes.

2. Add the stock and wine and simmer uncovered for 1½ hours.

3. Meanwhile, halve the acorn squashes crosswise and remove the seeds. Using a melon baller or spoon, scoop out the squash, leaving a ½-inch-thick shell; reserve the squash. If necessary, shave a thin slice off the bottom of each shell so they stand upright.

4. Add the reserved squash to the soup. Simmer until cooked, about 25 minutes. Add the Cognac and vinegar and cook for 5 minutes.

5. Preheat the oven to 350°. Working in batches, puree the soup in a blender. Season the pureed soup with salt and pepper to taste. **(The recipe can be prepared ahead to this point. Reheat the soup before proceeding.)**

6. Place the squash shells on a baking sheet and divide the hot soup among them. Bake for 20 minutes, or until the shells are heated through. Gently break 1 egg into each of the 6 shells. Return to the middle shelf of the oven and bake for 5 to 10 minutes, until the eggs are set.

7. Garnish each poached egg with a dollop of sour cream and a sprinkling of chives. Serve hot.

Trumps' Corn Soup with Red Pepper Puree

6 SERVINGS

2 red bell peppers
2 tablespoons unsalted butter
2 medium onions, chopped
3 cups of corn kernels, cut from 6 ears of corn
2 cups chicken stock or canned broth
1 cup heavy cream
½ teaspoon salt
¼ teaspoon freshly ground white pepper

1. Roast the peppers over an open flame or broil 4 inches from the heat, turning, until charred all over, about 5 minutes. Seal the peppers in a paper bag and let "sweat" for 10 minutes. With your fingers, rub off the charred skin and rinse briefly under cold running water; pat dry. Remove the seeds, stems and ribs and coarsely chop the peppers. Puree in a blender or food processor; strain and set aside.

2. In a large heavy saucepan, melt the butter over moderately high heat. Add the onions and sauté until translucent, 2 to 3 minutes.

3. Add the corn to the onions and continue cooking, stirring occasionally, for 5 minutes. Add the stock, reduce the heat to moderately low, cover the pan and cook for 15 minutes.

4. Working in batches, puree the soup in a food processor or blender; strain and return to the saucepan.

5. Add the cream and cook over low heat, stirring, until just heated through, about 5 minutes. Add the salt and pepper. Ladle the soup into serving bowls. Drizzle a few spoonfuls of the reserved red pepper puree across each bowl of soup and swirl decoratively. Serve hot or cold.

Asparagus Soup

Here's a good use for the tough ends and peelings removed from asparagus spears. Save them in the freezer until you have enough.

4 SERVINGS

6 cups tough asparagus ends (from about 4 pounds of asparagus), cut into 1-inch pieces
1 teaspoon salt
6 cups asparagus peelings
¼ teaspoon white pepper
2 tablespoons heavy cream (optional)
2 tablespoons unsalted butter (optional)
8 cooked asparagus spears, cut into small pieces, for garnish

1. In a large saucepan or stockpot, place the asparagus ends and enough water to half cover them. Add ½ teaspoon of the salt and bring to a boil over high heat. Reduce the heat and simmer, uncovered, until the asparagus is very soft, 15 to 20 minutes.

2. Add the peelings and cook, stirring, until the peelings are limp and color the liquid bright green, 3 to 5 minutes.

3. In a blender or food processor, puree the stems and peelings with their cooking liquid, in batches if necessary. Press through a fine sieve to remove stringy or coarse pieces. Return the soup to the saucepan. If the soup is too thick, thin it with a little water.

4. Season with the remaining ½ teaspoon salt and the pepper. For a richer soup, stir in the cream and/or the butter. Garnish each serving with the asparagus spears.

Rich Pea Soup

8 SERVINGS

6 packages (10 ounces each) frozen peas, thawed
1 bunch of scallions (8 to 10)
½ bunch of parsley (or stems from 1 bunch)
6 medium garlic cloves, unpeeled
10 peppercorns
3 cups canned chicken broth
⅔ cup heavy cream
¼ teaspoon salt
⅛ teaspoon white pepper
3 tablespoons all-purpose flour
3 tablespoons unsalted butter, softened

1. In a large saucepan or flameproof casserole, combine 3 packages of the peas, the white parts of the scallions (reserve the green tops), the parsley, garlic, peppercorns, chicken broth and 3 cups of water. Bring to a boil, reduce the heat to a simmer and cook uncovered over low heat for 30 minutes.

2. While the soup base is simmering, puree the remaining peas with ⅓ cup of the heavy cream. Press through a fine sieve to remove all the bits of skin.

3. Strain the soup base and discard the solids. Return the broth to the saucepan. Add the pureed peas to the broth, whisk to blend and heat through but do not boil. Season with the salt and pepper. **(The recipe can be prepared to this point up to a day ahead.)**

4. Beat the remaining ⅓ cup heavy cream until stiff. Cut the scallion greens into thin strips.

5. Knead the flour and butter until smooth to make a *beurre manié*. Whisk into the soup. Cook over moderately high heat, whisking, until the soup thickens and comes just to a boil. Remove from the heat and ladle into soup bowls. Garnish each serving with a small dollop of whipped cream and a pinch of scallion strips.

Egg Drop Soup

4 TO 6 SERVINGS

½ ounce dried Chinese
  mushrooms (about 4)
4 cups chicken stock or canned
  broth
1 tablespoon water chestnut
  powder* or cornstarch
¼ cup chopped scallions
¼ cup sliced water chestnuts,
  preferably fresh*
⅛ teaspoon ground white pepper
1 egg, slightly beaten
½ tablespoon Oriental sesame oil
*Available at Oriental groceries

1. Rinse the mushrooms under cool water. Put in a small bowl, cover with about 1 cup of cold water and soak until soft, about 1 hour.

2. Remove the mushrooms from their soaking water. Squeeze the mushrooms over the bowl to extract as much liquid as possible; reserve the soaking water. Cut off and reserve the mushroom stems. Cut the caps into small dice.

3. In a small saucepan, boil the mushroom water and stems over moderately high heat until reduced to about 2 tablespoons. Strain the liquid and set aside to cool. Discard the stems.

4. In a 2-quart saucepan, bring the chicken stock to a simmer. Add the diced mushrooms, reduce the heat to low and simmer for 2 minutes, stirring occasionally.

5. In a small bowl, dissolve the water chestnut powder in the cooled mushroom liquid to make a binder. Gradually stir into the stock. Simmer the soup until it thickens slightly, about 1 minute.

6. Add the scallions, sliced water chestnuts and white pepper. Simmer for another 30 seconds. Remove from the heat and slowly pour in the egg while stirring constantly. Add the sesame oil and stir again. Serve hot.

Roquefort Soup

8 SERVINGS

3 tablespoons unsalted butter
1 large onion, minced (1½ cups)
2 celery ribs, minced (1 cup)
2 medium carrots, minced (1½
  cups)
6 cups chicken broth
1 small potato, cut into ¼-inch dice
  (½ cup)
3 ounces Roquefort cheese
3 tablespoons heavy cream
2 egg yolks
Salt and freshly ground pepper
1 tablespoon minced celery leaves

1. In a large saucepan, melt the butter over low heat. Add the onion, celery and carrots and cook, stirring occasionally, until softened but not browned, about 10 minutes.

2. Add the broth and potato and bring to a boil over high heat. Reduce the heat, cover and simmer until the vegetables are quite tender but not mushy, about 15 minutes.

3. Meanwhile, in a small bowl, mash together the Roquefort and heavy cream until smooth. Add the egg yolks one at a time, mixing well.

4. Stir ¼ cup of hot soup into the Roquefort mixture. Remove the soup from the heat and stir in the Roquefort mixture. Return to low heat, stirring for about 1 minute, to heat through. Do not allow to boil. Season with salt and pepper to taste.

5. Serve hot in soup plates, garnished with a sprinkling of minced celery leaves.

Cream of Pumpkin Soup

8 SERVINGS

4 tablespoons unsalted corn oil
  margarine
1 medium onion, coarsely chopped
3 large shallots, coarsely chopped
1 leek (white part only), coarsely
  chopped
1 small baking potato, peeled and
  coarsely chopped
3 celery ribs, coarsely chopped
2 medium carrots, coarsely
  chopped
¼ cup dry Madeira
6 to 8 cups chicken stock
1½ teaspoons dried thyme or 2
  sprigs of fresh
1 imported bay leaf
1 small pumpkin (2½ to 3
  pounds)—peeled, seeded and cut
  into 1-inch cubes, or 3 cups
  pumpkin puree
¼ teaspoon freshly ground pepper
½ cup evaporated milk
Salt (optional)

1. In a large saucepan, melt the margarine over low heat. Add the onion, shallots, leek, potato, celery and carrots and toss to coat with the margarine. Cook over moderate heat until the vegetables are softened, 10 to 15 minutes.

2. Add the Madeira, cover and cook for 5 minutes. Add 6 cups of the stock, the thyme, bay leaf and pumpkin. Bring to a boil, then reduce to a simmer and cook, partially covered, until the pumpkin is very soft, about 30 minutes.

3. Strain the soup, reserving both the solids and the liquid. Discard the bay leaf. In a blender or food processor, puree the solids, in batches if necessary, with about ½ cup of the liquid. Return the strained liquid and the puree to the saucepan. Add the pepper and evaporated milk. Thin to desired consistency with up to 2 cups additional stock.

4. Before serving, reheat the soup gently. Season with salt to taste if desired.

Creamy Cold Avocado Soup

6 SERVINGS

3 tablespoons unsalted butter
3 tablespoons all-purpose flour
3 cups canned chicken broth
3 avocados, peeled and pitted
1 cup sour cream
¼ cup dry vermouth
1½ tablespoons fresh lemon juice
½ teaspoon white pepper
2 scallions, minced
1 small fresh hot red pepper,
    minced, or ¼ teaspoon cayenne
    pepper
1 tablespoon olive oil

1. In a heavy medium saucepan, melt the butter over low heat. Whisk in the flour until smooth and cook, stirring, for 2 minutes without coloring to make a roux. Add the chicken broth and whisk until smooth. Bring to a boil, stirring; reduce the heat to low and simmer, uncovered, for 5 minutes. Pour into a shallow container and place in the freezer until cool, 20 to 30 minutes.

2. Cut the avocados into large chunks and puree in a blender or food processor. Add the sour cream and puree until blended.

3. Pour in half of the chicken broth and puree until well blended. Pour into a large bowl. Whisk in the remaining broth, the vermouth, lemon juice, white pepper and ½ cup of cold water. Refrigerate, covered, until chilled, about 3 hours.

4. In a small bowl, combine the scallions, hot red pepper and olive oil. To serve, divide the soup among 6 bowls and drop about ½ tablespoon of the scallion-pepper oil into the center of each.

FISH
& SHELLFISH

Trout Portugaise

F&W Beverage Suggestion:
Muscadet de Sèvre-et-Maine

2 SERVINGS

1 trout (about 1 pound), gutted
3 tomatoes, quartered
3 green bell peppers, cut lengthwise into eighths
4 tablespoons unsalted butter, melted
¼ cup olive oil, preferably extra-virgin
Salt and pepper
1½ teaspoons chopped fresh oregano or ½ teaspoon dried
1 stuffed green olive, sliced
3 black olives, halved
6 anchovy fillets
1 teaspoon grated lemon zest

1. Preheat the oven to 350°. Lay the trout in a large baking dish and arrange the tomatoes and peppers around it.

2. In a small bowl, combine the melted butter and the oil. Pour about half the butter-oil mixture over the fish and vegetables. Season with salt and pepper to taste and sprinkle with half the oregano. Bake, uncovered, for 15 minutes.

3. Remove from the oven and with a fork gently lift off the top skin of the trout. Place a green olive slice on the eye. Arrange the black olive halves and anchovy fillets on the trout in a "backbone and rib" pattern. If your anchovies are too soft to make neat "rib" strips, coarsely chop the olives and anchovies and distribute them over and inside the trout.

4. Pour the remaining butter-oil mixture over the fish, and sprinkle with the remaining oregano and the grated lemon zest. Season with salt and pepper to taste. Return to the oven until the flesh at the backbone is still slightly translucent, about 15 minutes. Accompany with rice.

Blue Trout (Truite au Bleu)

Virtually all blue trout recipes require that the fish be cooked in what amounts to vinegared water; this inevitably results in a trout that tastes like vinegar. To retain a delicate flavor, use this two-step procedure, which produces instant bluing and more aromatic poaching.

Traditionally, a live fish is used for *truite au bleu*; at the least the fish should be killed and gutted as soon as possible before cooking to retain the characteristic blue color and curled shape of this dish.

F&W Beverage Suggestion:
Gewürztraminer, such as Clos St. Landelin (Muré)

4 SERVINGS

1 cup dry white wine
1 tablespoon fresh lemon juice
2 celery ribs, cut into ½-inch pieces
½ cup celery leaves
1 large carrot, sliced ½ inch thick
1 medium onion, quartered
6 parsley sprigs, plus additional sprigs for garnish
1 tablespoon chopped fresh tarragon or 1 teaspoon dried
3 bay leaves
6 peppercorns, bruised
¼ teaspoon salt
2 cups tarragon vinegar
2 trout (1 pound each), gutted

1. In a noncorrodible pan with a lid, large enough to poach the trout, combine the wine, lemon juice, celery and celery leaves, carrot, onion, parsley, tarragon, bay leaves, peppercorns and salt with 2 quarts of water and bring to a boil. Boil for 30 minutes, then strain through a fine-mesh sieve, discarding the solids. Return the court bouillon to the pan; bring to a boil.

2. In another large noncorrodible pot, combine the vinegar with 1 quart of water and bring to a boil.

3. With large kitchen tongs, grasp one trout by the lower jaw and, tilting the pot, lower it into the hot vinegar mixture. Boil for 30 seconds to a minute;

when the trout is properly bluish-grey, transfer to the boiling court bouillon. Repeat the process with the second fish.

4. When the court bouillon returns to a boil after adding the second fish, remove the pot from the heat and cover. Let stand for 15 minutes, until the trout are cooked.

5. Remove the fish with a large spatula. Drain and serve on a warmed platter. Garnish with the parsley sprigs.

Trout Grenobloise

F&W Beverage Suggestion:
California Chardonnay, such as Kendall-Jackson

2 SERVINGS

1 cup all-purpose flour
½ teaspoon salt
¼ teaspoon freshly ground pepper
2 trout (8 ounces each), gutted
½ cup peanut or cottonseed oil
2 tablespoons clarified butter
2 tablespoons capers
1 tablespoon diced lemon pulp
1 teaspoon fresh lemon juice
Lemon wedges and parsley sprigs, for garnish

1. In a shallow bowl, combine the flour, salt and pepper. Wash the trout under cold running water and drain thoroughly, but do not pat dry. Dust each fish while still damp with the seasoned flour so that it's lightly coated; shake off the excess. Place on a cooking rack and refrigerate for 3 to 4 hours, or overnight, for a crisper skin.

2. Pour the oil into a heavy skillet large enough to hold both trout and place over moderately high heat. Add the trout and cook, turning once, until crisp and well browned, about 5 minutes on each side. Remove the trout to absorbent paper, then transfer to a serving platter.

3. In a small skillet, combine the clarified butter, capers, lemon pulp and lemon juice over high heat until warmed through; pour over the fish. Garnish the platter with lemon wedges and parsley.

Seasons' Salmon Napoleon

Beverage Suggestion:
Fumé Blanc, such as Chateau Ste. Michelle or Mondavi

8 SERVINGS

½ pound prepared puff pastry
4 tablespoons minced shallots
¼ cup dry white wine
¼ cup white wine vinegar
3 sticks (¾ pound) unsalted butter, cut into tablespoons
¾ teaspoon salt
¼ teaspoon white pepper
1½ pounds thinly sliced fresh salmon fillet
2 tablespoons minced fresh parsley
Sprigs of watercress, for garnish

1. Roll out the puff pastry to a 16-by-10-inch rectangle. Transfer to a cookie sheet, cover and refrigerate for 40 minutes. Meanwhile, preheat the oven to 400°.

2. Prick the pastry all over evenly with a rolling pastry piercer or a fork. Cover with a sheet of parchment paper and pie weights or dried beans. Bake for 10 minutes. Remove the parchment and weights and bake until the pastry is golden brown, about 5 minutes. Remove from the oven and slide the pastry onto a rack; let cool. Leave the oven on.

3. Meanwhile, prepare a *beurre blanc* sauce: In a small noncorrodible saucepan, combine 2 tablespoons of the shallots, the wine and vinegar. Bring to a boil over high heat and boil until the liquid is reduced to 1 tablespoon, about 4 minutes.

4. Remove from the heat and whisk in 4 tablespoons of the butter, 2 tablespoons at a time. Return the pan to very low heat and gradually whisk in the remaining butter, 2 tablespoons at a time just until

incorporated; remove from the heat. Season with ½ teaspoon of the salt and ⅛ teaspoon of the pepper. Keep warm.

5. Season the salmon with the remaining ¼ teaspoon salt and ⅛ teaspoon white pepper. Arrange the salmon slices on the sheet of puff pastry, covering it totally in a single layer. Bake for about 5 minutes, until the fish is opaque.

6. Remove from the oven and cut the salmon pastry sheet into 16 even rectangles, 5 by 2 inches each. Place one rectangle, salmon-side up, on each of 8 warmed plates. Spoon 1 teaspoon of the *beurre blanc* sauce over each piece of salmon. Top with the remaining pastry rectangles, salmon-side up, to form napoleons, and surround with the remaining *beurre blanc*. Sprinkle each with a pinch of the remaining shallots and the minced parsley. Garnish with sprigs of watercress.

Gravetye Manor's Braised Salmon with Pike Mousse

F&W Beverage Suggestion:
California Chardonnay, such as Franciscan

6 SERVINGS

Sauce:
⅓ cup fish stock or bottled clam juice
⅓ cup dry white wine
1 cup chopped plum tomatoes (about 4)
¼ cup minced mushrooms
3 tablespoons chopped shallots
1 cup heavy cream
Salt and freshly ground black pepper

Pike Puree:
8 ounces pike or sole fillets
1 egg
½ teaspoon salt
Dash of white pepper
1 cup heavy cream

Salmon:
6 salmon fillets, about 4 ounces each

1⅔ cups fish stock or ⅔ cup bottled clam juice combined with ⅔ cup water and ⅓ cup dry white wine
Sprigs of parsley, for garnish

1. Make the sauce: In a noncorrodible medium saucepan, combine the fish stock, wine, tomatoes, mushrooms and shallots. Bring to a boil and continue to cook over moderately high heat until the liquid is reduced by half, about 10 minutes. Reduce the heat to moderate, add the heavy cream and cook for 5 minutes longer. Pour into a blender or food processor and puree. Strain through a fine sieve. Season with salt and black pepper to taste.

2. Make the pike puree: Preheat the oven to 400°. In a food processor, puree the pike until smooth. Add the egg, salt and white pepper and mix until well blended. If a finer texture is desired, press the mixture through a fine sieve, a small amount at a time.

3. Place the pike puree in a medium bowl over ice. Gradually beat in the cream with a wooden spoon. Continue beating over ice until the mousse is thick and firm, about 5 minutes.

4. Prepare the salmon: Arrange the salmon in a single layer in a large buttered baking dish. Spread the pike mousse evenly and smoothly over the fillets. Add the fish stock to the dish.

5. Bake for 15 minutes, or until the salmon is just opaque in the center. For a professional finish, broil the fish about 4 inches from the heat for 1 to 2 minutes to glaze the top.

6. While the fish is cooking, reheat the sauce. To serve, spoon ¼ cup of the sauce onto each of 6 dinner plates. Place the fish on top. Garnish with parsley.

Seppi Renggli's Roasted Whole Salmon

This fabulous fish makes a grand presentation for an important party. A large, whole salmon is expensive, but preparation is extremely simple. Roasting brings out the finest flavor of the fish and doesn't perfume your kitchen with the smells of the sea the way poaching does. Order your fish well in advance so it comes in fresh on the day of your party. Begin preparations three to four hours before you plan to serve the fish.

F&W Beverage Suggestion: California Chardonnay, such as Lambert Bridge

18 TO 24 SERVINGS

8-pound whole salmon, as fresh as possible
2 tablespoons salt
1 tablespoon freshly ground pepper
2½ lemons
Large bouquet of mixed fresh herbs such as tarragon, oregano, rosemary, basil, dill, sage
Green tops from 1 or 2 leeks
4 or 5 dried fennel branches (optional)
Parsley or Japanese radish sprouts and lemon slices, for garnish
Fresh Herb Dressing (recipe follows)
Lemon wedges

1. Rinse the fish and dry well. With a very sharp knife, score the fish in a chevron pattern at ¼-inch intervals, cutting ½-inch deep from the backbone halfway down the side of the fish on a diagonal away from the head and then scoring the bottom half in the same way, slanting in the opposite direction.

2. Combine the salt and pepper. (Chef Renggli grinds 2 parts coarse salt to 1 part black peppercorns in a coffee-spice mill.) Liberally season one side of the fish with 2 to 3 teaspoons of this mixture. Squeeze on the juice of 1 lemon and rub the seasonings into the fish. Turn the salmon over and season the second side in the same way. Season the cavity of the fish with about ½ tablespoon of the salt and pepper mixture

and the juice of half a lemon. Stuff the cavity with the herbs, leek greens and dried fennel if you have it; there should be plenty of greenery sticking out of the fish. Place on a rack or a tray lined with paper towels and refrigerate uncovered for 2 to 3 hours.

3. Preheat the oven to 400°. Turn a large jelly roll pan upside-down and oil the bottom. Remove the salmon from the refrigerator and pat dry with paper towels. Place on the inverted pan, diagonally if necessary to fit. Place the pan in a larger pan or on a very large piece of aluminum foil with a lip to catch any drippings. Roast uncovered in the middle of the oven without turning for 40 minutes, or until the center of the fish registers 125° on an instant-reading thermometer.

4. If the skin is not lightly browned and crisp at this point, broil about 4 inches from the heat for 2 to 3 minutes. If the salmon won't fit in your broiler, don't worry, it will taste delicious anyway.

5. Slide the fish from the pan onto a large platter or attractive cutting board. Garnish simply with parsley or Japanese radish sprouts and lemon slices. Let sit for 10 minutes.

6. To serve, slice the crisp skin down the length of the backbone. Then cut through the skin crosswise at 3-inch intervals. Remove the skin (it will lift or peel right off the fish) and carve sepa-

rately into 18 to 24 pieces, depending on how many people you are serving. Then carve the salmon down to the backbone into roughly 3-by-1- to 1½-inch pieces, transferring each piece to a plate as you carve. Spoon 1 to 2 teaspoons of Fresh Herb Dressing over each piece of fish and add a piece of the crackly skin to each plate. Encourage guests to help themselves to lemon wedges, set out in 3 or 4 bowls.

Fresh Herb Dressing

Use any or all of the herbs called for. If you do not have fresh tarragon or chervil, increase the parsley and chives.

MAKES ABOUT 1 CUP

¼ cup minced fresh parsley
¼ cup minced fresh chives
2 tablespoons minced fresh tarragon
2 tablespoons minced fresh chervil
2 tablespoons minced Japanese radish sprouts ("2-Mamina"), optional
3 tablespoons fresh lemon juice
½ teaspoon freshly ground pepper
½ teaspoon minced fresh jalapeño pepper or several dashes of cayenne
½ cup extra-virgin olive oil

Shortly before serving the fish, stir together all of the ingredients.

Salmon with Shrimp and Dill en Papillote

The two large papillotes used in the presentation of this dish are just as dramatic as eight individual envelopes and much more efficient. Serving is a breeze—the salmon and julienned vegetables are easily transferred from packet to plate with a spatula and any juices are spooned on top.

8 SERVINGS

24 raw small shrimp, in the shell
2 carrots
½ cup plus 3 teaspoons melted unsalted butter
2 medium shallots, finely chopped

2 tablespoons Cognac or brandy
4 salmon steaks, preferably
 Norwegian, cut 1 inch thick
 (about ½ pound each)
1 leek (white and tender green),
 cut into 2-inch-long julienne
 strips
2 whole branches plus 24 small
 sprigs of fresh dill
1 tablespoon plus 1 teaspoon fresh
 lemon juice
½ teaspoon salt
¼ teaspoon freshly ground pepper

1. Shell and devein the shrimp. Set the shrimp aside, reserving the shells.

2. Finely chop one of the carrots. Cut the other into 2-inch-long julienne strips.

3. Make a shrimp butter: In a large skillet, warm 2 teaspoons of the butter over moderate heat. When the foam subsides, add the shallots and chopped carrot. Cook until softened but not browned, about 4 minutes. Add the shrimp shells and continue cooking, tossing frequently, until the shells are opaque, 2 to 3 minutes longer.

4. Add the Cognac to the pan, warm for about 30 seconds, then ignite with a match. Cook, tossing the shell mixture, until the flames subside.

5. Scrape the mixture into the bowl of a blender or a food processor. Add ½ cup of the butter (1 teaspoon will still remain) and process to a thin paste, stopping twice to scrape down the sides of the bowl with a rubber spatula, about 2 minutes. Pass the mixture through a fine mesh sieve. Set the shrimp butter aside.

6. Preheat the oven to 400°. Butterfly the salmon steaks: Using a sharp knife, cut each salmon steak in half vertically from the top of the fish, cutting right through the bone. Remove the bones and any membranes. Now, with skin-side down, draw the knife down the length of each piece, cutting through the flesh to within ½ inch of the skin. Using your hands, flatten each piece into a fish-shaped steak. Cover with plastic wrap to prevent drying out and set aside.

7. Fold a 16-by-24-inch piece of parchment paper or aluminum foil in half crosswise to make a double sheet 16 by 12 inches. Using scissors, cut a heart from the paper, with the fold vertically down the center, as in a valentine. Center the folded heart on a large baking sheet. Open the heart-shaped paper. Brush the interior of the paper with half the remaining butter.

8. Sprinkle ½ of the julienne of carrot and ½ of the julienne of leek over the center of half the paper. Put 1 branch of dill down the center of the vegetables. Put 4 pieces of salmon on top, lined up parallel to each other, slightly on the diagonal.

9. Sprinkle ½ teaspoon of lemon juice over each piece of salmon. Season with the salt and pepper. Spread each piece with 1 tablespoon of the reserved shrimp butter. Arrange 3 shrimp in a row down the length of each piece of fish. Place a small sprig of dill on each shrimp.

10. Fold the paper over the fish and make a series of tight overlapping folds along the edge of the papillote to seal the package. Repeat with a second piece of parchment and the remaining vegetables, dill, fish, shrimp butter and shrimp.

11. Put the papillotes in the oven and bake for 15 minutes. Remove the papillotes to 2 serving platters. Present sealed, then with a knife slash the papillote and serve a piece of salmon with some of the vegetables on individual warmed plates.

Steamed Sea Bass with Ginger Sauce

2 TO 4 SERVINGS

1½-pound whole sea bass or red
 snapper
1 tablespoon dark soy sauce*
1 tablespoon Oriental sesame oil
2 tablespoons medium-dry sherry
1 tablespoon shredded fresh
 ginger
2 scallions, shredded
½ teaspoon water chestnut powder*
 or cornstarch
*Available at Oriental groceries

1. Make 3 shallow crescent-shaped incisions on each side of the fish. Place the fish on a large oval-shaped platter with at least a 1-inch lip that will fit into a turkey roaster or a large deep roasting pan.

2. Combine the soy sauce, sesame oil and 1 tablespoon of the sherry. Spoon this seasoning sauce over the fish.

3. Put half of the ginger and scallions in the cavity of the fish. Arrange the remainder on top of the fish in a criss-cross pattern.

4. Dissolve the water chestnut powder in the remaining 1 tablespoon sherry to make a binder.

5. Fill the turkey roaster with about 3 inches of water. Put the platter with the fish on a high-legged rack above the water level, or on 2 tin cans (whose tops and bottoms have been removed) measuring about 3 inches high. Bring the water to a boil over high heat, reduce the heat to moderate, cover and steam the fish for 15 minutes, or until the eyes bulge.

6. Pour the juices accumulated on the platter into a saucepan. Bring to a boil over high heat; reduce the heat to moderate. Stir the binder and stir it into the sauce. Cook, stirring constantly, until the sauce thickens. Pour over the fish and serve immediately.

Le Divellec's Oven-Roasted Red Snapper with Fresh Mint

At Le Divellec restaurant in Paris this dish is made with a fish called Saint-Pierre, or John Dory. Although found in North Atlantic waters, it is rarely available in American markets, and we suggest red snapper as a delicious substitute.

🍷 **F&W Beverage Suggestion:** Light white Burgundy, such as Louis Latour Mâcon-Villages

4 SERVINGS

1 red snapper, about 3 pounds
1 teaspoon salt
½ teaspoon freshly ground pepper
15 sprigs of fresh mint
1 stick (¼ pound) unsalted butter, clarified
3 tablespoons fresh lemon juice
1 tablespoon chopped parsley

1. Preheat the oven to 400°. Season the inside of the fish with ¾ teaspoon of the salt and ¼ teaspoon of the pepper. Stuff the cavity with half the mint sprigs and skewer closed.

2. Rub the fish with ½ tablespoon of the butter and sprinkle with the remaining salt and pepper. Put the fish on an oiled baking sheet and bake for about 20 minutes, until just opaque near the bone.

3. Meanwhile, finely chop the remaining mint. In a small saucepan, melt the remaining 7½ tablespoons butter over low heat. Add the mint and lemon juice. Strain the sauce and keep warm.

4. To serve, remove the skewers and lift the fillets from the fish, keeping the crisp skin on top intact. Pour the sauce over the fish and sprinkle with the chopped parsley.

Flounder Stuffed with Clams

🍷 **F&W Beverage Suggestion:** Portuguese *vinho verde,* such as Aveleda

4 SERVINGS

4 whole flounder, about 1 pound each
7 tablespoons unsalted butter
2 tablespoons vegetable oil
1½ cups stale bread crumbs
3 large shallots, minced
4 medium garlic cloves, minced
2 dozen large cherrystone clams, coarsely chopped
¼ cup clam liquor
½ cup chopped parsley
½ teaspoon salt
½ teaspoon freshly ground pepper
4 teaspoons fresh lemon juice
Lemon wedges and sprigs of parsley, for garnish

1. With a filleting knife, remove the skin from one side of the flounder. Skinned-side up, make a cut down the center line of the fish and separate the flesh from the backbone. Free the backbone from the fish.

2. Preheat the oven to 400°. In a large skillet, melt 2 tablespoons of the butter in the oil over moderate heat. When the foam subsides, add the bread crumbs and sauté, tossing frequently, for 2 to 3 minutes, or until crisp and browned. Drain on paper towels.

3. Wipe out the pan and melt 3 tablespoons of butter over moderate heat. Add the shallots and garlic and sauté until translucent and tender, about 3 minutes.

4. Add the clams and clam liquor and cook, tossing, for 30 seconds. Remove from the heat. Stir in the bread crumbs, parsley, salt and pepper. Let cool to room temperature.

5. In a small saucepan, melt the remaining 2 tablespoons butter. Generously butter a large cookie sheet with about ½ tablespoon of the melted butter. Place the fish on the sheet. Sprinkle the inside of each fish with 1 teaspoon of lemon juice and season lightly with salt and pepper. Mound about 1 cup of the stuffing into each fish. Brush any exposed area of the fish with the remaining melted butter.

6. Bake in the center of the oven for 10 minutes, or until the fish is white and opaque throughout. Serve garnished with lemon wedges and parsley.

Flounder Stuffed with Garlic Potatoes and Celery

🍷 **F&W Beverage Suggestion:** Colombard, such as Souverain

2 SERVINGS

2 whole flounder, about 1 pound each
1 cup diced (¼-inch) celery
1 cup diced (¼-inch) onion
4 garlic cloves
1 cup heavy cream
¼ teaspoon thyme

¾ teaspoon salt
¼ teaspoon finely ground white
  pepper
1 large baking potato (about ½
  pound), peeled and cut into 1-
  inch cubes
2 egg yolks
4 tablespoons unsalted butter,
  melted

1. With a filleting knife, remove the skin from one side of the flounder. Skinned-side up, make a cut down the center line of the fish and separate the flesh from the backbone. Free the backbone from the fish.

2. In a medium saucepan, combine the celery, onion, garlic, cream, thyme, ½ teaspoon of the salt and ⅛ teaspoon of the white pepper. Cover and simmer over moderately low heat until the vegetables are soft, 15 to 20 minutes. Drain, reserving the cream and the vegetables separately.

3. Preheat the oven to 400°. In a small pot of boiling salted water, cook the potato until soft, about 10 minutes. Drain and return to the pan. Toss over low heat to dry, 1 to 2 minutes.

4. Pick the whole garlic cloves out of the reserved vegetables. Mash the potato and garlic by passing through a sieve, ricer or food mill. Beat in the reserved cream, 1 of the egg yolks, 2 tablespoons of the butter and the remaining ¼ teaspoon salt and ⅛ teaspoon white pepper.

5. Generously brush a large cookie sheet with about ½ tablespoon of the melted butter. Place the fish on the

sheet. Spoon the celery and onion mixture into the cavities of the fish, dividing evenly. Cover with the mashed potato. Smooth the potato with a narrow metal spatula dipped in melted butter. Make diagonal ridges on the potato with the long side of the spatula. Brush any exposed areas of the fish with the remaining melted butter.

6. Beat the remaining egg yolk with 1 tablespoon of water and lightly brush over the potato.

7. Bake for 8 minutes. Transfer to the broiler and broil for about 2 minutes, until browned.

Sole and Shrimp à la Nage

The Champagne sauce in this dish is flavored with vegetables, shrimp shells, crème fraîche and butter. The taste is stunning and, happily, there is plenty of it.

6 SERVINGS

½ bottle (750 ml) brut Champagne
4 medium carrots, peeled and
  thinly sliced
2 small leeks (white and tender
  green), thinly sliced
3 celery ribs, thinly sliced
20 small white onions, peeled and
  thinly sliced
2 garlic cloves, thinly sliced
Bouquet garni: 6 parsley sprigs, ½
  bay leaf and ¼ teaspoon thyme
  tied in cheesecloth
5 peppercorns
5 coriander seeds
¼ teaspoon tarragon
1½ pounds medium shrimp
1 cup crème fraîche
1 teaspoon salt
¼ teaspoon freshly ground pepper
10 tablespoons unsalted butter,
  chilled and cut into tablespoons
1½ pounds sole fillets, cut into
  strips about 4 by ½ inch

1 tablespoon chopped fresh chervil
  or parsley

1. In a large noncorrodible saucepan or flameproof casserole, combine the Champagne and 4 cups of water. Add half of the sliced carrots, leeks, celery and onions; reserve the remainder. Add the garlic, bouquet garni, peppercorns, coriander seeds and tarragon. Bring to a boil, reduce the heat and simmer, uncovered, for 30 minutes. Strain through a fine mesh sieve and return the stock to the saucepan.

2. Bring the stock to a boil over high heat. Add the shrimp and cook until just pink and curled, about 1 minute. Remove with a slotted spoon and let cool. Remove the stock from the heat.

3. When the shrimp are cool enough to handle, peel them and add the shells to the stock. (Cover the shrimp to prevent them from drying out.) Simmer the shells for 15 minutes. Strain through a sieve, pressing on the shells to extract as much flavor as possible. Return the stock to the saucepan; there should be about 2¼ cups.

4. Add the remaining sliced carrots, leeks, celery and onions to the stock and boil over high heat until the liquid is reduced by half, about 15 minutes. (**The recipe can be prepared ahead to this point. Reheat the stock before proceeding.**)

5. Stir in the crème fraîche, salt and pepper and bring to a boil. Reduce the heat to low and gradually whisk in the butter, 1 or 2 tablespoons at a time, until the sauce is smooth and thickened; do not boil.

6. Add the sole and poach gently until almost opaque, 2 to 3 minutes. Add the reserved shrimp and cook until just heated through, about 1 minute longer. Serve in soup plates, garnished with chervil.

L'Ermitage's Fillet of Lotte with Two Butters and Two Caviars

F&W Beverage Suggestion: California Chardonnay, such as Acacia

6 SERVINGS

1 pound fresh spinach, stemmed and rinsed
2 cups heavy cream
4 sticks (1 pound) plus 3 tablespoons unsalted butter
1 teaspoon salt
¼ teaspoon freshly ground white pepper
1 cup freshly stewed tomatoes or 1 can (14 ounces) Italian peeled tomatoes, well drained
1 tablespoon tomato paste
3-pound fillet of monkfish (*lotte*), turbot or halibut, cut into 24 medallions or 1½-inch squares
2 ounces of red caviar
2 ounces black caviar, preferably sevruga

1. Preheat the oven to 450°. In a medium noncorrodible saucepan, cover and steam the spinach in the water clinging to its leaves over high heat, until just wilted, about 2 minutes. Drain and rinse under cold running water; squeeze to remove as much water as possible.

2. In a large saucepan, combine 1 cup of the cream and the spinach. Bring to a boil over moderately high heat and cook, uncovered, until reduced by half, 10 to 12 minutes. Remove from the heat and whisk in 2 sticks of the butter, 1 tablespoon at a time. Season with half of the salt and pepper. Puree in a blender, then strain into a saucepan and keep warm over very low heat.

3. Meanwhile, in a large saucepan, combine the remaining 1 cup cream, the stewed tomatoes and the tomato paste. Bring to a boil over moderately high heat, and cook, uncovered, until reduced by half, 10 to 12 minutes. Remove from

the heat and whisk in 2 sticks of butter, 1 tablespoon at a time. Season with the remaining salt and pepper. Puree in a blender, then strain into a saucepan and keep warm over very low heat.

4. In a large skillet over moderately high heat, melt 1½ tablespoons of butter until it foams. Working in 4 batches, add 6 medallions of fish and sauté, turning once, until lightly browned on each side, about 2 minutes. Transfer to an ovenproof dish; cover with foil to keep warm. After 2 batches, wipe out the skillet with a paper towel, then melt the remaining 1½ tablespoons butter and sauté the remaining 2 batches of fish. Remove the foil and bake the fish, uncovered, for 5 minutes.

5. To serve, divide each plate into quarters, spreading 1 tablespoon of the spinach butter in each of the 2 diagonally opposite quarters and 1 tablespoon of the tomato butter in each of the other 2 quarters, to form a harlequin pattern. Place a medallion of fish in the center of each quadrant. (See photo, page 69.)

6. Top each medallion on the spinach butter with a small dollop of red caviar. Top each medallion on the tomato butter with a small dollop of black caviar.

NOTE: An easier, though no less striking, presentation is achieved by dividing the plate in half, spreading 2 tablespoons of the spinach butter on one half of the plate and 2 tablespoons of the tomato butter on the other half. Place the 4 medallions of fish in the center and top with caviar as indicated.

Oyster Stew with Ham

Oyster stew is always a welcome delicacy. This smooth version tastes rich, but it contains no cream—a bonus for weight-conscious oyster fanciers.

4 TO 6 SERVINGS

2 dozen oysters, shucked, with their liquor reserved
3 tablespoons unsalted butter
1 quart milk
2 teaspoons Worcestershire sauce
¼ cup finely diced cooked ham

¼ cup finely diced prosciutto
Freshly ground pepper

1. In a heavy medium saucepan, place the oysters with their liquor and the butter. Warm over low heat until the butter melts and the oysters begin to lose their translucency, about 5 minutes.

2. Add the milk, Worcestershire sauce, ham and prosciutto. Cook over moderately high heat, covered, until the liquid is hot and the oysters are plump, 5 to 7 minutes. Season with pepper to taste.

Trumps' Mussels with Bacon, Fennel and Cream

This recipe can be easily doubled and also works well as a first course for four.

F&W Beverage Suggestion: Italian Chardonnay, such as Bollini

2 SERVINGS

½ pound slab bacon, thickly sliced and cut crosswise into ¼-inch strips
2 medium fennel bulbs, slivered
3 pounds mussels, scrubbed and debearded
8 garlic cloves, chopped
2 large shallots, chopped
1 cup dry white wine
2 tablespoons Pernod
½ cup heavy cream
8 sprigs of fresh tarragon, chopped or 1 teaspoon chopped fresh parsley

1. In a large flameproof casserole, sauté the bacon over moderately high heat until the fat is released and the bacon begins to soften, about 3 minutes.

2. Add the fennel and continue to sauté until tender, about 5 minutes.

3. Pour off the bacon fat. Add the mussels, garlic, shallots, wine and Pernod. Cover and cook until the mussels open, 3 to 4 minutes.

4. Add the cream and the tarragon, bring to a boil over high heat and cook, uncovered, for 1 minute. Divide the mussels and the sauce among 4 warmed bowls, discarding any mussels that have not opened.

Scallops and Mussels with Saffron Sauce

In this unusual cold main course, the scallops are "cooked" by marinating them in lime and orange juice, much like ceviche.

 F&W Beverage Suggestion:
California Fumé Blanc, such as Dry Creek

4 SERVINGS

1 pound bay scallops, rinsed and drained
½ cup fresh orange juice
½ cup fresh lime juice
¼ pound fresh asparagus—trimmed, peeled and cut on the diagonal into 1-inch pieces
3 medium shallots, minced
½ cup dry white wine
3 pounds fresh mussels, scrubbed and debearded
½ cup Fromage Blanc (p. 117)
½ teaspoon fresh lemon juice
Pinch of powdered saffron
Pinch of nutmeg
¼ pound fresh spinach, torn into bite-size pieces
1 tablespoon olive oil
½ teaspoon freshly ground pepper
Saffron threads, for garnish

1. Spread the scallops in a single layer in a noncorrodible flat-bottomed pan. Combine the orange and lime juices and pour over the scallops. Cover and marinate in the refrigerator for 3 to 4 hours; the scallops will become opaque throughout, as if cooked.

2. In a large pot of boiling water, blanch the asparagus until bright green and crisp-tender, 45 to 60 seconds. Drain and rinse under cold running water; drain and pat dry.

3. In a large, heavy, noncorrodible saucepan, combine the shallots and wine. Bring to a boil over high heat. Add the mussels, cover and cook, shaking the pan occasionally, until the mussels open, 5 to 6 minutes. With a slotted spoon, remove the mussels and set aside. Discard any that have not opened. Strain the cooking liquid through a fine mesh sieve lined with several layers of dampened cheesecloth.

4. Rinse out the saucepan. Return the cooking liquid to the pan and boil over high heat until reduced to 3 tablespoons, about 15 minutes. Meanwhile, remove the mussels from their shells and place in a medium bowl.

5. In a small bowl, whisk the Fromage Blanc, lemon juice, powdered saffron, nutmeg and 1 tablespoon of the reduced cooking liquid until smooth.

6. In a medium bowl, toss the spinach with the olive oil, remaining 2 tablespoons of the cooking liquid and ¼ teaspoon of the pepper. Arrange in a bed on a serving platter.

7. Drain the scallops and add them to the mussels. Toss with the saffron sauce. Mound in the middle of the spinach and arrange the asparagus pieces around them. Spoon any remaining saffron dressing on top, and sprinkle with the remaining ¼ teaspoon pepper and the saffron threads if desired.

Gratinéed Scallops on a Bed of Sliced Endives

 F&W Beverage Suggestion:
Mâcon-Villages or Fetzer Pinot Blanc

4 SERVINGS

1 pound bay scallops, cut in half crosswise if large
¾ cup milk
4 tablespoons unsalted butter
3 large Belgian endives—trimmed, cut crosswise into ¼-inch slices and separated into pieces
2 tablespoons superfine sugar
1 tablespoon fresh lime juice
2 teaspoons salt
½ teaspoon freshly ground pepper
½ cup hard apple cider, preferably French
¾ cup crème fraîche
¼ cup heavy cream
1 tablespoon minced chives

1. Place the scallops in a small bowl, add the milk and set aside.

2. In a large noncorrodible skillet, melt 2 tablespoons of the butter over low heat. Add the endives, sugar, half the lime juice, 1 teaspoon of the salt and ¼ teaspoon of the pepper. Cook over low heat, stirring frequently, until all the liquid has evaporated, 10 to 12 minutes. Divide the endives evenly among 4 large scallop shells and set aside.

3. Meanwhile, drain the scallops and pat dry. In a large heavy noncorrodible skillet, melt 1 tablespoon of the butter until it is just starting to turn golden; immediately add half the scallops. Stir to coat with butter and sauté, tossing, for 1 minute. Remove the scallops to a strainer set over a bowl to catch the juices. Repeat with the remaining scallops and 1 more tablespoon of the butter.

4. Preheat the broiler. Pour out any excess fat from the skillet and add the remaining lime juice, the cider and any reserved juices from the scallops. Boil, uncovered, until reduced to a glaze. Stir in the crème fraîche, heavy cream and the remaining 1 teaspoon salt and ¼ teaspoon pepper. Boil until reduced to a thick sauce, 2 to 3 minutes.

5. Divide the drained scallops among the 4 shells and spoon the sauce evenly over them. (**The recipe can be done ahead to this point.** Cover and refrigerate the scallop shells; bring back to room temperature before proceeding.)

6. Place the shells on a baking sheet and broil 5 to 6 inches from the heat for 2 to 3 minutes, until bubbly and light brown. Sprinkle with the chives and serve at once.

Pastry Seashells Filled with Scallops in Cream Sauce

To make the pastry shells for this recipe you will need eight 5- to 6-inch scallop shells. They are available in most kitchen equipment shops.

F&W Beverage Suggestion: Chablis, such as Moreau

8 SERVINGS

Pastry:

2½ cups all-purpose flour
¼ teaspoon salt
14 tablespoons cold unsalted butter, cut into small bits
1 egg yolk
About 5 tablespoons ice water

Filling:

6 scallions, coarsely chopped (about ¾ cup)
½ cup bottled clam juice
½ cup dry white wine
½ cup canned chicken broth
Grated zest of 1 lemon
2 peppercorns
1 small bay leaf
1¼ pounds bay scallops, or small sea scallops cut in thirds
½ cup heavy cream
3 egg yolks
1 teaspoon fresh lemon juice
Minced fresh chives and paprika, for garnish

1. Prepare the pastry: In a large bowl, combine the flour and salt. Cut in the butter until the mixture resembles coarse meal. Mix together the egg yolk and 5 tablespoons of ice water. Stir all but 1 tablespoon of the liquid into the flour mixture until it is well distributed. Sprinkle the remaining tablespoon of liquid over areas that are not moist enough. Gather the dough loosely into a ball. If there are dry bits that do not adhere easily, sprinkle with a few extra drops of water. Turn out the dough onto a lightly floured surface and knead gently for about 30 seconds to complete the blending. Divide the dough in half. Pat the dough into two 6-inch disks, wrap tightly in plastic wrap and refrigerate for at least 1 hour, or overnight.

2. On a lightly floured surface, roll out one disk of dough into a 14-by-14-inch square, between ⅛ and ¼ inch thick.

3. Place a scallop shell, curved-side up, on one corner of the pastry. Allowing a ½-inch rim all the way around, cut out a scallop shape using a sharp knife. Place the pastry on the outside of the shell and press firmly so that it will pick up the ridged relief of the shell. Cut off any excess pastry with a sharp knife. Prick the pastry all over with a fork. Refrigerate the pastry on the shell, pastry-side up, and cut out 3 more shells. (Discard the remaining pastry or knead the scraps together and refrigerate for another purpose.) Roll out the second round of pastry as before and cut out another 4 pastry shells, refrigerating them as you finish. Meanwhile, preheat the oven to 375°.

4. Place the shells, pastry-side up, on a baking sheet and bake in the middle of the oven until golden, 20 to 25 minutes, pricking any bubbles after 10 minutes. Let the pastry cool on the shells.

5. Prepare the filling: In a medium noncorrodible saucepan, combine the chopped scallions, clam juice, white wine, chicken broth, lemon zest, peppercorns and bay leaf. Bring to a boil, reduce the heat to moderately low and simmer, covered, for 20 minutes. Strain and measure the liquid; add water if necessary to equal 1¼ cups. Return the liquid to the saucepan.

6. Add the scallops. Cook over moderate heat, until simmering, 3 to 4 minutes, or until the scallops are just opaque but still tender. Strain the liquid into a bowl; reserve the scallops. Return the liquid to the saucepan. Boil uncovered until reduced to 1 cup, about 5 minutes. Remove from the heat. Stir in the heavy cream. Beat the egg yolks slightly. Add them to the liquid.

7. Stir the egg-cream mixture over moderately low heat until the custard thickens enough to coat a spoon lightly; do not allow to simmer, or the custard will curdle. Immediately strain into a bowl. Stir in the lemon juice. (**The sauce can be made ahead to this point.** Cover with waxed paper to prevent a skin from forming.)

8. Assemble the pastry shells: Preheat the oven to 400°. Gently transfer the pastry from the shells to a baking sheet. Heat for 3 to 4 minutes. Warm the sauce over moderately low heat, stirring, until hot to the touch, 2 to 4 minutes. Add the scallops and cook, stirring, to warm them through, 1 to 2 minutes; do not let boil.

9. Place the pastry shells on individual plates. Spoon the scallops and sauce into each shell, leaving about 1 inch of pastry showing around the edge. Sprinkle with chives and a dusting of paprika.

Fragrant Scallops and Lime in Parchment

4 SERVINGS

2 medium carrots, cut into 2-by-⅛-inch julienne strips
2 pounds sea scallops, halved or quartered if large
½ pound mushrooms, thinly sliced
4 scallions, sliced
4 sprigs of parsley
8 thin slices of lime
6 tablespoons fresh lime juice (from about 3 limes)
6 tablespoons dry white wine
4 tablespoons unsalted butter, cut into thin slices
4 teaspoons olive oil
1 teaspoon salt
½ teaspoon freshly ground pepper

1. Have ready 4 sheets of aluminum foil, each measuring 12 by 36 inches, and 4 sheets of cooking parchment or waxed paper that measure 12 by 18 inches. Fold one sheet of aluminum foil over to make a double sheet 12 by 18 inches and place one sheet of parchment or waxed paper over it to prevent the acid of the lime from reacting with the foil. Repeat with the remaining foil and parchment.

2. Preheat the oven to 475°. In a medium saucepan, bring 4 cups of water to a boil. Add the carrots and when the boiling resumes, boil for 3 minutes; drain.

3. In the center of each piece of parchment-lined foil place one-fourth each of the carrots, scallops, mushrooms, scallions, parsley and lime slices; toss together. Over each, drizzle 1½ tablespoons lime juice and 1½ tablespoons white wine. Add 1 tablespoon butter and 1 teaspoon of the olive oil to each. Sprinkle each with ¼ teaspoon salt and ⅛ teaspoon pepper.

4. Roughly shape the mixture into a narrow rectangle in the center of the parchment. Bring the two long sides of the paper-lined foil upward to meet in the center and fold twice to make a double seam. Tightly roll the ends inward until they meet the filling and fold to close. Seal the remaining pouches in the same manner. Evenly space them on the baking sheet and bake for 20 minutes.

5. Transfer the unopened pouches to individual serving plates and serve hot. Let guests open the pouches at table.

Shrimp and Scallops en Brochette

F&W Beverage Suggestion:
California Sauvignon Blanc, such as Franciscan

4 SERVINGS

16 small white boiling onions, peeled
16 large shrimp
16 sea scallops
6 slices of bacon, cut into 1-inch squares
⅓ cup olive oil
1 stick (¼ pound) unsalted butter, melted
1 tablespoon plus 1 teaspoon chopped fresh dill

½ teaspoon salt
¼ teaspoon freshly ground pepper
Lemon wedges

1. In a pot of boiling salted water, parboil the onions until the outer layers are tender, about 5 minutes. Drain and rinse under cold running water; drain well and pat dry.

2. Shell and devein the shrimp, slicing through to within ⅛ inch of the back of the shrimp. Spread the sides flat to butterfly the shrimp.

3. Thread the shrimp, the scallops, bacon and onions onto long metal skewers, alternating the ingredients and anchoring the ends with an onion.

4. In a small bowl, mix together the oil, melted butter and dill. Generously baste the brochettes with the marinade; reserve leftover marinade. Sprinkle the brochettes with the salt and pepper. **(The brochettes may be made 2 to 3 hours ahead to this point** and refrigerated until cooking time.)

5. Light the charcoal or preheat the broiler. Lightly oil the barbecue rack to prevent sticking. Grill the brochettes 4 to 6 inches from the heat, basting frequently with the reserved marinade and turning once, until the scallops are opaque throughout, 3 to 4 minutes on each side. Serve with lemon wedges.

Lemon-Fried Shrimp

The tart flavor of lemon is captured in this batter for the shrimp. If not eaten right away, they can be crisped for a few seconds in hot oil before serving.

F&W Beverage Suggestion:
Spanish white, such as C.U.N.E. Monopole

4 SERVINGS

1 pound large shrimp, shelled and deveined with the tails left on
¾ cup plus 1 tablespoon all-purpose flour
½ cup cornstarch
¾ teaspoon salt
¼ cup fresh lemon juice
2 tablespoons melted butter
Vegetable oil, for deep frying

1. Let the shrimp stand at room temperature for about 30 minutes before cooking.

2. In a medium bowl, combine the flour, ¼ cup of the cornstarch and the salt. In a cup, combine the lemon juice with ½ cup of water. Pour the liquid all at once over the dry ingredients and whisk just until smooth. Stir in the melted butter. Place the remaining ¼ cup cornstarch on a plate.

3. Heat about 1½ inches of vegetable oil in a deep fryer or large heavy saucepan until it registers 375° to 380°. Dredge the shrimp in the cornstarch and shake off the excess. One at a time, pick up a shrimp by the tail, dip it in the batter, then lower it into the hot oil. Fry in batches without crowding until the shrimp are crisp and golden brown, 2½ to 3 minutes. Drain on paper towels and keep the cooked shrimp warm in a low oven while you fry the remaining shrimp.

Sautéed Crab Cakes with Thyme

These lightly spiced crabcakes have a fresh, delicate flavor and a moist, tender texture. Serve them plain with lemon wedges or on lightly toasted buns.

4 SERVINGS

1 egg, beaten
1 teaspoon Dijon-style mustard
1 tablespoon fresh lemon juice
¾ teaspoon thyme
6 tablespoons olive oil
¼ teaspoon salt
¼ teaspoon freshly ground pepper
1 pound lump crabmeat, picked over to remove any bits of cartilage, then flaked
½ cup fine dry bread crumbs
2 tablespoons unsalted butter
Fresh lemon wedges

1. In a medium bowl, whisk the egg, mustard, lemon juice and thyme until blended. Slowly whisk in 4 tablespoons of the oil in a thin stream. Season with the salt and pepper. Stir in the crabmeat; add the bread crumbs and mix until blended. Shape the crabmeat mixture into eight ½-inch-thick patties.

2. In a large heavy skillet, melt 1 tablespoon of the butter in 1 tablespoon of the remaining oil until sizzling. Add 4 of the crabcakes and sauté, turning once, until crisp and brown, about 2½ minutes on each side. Drain on paper towels and cover loosely with foil to keep warm. Sauté the 4 remaining crab cakes in the remaining oil and butter. Serve with lemon wedges.

Indonesian Crab Fritters

These fritters have a very mild flavor. For contrast, accompany them with Sambal (p. 223) a fiery Indonesian condiment.

MAKES 10 TO 12 FRITTERS

½ pound baking or all-purpose potatoes
2 eggs, lightly beaten
2 teaspoons cornstarch
½ teaspoon salt
¼ teaspoon freshly ground pepper
1 scallion, thinly sliced
1 can (6 ounces) crab meat, flaked and picked over to remove bits of cartilage
¼ cup corn or peanut oil

1. In a medium saucepan of boiling salted water, cook the potatoes until tender throughout, 25 to 30 minutes; drain. As soon as they are cool enough to handle, peel the potatoes and then mash them with a ricer, food mill or potato masher. Measure out 1 cup.

2. In a medium bowl, mix the eggs, cornstarch, salt and pepper until smooth. Add the cup of mashed potatoes, the scallion and crab and blend well.

3. In a large skillet or wok, heat the oil over moderately high heat. Form fritters by scooping heaping tablespoons of the mixture into the skillet, then flattening them slightly with the back of an oiled fork. Fry, turning once, for about 3 minutes per side, until browned. Drain on paper towels. Serve warm or at room temperature.

Broiled Stuffed Lobster

🍷 **F&W Beverage Suggestion:**
Dry white Bordeaux, such as Chevalier de Vedrines

2 SERVINGS

2 live lobsters (1 pound each)
Pinch of salt
Pinch of freshly ground pepper
¼ cup dry white wine
¼ cup white wine vinegar
2 tablespoons minced shallots
1 cup broccoli florets
4 tablespoons cold unsalted butter
1 teaspoon crème fraîche or heavy cream
¼ cup Fromage Blanc (p. 117)
2 tablespoons minced fresh *fines herbes* (equal amounts of tarragon, chives and parsley, mixed together)
1 teaspoon fresh lemon juice

1. Bring a large pot of water to a boil. Add the lobsters and cook just until the color of the shell begins to change, about 2 minutes. (The lobster will finish cooking later.) Remove and drain. Break off the claws. Return the claws to the boiling water for an additional 4 minutes.

2. With a pair of kitchen scissors, carefully cut away the white underside of the lobster tail shell; do not break the shell. Remove the tail meat, cut into chunks and set aside. Crack the claws and remove the meat in one piece if possible (if the meat tears, cut into chunks and add to the tail meat); set aside. Reserve the lobster shells.

3. Lightly salt and pepper the lobster shells and lay them on their backs in a flameproof baking pan. Place the chunks of tail meat back in the tail cavity; lay the claw meat on top of the body. (**The recipe may be prepared up to this point 3 hours in advance.** Cover and refrigerate. Bring back to room temperature before proceeding.)

4. Preheat the broiler. Bring a medium saucepan of water to a boil in preparation for steaming the broccoli in Step 6.

5. In a small, heavy, noncorrodible saucepan, combine the wine, vinegar and shallots. Bring to a boil over moderately high heat and cook until reduced to 3 tablespoons, about 6 minutes.

6. Meanwhile, broil the lobster for about 4 minutes, until the flesh is creamy

white and firm. Steam the broccoli until bright green and crisp-tender, about 6 minutes.

7. Remove the sauce from the heat and whisk in the butter, 1 tablespoon at a time. Stir in the crème fraîche and Fromage Blanc. Stir in the herbs and lemon juice. Season with salt and pepper to taste.

8. To serve, place each lobster on a warmed plate. Spoon 3 tablespoons of sauce over each lobster. Garnish with the broccoli. Pass any remaining sauce separately.

Seasons' Lobster Flamed with Drambuie

Beverage Suggestion:
Acacia Iund Vineyard Pinot Noir

4 SERVINGS

4 live lobsters (1½ pounds each)
12 tablespoons (1½ sticks) unsalted butter
1 cup Scotch whisky
½ cup Drambuie
½ cup fish stock or bottled clam juice
⅓ cup peas, fresh or frozen, thawed
⅓ cup julienned rutabaga
⅓ cup julienned sweet potato
⅓ cup julienned carrot
1 tablespoon fresh lemon juice
¼ teaspoon salt
⅛ teaspoon freshly ground pepper
2 cups fresh spinach leaves (about 1 large bunch)
16 sprigs of fresh coriander
1 small truffle, shaved (optional)

1. In a large pot of rapidly boiling water, cook the lobsters for 8 minutes. Immediately transfer to a basin of cold water to stop the cooking.

2. Twist off the tails from the lobsters and cut them lengthwise in half. Remove the meat. Twist off the claws, crack them and remove the meat. Reserve the tomalley and roe for the sauce. Discard the shells.

3. In a large skillet, melt 4 tablespoons of the butter over moderate heat. Add the lobster and toss to coat with the butter. Pour in the Scotch and the Drambuie, warm for 10 seconds, then carefully ignite with a match. Cook, shaking the pan, until the flames subside. Remove the lobster to a warm plate.

4. Whisk in the fish stock. Add the peas (if fresh), rutabaga, sweet potato and carrot. Boil over moderately high heat until the liquid is reduced by half, about 8 minutes. Whisk together the reserved tomalley and roe and stir into the sauce.

5. Add the remaining 8 tablespoons butter to the pan, 1 tablespoon at a time, swirling until just melted. Season with the lemon juice, salt and pepper. Add the spinach leaves and the peas, if frozen, and cook until the spinach is just wilted.

6. To serve, arrange the lobster meat on 4 warm plates. Pour the sauce with the vegetables over the lobster. Garnish with sprigs of coriander and truffle slices if desired.

Lobster Cantonese

2 SERVINGS

1 lobster, preferably female (about 2 pounds)
⅔ cup chicken stock or canned broth
1 whole egg
2 egg whites
1 tablespoon water chestnut powder* or cornstarch

3 tablespoons medium-dry sherry
½ tablespoon dark soy sauce*
1 teaspoon sugar
3 tablespoons peanut oil
1 tablespoon fermented black beans,* minced
3 medium garlic cloves, minced
2 teaspoons minced fresh gingerroot
¼ pound ground pork
⅓ cup scallions, thinly sliced
*Available at Oriental groceries

1. Using a heavy cleaver, chop the body of the lobster into 2-inch sections. Discard the head. Crack the claws. (If the lobster is cut at the fish store, refrigerate it and use within 3 hours.) Add the roe (if you have a female) and tomalley to the chicken stock. Place the lobster pieces in a strainer set over a bowl; reserve the drained juices to add to the stock.

2. Beat the egg and the egg whites slightly; the yellow and white should not be completely mixed.

3. Dissolve the water chestnut powder in 2 tablespoons of the sherry to make a binder.

4. In a small bowl, combine the remaining 1 tablespoon sherry, the dark soy sauce and sugar.

5. Place a large wok over high heat for about 1½ minutes. Add the oil and heat to just below the smoking point. Add the black beans, garlic and ginger; stir-fry for 15 seconds. Add the pork; stir-fry until the pork turns white, about 3 minutes.

6. Add the lobster pieces; stir-fry for 2 minutes. Add the soy sauce mixture; mix well. Add the scallions and the stock; mix again. Bring to a boil. Cover tightly and cook over moderately high heat until the shells turn red, 3 to 5 minutes.

7. Stir the binder and add to the wok. Cook, stirring constantly, until the sauce thickens. Stir in the eggs; immediately turn off the heat. Transfer the mixture to a heated serving platter and serve hot.

Saffron Shellfish Stew with Leek and Red Pepper Marmalade

If you precede this gloriously rich and elegant stew with a noncreamy herbed pasta or risotto, you will need no other starchy accompaniment. Provide guests with soup spoons and forks and encourage them to stir the pepper marmalade into the sauce after admiring the arrangement of shellfish and garnish.

F&W Beverage Suggestion:
California Sauvignon Blanc, such as Chateau St. Jean or Preston

6 SERVINGS

10 tablespoons unsalted butter
½ teaspoon crushed hot red pepper
4 cups diced red bell peppers, (about 6 large)
4 cups coarsely chopped leeks (white part only), from about 4 large leeks
1 teaspoon salt
5 egg yolks
2 cups heavy cream
¼ teaspoon crumbled saffron threads
2 medium onions, finely chopped
3 carrots, finely chopped
2 small celery ribs, finely chopped
6 sprigs of Italian flat-leaf parsley
¼ teaspoon thyme
2 bay leaves
1½ pounds medium shrimp, cleaned, with shells reserved
2 cups dry white wine
2 cups fish stock or bottled clam juice
¼ teaspoon freshly ground black pepper
1½ pounds sea scallops
12 to 15 mussels, well scrubbed and debearded
Parsley sprigs, for garnish

1. In a large heavy saucepan, melt 5 tablespoons of the butter over moderate heat until foaming. Add the hot pepper and cook for 1 minute. Stir in the bell pepper, 3 cups of the leeks and ½ teaspoon of the salt. Cover, reduce the heat to low and simmer, stirring occasionally, until the vegetables are very soft but not browned, about 30 minutes.

2. Uncover, increase the heat to moderately high and cook, stirring constantly, until any excess moisture is evaporated and the vegetable mixture is thick enough to mound in a spoon, about 15 minutes. Remove from the heat; let cool slightly.

3. Transfer the vegetable mixture to a food processor. Turn the machine quickly on and off 4 or 5 times, until the vegetables are coarsely chopped. Scrape into a bowl, cover and reserve at room temperature. (**This marmalade can be prepared a day in advance.** Refrigerate and return to room temperature before using.)

4. At least 30 minutes before beginning the stew, whisk together the egg yolks and cream in a medium bowl. Stir in the saffron and set aside to steep.

5. In a large noncorrodible saucepan, melt the remaining 5 tablespoons butter over moderate heat until foaming. Add the onions, carrots, celery, parsley, thyme, bay leaves and remaining 1 cup leeks. Reduce the heat to low, cover and cook, stirring occasionally, for 20 minutes.

6. Add the reserved shrimp shells and cook for 10 minutes longer. Add the wine, fish stock, remaining ½ teaspoon salt and the black pepper. Bring to a boil over high heat. Reduce the heat to moderately low, partially cover and simmer the stock, stirring and skimming occasionally, for 20 minutes.

7. Strain the stock into a large saucepan, pressing on the vegetables and shrimp shells with the back of a spoon to extract as much liquid as possible. Discard the solids.

8. Bring the stock to a full boil over high heat. Add the shrimp and scallops all at once, then remove from the heat. Gently stir the seafood until somewhat stiffened and partially opaque, about 3 minutes; they should be only partially cooked at this point. With a slotted spoon, remove the shellfish to a bowl and set aside.

9. Bring the stock to a simmer over moderate heat. Add the mussels, cover and cook, turning the mussels and shaking the pan occasionally, until the mussels open, 5 to 7 minutes. With a slotted spoon, remove the opened mussels and set aside. Discard any that have not opened. Pour the stock through a fine-mesh strainer or a strainer lined with a double thickness of dampened cheesecloth.

10. Rinse out the saucepan. Return the stock to the saucepan and boil over high heat until reduced to 1 cup, about 20 minutes.

11. Slowly whisk the hot stock into the reserved saffron cream. Return this mixture to the saucepan. Add the reserved shrimp and scallops and cook very gently over low heat, stirring occasionally, until the stew is hot and slightly thickened, 5 to 7 minutes; do not overcook or the sauce will curdle.

12. Remove from the heat, add the reserved mussels and let stand, covered, for 1 minute to warm the mussels. Taste and season with additional salt and pepper if necessary.

13. Ladle the stew into soup plates. Arrange 2 mussels in each dish. Garnish each with a sprig of parsley and a heaping tablespoon of the leek and red pepper marmalade.

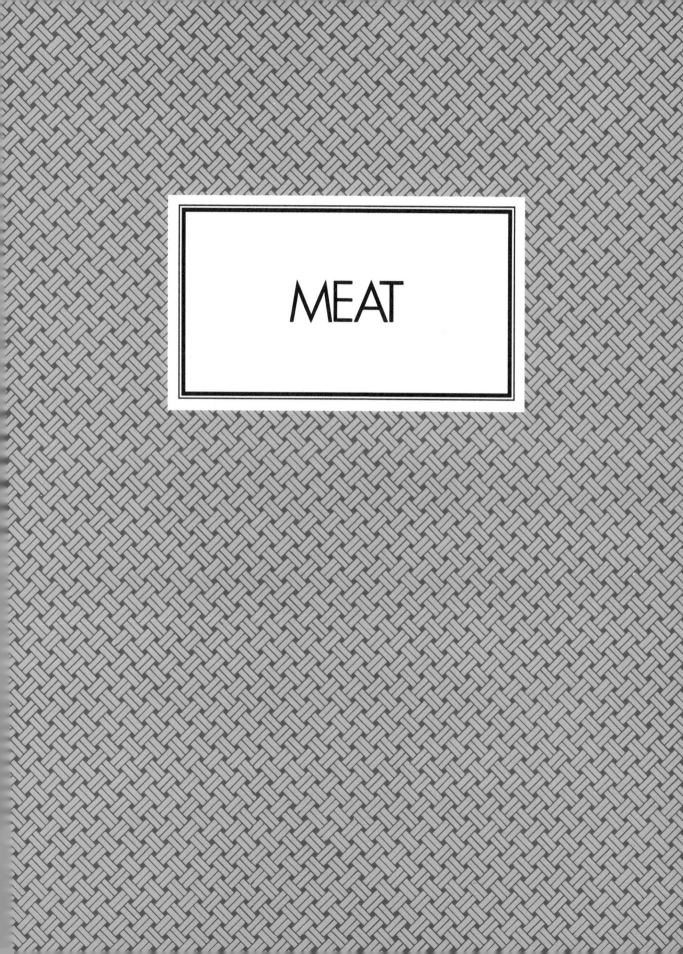

MEAT

Veal and Asparagus with Paprika Bread Crumbs

F&W Beverage Suggestion:
California Gamay Beaujolais, such as Mirassou

2 SERVINGS

10 large asparagus spears, trimmed and peeled
2 tablespoons unsalted butter
2 tablespoons olive oil
½ pound veal scallops
2 teaspoons sweet Hungarian paprika
¼ teaspoon salt
¼ teaspoon coarsely ground pepper
½ cup coarse fresh whole wheat bread crumbs
2 tablespoons finely chopped parsley

1. In a large pot of boiling salted water, cook the asparagus until tender but still bright green, about 3 minutes. Drain and wrap in a clean kitchen towel to keep warm until ready to use (the asparagus will continue to cook as they wait).

2. In a large skillet, melt 1 tablespoon of the butter in 1 tablespoon of the oil over moderately high heat. Pat the veal scallops dry. When the foam in the skillet subsides, sauté the scallops, turning once, until opaque, about 2 minutes on each side. As they are cooking, sprinkle them on both sides with the paprika, salt and pepper.

3. Remove the scallops to a warm platter and cover loosely with foil to keep warm.

4. Add the remaining tablespoon each of oil and butter to the pan. When the foam subsides, add the bread crumbs. Toss the crumbs until all the butter has been absorbed, then cook, stirring occasionally, until crisp, 5 to 10 minutes. Add the parsley and salt and pepper to taste.

5. Roll the asparagus spears in the crumbs, then divide the asparagus and the veal between 2 plates. Pour any accumulated juices over the veal. Sprinkle the crumbs over all.

Veal Cutlets with Lime-Spiked Mayonnaise

This dish can be served as an hors d'oeuvre by slicing the cutlets crosswise into ½-inch strips and serving the lime-spiked mayonnaise as a dip. And you don't have to use veal; chicken cutlets taste just as good. This zesty mayonnaise enhances seafood and vegetables as well.

F&W Beverage Suggestion:
Light red wine, such as Bodegas Olarra Rioja

6 MAIN-COURSE SERVINGS

Lime-Spiked Mayonnaise:

1 egg yolk, at room temperature
1½ tablespoons fresh lime juice
⅓ cup vegetable oil
¼ cup olive oil
1 teaspoon grated lime zest
¼ teaspoon salt

Veal Cutlets:

6 veal cutlets, sliced ¼-inch thick (about 1¼ pounds)
⅓ cup all-purpose flour
2 eggs, lightly beaten
1½ cups dry bread crumbs
½ cup olive oil
Salt and freshly ground pepper
Lime slices, for garnish

1. Prepare the mayonnaise: In a deep bowl, beat the egg yolk with 1 tablespoon of the lime juice until pale yellow.

2. Combine the vegetable oil and the olive oil. Beat the egg yolk at a moderate speed while you begin to add the oil drop by drop. After you have added about 2 tablespoons, begin adding the oil in a thin stream, stopping occasionally to make sure that all has been incorporated before adding more. When all the oil has been added and the mayonnaise is thick, beat in the remaining ½

tablespoon lime juice, the zest and the salt. Cover and refrigerate until serving time.

3. Prepare the veal: Place one veal cutlet between two sheets of waxed paper and pound with a smooth meat pounder or heavy cleaver until about ⅛ inch thick. Repeat with the remaining cutlets.

4. Place the flour on a sheet of waxed paper, the eggs in a shallow bowl and the bread crumbs on a plate. Dredge one cutlet in the flour, dip it into the egg and then into the crumbs, making sure the crumbs adhere. Place on a rack or platter and repeat with the remaining cutlets.

5. In a large heavy skillet, warm the olive oil over moderately high heat until hot but not smoking. Place two cutlets in the skillet and sauté until crisp and golden brown, about 2 minutes on each side. Drain on paper towels and repeat with the remaining cutlets.

6. Sprinkle the cutlets with salt and pepper to taste. Serve hot, warm or at room temperature with the cool mayonnaise. Garnish the plate with a slice of lime if desired.

Veal Scallopini with Zucchini

F&W Beverage Suggestion:
Italian white, such as Contratto Gavi

2 SERVINGS

1½ teaspoons unsalted corn oil margarine
1 medium zucchini, cut lengthwise into 4 slices
¼ cup all-purpose flour
¼ teaspoon chopped fresh rosemary or ⅛ teaspoon dried
4 small veal scallops (5 ounces total), pounded thin

1 tablespoon fresh lemon juice
6 capers, rinsed and drained

1. In a large skillet, melt ½ teaspoon of the margarine over moderate heat. Dredge the zucchini slices in the flour and shake off the excess; reserve the flour. Add to the skillet and cook about 2 minutes on each side until lightly browned. Keep warm in the oven.

2. Press the rosemary into both sides of the veal scallops and dredge them in the flour, shaking off any excess. Add the remaining 1 teaspoon margarine to the skillet and melt over moderately high heat. Add the veal and cook for 1 to 2 minutes on each side, until lightly browned.

3. Transfer to a warm platter and top with the reserved zucchini slices. Add the lemon juice and 1 tablespoon of water to the skillet. Bring to a boil, scraping up any browned bits from the bottom of the pan. Add the capers and pour the pan juices over the veal and zucchini.

Herbed Veal Stew with Winter Root Vegetables

This delicately creamy stew with its garnish of winter vegetables is unthickened, and the flavor of the veal is richly apparent. If you cannot locate fresh dill (a year-round staple in some areas), increase the mustard and parsley slightly, to taste. No additional starch or vegetable is needed, but pumpernickel bread makes a good accompaniment.

🍷 **F&W Beverage Suggestion:**
Italian Chianti, such as Antinori

<u>6 SERVINGS</u>

4 tablespoons unsalted butter
3 tablespoons vegetable oil
3 pounds boneless veal shoulder or leg, cut into 1½-inch cubes
Salt and freshly ground pepper
¼ cup brandy
2 leeks (white part only), partially split and thoroughly cleaned
3 carrots, coarsely chopped
1 medium onion, quartered and separated into layers
1 teaspoon thyme
1 cup dry white wine

4 cups chicken or veal stock or canned chicken broth
12 small white onions, about 1 inch in diameter
3 small turnips, about 2 inches in diameter
6 small red potatoes, 1 to 2 inches in diameter, scrubbed
1 cup heavy cream
1½ tablespoons Dijon-style mustard
⅓ cup chopped fresh dill
½ cup chopped Italian flat-leaf parsley

1. Preheat the oven to 350°. In a large, noncorrodible, flameproof casserole, melt 2 tablespoons of the butter in 1 tablespoon of the oil over moderately high heat until almost smoking. Add about one-third of the veal, being careful not to crowd the casserole. Season with salt and pepper to taste. Cook,, turning occasionally, until lightly browned, about 5 minutes. With a slotted spoon, transfer the veal to a bowl. Repeat with the remaining veal, adding 1 tablespoon of oil with each batch if the meat begins to stick to the bottom of the casserole.

2. When all the veal is browned, remove the casserole from the heat. Add the brandy, swirl to warm it in the pan and, averting your face, ignite with a match. When the flames die down, return the casserole to moderate heat and add the remaining 2 tablespoons butter. When the butter foams, add the leeks, carrots, quartered onion layers and thyme. Cover, reduce the heat to low and cook, stirring occasionally until the onion is soft but not browned, about 15 minutes.

3. Add the wine and stock to the pan, stirring well to scrape up any browned bits from the bottom of the pan. Add the browned veal and any juices that have accumulated in the bowl. Bring to a boil, skimming off any scum that forms on the surface. Cover and bake for 45 minutes.

4. Meanwhile, cut a shallow X in the root end of each white onion. Bring a medium saucepan of water to a boil, drop in the onions and boil for 5 minutes. Drain and rinse under cold running water; peel and set aside.

5. Peel the turnips; cut them in half and hold in a bowl of cold water. Peel a strip from around the middle of each potato and hold in a bowl of cold water.

6. Remove the stew from the oven but leave the oven on. Pour the stew into a strainer set over a bowl. Reserve the liquid. Pick the meat out of the vegetables and set aside; discard the cooked leeks, carrots and onion layers. Wipe out the casserole. Return the veal and liquid to the pan. Add the white onions, turnips and potatoes. (**The stew may be prepared up to this point a day ahead.** Let cool to room temperature, cover and refrigerate. Bring to a simmer on top of the stove, stirring, before proceeding.)

7. Return the stew to the 350° oven and bake uncovered for about 45 minutes, until the veal and vegetables are tender.

8. Pour the stew into a strainer set over a bowl. Set aside the meat and vegetables, covered loosely to keep warm. Return the liquid to the casserole and add the cream. Bring to a boil over high heat, reduce the heat slightly and boil until reduced by half, about 10 minutes. Whisk in the mustard; taste and correct the seasoning if necessary. Add the dill and parsley and the reserved veal and vegetables. Cover and let stand for 1 minute before serving.

Veal Chops Westcott

Easy and elegant, these breaded chops are well complemented by sautéed mushrooms and a simple green salad.

🍷 **F&W Beverage Suggestion:**
Beaujolais or California Gamay

<u>2 SERVINGS</u>

2 veal chops, cut 1 inch thick and trimmed of excess fat
¼ teaspoon salt
¼ teaspoon freshly ground pepper
1½ tablespoons all-purpose flour
½ cup fine dry bread crumbs, preferably onion-rye
1 egg, beaten
2 tablespoons unsalted butter
2 tablespoons corn oil
Lemon slices, for garnish

1. Preheat the oven to 350°. Season the veal chops on both sides with the salt and pepper. Place the flour in a shallow bowl. Place the bread crumbs in a second shallow bowl.

2. Lightly dredge the chops in the flour, shaking off any excess, dip into the beaten egg, then coat well with the bread crumbs. Refrigerate the breaded chops for 5 minutes to set the coating.

3. In a large heavy skillet, melt the butter with the oil over moderately high heat until bubbling. Add the veal chops and sauté until golden brown, about 2 minutes on each side. Drain on paper towels and place on a rack in a small roasting pan.

4. Bake for about 30 minutes, until the center of each chop is white throughout. To serve, garnish with lemon slices.

Broiled Butterflied Leg of Lamb

A whole leg of lamb usually weighs between five and nine pounds; the meat should be pink, and the surrounding fat white and brittle. A three-quarter leg refers to a leg from which the sirloin section at the larger, butt end has been removed, making the lamb easier to bone and butterfly. Have your butcher bone and butterfly the leg, or do it yourself following the method detailed below.

F&W Beverage Suggestion:
Napa Valley Cabernet Sauvignon, such as Robert Mondavi

6 SERVINGS

6- to 7-pound leg of lamb with sirloin section removed
⅓ cup vegetable oil
⅓ cup fresh lemon juice
1 tablespoon ground cumin
2 teaspoons ground coriander
1 teaspoon salt

1. Bone the leg: With a sharp knife, slit the meat from the butt end to the shank, right down to the bone. Scraping against the bone, gently work the meat away from the bone from both sides, then work around the bones until they can be removed. Spread the meat out, outerside down. Make shallow vertical slits into the thick parts of the leg and spread the slits open to flatten and butterfly the

meat. Remove excess fat and membranes. Place the meat in a large noncorrodible container.

2. In a small bowl, whisk the oil and lemon juice together. Sprinkle each side of the meat with half of the cumin and coriander and rub the spices in well. Pour the oil and lemon juice over the meat, turning to coat. Cover and marinate in the refrigerator for 8 to 24 hours, turning several times.

3. Preheat the broiler. Remove the meat from the marinade and scrape the spices off the meat; pat dry with paper towels. Strain and reserve the marinade.

4. Broil the meat about 4 inches from the heat for 5 minutes. Baste with the marinade and cook for 5 minutes longer until the top is browned. Sprinkle with ½ teaspoon of the salt. Turn the meat and broil, basting once, for about 7 minutes for rare, 10 minutes for medium rare. Sprinkle with the remaining ½ teaspoon of salt. Let rest, loosely covered with foil, for 10 minutes before serving. Carve across the grain.

Leg of Lamb Michoacan Style (Tatamado de Borrego)

Serve this on a platter garnished with shredded lettuce, sweet onion rings and cooked asparagus spears. Pass hot flour tortillas and Fresh Tomato Salsa (p. 223) on the side.

F&W Beverage Suggestion:
Spicy red wine, such as Bandiera Wildflower red or California Zinfandel

8 TO 12 SERVINGS

2 dried *pasilla* chilies
2 dried *ancho* chilies
1 dried *mulato* chili
1 teaspoon salt
4 fresh *tomatillos* or half a 13-ounce can, drained (see Note)
1 medium onion, minced
1 tablespoon fresh lime juice or distilled white vinegar
1 leg of lamb (7 to 8 pounds)

1. Soften the three kinds of dried chilies by toasting them lightly on a hot griddle

or skillet for about 30 seconds on each side. Do not allow them to brown or they will become bitter. Cut the chilies open and remove the stems, seeds and ribs. Wash and cut into large pieces.

2. Put the chilies in a bowl and cover with hot water. Let soak for about 30 minutes, until soft.

3. Using a slotted spoon, transfer the chilies to a blender or food processor. Puree to a thick paste, adding some of the soaking liquid if necessary. Add the salt. Set the chili paste aside. (**The recipe can be prepared days ahead to this point.** Store the chili paste tightly covered in the refrigerator.)

4. Preheat the oven to 350°. In a medium saucepan, boil the *tomatillos* if they are fresh for 8 to 10 minutes, until soft. Drain and peel. Puree the *tomatillos*.

5. Blend together the *tomatillos,* onion and lime juice and rub over the leg of lamb. Put the lamb on a rack in a roasting pan. Cover tightly with a tent of aluminum foil. Bake for 1½ hours.

6. Remove the foil tent and spread the chili paste all over the meat. Return the lamb to the oven and roast, uncovered, until fork tender, 35 to 45 minutes longer. Let the lamb rest for about 15 minutes before carving.

NOTE: Also called Mexican green tomatoes, *tomatillos* are available in Latin American groceries.

Grilled Lamb with Lemon-Soy Marinade

These juicy chunks of lamb are good in a sandwich—use warmed pita bread rounds, and sprinkle in chopped scallion, tomatoes and fresh mint.

6 SERVINGS

½ cup plus 2 tablespoons fresh lemon juice
¼ cup olive oil
2 tablespoons soy sauce
1 small onion, minced
½ teaspoon freshly ground pepper
2 pounds boneless leg of lamb, trimmed and cut into 1-inch cubes

2 tablespoons unsalted butter, melted
1 tablespoon plain yogurt, at room temperature
½ teaspoon cumin
Salt

1. In a medium noncorrodible container, whisk the lemon juice, olive oil and soy sauce until blended. Stir in the onion and pepper. Add the lamb and toss to coat with the marinade. Cover and refrigerate for several hours or overnight, stirring the meat occasionally. Remove from the refrigerator 1 hour before grilling.

2. Light the charcoal or preheat the broiler. Thread the lamb cubes onto 6 metal skewers. In a small bowl, whisk together the melted butter, yogurt and cumin.

3. Grill the meat 4 to 6 inches from the heat, turning occasionally and basting twice with the butter-yogurt mixture, until lightly browned, 8 to 10 minutes. Season with salt to taste.

Rioja-Style Roast Lamb and Potatoes

An easy dish to prepare, since the oven does practically all of the work. The result: lamb and potatoes given a deliciously different edge by the sharpness of vinegar.

F&W Beverage Suggestion:
Red Rioja, such as Olarra Reserva

8 TO 10 SERVINGS

1 head of garlic, divided into individual cloves and peeled
8-pound leg of lamb, trimmed of excess fat
½ cup plus 3 tablespoons olive oil
5 baking potatoes, peeled and cut into ¼-inch slices
1 tablespoon coarse (kosher) salt
½ teaspoon freshly ground pepper
6 tablespoons chopped parsley
1 cup red wine vinegar

1. Preheat the oven to 350°. Slice 3

cloves of garlic in half lengthwise. Cut 6 slits in the lamb; insert a half-clove in each slit.

2. Grease a shallow roasting pan with 3 tablespoons of the olive oil. Place the lamb in the center of the pan and arrange the potatoes around the edges. Sprinkle the remaining oil evenly over the potatoes and the lamb. Sprinkle the lamb with the salt, pepper and 3 tablespoons of the parsley. Roast in the oven for 45 minutes.

3. Meanwhile, in a blender, combine the remaining garlic with the remaining 3 tablespoons parsley to form a paste. Blend in the vinegar.

4. Remove the lamb from the oven and spoon the vinegar mixture over the leg. Turn the potatoes. Return the pan to the oven and continue roasting, turning the potatoes occasionally, for 35 to 45 minutes, until the lamb registers 125° on an instant-reading meat thermometer for rare, or 135° for medium rare. Turn the oven off.

5. Remove the lamb to a carving board and let rest, loosely covered with foil, for 10 to 15 minutes. Cover the roasting pan with foil and leave the potatoes in the oven until ready to serve.

Crown Roast of Lamb

F&W Beverage Suggestion:
Red Bordeaux, such as Cos d'Estournel

6 TO 8 SERVINGS

2 racks of lamb (8 chops each, see Note)
1 large garlic clove, cut in half
2 tablespoons olive oil
1 teaspoon salt
1 teaspoon freshly ground pepper
1 tablespoon dried tarragon
1 bunch of watercress
Vegetable Mélange (recipe follows) or Sweetbread, Kidney and Potato Sauté (p. 66), for accompaniment
Béarnaise Sauce (p. 221)

1. Preheat the oven to 375°. "French" the rib bones by cutting down about 2 inches between the bones and trimming the meat from between the bones. With the edge of the knife, scrape the meat and membranes from the bones.

2. Line the two racks up end to end. With a trussing needle and three 10-inch lengths of heavy kitchen string, sew the racks together near the bone at three points: on the top meat next to the exposed rib bones, through the top of the loin and below the loin where the rib bones meet the chine bone. Tie the ends of the strings together on the bony side of the roast; trim off the extra string.

3. With the meaty loin part on the inside, bend the connected racks into a circle. Tie and sew the other two end ribs together as before to secure the roast.

4. Rub the cut sides of the garlic clove over the entire surface of the roast. Brush with the olive oil. Sprinkle with the salt and pepper. Rub the tarragon into the cut surfaces between each chop.

5. Put the crown roast in a shallow heavy roasting pan without a rack. Push a ball of crumbled aluminum foil tightly into the space in the center of the crown to mold the roast into a rounder circle. Wrap the exposed rib bones with a strip of aluminum foil to prevent them from burning during cooking.

6. Place in the lower third of the oven and roast for about 45 minutes, until the meat is firm and resistant to the touch, 145° for medium rare.

7. Transfer the roast to a larger platter and surround the base with the watercress for decoration. Let stand for 10 to 15 minutes to allow the juices to set. Remove the foil from the bones. Remove the top and bottom strings; the middle one will help the roast keep its shape. Fill the center with one of the suggested accompaniments. Present the roast, then carve into individual chops. Serve with the Béarnaise Sauce on the side.

NOTE: Choose two racks as uniform in size as possible. Have your butcher prepare each rack for roasting by trimming the rib bones evenly, removing the back strap—a flat piece of cartilage between the rib muscles—and trimming off excess fat and membranes. Be sure he cuts through the chine bone (backbone) so that the chops can be divided easily at table.

Vegetable Mélange

6 TO 8 SERVINGS

4 medium carrots
4 medium turnips
18 small white onions (about 1 inch in diameter)
1 bunch of broccoli, stemmed and cut into 1-inch florets
2 tablespoons olive oil
18 cherry tomatoes
1½ teaspoons dried tarragon
1 teaspoon salt
½ teaspoon freshly ground pepper

1. Peel the carrots and cut them into 2-inch lengths. Peel and quarter the turnips. "Turn" the carrot and turnip pieces by carving them with a paring knife into oval football shapes. Keep the carrots and turnips separate. Place the turned turnips in a bowl of cold water.

2. In a large saucepan of boiling salted water, cook the carrots over high heat until just tender, 3 to 5 minutes. Remove with a slotted spoon, rinse under cold running water and drain well. Place in a bowl.

3. Add the turnips to the same saucepan of boiling water and cook until just tender, about 3 minutes. Remove with a slotted spoon, rinse under cold running water and drain well. Add to the carrots.

4. Add the onions to the saucepan of boiling water and cook until just tender, about 2 minutes. Remove with a slotted spoon, rinse under cold running water and drain. Cut off the roots and remove the outer skin. Add to the carrots and turnips.

5. Add the broccoli florets to the boiling water and cook until barely tender but still bright green, about 1 minute. Drain, rinse under cold running water and drain well. Set aside separately. **(The recipe can be prepared ahead to this point.)**

6. In a large skillet, heat the oil. Add the carrots, turnips and onions and sauté over moderately high heat, tossing frequently until the vegetables begin to warm through, about 1 minute.

7. Add the tomatoes, broccoli, tarragon, salt and pepper. Cook, tossing frequently, until all the vegetables are heated through, 2 to 3 minutes.

Sweetbread, Kidney and Potato Sauté

This elegant dish was inspired by a creation of Chef Claude Deligne of Taillevent in Paris, Panaché d'Agneau, which presents lamb chops garnished with lamb kidneys and lamb sweetbreads in tarragon sauce. With all the preliminary preparations done ahead, the dish can be sautéed at the last moment while the rack of lamb is resting.

6 TO 8 SERVINGS

1 pound lamb or veal sweetbreads (see Note)
1 pound lamb kidneys
3 cups milk
24 small red potatoes
3 teaspoons salt
½ cup all-purpose flour
1 teaspoon freshly ground pepper
About 9 tablespoons olive oil

1. Soak the sweetbreads in 3 or 4 changes of cold water for 2 hours. Soak the kidneys in the milk for 1 hour.

2. Meanwhile, peel the potatoes and "turn" them by carving them with a paring knife into oval football shapes. As they are prepared, drop them in a bowl of cold salted water.

3. Drain the kidneys and pat dry; discard the milk. With a sharp knife, cut each kidney horizontally in half through the connective tubes to form two roughly crescent shapes. Cut out the tubes and remove as much tough connective tissue as possible. Set aside.

4. Put the sweetbreads in a large saucepan. Add cold water to cover and 2 teaspoons of the salt. Bring to a boil over moderately high heat. Reduce the heat to moderate and simmer until the sweetbreads are firm, about 15 minutes.

5. Remove the sweetbreads with a slotted spoon and drain on paper towels. Let stand until cool enough to handle. Peel off the outer membranes that cover the sweetbreads. Cut out any tubes and tough connective tissues. **(The recipe may be prepared ahead to this point.** Wrap and refrigerate the sweetbreads and kidneys separately. Let return to room temperature before proceeding.)

6. Place the potatoes in a large saucepan of salted cold water. Bring to a boil over high heat. Reduce the heat to moderate and simmer the potatoes until almost tender when pierced with a fork (they will finish cooking later), about 5 minutes. Drain and pat dry.

7. Slice the sweetbreads into medallions about ¼ inch thick. Sift together the flour, pepper and remaining 1 teaspoon salt onto a sheet of waxed paper.

8. About 15 minutes before you plan to serve the dish, heat 3 tablespoons of the oil in a large skillet until shimmering. Add the potatoes and sauté over moderately high heat, turning frequently, until tender and browned all over, 8 to 10 minutes.

9. Meanwhile, in another large skillet, heat 3 tablespoons of the oil until shimmering. Add the kidneys and sauté over moderately high heat, tossing frequently, until browned outside but rare inside, 2 to 3 minutes. Remove and drain on a plate lined with paper towels. Cover loosely with foil to keep warm.

10. Pour the oil out of the skillet. Carefully wipe out the pan with paper towels.

Add the remaining 3 tablespoons oil to the skillet; place over moderately high heat.

11. Quickly dredge the sweetbreads in the seasoned flour; shake off any excess. Add as many slices to the hot oil as fit in a single layer. Sauté, turning once, until golden brown, 2 to 3 minutes. Remove and drain on paper towels. Add more oil to the pan if necessary to sauté the remaining sweetbreads.

12. To assemble, add the kidneys and sweetbreads to the skillet with the potatoes. Toss over moderate heat just to warm through, about 1 minute. Season liberally with salt and pepper.

NOTE: Ask your butcher for the higher quality round sweetbreads, if available.

Roast Rack of Lamb with Thyme and Mint

Have your butcher remove the chine bones on the rack to facilitate carving. You may also ask him to "french" the ends of the chops, or you can do it as detailed below.

🍷 **F&W Beverage Suggestion:**
Moulin à Vent, such as Louis Latour

4 SERVINGS

8-chop rack of lamb (about 2 pounds) or two 4-chop racks, chine bones removed
Salt and freshly ground pepper
¼ cup melted unsalted butter
2 tablespoons peanut oil
1 tablespoon thyme
2 teaspoons dried mint

1. Preheat the oven to 425°. Trim the lamb of excess fat, leaving a ¼-inch layer of fat over the meaty part of the rack. With a sharp knife, "french" the ends of the bones by cutting down about 2 inches between the end of the bones and removing all the meat and fat. Scrape the exposed bone ends clean. Sprinkle the lamb lightly with salt and pepper.

2. Place the rack, meaty-side up, in a roasting pan. Mix the melted butter and

oil together and pour over the meat to coat lightly.

3. Roast the lamb in the center of the oven for 20 minutes; then sprinkle with the thyme and mint. Continue roasting for 10 minutes to an internal temperature of 125° on an instant-reading thermometer for rare, 20 minutes and 135° for medium rare.

4. Let the lamb rest at room temperature, loosely covered with foil, for 10 minutes. Slice into 2-chop serving portions.

Lamb Chops with Sorrel Sauce

🍷 **F&W Beverage Suggestion:**
Mature California Cabernet Sauvignon, such as Robert Mondavi, or mature Bordeaux

4 SERVINGS

1 cup heavy cream
4 tablespoons unsalted butter
2 tablespoons olive oil
8 rib lamb chops, cut 1 inch thick
Salt and freshly ground pepper
1⅓ cups dry white wine
5 ounces fresh sorrel leaves, finely chopped, or ¼ cup pureed jarred sorrel
½ cup chopped fresh mint
Fresh mint sprigs, for garnish

1. Preheat the oven to 200°. In a medium saucepan, bring the cream to a boil over moderate heat. Cook, stirring occasionally and taking care that the cream doesn't boil over, until reduced to ½ cup, 5 minutes.

2. Meanwhile, in a large skillet (or two if necessary), melt the butter in the oil over moderate heat. When the foam subsides, add the lamb chops and sauté, turning once, until browned outside but still pink in the center, 3 minutes on each side for rare, 4 for medium rare, 5 for well done. They should be slightly underdone. Transfer to a platter, season with salt and pepper to taste, cover loosely with foil and keep warm in the oven.

3. Pour off and discard the fat from the skillet. Add the wine and bring to a boil,

scraping up any browned bits from the bottom of the pan. Boil over high heat until reduced by half, about 7 minutes. Add the sorrel and cook for 2 minutes. Add the reduced cream and cook until heated through, about 2 minutes. Season with salt and pepper to taste.

4. Pour the sauce over the lamb and sprinkle with the chopped mint. Garnish with the sprigs of mint.

Grilled Lamb Patties

🍷 **F&W Beverage Suggestion:**
Rosé of Cabernet Sauvignon, such as Simi

2 OR 3 SERVINGS

1 pound lean ground lamb, preferably shoulder
2 tablespoons finely chopped onion
2 garlic cloves, finely chopped
1 tablespoon finely chopped parsley
1 teaspoon salt
¼ teaspoon freshly ground pepper
2 tablespoons unsalted butter
1 tablespoon olive oil
Avgolemono Sauce (p. 222)

1. Lightly mix the lamb with the onion, garlic, parsley, salt and pepper; do not mash or press. Form the meat into 2 or 3 patties, each slightly less than 1 inch thick.

2. In a large heavy skillet, melt the butter in the oil over high heat. When the foam subsides, add the patties and cook until well browned on the bottom, 4 to 5 minutes. Turn and cook for 2 to 3 minutes for rare. If you want to cook the meat further, reduce the heat to moderate and cook until the patties reach the desired degree of doneness. Serve immediately with Avgolemono Sauce.

Donatello's Lamb Chops Milanese

🍷 **F&W Beverage Suggestion:**
Italian Merlot, such as Friulvini

4 SERVINGS

12 rib lamb chops, cut no more
  than ¾ inch thick—trimmed,
  frenched and pounded ½ inch
  thick
⅓ cup finely chopped fresh basil
1 large sprig of fresh rosemary or 2
  teaspoons dried, crumbled
4 imported bay leaves
8 medium garlic cloves, bruised
  and peeled
2 cups olive oil, preferably extra-
  virgin
½ cup all-purpose flour
3 egg whites
½ teaspoon salt
¼ teaspoon freshly ground pepper
1½ cups fresh bread crumbs,
  preferably from egg bread
4 tablespoons unsalted butter
⅔ cup vegetable oil

1. Place the lamb chops close together
in a single layer in a shallow container.
Sprinkle with the basil, rosemary, bay
leaves and garlic and pour the olive oil
over all. Marinate, turning frequently, at
room temperature for 3 hours or refrigerate, covered, for up to 3 days.

2. Place the flour in a shallow dish. Beat
the egg whites in a wide bowl with the
salt and pepper until foamy. Place the
bread crumbs in a shallow dish.

3. Preheat the oven to 350°. One by one,
remove the chops from the marinade,
scrape off the herbs and blot any excess
oil with paper towels. Bread each chop
by first dredging in the flour and shaking
off any excess. Then dip in the egg
white, drawing each side over the side of
the bowl to remove any excess. Then
coat with the bread crumbs, pressing so
that they adhere. Shake off excess
crumbs, then place the chops on a rack.

4. In a large skillet, warm 2 tablespoons
of the butter in ⅓ cup of the vegetable
oil over high heat until shimmering.
Working in 4 batches, add 3 chops at a
time and sauté, turning once, until well
browned, about 30 seconds on each side
(they will finish cooking later). Transfer

to a large baking sheet and cover loosely
with foil. After 2 batches, discard the oil
and wipe out the skillet with a paper
towel. Heat the remaining 2 tablespoons
butter and ⅓ cup oil and sauté the remaining 2 batches.

5. Uncover the chops and bake for 2 to
3 minutes for rare, 3 to 4 minutes for
medium rare. Serve immediately.

Norwegian Boiled Lamb in Dill Sauce

This dish is traditionally served with
boiled new potatoes.

🍷 **F&W Beverage Suggestion:**
St. Emilion, such as Château Belair

10 TO 12 SERVINGS

Lamb:

3 pounds boneless lamb shoulder
  or leg, trimmed of excess fat and
  cut into 1-inch cubes
1 teaspoon salt
10 white peppercorns
4 allspice berries
1 bay leaf
1 teaspoon thyme
1 medium onion, coarsely chopped
2 carrots, coarsely chopped
1 large leek (white part only),
  coarsely chopped
1 large celery rib with leaves,
  coarsely chopped
⅓ cup finely chopped fresh dill

Dill Sauce:

2 tablespoons unsalted butter
2 tablespoons all-purpose flour
2 tablespoons distilled white
  vinegar
1 tablespoon sugar
½ cup heavy cream
2 egg yolks
½ cup finely chopped fresh dill
1 teaspoon fresh lemon juice
1 teaspoon coarse (kosher) salt
½ teaspoon freshly ground white
  pepper

1. **Prepare the lamb:** Place the lamb in
a large flameproof casserole. Add the salt
and 1½ quarts of cold water and bring to
a boil over high heat, skimming as scum
forms on top. Continue to cook, skimming occasionally, for 15 minutes to remove all impurities. Add the remaining
ingredients for the lamb, reduce the
heat, cover and simmer until the meat is
tender, 1½ to 2 hours.

2. Preheat the oven to 200°. With a slotted spoon, transfer the meat to a medium casserole. Strain the cooking liquid;
reserve the stock and discard the vegetables. Moisten the meat with ¼ cup of the
stock; pour the remainder into a large
heavy saucepan. Cover the casserole and
keep warm in the oven.

3. **Make the dill sauce:** Boil the lamb
stock over high heat until reduced to 2
cups, about 15 minutes.

4. In a medium saucepan, melt the butter over moderately low heat. Add the
flour and cook, stirring, for about 2 minutes without allowing the flour to color
to make a roux. Add the stock all at once.
Bring to a boil over moderate heat,
whisking constantly. Cook, stirring frequently, for 5 minutes. Remove the sauce
from the heat.

5. In a small noncorrodible saucepan,
bring the vinegar and sugar to a boil
over high heat. Lower the heat to moderate and boil until reduced to a light syrup, about 3 minutes. Remove from the
heat. Stir the syrup into the sauce.

6. Whisk the cream and egg yolks together until well blended. Stir a little of
the sauce into the cream-yolk mixture,
then stir all of the mixture into the
sauce. Cook over low heat, stirring constantly until warmed through, about 3
minutes; do not boil.

7. Remove the sauce from the heat. Stir
in the dill, lemon juice, salt and pepper.
Pour over the meat and serve.

*Right, Flounder Stuffed with Garlic
Potatoes and Celery (p. 52).*

Clockwise from far left: Snow Pea Salad with Walnut Vinaigrette (p. 153), Lemon-Orange Broth with Scallions and Dill (p. 41), Creamy Pineapple Pie (p. 198) and Scallops and Mussels with Saffron Sauce (p. 55).

Left, Rioja Style Roast Lamb (p. 65). Above, top, Pork Loin Smothered with Onions and Gruyère (p. 78). Above, bottom, Pork Chili with Cinnamon and Chocolate (p. 82).

Left, Veal Scallopini with Zucchini (p. 62) and Stuffed Mushroom Caps Monégasque (p. 26). Right, top, Fragrant Scallops and Lime in Parchment (p. 56). Right, bottom, Fillet of Lotte with Two Butters and Two Caviars (p. 54).

Blanquette of Lamb with Asparagus and Morels

Lamb, morels and asparagus are three of America's finest natural resources, and they combine spectacularly in this "white" stew. When asparagus is out of season, simply accompany the blanquette with a buttered seasonal green vegetable of your choice.

F&W Beverage Suggestion: Bordeaux, such as Château Pichon-Lalande, or California Cabernet Sauvignon, such as Chateau Montelena

6 SERVINGS

About 5 cups chicken stock or canned broth
1 ounce (about 1 heaping cup) dried morels
3 pounds boneless lean lamb shoulder or leg, cut into 1½-inch cubes
1 large onion
1 whole clove
1 large leek (white part only), partially split and thoroughly cleaned
2 celery ribs, including leafy tops
1 bay leaf
6 sprigs of Italian flat-leaf parsley
1 carrot, trimmed but not peeled
½ teaspoon thyme
Tips from 2 pounds of asparagus, 30 to 40 stalks (reserve the stalks for another use)
4 tablespoons unsalted butter
¼ cup all-purpose flour
2 tablespoons fresh lemon juice
½ teaspoon salt
¼ teaspoon freshly ground pepper
3 egg yolks
½ cup heavy cream

1. In a small saucepan, bring 2 cups of the chicken stock to a boil. Rinse the morels under cold running water and place in a small heatproof bowl. Pour the boiling stock over them and let stand, stirring occasionally, until softened, about 1 hour. Remove the morels with a slotted spoon and set aside. Let the liquid settle, then strain through a coffee filter or a strainer lined with a paper towel; discard the sandy residue. Add additional stock to the mushroom liquid to equal 5 cups.

2. In a large flameproof casserole, combine the lamb and stock. Gradually bring to a simmer over moderate heat, skimming as scum forms on the top. Continue to cook, skimming, for 10 to 15 minutes to remove all impurities.

3. Meanwhile, stick the onion with the clove. With kitchen twine, tie the leek, celery ribs, bay leaf and parsley into a bundle.

4. Add the onion, leek bundle, whole carrot and thyme to the casserole. Partially cover and simmer until the lamb is very tender, 1¼ to 1½ hours.

5. Meanwhile, in a large saucepan of boiling salted water, cook the asparagus tips, uncovered, until crisp-tender, about 3 minutes. Drain and rinse under cold running water; drain well.

6. Discard the onion, carrot and leek bundle. Strain the stew, reserving the liquid. Rinse and dry the casserole. Measure the strained liquid; there should be 3⅓ cups of stock. If not, add water or boil until reduced to the correct quantity. Skim off surface grease. In a medium saucepan, bring the stock to a boil.

7. Melt the butter in the casserole over moderate heat. Add the flour and cook, stirring constantly, for 5 minutes, without letting the flour color to make a roux. Whisk in the boiling stock. Reduce the heat to moderately low and simmer, stirring, until slightly thickened, about 5 minutes. Season with the lemon juice, salt and pepper. Add the lamb and morels. (**The recipe can be prepared to this point up to a day ahead.** Let cool; then refrigerate, tightly covered.)

8. To complete the stew, warm it over low heat, stirring frequently. In a small bowl, whisk the egg yolks and cream until blended. Gradually whisk in 1 cup of the hot stew liquid. Stir the warmed egg mixture back into the stew. Cook over low heat, stirring occasionally, for 5 minutes; do not allow the stew to boil or the sauce will curdle. Add the asparagus and cook until the stew is creamy and thickened, about 5 minutes longer.

Lamb Shish Kebab

F&W Beverage Suggestion: California Cabernet Sauvignon, such as San Martin

8 SERVINGS

½ cup tomato paste
½ cup olive oil
¼ cup red wine vinegar
3 garlic cloves, finely chopped
2 teaspoons oregano
½ teaspoon salt
¼ teaspoon freshly ground pepper
5-pound leg of lamb—boned, trimmed of fat and cut into 1-inch cubes (to yield about 3½ pounds of meat)
2 green bell peppers, cut into 1-inch squares
2 medium onions, cut into 8 wedges
1 pound medium mushrooms
1 pint cherry tomatoes

1. In a large bowl, combine the tomato paste, olive oil, vinegar, garlic, oregano, salt and pepper. Stir until blended. Add the lamb, green peppers and onions to the marinade; toss to coat well. Cover and marinate at room temperature for 3 to 4 hours, tossing occasionally, or refrigerate overnight.

2. Light the charcoal or preheat the broiler. Loosely thread the peppers, lamb and onions onto long metal skewers, alternating the ingredients and allowing 6 to 8 pieces of lamb per skewer. Thread the mushrooms onto thin metal skewers through the caps. Thread the tomatoes onto separate skewers.

3. Lightly oil the barbecue rack to prevent sticking. Grill the lamb 4 to 6 inches from the heat, turning the meat frequently until browned outside and tender and pink inside, 10 to 12 minutes. Grill the tomatoes on the cooler, outer edge of the grill; grill the mushrooms in the center, basting with the marinade and turning frequently, for about 3 minutes.

Left, rich and savory Baked Jambonneaux with Mushroom and Wild Rice Stuffing (p. 98).

Pork Loin Smothered with Onions and Gruyère

A pork loin is one of the simplest and most satisfying roasts to prepare. Boned and tied, it presents a tidy, symmetrical package that is quick to cook and a snap to carve. If you want a simple, elegant piece of meat to serve hot or cold, the loin is a good choice.

Like pork in general, the loin takes well to embellishment, and this dish, which combines hearty, crowd-pleasing flavors with spectacular presentation, is a good example. Since the roasting of the pork and the preparation of the onion mixture can both be done hours ahead, the last-minute touches necessary to put the finished dish on the table take a mere 20 minutes.

Serve with mashed or parslied potatoes, black bread and cornichons.

F&W Beverage Suggestion:
Alsatian Gewürztraminer

6 SERVINGS

3-pound boneless pork loin roast, rolled and tied
1 teaspoon salt
¼ teaspoon freshly ground black pepper
4 tablespoons unsalted butter
2 large Spanish onions (2 pounds), thinly sliced
1 teaspoon thyme
¼ teaspoon freshly grated nutmeg
1 cup dry white wine
1 cup shredded, imported Gruyère cheese
Watercress, for garnish

1. Preheat the oven to 325°. Set the pork roast in a shallow baking dish, season with half of the salt and pepper and roast for 1½ hours, until 165° on an instant-reading thermometer. Remove from the oven and let stand for 20 minutes.

2. Meanwhile, in a large noncorrodible skillet, melt the butter over moderate heat. Add the onions, thyme, nutmeg and remaining salt and pepper and toss to coat. Cover the skillet, reduce the heat to low and cook, stirring occasionally, until the onions are very soft and golden, about 45 minutes.

3. Stir in the white wine and simmer, uncovered, until all the liquid has evaporated and the onions begin to sizzle, about 45 minutes. Cook, stirring frequently to prevent sticking, until the onions are lightly browned, 5 to 10 minutes longer.

4. Remove the strings from the roast and carve into at least 12 thick slices. In a shallow oval gratin dish, arrange the slices, overlapping slightly. Spoon the onion mixture evenly over the pork slices. (**The recipe can be prepared up to this point a day in advance.** Let cool to room temperature, cover and refrigerate. Bring the dish back to room temperature before proceeding.)

5. Increase the oven temperature to 350°. (If the roast was prepared the day before, reheat it on the lower rack of the oven for 10 to 15 minutes.) Sprinkle the Gruyère over the onions and bake it in the middle of the oven for 10 minutes, until the cheese is melted and lightly browned. Garnish with watercress before serving.

Sweet and Spicy Pork Chops

F&W Beverage Suggestion:
Chilled lager

8 SERVINGS

⅓ cup chili sauce
¼ cup vegetable oil
¼ cup strained apricot preserves
¼ cup hoisin sauce*
1 tablespoon plus 1 teaspoon cider vinegar
2 teaspoons *sambal ulek* (Indonesian hot pepper sauce) or Tabasco sauce to taste**

1 teaspoon powdered mustard
2 garlic cloves, minced
8 loin pork chops, cut ½ inch thick, trimmed of excess fat
***Available in Oriental groceries**

1. Light the charcoal or preheat the broiler. Lightly oil the barbecue rack to prevent sticking. In a small bowl, combine the chili sauce, oil, apricot preserves, hoisin sauce, vinegar, *sambal ulek*, mustard and garlic to form a glaze. Stir until blended.

2. Cut through the remaining fat on the curved edge of the chops every ½ inch to prevent curling when cooked.

3. Brush both sides of the chops with the glaze. Grill 4 to 6 inches from the heat, basting frequently with the glaze, for 4 minutes on each side, until the chops are lightly browned and the juices run clear when the chops are pierced.

Braised Pork with Apples

F&W Beverage Suggestion:
French hard cider, such as Purpom, or California Gewürztraminer, such as Monterey Vineyard

4 SERVINGS

2 tablespoons unsalted butter
2 large tart apples, such as Granny Smith—peeled, cored and cut into ½-inch slices
½ cup Calvados
4 pork loin chops (cut 1½ inches thick)
¾ cup plus 2 tablespoons hard apple cider, preferably French
1 small sprig of fresh sage or ½ teaspoon crumbled dried

2 small sprigs of fresh thyme or ¼ teaspoon dried
⅛ teaspoon freshly ground pepper
¾ cup heavy cream
¼ teaspoon salt
Sprigs of fresh sage, watercress or parsley, for garnish

1. In a large noncorrodible skillet, melt the butter over moderately high heat until sizzling. Add the apple slices, toss to coat with the butter and sauté, tossing once or twice, until golden but still firm, 3 to 4 minutes. Remove from the heat.

2. Pour ¼ cup of the Calvados into the skillet, return to low heat, warm gently and ignite with a match. Shake the pan until the flames subside. Remove the apples to a plate with a slotted spoon and set aside. Reserve the apple cooking juices for the sauce. **(The recipe can be prepared several hours ahead to this point.** Cover and refrigerate the apples.)

3. Trim any excess fat from the chops. Place the fat in a large heavy noncorrodible skillet over moderate heat until a good film of fat has been rendered. Remove and discard any pieces of unrendered fat. (If the chops have no extra fat, use a little vegetable oil.) Pat the chops dry and place in the hot skillet. Brown well for about 5 minutes on each side.

4. Remove the pan from the heat. Pour off any excess fat that has accumulated and pour in the remaining ¼ cup Calvados. Return to low heat, warm gently and ignite with a match. When the flames subside, add the cider, sage, thyme and pepper. Cover and let cook at a bare simmer, turning once, until the juices run clear, 140° on an instant-reading thermometer, about 10 minutes.

5. Remove the chops to a baking sheet and arrange overlapping apple slices on top. Lay any extra apple slices on the sheet. Preheat the broiler.

6. Add the reserved apple cooking juices to the skillet and boil until reduced to a syrup, 2 to 3 minutes. Re-move the sage and thyme sprigs. Paint the apple slices lightly with some of the syrup and broil 6 inches from the heat until the apples are nicely browned on the edges, 2 to 3 minutes.

7. Meanwhile, stir the cream into the remaining glaze in the skillet and boil until reduced to the consistency of a medium gravy, 3 to 4 minutes. Stir in the salt.

8. To serve, place the chops on a serving platter and drizzle the gravy evenly over or around them. Garnish the platter with the remaining few apple slices and sprigs of fresh sage, watercress or parsley.

Braised Pork Chops with Vegetables

Pork chops are among the most familiar and available cuts of pork, and are often the most disappointing as well. When cut thin and cooked quickly, they can be dry, tough and boring. Buy center-cut loin chops about 1 inch thick. To be tender and juicy they should be braised—that is, cooked with moisture in a tightly covered vessel. The recipe given here is a good illustration and can serve as a model for future improvisations. The chops are baked on a bed of potatoes, carrots and onions moistened with apple cider. The result is a delicious, country-style one-dish meal that, with a glass of beer or Beaujolais and a green salad, is utterly satisfying.

4 SERVINGS

¼ pound bacon, cut into 1-inch pieces
4 center-cut loin pork chops, cut 1 inch thick, trimmed of excess fat
1 teaspoon salt
½ teaspoon freshly ground pepper
1 small onion, thinly sliced
¾ teaspoon thyme
1 pound carrots, cut on the diagonal into ¼-inch slices
3 large boiling potatoes, peeled and cut into ¼-inch slices
⅓ cup chopped Italian flat-leaf parsley

½ cup fresh apple cider or apple juice
½ cup chicken stock or canned broth

1. Preheat the oven to 375°. In a flame-proof casserole large enough to hold the pork chops in a single layer, cook the bacon over moderate heat, stirring occasionally, until crisp and brown, about 10 minutes. With a slotted spoon, remove the bacon and drain on paper towels. Reserve the bacon grease in the pan.

2. Add the pork chops, season with half the salt and pepper and cook over moderate heat, turning once, until browned, about 5 minutes per side. Transfer the chops to a plate and set aside. Pour off all but 1 tablespoon of the fat in the pan.

3. Reduce the heat to moderately low. Add the onion and thyme to the casserole, cover and cook until the onion is softened and translucent, about 10 minutes. Add the carrots, potatoes and the remaining salt and pepper. Increase the heat to moderately high and cook, uncovered, stirring occasionally, until the vegetables are lightly browned, about 15 minutes.

4. Add the parsley, apple cider, chicken stock and reserved bacon. Transfer the casserole to the oven and bake, uncovered, for 30 minutes.

5. Reduce the oven temperature to 325°. Arrange the pork chops in a single layer over the vegetables, cover and bake for 20 to 30 minutes, until the chops are cooked through, but still moist and tender.

Pork Chops Smothered in Sweet and Sour Onions

Subtly sweet and sour, this delicious dish is one that improves if you bake it several hours ahead of time and reheat gently before serving. The sauce—a beautiful deep red color—goes well with roasted, boiled or mashed potatoes.

F&W Beverage Suggestion: Gewürztraminer, from Alsace or California, such as Trimbach or Rutherford Hill

6 SERVINGS

⅓ cup raisins
½ cup brandy
1½ pounds small white boiling onions (about 24)
2 tablespoons olive oil
6 center-cut loin pork chops, about 1 inch thick (about 2½ pounds)
1 tablespoon sugar
1 can (16 ounces) whole tomatoes with their juice
2 tablespoons red wine vinegar or cider vinegar
½ teaspoon salt
½ teaspoon thyme
¼ teaspoon freshly ground pepper

1. Place the raisins and brandy in a small saucepan and bring to a simmer over low heat. Remove from the heat and let stand for 30 minutes.

2. Trim a small slice away from both ends on each onion; peel off and discard the thin outer layer.

3. Place the oil in a large noncorrodible skillet over moderate heat. Add the pork chops in batches, without crowding, and sauté, turning once, until browned, about 3 minutes on each side. As they are browned, transfer to a large baking dish.

4. Preheat the oven to 350°. Place all of the onions into the skillet and sauté over moderate heat, shaking the pan frequently, until speckled brown all over, about 5 minutes. Sprinkle on the sugar and cook, tossing, for 3 minutes to caramelize. Add the tomatoes and their juice, the vinegar, salt, thyme, pepper and the raisins and brandy. Break up the tomatoes with a spoon and bring to a boil

over moderate heat, scraping the bottom of the pan to incorporate any bits of caramelized sugar. Pour the contents of the skillet over the pork chops.

5. Cover the baking dish tightly in a double layer of aluminum foil and bake for 1¾ hours, or until the pork chops are tender. Let rest for about 15 minutes before serving hot or warm.

Pork Scallops with Raisins and Vinegar

This dish is elegant and ready in minutes. It is made with pork tenderloin, as tender and flavorful as good veal, but much more affordable. The sauce is quickly concocted of such pantry staples as chicken broth, raisins and vinegar. The entire operation, in fact, will take much less time than the suggested accompaniment of wild rice cooked with mushrooms. Maintain the elegance by pouring a rich oaky California Chardonnay.

2 SERVINGS

¼ cup (packed) mixed dark and golden raisins
½ cup chicken stock or canned broth
1 pork tenderloin (about ¾ pound)
6 tablespoons unsalted butter
All-purpose flour, for dredging
¼ cup sherry vinegar
¼ teaspoon salt
¼ teaspoon freshly ground white pepper

1. Place the raisins in a small bowl. In a small saucepan, bring the chicken stock to a boil, then pour it over the raisins. Let stand until the raisins are soft, about 30 minutes.

2. Starting at the larger end of the tenderloin, slice off six pieces ½ inch thick. (The remaining, tapered end of the loin is unsuitable for this recipe. Reserve for pâtés or other use.) One at a time, place the pork pieces between the two sheets of waxed paper and pound lightly with a meat pounder or the bottom of a skillet or saucepan, to form circles about 3 inches in diameter.

3. In a large skillet, melt 2 tablespoons of the butter over moderate heat until

foaming. Dredge the scallops in the flour and shake off any excess flour. Working in batches, sauté 3 of the scallops, turning once, until lightly colored, about 4 minutes per side. Transfer the scallops to a plate and set aside. Sauté the remaining 3 scallops.

4. Add the vinegar to the skillet, increase the heat to high and boil, scraping up any browned bits from the bottom of the pan, until the vinegar is reduced to a thick, syrupy glaze, about 5 minutes.

5. Add the raisins and chicken stock to the skillet and bring to a boil. Return the scallops to the skillet and season with the salt and pepper; lower the heat, cover and simmer for 5 minutes.

6. Transfer the pork to warmed serving plates. Reduce the heat to low and whisk the remaining 4 tablespoons of butter into the sauce, 1 tablespoon at a time. Taste and add a splash more vinegar if desired. Pour the sauce over the scallops and serve at once.

Spareribs with Molasses-Mustard Glaze

4 SERVINGS

2 racks (about 6 pounds) baby pork spareribs, trimmed of excess fat and cracked for barbecuing
1 teaspoon salt
1¼ teaspoons freshly ground pepper
¾ cup Molasses-Mustard Glaze (recipe follows)

1. Preheat the oven to 350°. Season the ribs on both sides with the salt and pepper and lay them meaty-side down on a large baking sheet. Bake on the middle rack of the oven for 1 hour, turning once after 30 minutes. Drain off any excess fat.

2. Increase the oven temperature to 400°. Generously brush the meaty side of the ribs with the Molasses-Mustard Glaze and bake for 5 minutes; repeat 2 more times, letting the ribs bake for 10 minutes after their third coating.

3. Remove the ribs from the oven. When cool enough to handle, cut the ribs apart with a thin, sharp knife. Serve warm. (**The ribs can be made ahead and reheated loosely covered with foil.**)

Molasses-Mustard Glaze

MAKES ABOUT 1½ CUPS

½ cup Dijon-style mustard
⅓ cup cider vinegar
⅓ cup packed dark brown sugar
½ cup unsulphured molasses
1 teaspoon hot pepper sauce, or to taste
1 teaspoon thyme
1 tablespoon powdered mustard
½ teaspoon salt

In a small saucepan, whisk all the ingredients together until thoroughly mixed. Bring to a boil over moderate heat. Reduce the heat and simmer uncovered for 5 minutes. Remove the glaze from the heat, transfer immediately to a bowl and cool to room temperature before using.

NOTE: The glaze can be stored, covered, in the refrigerator for several weeks, although the flavors will diminish.

Chinois' Honey-Glazed Pork Ribs

The ribs for this recipe must marinate for 24 hours, so plan accordingly.

F&W Beverage Suggestion:
Chianti, such as Antinori

10 SERVINGS

Marinade:

3 cups rice wine vinegar*
1 cup mushroom soy sauce*
1¼ cups honey, preferably clover
6 jalapeño peppers, seeded and chopped
6 medium shallots, chopped
10 garlic cloves, chopped
2 tablespoons chopped fresh ginger
5 racks of baby pork ribs (4 to 5 pounds)

Sauce:

4 medium red onions, chopped
1 cup rice wine vinegar*
6 tablespoons mushroom soy sauce*
½ cup honey, preferably clover
1 cup chicken stock or canned broth
¾ cup plum wine
3 tablespoons fresh lemon juice
3 jalapeño peppers, seeded and chopped
2 medium shallots, chopped
½ cup chopped fresh coriander
½ cup chopped Italian flat-leaf parsley
4 sticks (1 pound) unsalted butter

*Available at Oriental groceries

1. In a noncorrodible container large enough to hold all of the ribs, combine all of the marinade ingredients; mix well. Lay the ribs in the marinade, cover and marinate in the refrigerator, turning occasionally, for 24 hours.

2. Preheat the oven to 450°. Set one oven rack in the middle and one on the lowest level. Place a foil-covered pan on the lower rack to catch the drippings from the ribs.

3. In a large noncorrodible saucepan, combine the onions, vinegar, soy sauce, honey, stock, plum wine, lemon juice, peppers, shallots, coriander and parsley. Cook, uncovered, over moderately high heat until reduced to one-fourth of the original volume, 15 to 20 minutes. Remove the sauce from the heat and whisk in the butter, 1 tablespoon at a time.

4. Working in batches, puree the sauce in a food processor or blender. Return to the saucepan and set aside.

5. Lift the ribs from the marinade and place 2 racks of ribs directly on the top rack in the oven or place the ribs on a rack in a roasting pan. Roast the ribs for 35 minutes until well glazed. Remove from the oven and, using a sharp knife, separate the racks into individual ribs. Roast the remaining racks. (**The recipe may be made ahead to this point.** Wrap the ribs in foil and refrigerate. Cover and refrigerate the sauce.)

6. Before serving, reheat the ribs in a 350° oven for 15 minutes, or until warmed through. Reheat the sauce and pass separately with the ribs.

Savory Pork Ragout with Carrots

This combination of pork and cinnamon, with garlic added at the last minute for extra emphasis, is particularly exciting. The resulting stew is rich and warming, all one could ask for on a cold winter's night. Since the seasoning gives it a mildly Middle Eastern air, serve the stew with a bulgur pilaf, tossed just before serving with sautéed mushrooms.

F&W Beverage Suggestion:
Dark beer, such as Dos Equis or Prior Double Dark

6 SERVINGS

About 5 tablespoons olive oil
3 pounds boneless lean pork shoulder, cut into 1½-inch cubes
2 medium onions, finely chopped
3 tablespoons all-purpose flour
1 cup dry red wine
1½ cups chicken stock or canned broth
1 cup canned crushed tomatoes
1 tablespoon cinnamon
1 teaspoon thyme
1 bay leaf
1 teaspoon salt
½ teaspoon freshly ground pepper
1 pound carrots, cut on the diagonal into 2-inch pieces
5 large garlic cloves, minced
1 cup chopped Italian flat-leaf parsley

1. Preheat the oven to 350°. In a large flameproof casserole, warm 2 tablespoons of the oil over moderately high heat until smoking. Working in batches, add one-third of the pork and cook, turning frequently, until lightly browned, about 5 minutes. With a slotted spoon, transfer the browned meat to a bowl. Repeat with the remaining pork, adding 1 tablespoon of oil with each batch if the casserole seems dry and the meat sticks to the bottom.

2. Add the onions and 1 tablespoon oil if the pan seems dry. Reduce the heat to moderately low and cook, stirring occasionally, until soft and golden, 15 to 20 minutes. Sprinkle on the flour and cook, uncovered, stirring frequently, without letting the flour color, for 5 minutes to make a roux.

3. Add the wine, stock, tomatoes, cinnamon, thyme, bay leaf, salt and pepper. Slowly bring to a boil, stirring to scrape up any brown bits on the bottom of the pan. Add the browned pork and any juices that have accumulated in the bowl. Cover and bake for 45 minutes. (**The recipe can be prepared up to this point a day in advance.** Let cool to room temperature, cover and refrigerate. Bring the stew to a simmer before proceeding.)

4. Add the carrots and bake uncovered until the vegetables and meat are tender and the sauce is slightly thickened, 30 to 45 minutes. Stir in the garlic and parsley, cover and let stand for 1 minute before serving.

Pork Chili with Cinnamon and Chocolate

This chili uses pork—it makes an excellent chili meat—and is seasoned liberally with cinnamon and unsweetened cocoa. Both have precedent in Mexican and Spanish cookery, and the combination contributes an unusual but delicious difference to America's favorite stew.

Precede the chili with guacamole salad or seviche and follow it with a green salad garnished with oranges. As an accompaniment serve corn bread, but flour tortillas are good, too. If for some reason you've made the chili relatively mild, you could pour a big but uncomplicated red wine (like the jug Zinfandel from C. K. Mondavi), slightly chilled. For hotter chili, an ice-cold beer (or several) is the beverage of choice.

And as for beans, you can serve them on the side, if you prefer, but don't omit them altogether. This chili is rich, and beans are the perfect foil.

8 SERVINGS

3 pounds finely diced or coarsely ground lean pork
¼ cup olive oil
4 medium onions, coarsely chopped
4 cups tomato juice

3 to 5 tablespoons chili powder, to taste
3 tablespoons ground cumin
3 tablespoons oregano (see Note)
3 tablespoons unsweetened cocoa powder
3 tablespoons cinnamon
1 tablespoon salt
8 medium garlic cloves, finely chopped
3 tablespoons stone-ground white cornmeal
2 cans (1 pound each) red kidney beans, drained and rinsed

1. In a stockpot or large flameproof casserole, cook the pork over moderate heat, stirring frequently, until it loses all pink color, about 20 minutes; do not brown.

2. Meanwhile, in a large heavy skillet, heat the oil. Add the onions, cover and cook over moderate heat, stirring occasionally, until softened and translucent, about 20 minutes.

3. Scrape the onions into the pork. Add the tomato juice and 3 cups of water; stir in 3 tablespoons of the chili powder, the cumin, oregano, cocoa, cinnamon and salt. Bring the chili to a boil; then reduce the heat and simmer, uncovered, stirring occasionally, for 1 hour.

4. Taste for seasoning, adding up to 2 tablespoons more chili powder if necessary. Cook for 30 minutes longer. Resist the temptation to skim off the fat; it adds flavor.

5. Stir in the garlic, cornmeal and beans; simmer until the beans are just heated through, about 10 minutes.

NOTE: If you can locate Mexican oregano, available in spice stores and Latin markets, use it. Its pungent flavor is especially welcome here.

Cantonese Barbecued Spareribs

6 SERVINGS

2 tablespoons grated fresh ginger
½ cup thinly sliced scallions
4 medium garlic cloves, minced
½ teaspoon freshly ground pepper
¼ cup dark soy sauce*
½ cup hoisin sauce*
2 tablespoons Chinese plum sauce*
2 tablespoons light miso*
¼ cup American chili sauce
¼ cup medium-dry sherry
¼ cup honey
1 rack of pork spareribs (about 4 pounds)
***Available at Oriental groceries**

1. Stir together all of the ingredients, except the ribs, to make a marinade.

2. Leave the rack of spareribs whole, or cut them in half if they are too long for the oven. Remove the skin from the concave side of the rack or have your butcher do this. Trim off excess fat. On the thicker end of the rack, make shallow cuts, about 4 inches long, between each rib.

3. Place the ribs in a shallow noncorrodible pan and rub the marinade all over them. Refrigerate, covered, for 4 to 8 hours, turning occasionally. Let return to room temperature before roasting.

4. Preheat the oven to 350°. Transfer the ribs, meaty-side up, to a rack set in a roasting pan (see Note) filled with 1 inch of water; reserve the marinade.

5. Roast in the middle of the oven for 40 minutes, turning once after 20 minutes. Increase the oven temperature to 450° and turn the ribs meaty-side up again. Roast for another 10 to 15 minutes, or until the spareribs are dark and crisp.

6. Remove the ribs from the oven and let stand uncovered for about 10 minutes while you make the sauce. Remove the fat from the drippings that have collected in the roasting pan. Boil the remaining liquid until reduced to ½ cup, about 10 minutes. Add 3 tablespoons of the reserved marinade and boil for 1 minute longer.

7. Leave each rib whole or chop crosswise with a heavy cleaver into 2-inch segments, Chinese style, if desired. Pass the sauce separately for dipping.

NOTE: To simulate a Chinese oven and produce crisp, succulent ribs, roast the spareribs directly on the middle rack of the oven. Place a shallow pan filled with 1 inch of water on the lowest rack to catch the drippings. Cooking time is the same, but the ribs need no turning.

Stir-Fry of Asparagus, Pork, and Shiitake Mushrooms

2 SERVINGS

1 pound center-cut pork chops—boned, trimmed and cut into ¼-inch-wide strips
2 tablespoons soy sauce, preferably dark*
3 teaspoons Oriental sesame oil
2 tablespoons dry sherry
Pinch of salt and freshly ground pepper
½ teaspoon chili paste*
2 cups peanut oil
1 pound asparagus—trimmed and cut into 2-inch lengths
¼ pound fresh shiitake mushrooms,* washed, stemmed and cut into thick slices (see Note)
3 water chestnuts, preferably fresh,* peeled and thinly sliced
***Available at Oriental groceries**

1. In a medium bowl, toss the pork with 1 tablespoon of the soy sauce. Add 1 teaspoon of the sesame oil, 1 tablespoon of the sherry and the salt and pepper and toss again. Marinate at room temperature for 30 minutes.

2. Meanwhile, make the sauce. In a small bowl, combine the remaining 1 tablespoon soy sauce, 2 teaspoons sesame oil, 1 tablespoon sherry and the chili paste.

3. Place a wok over high heat for about 1 minute. Pour in the peanut oil and heat until the oil begins to shimmer. Drain

the pork, add it to the wok and fry until lightly browned, about 2 minutes.

4. Drain the pork in a colander set over a large bowl. Measure out ¼ cup of the oil and reserve the remainder for another use.

5. Return the wok to high heat. After 1 minute add the ¼ cup of oil. When the oil shimmers, add the asparagus and reduce the heat to moderate. Stir-fry the asparagus until almost tender, about 2 minutes.

6. Add the mushrooms and the water chestnuts and continue stir-frying for 1 minute longer.

7. Add the pork and the sauce and stir-fry until heated through, about 1 minute.

NOTE: One ounce dried shiitake mushrooms (available in Oriental and specialty grocery stores) may be substituted, although the flavor and texture of the dish will be altered. To reconstitute, soak the dried mushrooms in boiling water to cover until soft, about 20 minutes. Squeeze dry before using.

Beef, Pork and Pumpkin Stew with White Beans and Tomatoes

Since fresh pumpkin is unavailable much of the year, you may substitute chunks of any firm-fleshed winter squash. This stew, like most, is best if made one day and served the next.

F&W Beverage Suggestion: California Zinfandel, such as Ridge

8 TO 10 SERVINGS

1 cup dried navy or pea beans, rinsed and picked over to remove any grit
1 pound trimmed, lean, boneless beef chuck, cut into 1-inch cubes
1 pound trimmed, lean, boneless pork shoulder, cut into 1-inch cubes
½ cup all-purpose flour
3 to 4 tablespoons olive oil
2 tablespoons unsalted butter
3 large onions, coarsely chopped
4 large garlic cloves, minced
1 green bell pepper, coarsely chopped
1 red bell pepper, coarsely chopped
½ teaspoon oregano
¼ teaspoon crumbled rosemary
½ teaspoon thyme
1 can (28 ounces) tomatoes with their juice
1 can (13¾ ounces) chicken broth
2 strips, 2 by ½ inch, orange zest
2 pounds pumpkin, butternut or Hubbard squash—peeled, seeded and cut into 1-inch chunks
2 teaspoons salt
½ teaspoon freshly ground pepper

1. In a large heavy saucepan, bring the beans and 2 cups of cold water to a boil over moderate heat. Cover tightly, turn the heat off and let cool to room temperature, about 1 hour.

2. Meanwhile, working in batches, dredge the beef and pork cubes in the flour until well coated. In a large heatproof casserole, warm 2 tablespoons of the olive oil over moderately high heat until shimmering. Brown the meat on all sides in batches, adding more oil if needed to prevent sticking. As the meat browns, transfer it with a slotted spoon to a large bowl.

3. Add the butter to the casserole. Add the onions, garlic, green and red peppers, oregano, rosemary and thyme. Reduce the heat to moderate and sauté, stirring frequently, until the onions are lightly browned, 8 to 10 minutes. There should be enough drippings in the casserole to brown the vegetables; if not, add another tablespoon of oil.

4. Return the meat to the casserole. Add the tomatoes and their juice, the broth and the orange zest. Bring to a simmer, cover and simmer gently for about 2 hours, until the beef and pork are almost tender.

5. Meanwhile, check the beans. If they have reached room temperature, add another 2 cups of cold water, set over moderate heat and bring to a boil. Reduce the heat, cover tightly and simmer for 1 to 1½ hours, until tender but still firm. Drain well.

6. Add the pumpkin chunks and the beans to the stew and simmer gently, partially covered, for 45 to 60 minutes, until the pumpkin and meats are both tender when pierced with a fork. Season with the salt and pepper.

Stuffed Leeks

6 SERVINGS

12 leeks, 1½ to 2 inches in diameter
1 cup (8 ounces) bulk sausage meat, or 8 ounces breakfast sausage links
1¼ cups (about 5 ounces) minced mushrooms
6 garlic cloves, minced
1¼ cups cooked rice
½ cup minced fresh parsley
2 teaspoons minced fresh dill or ½ teaspoon dried dillweed
½ teaspoon aniseed
1½ teaspoons sugar
¾ teaspoon salt
⅛ teaspoon freshly ground pepper
2 cups chicken broth
½ cup cream sherry
1 tablespoon unsalted butter

1. Trim the roots from the leeks and cut off enough of the green so that the leeks measure 6 inches. Cutting only halfway through, slit the entire length of each leek. Remove enough of the central core to leave a ¼-inch cylindrical shell. Soak the cores and shells and rinse thoroughly under cold running water to remove all grit. Finely chop the cores; set the shells aside.

2. If using links, remove the sausage meat from the casing. In a large skillet, cook the sausage, chopped leeks, mushrooms and garlic over moderate heat, stirring occasionally to mix and to break up the meat, until the sausage is cooked through and the leeks are softened, 5 to 7 minutes. Remove from the heat and drain off any excess fat. Add the rice, parsley, dill, aniseed, sugar, salt and pepper. Lightly toss to mix. Let stand until cool enough to handle, about 10 minutes.

3. Preheat the oven to 350°. Pack the stuffing into the leek shells, filling to

about one-half inch of either end and allowing room for the edges of the leeks to close around the filling. Tie each leek in the middle to seal. Place in a baking dish large enough to hold them in a single layer, or in two smaller pans. Combine the broth and sherry and pour over the leeks. Cover the dish tightly with aluminum foil.

4. Bake for 40 to 60 minutes, until the leeks are very tender when pierced with the tip of a knife.

5. Transfer the leeks to a serving platter. Strain the cooking liquid into a small saucepan and boil rapidly over high heat until reduced to 1 cup, about 5 minutes. Meanwhile, remove the strings from the leeks.

6. Whisk the butter into the reduced cooking liquid and season to taste with salt and pepper. Pour the sauce over the leeks and serve hot.

Leek and Sausage Pasties

F&W Beverage Suggestion: Good British ale, such as Bass

MAKES 4 PASTIES

2 cups all-purpose flour
¼ teaspoon salt
6 tablespoons unsalted butter, chilled and cut into ¼-inch bits
6 tablespoons (3 ounces) lard, chilled and cut into small bits
4 Italian sweet sausages (about 4 inches long), casings removed
1⅓ cups chopped leeks (white part only, 2 or 3 medium)
¼ cup chopped parsley
Freshly ground pepper
1 egg, lightly beaten

1. In a medium bowl, combine the flour and salt. Cut in the butter and lard until the mixture resembles coarse meal. Sprinkle on about ⅓ cup water while tossing with a fork. Gather the dough into a ball, adding a few drops of water if the pastry seems dry or crumbly.

2. Turn the pastry out onto a board and gently push it away from you with the heel of your hand to blend slightly. Form the dough into a 6-inch disk. Wrap and refrigerate for at least 1 hour.

3. Preheat the oven to 375°. Divide the dough into four equal pieces. On a lightly floured surface, roll out each piece into a 7½-inch circle, ⅛ inch thick. Place 1 sausage in the center of a pastry circle, cover with ⅓ cup of chopped leeks, 1 tablespoon of parsley and a pinch of pepper. Brush the edges of the pastry with beaten egg, bring together on top and pinch to close; crimp to seal. Brush the pastry with beaten egg. Make ½-inch vents on each side of the pastry "ridge" and place the pasty on a lightly greased baking sheet. Repeat to make three more pasties.

4. Bake in the center of the oven for 10 minutes; reduce the heat to 350° and bake for 40 to 50 minutes longer, until the pasty is golden brown. Serve hot, warm or at room temperature.

Roast Beef with Pan Gravy

F&W Beverage Suggestion: California Merlot, such as Rutherford Hill

8 SERVINGS

4 to 4½ pounds eye of round, including a thin layer of fat, rolled and tied
½ teaspoon freshly ground pepper
4 ounces beef suet
Pan Gravy (recipe follows)

1. Preheat the oven to 350°. Heat a heavy roasting pan over moderate heat until very hot.

2. Sprinkle the meat with the pepper and place it, fat-side down, in the hot pan. Increase the heat to high and cook the roast, turning without piercing the meat, until browned all over, about 8 minutes.

3. Add the piece of suet to the pan, turn the roast fat-side up and place the pan on the middle rack of the oven. Roast for 20 minutes.

4. Remove the roasting pan from the oven. Tilt the pan and draw off the melted, or rendered, fat with a bulb baster (see Note). Return to the oven and roast for 40 minutes for rare roast beef, 120° to 125° on an instant-reading thermometer; for medium rare, roast about 20 minutes longer to 135°.

5. Transfer the roast to a carving board, cover very loosely with aluminum foil and let rest for 20 to 30 minutes before carving into thin slices. Meanwhile discard the suet in the roasting pan. Pour off the melted fat in the pan, reserving 3 tablespoons; use the pan to make Pan Gravy.

NOTE: To accompany this hearty Roast Beef with Pan Gravy we suggest the Mini-Yorkshire Puddings (p. 137) and Roast Potatoes and Shallots (p. 128). Reserve ¼ cup of the drippings for the puddings and ⅓ cup for the potatoes. Remove more fat from the pan after the final roasting if necessary.

Pan Gravy

MAKES ABOUT 2 CUPS

3 tablespoons melted beef fat, reserved from Roast Beef (above)
3 tablespoons all-purpose flour
2 tablespoons Madeira or port (optional)
2 cups homemade beef stock (p. 218) or canned broth
Salt and freshly ground pepper

1. Return the reserved 3 tablespoons of fat to the roasting pan. Sprinkle in the flour and cook, stirring constantly, over moderately low heat until lightly browned, 2 to 3 minutes.

2. Whisk in the Madeira and beef stock. Bring to a boil, reduce the heat and simmer, stirring occasionally, for 3 minutes. Add any juices that may have collected on the platter on which the roast is resting.

3. Season with salt and pepper to taste. Strain and serve in a sauceboat.

Entrecôte au Roquefort

4 SERVINGS

5 tablespoons unsalted butter, slightly softened
2 tablespoons Roquefort cheese
2 tablespoons minced fresh parsley
½ teaspoon fresh lemon juice
4 Delmonico or rib-eye steaks, cut ¾ inch thick (about 8 ounces each)
Salt and freshly ground pepper
1 tablespoon vegetable oil

1. Mix 4 tablespoons of the butter with the Roquefort cheese until blended. Stir in the parsley and lemon juice. Wrap the Roquefort butter loosely in plastic wrap and roll between your hands to form a small log about 1 inch in diameter. Refrigerate until firm, at least 1 hour.

2. Season each steak with a pinch of salt and pepper. In a large skillet, heat the remaining 1 tablespoon butter and the oil. When the foam begins to subside, add the steaks and sauté over moderately high heat for 3 minutes. Turn the steaks and sauté for about 2 minutes longer for a medium-rare steak.

3. Remove the steaks to a heated platter. Unwrap the butter and slice the log into 8 disks. Arrange 2 disks of Roquefort butter on each steak and serve hot.

Flank Steak with Mustard Marinade

This is an easy dish to prepare but the steak must marinate a minimum of three to four hours, so plan accordingly.

🍷 **F&W Beverage Suggestion:** California Petite Sirah, such as Fetzer, or Côtes-du-Rhône

4 SERVINGS

½ cup vegetable oil
2 tablespoons white wine vinegar
2 tablespoons dry vermouth
2 tablespoons whole-grain mustard
1 tablespoon plus 1 teaspoon minced fresh rosemary or 1½ teaspoons dried, crumbled
¼ teaspoon freshly ground white pepper
1 flank steak (1¼ to 1½ pounds), trimmed of excess fat

1. In a shallow baking dish, stir together the oil, vinegar, vermouth, mustard, rosemary and white pepper to make a marinade. Add the steak and turn to coat. Cover and marinate at room temperature for 3 to 4 hours, turning the steak several times, or refrigerate overnight.

2. Light the charcoal or preheat the broiler. Lightly oil the barbecue rack to prevent sticking. Remove the steak from the marinade. Pour the marinade into a small saucepan and warm on the grill or over low heat.

3. Grill the steak 4 to 6 inches from the heat, basting occasionally with the marinade and turning once, for 5 minutes on each side for rare, 7 minutes for medium rare.

4. Remove the meat to a warmed platter, cover loosely with foil and let rest for 10 minutes. Thinly slice across the grain on the diagonal and serve with its juices.

Beef and Broccoli with Oyster Sauce

4 TO 6 SERVINGS

1 bunch of broccoli
1 pound flank steak or boneless sirloin, partially frozen
1 egg white
1 tablespoon water chestnut powder* or cornstarch
3 tablespoons medium-dry sherry
¼ cup oyster sauce*
1 tablespoon dark soy sauce*
1 teaspoon sugar
2 cups peanut oil
2 teaspoons minced fresh ginger
½ cup thinly sliced scallions
2 medium garlic cloves, minced
*Available at Oriental groceries

1. Separate the broccoli florets into 1- to 1½-inch pieces. Reserve the stems for another use or discard. Add the broccoli to a large saucepan of boiling salted water and blanch for 1 minute after the water returns to a boil. Drain and rinse under cold running water until cool; drain well.

2. Cut the meat in half along the grain; slice across the grain into ¼-inch slices.

3. Put the pieces of beef in a medium bowl. Add the egg white, water chestnut powder and 1 tablespoon of the sherry. Stir to coat the beef well. Cover and refrigerate for at least 1 hour, or up to 12 hours.

4. In a small bowl, combine the remaining 2 tablespoons sherry, the oyster sauce, soy sauce and sugar. Set aside.

5. Put a large wok over high heat for about 1½ minutes. Pour in the oil and heat to 325°. Stir the marinated beef and carefully add it to the hot oil. Cook, stirring constantly, for about 1 minute or until the beef turns brown. Turn off the heat.

6. Pour the beef and oil into a colander set over a large bowl. Shake gently to drain off as much oil as possible. Reserve 2 tablespoons of the oil. If desired, the remaining oil can be strained and reserved for other frying, such as for Chicken Soong, page 102.

7. Return the wok to high heat and add the 2 tablespoons reserved oil. Add the ginger, scallions and garlic. Stir-fry for 30 seconds. Add the broccoli and stir-fry for 1 minute longer.

8. Return the cooked beef to the wok; toss to mix. Stir the oyster sauce mixture and add it to the wok. Cook, tossing for about 10 seconds, until the meat and vegetables are evenly coated with sauce.

Spicy Beef and Onion Curry

Full of spice and flavor, but not too hot. Serve this over hot rice and with condiments such as peanuts, raisins, grated coconut and diced banana.

2 OR 3 SERVINGS

4 tablespoons vegetable oil
1 pound boneless beef sirloin, cut into thin 2½-by-¾-inch strips
1 large onion, thinly sliced
1 teaspoon ground coriander
½ teaspoon minced fresh ginger
½ teaspoon minced garlic
½ teaspoon ground cloves
½ teaspoon ground cardamom
½ teaspoon cayenne pepper
½ teaspoon cinnamon
½ teaspoon chili powder
½ teaspoon ground cumin
½ teaspoon turmeric
1 cup canned beef broth
¼ cup canned coconut cream
1 tablespoon fresh lemon juice
Salt and freshly ground black pepper
1 cup plain yogurt (optional)

1. In a large heavy skillet, heat 2 tablespoons of the oil. Add the beef strips and sauté over high heat, stirring occasionally, until well browned and almost cooked through, about 3 minutes. With a slotted spoon, transfer to a plate and set aside.

2. Add the remaining 2 tablespoons oil to the skillet and reduce the heat to moderate. Add the onion and sauté, stirring occasionally, until softened, about 3 minutes.

3. Stir in the coriander, ginger, garlic, cloves, cardamom, cayenne, cinnamon, chili powder, cumin and turmeric. Cook for 1 to 2 minutes, until fragrant.

4. Add the beef broth, coconut cream, lemon juice and the reserved beef. Simmer for 10 minutes, until the sauce has thickened enough to coat the back of a spoon. Season with salt and black pepper to taste. Stir in the yogurt if desired.

Country Beef Stew with Whole Garlic Cloves

This is a sturdy and satisfying dish. Diners can mash the sweet, tender garlic cloves against the bowl, adding savor to the stew, or retrieve them and spread them on bread. For a slightly different presentation, omit the potatoes and accompany the stew with buttered noodles seasoned with fresh herbs.

F&W Beverage Suggestion:
Hearty red wine, such as Portuguese Dão or Côtes-du-Rhône

6 SERVINGS

3 pounds lean boneless beef chuck, cut into 1½-inch cubes
1 cup dry red wine
⅓ cup red wine vinegar
8 large garlic cloves, peeled and minced, plus 24 whole and unpeeled
2 teaspoons thyme
2 bay leaves
About 8 tablespoons olive oil, preferably extra-virgin
2 medium onions, finely chopped
¼ cup all-purpose flour
2 cups beef stock or canned broth
1 cup canned crushed tomatoes
1 teaspoon salt
½ teaspoon freshly ground pepper
4 large carrots, cut on the diagonal into 2-inch pieces
9 small red potatoes, scrubbed and halved
1 cup chopped Italian flat-leaf parsley

1. In a large bowl, combine the beef, wine, vinegar, minced garlic, thyme, bay leaves and 3 tablespoons of the oil; stir well. Marinate at room temperature, stirring occasionally, for 2 hours.

2. Drain the meat, reserving the marinade. In a large, noncorrodible, flameproof casserole, heat 3 tablespoons of the oil until smoking. Working in batches, add one-third of the meat; cook over moderately high heat, turning frequently, until well browned, about 7 minutes. With a slotted spoon, transfer the meat to a bowl. Repeat with the remaining meat, adding 1 tablespoon of oil per batch if the meat begins to stick to the bottom of the casserole.

3. Preheat the oven to 350°. Add the onions to the casserole, reduce the heat to low and cook, covered, stirring occasionally, until the onions are soft and golden, 15 to 20 minutes. Sprinkle on the flour and continue to cook for 5 minutes, stirring often and without allowing the flour to color, to make a roux.

4. Add the reserved marinade to the casserole and bring to a boil, stirring to scrape up any brown bits from the bottom of the pan.

5. Add the browned meat, any juices that have accumulated in the bowl, the stock, tomatoes, salt and pepper. Bring to a simmer over moderate heat. Cover and bake for 1 hour. (**The recipe can be prepared up to this point a day in advance.** Remove from the oven, let cool to room temperature and refrigerate, covered. Bring the stew to a simmer, stirring often, before proceeding.)

6. Add the carrots, potatoes and whole garlic cloves. Return the stew to the 350° oven and bake uncovered for 45 to 60 minutes, until the vegetables and meat are tender and the gravy is slightly thickened. Stir in the parsley just before serving.

Kentucky Burgoo

4 SERVINGS

¼ cup all-purpose flour
½ teaspoon salt
¼ teaspoon ground allspice
1¼ pounds lean chuck steak, cut into 4 pieces
4 chicken thighs or drumsticks, trimmed of extra fat
2½ tablespoons unsalted butter
2½ tablespoons corn oil
2 loin pork chops, about 1 inch thick, boned and cut into ¾-inch-wide strips
1 medium onion, chopped
1 shallot, minced
1 garlic clove, minced
¾ cup chopped, peeled and seeded fresh tomatoes or 1 can (16 ounces) peeled tomatoes— drained, seeded and coarsely chopped
¼ teaspoon basil
¼ teaspoon sugar
⅔ cup chicken stock or canned broth
⅓ cup dry white wine
½ teaspoon crushed dried hot red pepper
Salt and black pepper
1 teaspoon bourbon
1 tablespoon chopped fresh parsley

1. On a sheet of waxed paper, combine the flour, salt and allspice. Dredge the steaks in the flour mixture, pressing it into the meat. Coat the chicken lightly with the remaining flour mixture.

2. In a large heavy skillet, heat 2 tablespoons of the butter in 1 tablespoon of the oil. Add the steaks and sauté over moderately high heat, turning once, until golden brown on both sides, about 2 minutes per side. Transfer to a large casserole.

3. Add the chicken to the skillet and sauté, turning, until golden brown on all sides, about 6 minutes; transfer to the casserole.

4. Add the pork to the skillet and sauté until golden brown, about 2 minutes; transfer to the casserole.

5. Preheat the oven to 350°. Stir the chopped onion into the browned meats.

6. Drain any grease from the skillet and wipe it out with paper towels. Melt the remaining ½ tablespoon butter in the remaining 1½ tablespoons oil. Add the shallot and garlic and sauté over moderately low heat until golden, about 5 mintues. Stir in the tomatoes and sprinkle with the basil and sugar. Cook, stirring, over low heat, for 15 minutes. Add the tomato mixture to the meats.

7. Add the chicken stock, wine and hot pepper to the skillet. Bring to a boil over high heat, scraping up the browned bits that stick to the pan. Pour the hot liquid over the meats in the casserole. Bake, uncovered, until the steak is tender, about 1½ hours. (**This dish may be prepared 1 or 2 days ahead to this point and refrigerated.** Reheat before serving.)

8. Just before serving, season with salt and black pepper to taste. Stir in the bourbon and sprinkle with the parsley; serve hot.

Hearty American Meat Loaf

6 TO 8 SERVINGS

2 pounds ground round
1 pound sweet Italian sausage,
  casings removed
1 cup fresh bread crumbs
1 medium onion, chopped
2 garlic cloves, minced
1 teaspoon thyme
1 teaspoon ground allspice
1½ teaspoons freshly ground
  pepper
1½ teaspoons salt
2 eggs
½ cup milk
⅓ cup tomato paste

1. Preheat the oven to 350°. In a large bowl, crumble the ground beef and sausage meat. Add the bread crumbs, onion, garlic, thyme, allspice, pepper and salt; mix together.

2. In a small bowl, whisk the eggs, milk and tomato paste until smooth. Pour the liquid ingredients over the meat mixture and mix with a wooden spoon or your hands until well blended.

3. Pack the mixture into a 11½-by-5-by-2½-inch (8-cup) loaf pan and place on a cookie sheet. Bake for 1 hour and 20 minutes; if necessary, increase the oven temperature to 375° for the last 10 minutes of baking to brown the top.

4. Pour off the accumulated cooking fat, if desired, and serve hot.

Corned Beef Hash

6 SERVINGS

4 medium potatoes
½ pound lean slab bacon, sliced
2 teaspoons vegetable oil
2 pounds cold corned beef,
  coarsely chopped
1 large onion, minced
2 tablespoons bourbon
2 teaspoons Worcestershire sauce
1 teaspoon freshly grated nutmeg
Salt and freshly ground pepper
1 cup heavy cream
3 tablespoons finely chopped
  parsley
6 poached eggs

1. In a large saucepan of boiling salted water, cook the potatoes until tender, about 25 minutes; drain. As soon as the potatoes are cool enough to handle, peel and chop coarsely.

2. In a medium saucepan of boiling water, blanch the bacon over moderately high heat for 10 minutes; drain. Remove and discard any rind, pat the bacon dry and cut into ⅛-inch dice.

3. In a medium skillet, sauté the bacon in the oil over moderate heat until the bacon is browned and crisp, about 20 minutes. Drain on paper towels; reserve 4 tablespoons of the drippings and set aside.

4. In a large bowl, combine the corned beef, potatoes, bacon, onion, bourbon, Worcestershire sauce, nutmeg and salt and pepper to taste; mix well. Cover and refrigerate for at least 2 hours, or overnight.

5. Just before preparing the hash, place the cream in a medium saucepan and boil over moderate heat until reduced by half, about 20 minutes.

6. In a large ovenproof skillet (see Note), preferably nonstick, melt the reserved bacon drippings over moderately high heat until sizzling. Add the hash mixture, pressing down firmly with the back of a wooden spoon and cook uncovered for 15 minutes.

7. Add the reduced cream and stir well. Press the mixture down again, reduce the heat to moderate and cook until a dark golden crust forms on the bottom,

about 25 minutes. After about 15 minutes, preheat the broiler.

8. Transfer to a hot broiler and broil 4 inches from the heat until the top is browned, about 10 minutes. Turn the hash out onto a large platter and sprinkle with the parsley. Top each serving with a poached egg.

NOTE: If you do not have an ovenproof skillet, the hash can be prepared through Step 7 in a regular skillet. Then, instead of broiling, invert the hash onto a cookie sheet and slide it back into the pan to brown the second side.

Sesame-Cheddar Burgers

Initially seared over high heat to seal in the flavorful natural meat juices, then finished over moderate heat, these cheeseburgers, topped with sesame seeds, are mouth-wateringly juicy. Handle the ground meat lightly when forming the patties.

4 SERVINGS

1 pound lean ground round
1 teaspoon coarse (kosher) salt
½ teaspoon freshly ground pepper
¼ cup grated extra-sharp Cheddar
  cheese
1 tablespoon plus 1 teaspoon
  toasted sesame seeds

1. Pat the meat dry with paper towels to absorb any excess moisture. Divide into 4 equal portions. Lightly pat and shape each portion into a patty about 3 inches in diameter and ¾ inch thick.

2. Evenly sprinkle the salt over the bottom of a large heavy skillet. Warm the skillet over high heat until the salt smokes, about 3 minutes. Add the patties and cook for 2 minutes; reduce the heat to moderate and cook until well browned and crusty on the bottom, about 3 minutes longer.

3. Turn the burgers and sprinkle them with the pepper. Mound 1 tablespoon of the cheese on top of each burger. Cover the skillet and cook for 2 minutes for rare burgers, 3 minutes for medium rare, 4 for well done. Sprinkle 1 teaspoon toasted sesame seeds over each burger and serve hot.

POULTRY

Pan-Fried Quail with Country Ham

4 SERVINGS

2 teaspoons salt
½ teaspoon freshly ground pepper
1 teaspoon thyme
8 quail, split and flattened
½ cup (1 stick) unsalted butter
½ pound Smithfield ham, cut into
  2-by-¼-inch matchsticks

1. Mix together the salt, pepper and thyme, crushing the thyme with your fingertips. Sprinkle the birds lightly on both sides with this mixture.

2. In a large heavy skillet, melt the butter over moderately high heat until it foams and just begins to brown. Add the quail, skin-side down. Sprinkle on the ham, cover and cook until the skin is golden brown, 3 to 4 minutes. Turn the birds and continue cooking, covered, until the juices run clear, about 4 minutes longer. Remove from the heat and let rest, covered, for about 10 minutes. Arrange the quail on a platter and sprinkle the ham over them.

3. Pour off the fat from the skillet and add ¼ cup of water. Bring to a boil and cook for 1 minute, scraping up the browned bits from the bottom of the pan. Pour over the quail.

Jasper's Squab with Oysters and Zinfandel

At Restaurant Jasper in Boston, the squab breast and oysters are served together with wild rice. The tiny drumsticks and thighs are served separately afterward as a salad course, with bitter greens, such as arugula or endive, dressed with a simple vinaigrette.

Beverage Suggestion:
Grgrich Hills Zinfandel

4 SERVINGS

4 squab (¾ to 1 pound each)
5 tablespoons vegetable oil
1 medium onion, chopped
1 medium carrot, chopped
1 celery rib, chopped

2 medium garlic cloves, crushed
2¼ cups Zinfandel
1 cup veal or chicken stock or
  canned broth
¼ teaspoon salt
⅛ teaspoon freshly ground pepper
7 tablespoons unsalted butter
1 cup fresh white bread crumbs
1 tablespoon minced fresh chives
1 tablespoon minced fresh parsley
12 fresh oysters, shucked

1. Remove the legs from the squab in one piece. Carefully peel the skin from the breast and lift off the breast meat from each side in one piece. You will have 4 pieces of meat from each bird. Cover the meat and set aside. Chop the carcasses.

2. In a large skillet, heat 2 tablespoons of the oil. Add the chopped carcasses, the onion, carrot, celery and garlic and sauté over moderately high heat until browned, about 10 minutes.

3. Add 2 cups of the Zinfandel and the stock. Simmer, partially covered, for 1 hour. Strain the sauce, and set aside. (You should have about 1¼ cups of sauce.)

4. Preheat the broiler. Season the squab pieces with ⅛ teaspoon of the salt and a pinch of pepper. In a large skillet, melt 2 tablespoons of the butter in 1 tablespoon of the oil over moderately high heat. Add the breasts and legs, skin-side down, and sauté for 1 minute. Turn the breasts only and sauté for 1 minute longer. Then remove the breasts and cover loosely with foil to keep warm. Turn the legs and continue cooking for 2 minutes. Remove the legs from the pan and set aside for the salad course; they are served tepid.

5. Pour out the excess fat and add the remaining ¼ cup Zinfandel to the skillet. Bring to a boil, scraping up any brown bits from the bottom of the pan. Add the

reserved sauce and bring to a boil. Remove from the heat and stir in 4 tablespoons of butter, 1 tablespoon at a time. Season with the remaining ⅛ teaspoon salt and pepper.

6. In a shallow bowl, combine the bread crumbs, chives and parsley. Dip the oysters in the remaining 2 tablespoons vegetable oil. Then roll them in the herbed bread crumbs. Place them on a baking sheet. Melt the remaining 1 tablespoon butter and drizzle over the oysters. Broil for about 1 minute, or until golden brown.

7. To serve, coat the bottom of each of 4 warmed dinner plates with sauce. Cut the squab breasts in half lengthwise and alternate on the plate with the oysters.

Lime-Marinated Grilled Squab

The squab must be butterflied so that it will grill evenly. Ask your butcher to do this or do it yourself, following the method below. The birds need to marinate for 12 hours, so plan accordingly.

F&W Beverage Suggestion:
Fetzer Gewürztraminer

4 SERVINGS

4 squab or 2 Cornish game hens
1 small onion, thinly sliced
½ cup chicken stock
¼ cup fresh lime juice
1 tablespoon fresh orange juice
¼ teaspoon salt
¼ teaspoon freshly ground pepper
Zest of ½ lime, cut into julienne
  strips
Zest of ¼ orange, cut into julienne
  strips
2 tablespoons sugar
¼ cup red wine vinegar
1 teaspoon *glace de viande**
1 teaspoon crème fraîche or heavy
  cream
1 lime, peeled and thinly sliced, for
  garnish

*Available at specialty food stores

1. Butterfly the squab: With the knife inside the cavity of the bird, set breast-side up, cut through the small bones on either side of the backbone to remove it. Press the breast down firmly to flatten the squab. Twist the wings back so that they will remain flat during grilling. Repeat with the 3 remaining birds.

2. In a dish large enough to hold the birds in one layer, combine the onion, chicken stock, lime juice, orange juice, salt and pepper. Add the squab, cover and marinate in the refrigerator for 12 hours, turning occasionally.

3. Light the charcoal or preheat the broiler. Remove the birds from the marinade. In a medium noncorrodible saucepan, simmer the marinade, covered, until reduced to marmalade consistency, about 20 minutes.

4. Meanwhile, in a small saucepan of boiling water, blanch the lime and orange zests for 10 minutes. Drain and set aside.

5. In a small noncorrodible saucepan, combine the sugar and vinegar. Simmer for 5 minutes.

6. In a blender or food processor, puree the reduced marinade. Add the sweetened vinegar, the *glace de viande* and the crème fraîche and blend thoroughly. Return to the saucepan and keep warm over low heat.

7. Lightly oil the grill or the broiler pan. Place the squab skin-side to the heat and cook for 10 minutes. (If using a grill, rotate the birds a half-turn after 5 minutes to make crisscross grill marks.) Turn the birds over and cook for 5 minutes, or until well browned.

8. Pool the warm sauce on 4 hot plates. Place a squab in the center of each plate. Garnish with the slices of lime and the reserved zest.

Roast Cranberry-Glazed Ducklings with Cranberry Gravy

F&W Beverage Suggestion: Red Bordeaux, such as Château Pontet Canet or Château Lynch-Bages

6 TO 8 SERVINGS

Ducklings:
3 fresh ducklings (about 5 pounds each)
1½ teaspoons salt
½ teaspoon freshly ground pepper

3 small sprigs of fresh rosemary or ¾ teaspoon dried, crumbled
2 medium celery ribs, diced
2 medium onions, diced
2 medium tart apples—peeled, cored and diced

Cranberry Glaze:
½ cup light honey
2 cups fresh or frozen whole cranberries

Cranberry Gravy:
2 cups Savory Duck Stock (p. 220)
1 tablespoon red currant jelly
1 tablespoon fresh lemon juice
2 tablespoons unsalted butter, at room temperature
Salt and freshly ground pepper

1. **Prepare the ducklings:** Preheat the oven to 450°. Pull all the fat from the body and neck cavities of the ducklings and discard. Clip off the wing tips and reserve these, the giblets and necks for the Savory Duck Stock (p. 220). Rinse and dry each duckling thoroughly. Rub the body cavities with the salt and pepper (and, if you have no fresh rosemary, with the dried rosemary as well). If using fresh rosemary, tuck a sprig into each body cavity.

2. In a medium bowl, combine the celery, onions and apples and toss well to mix. Loosely fill the ducklings with the mixture. Close the body cavities with poultry pins and kitchen twine. Skewer the flaps of neck skin to the backs of the ducklings. **(The ducks can be prepared ahead to this point; keep loosely covered on a rack in the refrigerator.)**

3. Prick each duckling well all over with a fork and place breast side down on a rack in a very large shallow roasting pan. Roast the ducklings, uncovered, for 20 minutes. Lower the oven to 350°. Prick the ducklings well all over, turn onto one side and roast for another 20 minutes. Prick each well again, turn onto the opposite side and roast 20 minutes longer. (Remove the duck fat from the roasting pan as it accumulates to reduce spattering.) Once again prick the ducklings well, turn breast-side up and roast for 1 hour, pricking lightly about every 20 minutes and pouring off the fat as it collects.

4. **Meanwhile, prepare the cranberry glaze:** In a heavy medium saucepan, bring 2 cups of water and the honey to a boil over moderate heat. Add the cranberries and boil until the skins pop, about 5 minutes.

5. With a slotted spoon, remove the cranberries. Set half of them aside for the cranberry gravy. In a blender or food processor, puree the remaining cranberries with the honey mixture. Return the puree to the pan. Boil until reduced to about 1½ cups (the mixture should be glistening and about the consistency of corn syrup). Remove from the heat and cover to keep warm. **(The glaze can be prepared ahead to this point and reheated.)**

6. When the ducklings test done (the drumsticks should move easily in the hip joints), remove from the oven but leave the oven on. Remove the poultry pins, twine and stuffing (it was used for flavor only). Pour the pan drippings into a small bowl and skim off the fat; reserve the drippings for making the gravy.

7. Using a pastry brush, generously paint each duckling with the cranberry glaze. Return to the oven and roast, uncovered, for 5 to 10 minutes, or until the skin looks shiny and glazed. Remove the ducklings from the oven and again brush generously with the glaze (set the remainder aside). Transfer the ducklings to a large heated platter and let rest for about 20 minutes.

8. **Meanwhile, make the cranberry gravy:** Set the roasting pan over moderate heat, add ½ cup of water and stir, scraping up the browned bits that cling to the bottom to deglaze the pan.

9. Strain the mixture into a heavy medium saucepan and add the reserved cranberry glaze, the reserved duck drippings and the Savory Duck Stock. Set over high heat and boil, whisking frequently, until reduced by one-third, 15 to 20 minutes.

10. Whisk in the currant jelly, lemon juice and butter. Stir in the reserved whole cranberries. Season with salt and pepper to taste. Pour into a heated sauceboat and pass separately.

Grilled Breast of Duck

The duck must marinate for two days, so plan accordingly. This dish was designed to be served with the Ragout of Winter Vegetables (p. 127).

Beverage Suggestion:
California Pinot Noir, such as Acacia

4 SERVINGS

2 medium onions, thinly sliced
1 carrot, thinly sliced
4 parsley stems
15 black peppercorns
3 garlic cloves, crushed
1 sprig of fresh thyme or ⅛ teaspoon dried
1 sprig of fresh tarragon or ⅛ teaspoon dried
2 bay leaves
½ cup extra-virgin olive oil
1 bottle California Pinot Noir
4 duck breasts, preferably from 2 wild mallards (see Note)
4 medium shallots, finely chopped
2 cups Rich Duck Stock (p. 219) or chicken stock
4 tablespoons unsalted butter
½ teaspoon salt
⅛ teaspoon freshly ground pepper

1. In a noncorrodible dish or shallow bowl, combine the onions, carrot, parsley, peppercorns, garlic, thyme, tarragon and bay leaves with the olive oil and half of the wine. Add the duck breasts and refrigerate, covered, for 2 days, turning occasionally.

2. Remove the breasts from the marinade and pat dry. Pour the marinade into a large noncorrodible saucepan. Boil over moderately high heat until reduced to a glaze, 15 to 20 minutes. Add the remaining wine and the shallots and continue to boil again until reduced to a syrupy glaze, 15 to 20 minutes longer.

3. To finish the sauce, add the duck stock and simmer for 10 minutes. Off heat, stir in the butter. Strain the sauce into a double boiler. Season with the salt and pepper. Keep warm over low heat until ready to serve.

4. Lightly oil a hot grill. Season the duck breasts lightly with salt and put them skin-side down on the grill. Cook, turn-

ing them once, until rare, about 8 minutes. Remove the breasts from the grill; let rest in a warm place for 5 minutes.

5. Thinly slice the breasts on the diagonal. Fan out each breast in a crescent on a large dinner plate. Arrange the Ragout of Winter Vegetables (if serving) on the other side of the plate. Coat the breast with the sauce.

NOTE: This recipe may also be done with quail. The marinade ingredients and time will be the same. Substitute chicken bones for the duck bones in the stock recipe but roast at 375° for only 25 to 35 minutes in Step 1. Proceed as for the mallards. The grilling time for the quail will be 4 to 6 minutes. Serve 2 quail per person.

Roasted Cornish Hens with Cashew Stuffing

6 SERVINGS

6 Cornish hens (1¼ to 1½ pounds each)
1 large garlic clove, halved
1 teaspoon salt
¾ teaspoon freshly ground pepper
1 tablespoon unsalted butter
1 tablespoon vegetable oil
½ cup sliced mushrooms (about 3 ounces)
⅓ cup chopped scallions
2 cups cooked rice (wild, white or brown rice, or a combination)
⅓ cup cashews, coarsely chopped
1 tablespoon grated orange zest

1. Preheat the oven to 375°. Rub the inside of the birds with the cut sides of the garlic. Season with ¾ teaspoon of the salt and ½ teaspoon of the pepper.

2. In a medium skillet, melt the butter in the oil over moderate heat. Add the mushrooms and scallions and sauté until the mushrooms are golden, about 5 minutes. Remove from the heat. Stir in the rice, cashews, orange zest and the remaining ¼ teaspoon salt and pepper.

3. Stuff the cavity of each bird with ½ cup of stuffing. Place in a large shallow baking pan and roast for 1 hour, or until golden.

Grilled Cornish Game Hens with Bacon-Butter Stuffing

This marvelous dish can be done on an outdoor grill or under the broiler. Have your butcher butterfly the game hens.

2 TO 4 SERVINGS

7 slices lean bacon (⅓ pound)
2 medium shallots, minced
¼ cup minced parsley
3 garlic cloves, minced
8 tablespoons (1 stick) cold unsalted butter
⅛ teaspoon cayenne pepper
2 Cornish game hens (1¼ to 1½ pounds each), butterflied
Freshly ground black pepper

1. Light the grill or preheat the broiler.

2. In a large heavy skillet, cook the bacon over moderately high heat just until the fat is translucent, about 1 minute. Remove from the heat, drain and mince.

3. In a food processor or blender, combine the bacon, shallots, parsley and 2 of the minced garlic cloves. Process until the mixture is a very smooth paste. Add 4 tablespoons of the butter and process again until just blended.

4. In a small saucepan, melt the remaining 4 tablespoons butter with the remaining minced garlic clove over very low heat. Stir in the cayenne pepper; keep warm.

5. Place the hens breast-side up on a work surface. Use your fingers to gently separate the skin from the meat without tearing the skin. Stuff the bacon-butter mixture under the skin of the breast and thighs of each hen, spreading it into an even layer with your fingers.

6. Lightly oil the hot grill or broiling rack. Brush the hens with some of the garlic butter and place them, skin-side up, on the grill or rack. Cook for 10 minutes. Turn carefully and cook for 8 to 10 minutes more, basting once with the garlic butter, until crisp and brown. Season with salt and black pepper to taste.

Broiled Chicken and Caraway

This savory chicken makes a beautiful presentation served with apple and red onion slices that have been sautéed in butter, painted with a little of the glaze and sprinkled with caraway seeds. Plums, peaches or any other firm fruit can also be used.

F&W Beverage Suggestion:
Cabernet Sauvignon, such as Beringer State Lane

2 TO 4 SERVINGS

2 tablespoons unsalted butter
3 tablespoons minced onion
1 teaspoon caraway seeds
½ teaspoon salt
¼ teaspoon freshly ground pepper
1 whole chicken (about 3½ pounds)
2 teaspoons corn oil
1 can (6 ounces) frozen apple juice concentrate, thawed

1. In a small skillet, melt the butter. Add the onion, caraway seeds, ¼ teaspoon of the salt and the pepper. Cook over low heat until the onions are just softened, 2 to 3 minutes. Set aside to cool.

2. Using a pair of poultry shears, cut out the backbone of the chicken to butterfly the bird. Gently loosen the breast, thigh and leg skin by working your fingers carefully underneath. Using a sharp knife, score the thickest part of the meat along the back center of the thigh and leg down to the bone (this allows the legs to cook roughly as fast as the breast).

3. Preheat the broiler and broiler pan. Stuff the onion mixture under the chicken skin, spreading as evenly as possible. Sprinkle the skin with the remaining ¼ teaspoon salt.

4. Brush the hot broiler pan with the oil and place the chicken on it skin-side up. Broil about 5 inches from the heat until well browned, about 10 minutes.

5. Meanwhile, in a small saucepan, boil the apple juice concentrate until reduced by about one-fourth to a syrupy glaze, about 5 minutes.

6. Reduce the oven temperature to 375°, transfer the chicken to the middle of the oven and roast for 10 minutes. Brush the bird with the apple glaze. Roast for 10 minutes longer, basting twice. Serve hot or at room temperature.

Clay Pot Chicken with Olives

Parslied egg noodles and a green vegetable or two are a good accompaniment for this savory chicken.

F&W Beverage Suggestion:
Zinfandel, such as Sutter Home

4 TO 6 SERVINGS

20 tiny white boiling onions, peeled
1 tablespoon olive oil
1 whole chicken (about 3½ pounds)
2 imported bay leaves
Zest of 1 navel orange
6 whole garlic cloves, bruised and peeled
2 sprigs of fresh rosemary or ½ teaspoon dried
20 Calamata olives, halved and pitted
20 brine-cured green olives, halved and pitted
¼ teaspoon coarsely ground pepper
¾ cup chicken broth
¼ cup dry vermouth
2 teaspoons arrowroot

1. Soak the clay pot top and bottom in cold water for 15 minutes.

2. Cook the onions in a large pot of salted boiling water until almost tender, about 5 minutes. Drain well. Heat 1 teaspoon of the oil in a small skillet. Add the onions and sauté over high heat, shaking the pan, until browned all over.

3. Rinse and dry the chicken; remove excess fat from around the cavity. Stuff with 1 bay leaf, half of the orange zest, 2 garlic cloves and 1 sprig of rosemary. Truss the chicken. Rub the chicken with the remaining 2 teaspoons olive oil and place inside the pot. (If the bottom surface is not glazed, fold a piece of parchment or waxed paper to fit the bottom so the chicken doesn't stick.)

4. Distribute the onions, olives, remaining orange zest, bay leaf, rosemary and 4 garlic cloves around the chicken. Sprinkle with the pepper and pour on the broth and vermouth.

5. Cover and place the clay pot in the middle of a cold oven. Turn the oven on to 450° and bake the chicken for 1 hour. Remove the lid and bake uncovered for 15 minutes longer to brown the skin.

6. To serve, transfer the chicken to a carving board and cut into pieces. Arrange on a platter. Remove the onions and olives with a slotted spoon and scatter over the chicken. Skim the fat off the top of the cooking juices and pour into a small saucepan. Dissolve the arrowroot in 2 tablespoons of cold water and stir into the juices. Heat, stirring until slightly thickened. Serve this light gravy with the chicken.

Oven-Roasted Chicken and Potatoes with Rosemary and Lemon

4 SERVINGS

3 tablespoons olive oil
2½- to 3-pound chicken, cut into serving pieces
3 medium baking potatoes, scrubbed and cut into 1½-inch chunks
1 garlic clove, minced
2 teaspoons rosemary, crumbled
6 tablespoons fresh lemon juice
½ teaspoon salt
¼ teaspoon freshly ground pepper

1. Preheat the oven to 400°. Grease a large ovenproof skillet or baking pan with 1 tablespoon of the oil. Toss the chicken and potatoes with the remaining 2 tablespoons oil and arrange in the skillet in an even layer.

2. Sprinkle with the garlic, rosemary and 4 tablespoons of the lemon juice. Cover the skillet loosely with aluminum foil.

3. Bake for 30 minutes. Uncover and bake for 15 minutes longer, turning the chicken pieces occasionally to brown evenly.

4. To serve, divide the chicken among 4 plates and sprinkle with the remaining 2 tablespoons lemon juice; season with the salt and pepper. Spoon some of the pan juices over each plate.

Simple Roast Chicken with Parsley and Lemon

 F&W Beverage Suggestion:
Beaujolais-Villages or a light California Zinfandel, such as Simi

4 SERVINGS

1 whole chicken (about 3½ pounds)
1 lemon
½ teaspoon salt
½ teaspoon freshly ground pepper
10 sprigs of parsley with stems
5 tablespoons unsalted butter, melted

1. Preheat the oven to 400°. With paper towels, pat the chicken dry inside and out.

2. Squeeze the juice of the lemon into the cavity of the chicken; reserve the lemon rinds. Turn the bird to moisten all over inside with the juice.

3. Season the inside of the chicken with half the salt and pepper. Stuff the squeezed lemon rinds and the parsley into the cavity. Truss the chicken.

4. Baste well with one-third of the melted butter. Sprinkle with the remaining salt and pepper.

5. Put the bird on its side on a rack and roast for 25 minutes, basting with one-third of the remaining butter halfway through. Turn the bird over and roast on the other side for 25 minutes longer, basting again halfway through. Turn the bird breast-side up, baste one last time and roast for about 15 minutes, until the juices of the thigh run clear when pierced. Remove from the oven and let rest for 10 minutes before carving.

Olympe's Chicken in Beer with Leeks

 F&W Beverage Suggestion:
California Chardonnay, such as Beringer Private Reserve

4 SERVINGS

1 frying chicken (about 4 pounds)
1½ tablespoons unsalted butter
3 medium shallots, chopped

1 bottle (12 ounces) dark beer
¼ teaspoon thyme
1 bay leaf, preferably imported
1 teaspoon salt
½ teaspoon freshly ground pepper
4 large leeks (white part only), cut into 1-inch slices
¼ cup chicken stock or canned broth
1 cup crème fraîche or heavy cream
1 tablespoon chopped chives

1. Remove the chicken giblets and chop them coarsely. Quarter the chicken.

2. In a large skillet, melt the butter over moderately high heat. Add the giblets and chopped shallots and sauté, stirring, for 3 minutes.

3. Add the chicken and sauté, turning, until browned on both sides, about 10 minutes. Add the beer, thyme, bay leaf, ½ teaspoon of the salt and ¼ teaspoon of the pepper. Cover and cook over low heat until no longer pink but still juicy, about 12 minutes for the breast and wings, 20 minutes for the legs and thighs. Remove from the heat and return all the chicken to the pan; set aside.

4. Meanwhile, in a large saucepan of boiling salted water, cook the leeks until tender, about 12 minutes. Drain well.

5. In a medium saucepan, combine the leeks, stock, ½ cup of the crème fraîche, and the remaining ½ teaspoon salt and ¼ teaspoon pepper. Bring to a boil over moderately high heat. Boil for 4 minutes. Reduce the heat to low and keep warm.

6. Remove the skin from the pieces of chicken. Return the chicken to the skillet. Add the remaining ½ cup crème fraîche and cook over high heat for 5 minutes, until the chicken is hot and the sauce is slightly thickened. Remove and discard the bay leaf.

7. To serve, arrange the chicken on a warm platter. Add the leeks with their sauce to the platter. Spoon the sauce from the skillet over the chicken and sprinkle with the chives.

Braised Chicken with Cider-Cream Gravy

The apple cider you use for this recipe should be tart (hard), not sweet. Try to find a good imported French cider (many liquor stores now carry it) because it will have just the proper crispness and intense apple flavor.

 F&W Beverage Suggestion:
Chardonnay, such as Beringer Private Reserve

6 SERVINGS

3 tablespoons unsalted butter
2 chickens (about 2½ pounds each), cut into serving pieces
5 large shallots, minced (about ½ cup)
1 pound small mushrooms
½ cup Calvados
½ cup hard apple cider, preferably French
1 cup heavy cream
½ teaspoon salt
⅛ teaspoon freshly ground pepper
3 tablespoons minced parsley

1. In a large heavy noncorrodible skillet, melt 2 tablespoons of the butter over moderately high heat. When the butter is sizzling, add half the chicken pieces (don't crowd) and sauté until browned, about 5 minutes per side. Remove to a platter and brown the second half. Brown the hearts and livers for only about 1 minute at the end of the second batch and remove.

2. In the same skillet, melt the remaining 1 tablespoon of butter. Add the shallots and mushrooms and cook, stirring, until lightly browned, 2 to 3 minutes. Reduce the heat to low. Cover the skillet and cook until the shallots are soft, about 10 minutes.

3. Return the chicken to the skillet and spoon the mushroom mixture on top. Pour the Calvados over the chicken, warm gently over low heat and ignite with a match. When the flames subside, pour in the cider, cover the skillet and simmer over very low heat for 15 minutes. Remove the chicken breasts and mushrooms to an ovenproof platter, cover loosely and keep warm in a 250°

oven. Continue cooking the dark meat for 10 minutes longer, then add to the platter in the oven.

4. Boil the liquid in the skillet until it is reduced to a thin glaze, 12 to 15 minutes. Pour in the cream and continue to boil, uncovered, until the sauce is the consistency of moderately thin gravy, 4 to 5 minutes. Add the salt and pepper and half of the parsley.

5. To serve, spoon the sauce evenly over the chicken and mushrooms, then sprinkle with the remaining parsley.

Le Lion d'Or's Poulet au Poivre

Accompany this surprisingly easy dish with delicate fresh pasta, such as angel's hair, and fresh spinach, lightly steamed and buttered. Start with gravlax and serve with a full-bodied red wine.

F&W Beverage Suggestion: Zinfandel, such as Sebastiani Proprietor's Reserve

2 SERVINGS

2 tablespoons golden raisins
2 tablespoons Cognac or brandy
1 whole chicken (3½ pounds), quartered
1 tablespoon coarsely cracked peppercorns
½ teaspoon salt
2 tablespoons unsalted butter
1 tablespoon vegetable oil
¼ cup brown stock or canned chicken broth

1. Place the raisins in a small bowl. Cover with boiling water and let soak until softened, about 5 minutes. Drain; then toss with the brandy and macerate until ready to use.

2. Pat the chicken dry. Spinkle on both sides with the pepper and salt, pressing the peppercorns so that they will adhere to the chicken.

3. In a large skillet, melt 1 tablespoon of the butter in the oil over moderately high heat. When sizzling, add the chicken, skin-side down. Fry until well browned, turning once, about 8 minutes per side.

4. Cover and cook until the breasts are tender, 8 to 10 minutes. Remove the breasts to a warm plate and cover loosely with foil to keep warm. Cook the legs 5 minutes longer; add to the breasts.

5. Pour off any fat in the skillet. Add the raisins and brandy. Carefully ignite with a match. Shake the pan until the flames subside. Add the stock and bring to a boil, scraping up any browned bits from the bottom of the pan. Cook until reduced by one-third, about 2 minutes.

6. Remove from the heat and swirl in the remaining 1 tablespoon butter. Season to taste, adding more salt if necessary. Pour the sauce over the chicken.

Chicken in Champagne Sauce

4 SERVINGS

3½- to 4-pound broiler-fryer chicken, cut into 8 pieces
½ teaspoon salt
½ teaspoon freshly ground pepper
10 tablespoons unsalted butter
2 tablespoons olive oil
3 large shallots, minced (about ⅓ cup)
1¼ cups brut Champagne
1 cup chicken stock or canned broth
1 cup crème fraîche

½ pound mushrooms, quartered and sautéed (optional)

1. Preheat the oven to 375°. Pat the chicken dry with paper towels. Season all over with the salt and pepper.

2. In a large, heavy, ovenproof skillet, melt 4 tablespoons of the butter in the oil over moderate heat. When the foam begins to subside, add the chicken and sauté, turning once, until golden, about 5 minutes a side. Remove the chicken and set aside.

3. Add the shallots to the skillet, reduce the heat to moderately low and sauté, shaking the pan frequently, until just softened, about 1 minute. Return the chicken to the pan and stir to coat with the shallot butter. Pour the chicken, shallots and butter into a colander; let drain for 2 to 3 minutes to remove excess fat and return to the skillet.

4. Add the Champagne and bring to a boil over moderate heat. Cook for 2 minutes; turn the chicken and partially cover the skillet. Boil until the Champagne is reduced by half, about 5 minutes.

5. Add the stock, bring to a boil and cover tightly. Transfer the skillet to the oven and bake until the chicken is tender and its juices run clear when pierced with a fork, about 10 minutes.

6. Remove the chicken to a platter and cover loosely with foil to keep warm. Add the crème fraîche to the skillet and boil over moderate heat until the sauce is thick enough to coat a spoon lightly, 15 to 20 minutes.

7. Reduce the heat to low. Gradually whisk in the remaining 6 tablespoons butter, 1 or 2 tablespoons at a time, until the sauce is smooth and thickened. (Squeeze the butter into the sauce through your fingers so that it softens slightly and breaks into small bits. Then a simple stir or shake of the pan will form a smooth emulsion.) Season with salt and pepper to taste. Add the mushrooms, if you are using them, and the chicken. Serve hot.

Chicken Sauté with Tomatoes and Garlic

🍷 **F&W Beverage Suggestion:**
Beaujolais-Villages

4 SERVINGS

¼ **cup all-purpose flour**
¼ **teaspoon salt**
¼ **teaspoon freshly ground pepper**
1 **whole chicken (3 pounds), cut into 8 or 10 serving pieces**
¼ **pound small mushrooms**
2 **tablespoons fresh lemon juice**
3 **tablespoons olive oil**
2 **tablespoons unsalted butter**
4 **garlic cloves, minced**
¾ **cup dry white wine**
¼ **pound fresh plum tomatoes— peeled, seeded and cut lengthwise into ¼-inch strips**
2 **tablespoons minced fresh parsley, for garnish**

1. In a shallow container, mix the flour, salt and pepper. Lightly dredge the chicken pieces in the seasoned flour; shake off the excess.

2. In a small bowl, toss the mushrooms with the lemon juice until coated.

3. In a large noncorrodible skillet, heat the oil until sizzling. Add the chicken, skin-side down, and cook over high heat, shaking the pan occasionally to prevent sticking, until golden brown on the bottom, about 10 minutes. Turn and cook until golden brown on the second side, 8 to 10 minutes. Transfer the chicken to a platter. Pour the fat out of the skillet and gently blot any remaining fat with a paper towel.

4. Return the chicken to the skillet. Add 1 tablespoon of the butter and the mushrooms with the lemon juice. Cook over high heat, stirring and scraping up brown bits from the bottom of the pan, for 1 minute. Sprinkle in the garlic and cook, stirring, for 30 seconds. Add the wine, cover and cook for 5 minutes.

5. Add the tomato strips and the remaining 1 tablespoon butter. Cook uncovered for 30 seconds. To serve, arrange on a platter or individual plates and pour the pan juices over the chicken. Sprinkle the parsley on top.

Poached Chicken with Garden Vegetables

🍷 **F&W Beverage Suggestion:**
California Chenin Blanc, such as Fetzer

4 SERVINGS

1 **whole chicken (3 pounds), cut into 8 or 10 serving pieces**
1 **small head of green cabbage, chopped**
2 **medium carrots, cut into ½-inch cubes, plus 1½ medium carrots, shredded**
2 **small white turnips, peeled and cut into ½-inch cubes**
1 **medium onion, chopped**
2 **cups chicken stock or canned broth**
¾ **cup dry white wine**
1 **bay leaf**
1 **sprig of fresh thyme or ½ teaspoon dried**

½ **teaspoon salt (optional)**
¼ **teaspoon freshly ground pepper**
¾ **pound red potatoes, peeled and cut into ½-inch cubes**
1 **tablespoon Worcestershire sauce**
¼ **cup minced fresh parsley, for garnish**

1. In a large noncorrodible casserole, combine the chicken, cabbage, cubed carrots, turnips, onion, chicken stock, wine, bay leaf and thyme. Add the salt only if your chicken stock is unsalted. Sprinkle in the pepper. Bring the mixture to a boil over high heat. Reduce the heat to low, cover and cook until the chicken is cooked through and the vegetables are tender, 17 to 20 minutes.

2. Meanwhile, bring a medium saucepan of salted water to a boil over moderate heat. Add the potatoes and simmer for about 2 minutes, until partially cooked but still firm in the center (they will finish cooking later). Drain and set aside.

3. Transfer the chicken to a platter. Pour half of the cooked mixed vegetables and cooking liquid into a blender or food processor. Puree coarsely; small bits of the vegetables will still be visible. Pour back into the pot. Return the chicken to the pot. Add the potatoes, cover and bring the stew to a boil over high heat. Reduce the heat to low and simmer, uncovered, until the potatoes are tender, 5 to 10 minutes.

4. Stir in the shredded carrots and Worcestershire sauce. Serve in soup plates, garnished with the parsley.

Chicken with Apple and Calvados Sauce

🍷 **F&W Beverage Suggestion:**
California Chardonnay, such as Franciscan Napa

4 SERVINGS

2 **tablespoons clarified butter**
2 **tablespoons peanut oil**
3-**pound chicken, cut into 8 serving pieces**
1 **teaspoon salt**
½ **teaspoon white pepper**

½ cup Calvados
¼ cup cider vinegar
1 bay leaf
1 pound tart red apples, preferably Winesap or Cortland, cored and cut into eighths
1 cup chicken stock or canned broth
¼ cup heavy cream
2 tablespoons cold unsalted butter

1. Preheat the oven to 350°. In a large noncorrodible skillet, heat the clarified butter and oil until shimmering. Add the chicken in batches and sauté without crowding, turning, over moderately high heat until well browned, 6 to 8 minutes. Remove to a plate and season with ½ teaspoon of the salt and ⅛ teaspoon of the white pepper.

2. Pour off the fat from the skillet. Add ¼ cup of the Calvados and the vinegar and bring to a boil, scraping up any browned bits from the bottom of the pan. Add the bay leaf and remove from the heat.

3. Place the apples in a medium, noncorrodible casserole. Arrange the chicken on top. Pour the Calvados-vinegar mixture over the chicken and bake uncovered for 30 to 35 minutes, until the juices run clear when the thigh of the chicken is pierced.

4. Remove the chicken pieces and cover loosely with foil to keep warm. Discard the bay leaf. Pass the apples and the cooking juices through a food mill or puree in a food processor or blender. Pass through a fine sieve.

5. Pour the sauce into a noncorridible saucepan; add the stock and cream. Bring to a boil over moderately high heat and cook until the sauce is slightly thickened and darker in color, about 5 minutes. Add the remaining ¼ cup Calvados and remove from the heat. Stir in the cold butter. Season with the remaining salt and white pepper. Spoon about ¼ cup of the sauce onto each serving plate and arrange the chicken on top.

Country Fried Chicken

4 SERVINGS

1 egg
⅓ cup milk
1 cup all-purpose flour
1 tablespoon salt
1 teaspoon freshly ground pepper
1 teaspoon paprika
3-pound chicken, cut into 8 pieces
1 pound lard
¼ cup rendered bacon fat

1. In a medium bowl, lightly beat the egg and milk together. Set aside.

2. In a brown paper or plastic bag, combine the flour, salt, pepper and paprika.

3. Dip each piece of chicken in the egg-milk mixture. Allow the excess to drip off, then place one piece at a time in the bag with the seasoned flour. Close the bag and shake it gently to evenly coat each piece. Remove the chicken and shake off the excess flour.

4. In a large skillet, preferably cast iron, melt the lard over moderate heat. (It should be about ½ inch deep.) Add the rendered bacon fat. Increase the heat to moderately high and bring the fat to 375°, just below the smoking point.

5. Carefully place the chicken pieces, skin-side down, in the hot fat. Cook for 15 minutes, adjusting the heat if necessary to keep the fat at about 375°. Turn each piece and cook for about 15 minutes longer, until the chicken is golden brown. Remove and drain, preferably on brown paper bags, before serving.

Baked Chicken with Celery Sauce

This chicken is unusual in that it bakes—actively—for only 30 minutes. However, it sits in the still-hot oven and finishes cooking there. The result is tender and moist pieces of chicken that are warm and flavorful.

6 SERVINGS

3 cups coarsely chopped celery
Salt
10 medium chicken thighs (about 2 pounds)
2 whole small chicken breasts, cut in half (about 1½ pounds)
Sprigs of fresh chervil (optional)
Freshly ground pepper
1 teaspoon chopped fresh chervil or ½ teaspoon dried
About ¼ cup crème fraîche

1. Preheat the oven to 375°. Cover the bottom of a lasagna dish with the celery. Salt the chicken thighs and breasts very generously (including the areas under the skin where possible); if fresh chervil is available, tuck a sprig under the skin of each piece. Pack the chicken parts tightly together, skin-side up, in a single layer that completely covers the celery. Arrange any loose skin so that it completely covers the meat. Sprinkle generously with pepper.

2. Bake the chicken, uncovered, for 30 minutes. Turn off the oven (do not open the door) and let the chicken sit in the warm oven for 1½ hours.

3. Just before serving, transfer the celery pieces to a food processor; keep the chicken and juices warm in the oven. Add the chervil to the celery and puree. If the puree is very liquid, drain briefly in a sieve. Otherwise, transfer to a small heavy saucepan, add ¼ cup crème fraîche and correct the seasoning if necessary. Cook over moderate heat until warmed through; if the sauce seems too thick, add more crème fraîche and thin with some of the chicken juices from the baking dish. Serve a generous spoonful of the sauce with each piece of chicken.

Sautéed Jambonneaux with Mushroom and Wild Rice Stuffing

🍷 **F&W Beverage Suggestion:** California White Zinfandel, such as Sutter Home

8 SERVINGS

8 large chicken legs with thighs attached, at least 10 ounces each
½ cup wild rice, well washed
¼ pound sliced bacon
2 tablespoons unsalted butter
1 medium shallot, minced
1 cup finely chopped mushrooms (about 6 ounces)
1 tablespoon finely chopped fresh parsley
½ teaspoon salt
¼ teaspoon freshly ground pepper
2 tablespoons vegetable oil

1. Using a boning knife, cut through the meat down the inside of each thigh to expose the bone. Starting at the top and scraping against the bone, gently work the thigh meat down to expose the leg joint. Carefully cut the tendons at the joint, taking care not to pierce the skin. Continue to scrape the meat off the leg bone, turning it inside out as you go. As you reach the lower part of the drumstick where the meat is thin, use your fingers to pull the meat downward around the bone. Cut through the skin and remove the bones, reserving them for stock. Remove the white tendons by pulling them out with small pliers or your fingers while scraping against the tendon with a knife.

2. Place the wild rice in a medium saucepan and add 1½ cups of cold water. Bring to a boil over moderately high heat; reduce the heat to low and simmer, uncovered, stirring frequently, until tender, about 30 minutes. Drain the rice and set aside in a medium bowl.

3. In a large heavy skillet, sauté the bacon over moderate heat until crisp, about 5 minutes. Drain the bacon on paper towels. Drizzle 2 tablespoons of the fat in the skillet over the wild rice; reserve the remainder.

4. In a large skillet, melt the butter over moderate heat. When the foam subsides, add the shallot and mushrooms and sauté until the mushrooms release their juice and it evaporates, about 5 minutes.

5. Add the mushroom mixture to the rice. Crumble in the bacon and add the parsley and half the salt and pepper. Mix lightly to blend. Let the stuffing cool to room temperature.

6. Season each leg with the remaining salt and pepper and turn the meat skin-side out. Spoon 2 rounded tablespoons of the stuffing into the cavity of each leg. Fold down the top flap of the thigh, wrapping the meat around the stuffing so that each leg resembles a small ham, and tuck the thigh flap into the skin of the leg. With a trussing needle and butcher's twine, sew the skin together to seal.

7. Place the skillet with the remaining bacon fat over moderately high heat and add the vegetable oil. Add the *jambonneaux* and sauté, turning frequently, until golden and lightly crisped, about 20 minutes. Drain on paper towels. Remove the strings before serving.

Baked Jambonneaux with Italian-Style Stuffing

🍷 **F&W Beverage Suggestion:** Italian Chardonnay, such as Santa Margherita

6 SERVINGS

3 tablespoons olive oil, preferably extra-virgin

1 large garlic clove, minced
⅔ cup dry bread crumbs, preferably from Italian bread
⅓ cup minced prosciutto or good-quality cured ham (about 1½ ounces)
½ cup freshly grated Parmesan cheese
1½ tablespoons chopped fresh basil or 2½ teaspoons dried
1 tablespoon chopped fresh parsley
⅛ teaspoon freshly ground pepper
1 egg, lightly beaten
6 large chicken legs with thighs attached, at least 10 ounces each

1. In a small skillet, heat 1 tablespoon of the olive oil. Add the garlic and cook over low heat until the garlic is fragrant but not browned, about 1 minute.

2. Remove from the heat and add the bread crumbs. Scrape the mixture into a medium bowl and stir in the prosciutto, Parmesan, basil, parsley and pepper. Add the egg and mix lightly to combine.

3. Remove the bone from each leg as in Step 1 of the recipe for Sautéed Jambonneaux with Mushroom and Wild Rice Stuffing (at left).

4. Preheat the oven to 375°. Divide the stuffing into 6 to 8 equal portions, depending on the number of legs you are using. Turn the legs skin-side out. Spoon about 2 rounded tablespoons of the stuffing into the cavity of each chicken leg. Fold down the top flap of the thigh, wrapping the meat around the stuffing so that each leg resembles a small ham, and tuck the thigh flap into the skin of the leg. With a trussing needle and butcher's twine, sew the skin together to seal or fasten securely with a rounded toothpick. Rub the skin with the remaining 2 tablespoons olive oil and place the *jambonneaux*, seam-side down without crowding, in a shallow baking pan lined with foil.

5. Bake for 25 to 30 minutes, until light golden. Drain on paper towels. Remove the strings or toothpicks before serving. Serve whole or halved lengthwise.

Ston Easton's Breast of Chicken with Julienne of Vegetables in Cream Sauce

Fresh herbs impart a marvelously delicate flavor to the sauce. By all means, if you have them, use about a teaspoon of minced fresh herbs instead of the pinch of dried.

F&W Beverage Suggestion:
California Sauvignon Blanc, such as Dry Creek

4 SERVINGS

8 small skinless, boneless chicken breast halves (1½ to 2 pounds total)
⅔ cup white wine
⅔ cup dry sherry
1 bay leaf
2 medium carrots, cut into julienne strips
1 medium leek (white part only), cut into julienne strips
2 medium celery ribs, cut into julienne strips
Pinch of crushed fennel seeds
Pinch of basil
Pinch of mint
Pinch of thyme
1 teaspoon minced fresh chives
1¼ cups heavy cream
¾ teaspoon salt
⅛ teaspoon freshly ground pepper
Sprigs of parsley, for garnish

1. Place the chicken breasts in a large noncorrodible skillet. Pour in the wine and sherry; add the bay leaf. Arrange the julienned carrots, leek and celery over the chicken.

2. Cover the skillet and simmer over moderate heat for about 15 minutes, or until the chicken is tender and the juices run clear when pierced with a knife.

3. With a slotted spoon, transfer the chicken to a platter. Scatter the vegetables over the chicken. Cover with foil to keep warm.

4. Add the fennel, basil, mint, thyme and chives to the skillet and boil the mixture over high heat until reduced by half, about 6 minutes.

5. Add the cream and boil again until the sauce thickly coats the back of a spoon, about 6 minutes longer. Season with the salt and pepper. Pour the hot sauce around the chicken breasts. Garnish with sprigs of parsley.

Chicken Cutlets with Fresh Orange Sauce

The simple elegance of this chicken dish makes it appropriate for either a casual dinner or company.

F&W Beverage Suggestion:
German or California Riesling

4 SERVINGS

1 large navel orange
4 skinless, boneless chicken breast halves, pounded ¼ inch thick
½ teaspoon salt
¼ teaspoon freshly ground pepper
4 tablespoons unsalted butter
2 small shallots, minced
⅓ cup canned chicken broth
⅛ teaspoon curry powder
1 teaspoon fresh lemon juice

1. Grate the zest from the orange and reserve. Working over a bowl to collect the juices, peel and section the orange, removing the membrane. Reserve the orange sections and juice.

2. Season the chicken cutlets on both sides with the salt and pepper. In a large heavy skillet, melt 1 tablespoon of the butter over low heat. Add the shallots and sauté until translucent, about 1 minute. Transfer the shallots to a small bowl.

3. Increase the heat to high and add 1 tablespoon of butter to the skillet. Add 2 chicken cutlets and sauté, turning once, until lightly browned on both sides, 1 to 2 minutes. Remove the chicken and set aside. Add 1 tablespoon of butter and sauté the remaining cutlets in the same way.

4. Drain off any excess fat in the skillet. Pour in the broth and stir, scraping the bottom of the pan to incorporate any brown bits. Bring to a boil over high heat and stir in the curry powder, lemon juice, the reserved orange zest and juice and the shallots. Cook for 30 seconds. Return all the chicken to the pan. Reduce the heat to low, cover and simmer until

the chicken is cooked, 2 to 3 minutes.

5. Arrange the chicken cutlets, overlapping slightly, on a warmed platter. Add the remaining 1 tablespoon butter to the skillet, swirling to form a creamy sauce. Pour over the chicken and garnish with the reserved orange sections.

Crispy Chicken Strips with Lemon-Soy Dipping Sauce

These quickly sautéed strips of chicken breast are tender and succulent. Their flavor is enhanced by a zippy lemon-soy dipping sauce.

4 SERVINGS

½ cup soy sauce
¼ cup fresh lemon juice
1 garlic clove, minced or crushed through a press
1 tablespoon sugar
1 tablespoon Oriental sesame oil
2 scallions, minced (about 3 tablespoons)
1½ pounds skinless, boneless chicken breast halves
4 tablespoons all-purpose flour
About 4 tablespoons vegetable oil
½ teaspoon freshly ground pepper

1. Make a dipping sauce by combining the soy sauce, lemon juice, garlic, sugar, sesame oil and scallions in a small bowl. Stir until the sugar dissolves.

2. Trim away any fat or tendons from the chicken. Cut into 3-by-½-inch strips.

3. In a paper or plastic bag, combine the chicken with the flour; shake to coat the chicken. In a large heavy skillet, heat 2 tablespoons of the oil. When the oil is hot but not smoking, add as much of the floured chicken as will fit in a single layer without crowding. Sauté over moderately high heat until crisp and golden brown on the bottom, 1 to 2 minutes. Turn and cook the remaining side until just cooked, about 15 seconds. Drain on paper towels. Fry the remaining chicken in batches, adding more oil as necessary. Sprinkle the chicken with the pepper and serve with four individual bowls of the dipping sauce.

Spicy Chicken with Spring Peanut Sauce

Great for picnics. Serve this piquant chicken with fresh radishes, scallions, tomatoes and cucumbers, sprinkled lightly with black pepper and coarse salt.

F&W Beverage Suggestion:
English ale, such as Samuel Smith

4 SERVINGS

- **3 tablespoons smooth peanut butter**
- **1 cup chicken broth**
- **1 tablespoon fresh lemon juice**
- **1 teaspoon Oriental sesame oil**
- **2 scallions, minced**
- **1 large garlic clove, crushed through a press**
- **½ teaspoon coarse salt**
- **¼ teaspoon freshly ground black pepper**
- **⅛ to ¼ teaspoon hot pepper sauce, to taste**
- **2 to 3 teaspoons crushed hot pepper flakes**
- **½ cup finely chopped unsalted dry-roasted peanuts**
- **6 slices crisply cooked bacon, finely chopped**
- **4 skinless, boneless chicken breast halves**
- **2 eggs, separated**
- **½ cup corn oil**
- **Lemon wedges, for garnish**

1. Put the peanut butter in a medium bowl and gradually stir in the chicken broth until smooth. Add the lemon juice, sesame oil, scallions, garlic, ¼ teaspoon of the salt, the black pepper, hot sauce and ½ to 1 teaspoon hot pepper flakes, to taste. Cover and let stand at room temperature to let the flavors develop for at least 1 hour. **(The sauce can be made a day ahead.** Cover and refrigerate. Let return to room temperature before serving.)

2. Combine the chopped nuts, bacon, the remaining ¼ teaspoon salt and 1½ to 2 teaspoons hot pepper flakes, to taste.

3. Lightly pound the chicken breasts between two sheets of waxed paper to an even thickness of about ⅜ inch.

4. Beat the egg whites until soft peaks form; then beat in the egg yolks. Spread a thick layer of egg on one side of each breast. Sprinkle about 1½ tablespoons of the nut-bacon mixture over each and press firmly so that it adheres. Refrigerate for 30 minutes.

5. Repeat to coat the second side of each chicken breast with the nut mixture. Chill for 15 minutes longer.

6. In a large skillet, heat the oil until shimmering. Add the breasts and cook over moderately high heat for about 5 minutes until the nuts are brown on the bottom. Turn carefully and brown on the second side for 5 minutes. Drain on paper towels. Serve hot or at room temperature with the peanut butter sauce and lemon wedges.

Chicken Teriyaki with Mustard Sauce

This is a do-ahead recipe par excellence. The dipping sauce must mellow for three to four hours, the chicken must marinate for about two hours and the bamboo skewers should be soaked in water for at least three hours to prevent them from burning.

8 SERVINGS

- **½ cup mayonnaise, preferably homemade**
- **⅓ cup Dijon-style mustard**
- **1 teaspoon Worcestershire sauce**
- **½ teaspoon hot pepper sauce**
- **½ cup dry sherry**
- **½ cup soy sauce**
- **¼ cup vegetable oil**
- **¼ cup loosely packed light brown sugar**
- **2 large garlic cloves, crushed to a paste**
- **¼ teaspoon freshly ground pepper**
- **8 skinless, boneless chicken breast halves**
- **8 scallions, sliced on the diagonal into ½-inch lengths**
- **Escarole leaves, for garnish**

1. In a small bowl, stir together the mayonnaise, mustard, Worcestershire sauce and hot pepper sauce to make a dipping sauce. Cover and refrigerate for 3 to 4 hours before serving.

2. In a large bowl, stir together the sherry, soy sauce, oil, brown sugar, garlic and pepper to make a marinade.

3. Slice the breasts into 2-by-¼-inch strips. Place in the marinade and toss to coat. Cover loosely and marinate at room temperature for 2 hours.

4. Light the coals or preheat the broiler. Remove the chicken from the marinade and thread 2 strips with 2 or 3 pieces of scallion each onto 16 bamboo skewers, alternating the ingredients.

5. Lightly oil the barbecue rack to prevent sticking. Grill the chicken 4 to 6 inches from the heat, turning once, for 2 to 3 minutes on each side.

6. To serve, place the dipping sauce in the center of a large round platter. Arrange a bed of escarole leaves around the dipping sauce and lay the skewers on top.

Chicken Stir-Fry with Summer Squashes

Light and summery, this colorful green and yellow dish needs only some sliced ripe red tomatoes and good bread.

F&W Beverage Suggestion:
Chenin Blanc, such as Dry Creek

4 SERVINGS

- **4 skinless, boneless chicken breast halves**
- **1 egg white**
- **1 tablespoon dry white wine**
- **¾ teaspoon salt**
- **1 tablespoon cornstarch**
- **3 tablespoons olive oil**
- **½ medium onion, finely chopped**
- **2 or 3 garlic cloves, finely chopped**
- **½ pound small zucchini (about 2), cut into 2-by-¼-inch julienne strips**
- **½ pound small yellow summer squash (about 2), cut into 2-by-¼-inch julienne strips**
- **¼ teaspoon freshly ground pepper**
- **¼ cup coarsely chopped basil leaves**
- **Fresh spinach leaves, for garnish**

1. Trim any remaining fat or tendons from the chicken. Remove the small fillet section underneath each breast and cut it lengthwise into strips ¼ inch wide. Cut the chicken breast crosswise on the diagonal into long strips about ¼ inch wide.

2. Combine the egg white, wine, ½ teaspoon of the salt and the cornstarch in a food processor and mix until it becomes a very smooth emulsion, about 1 minute, scraping down the sides after 30 seconds.

3. Pour the egg white mixture into a bowl, add the chicken and toss to coat. Let marinate, covered, in the refrigerator for 3 hours or overnight. **(The recipe can be prepared ahead to this point.)**

4. When ready to assemble the dish, bring a large pot of water to a boil, reduce to a simmer and add the chicken, stirring gently to separate the pieces. Simmer until the chicken is almost done but still slightly pink in the center, about 2 minutes. Do not let the water boil. Drain into a colander and rinse under cold running water to cool; drain well. Dry on paper towels.

5. In a wok or large skillet, heat the oil. Add the onion and sauté over moderate heat for 1 minute. Add the garlic and cook for 30 seconds. Add the zucchini and yellow squash and stir-fry until just warmed through, about 3 minutes. Add the chicken and stir-fry to warm through and finish cooking, about 1 minute. Add the pepper and basil and toss well; then turn out onto a spinach-lined platter. Serve warm or at room temperature.

Szechuan Stir-Fried Leeks and Chicken

F&W Beverage Suggestion: California Gewürztraminer, such as Rutherford Hill

3 TO 4 SERVINGS

3 medium leeks (white and about 1 inch of tender green)
3 tablespoons peanut oil
4 garlic cloves, minced
1 pound skinless, boneless chicken breasts, shredded

½ green or red bell pepper, cut into thin strips
1 cup (4 ounces) thinly sliced mushrooms
1 teaspoon minced gingerroot
1 teaspoon hot pepper flakes
1 tablespoon sugar
1 tablespoon rice vinegar*
2 tablespoons Oriental sesame oil*
¼ cup chicken broth
*****Available in Oriental groceries**

1. Cut the leeks into thin slices crosswise on the diagonal. Wash thoroughly and drain well; dry on paper towels.

2. Heat the peanut oil in a wok over moderately high heat until the oil is shimmering; reduce the heat to moderate. Add the garlic and sauté for a few seconds, until fragrant. Add the shredded chicken and stir-fry until the chicken turns white, about 1 minute.

3. Add the leeks, bell pepper, mushrooms, gingerroot and hot pepper flakes. Continue to stir-fry for 1 minute longer, until the vegetables are barely tender. Add the sugar, vinegar, sesame oil and broth; increase the heat to moderately high and continue to cook until the vegetables are just tender, about 2 minutes. Serve with steamed white rice.

Curried Chicken with Yogurt

The list of ingredients for this mild curry is long, but the preparation is quite simple—particularly so if you use a food processor to chop the vegetables. The curry will keep well for two days. Serve over rice and accompany with a spicy chutney if desired.

F&W Beverage Suggestion: Dry rosé, such as rosé of Cabernet Sauvignon

6 SERVINGS

Chicken:
2 whole chicken breasts, skin removed
1 cup dry white wine
½ small onion, sliced
1 bay leaf
2 sprigs of fresh parsley
1 carrot, coarsely chopped

Curry:
2 tablespoons safflower oil
2 large garlic cloves, minced
2 tablespoons minced fresh gingerroot
2 tablespoons curry powder
3 medium onions, chopped
3 carrots, finely chopped
3 small celery ribs, chopped
4 small zucchini, chopped
1 tart apple, such as Granny Smith—peeled, cored and finely chopped
1 medium fennel bulb, trimmed and finely chopped
3 tomatoes, peeled and chopped
1 cup plain yogurt, at room temperature
Freshly ground pepper

1. Cook the chicken: In a large heavy saucepan, combine the chicken, wine, onion, bay leaf, parsley, carrot and 2 cups of water. Bring to a boil over high heat, reduce the heat to low and simmer, covered, until the chicken is tender and just cooked through, 10 to 12 minutes.

2. Strain out 1½ cups of the poaching liquid to use in the curry; let the chicken cool in the remaining broth while preparing the curry.

3. Make the curry: In a large skillet or flameproof casserole, warm the oil over moderately low heat. Add the garlic and ginger and sauté until softened but not browned, about 2 minutes.

4. Add the curry powder, onions, carrots, celery, zucchini, apple, fennel, tomatoes and the reserved 1½ cups poaching liquid. Simmer uncovered until the mixture is reduced to a thick sauce, 50 to 60 minutes. Add a little more poaching liquid if the consistency becomes too thick.

5. Meanwhile, remove the cooled chicken from the poaching liquid. Shred the chicken. Add to the curry sauce and cook until heated through, about 3 minutes. **(The recipe can be prepared a day ahead to this point.** Reheat over moderately low heat until warmed through.)

6. Remove from the heat and stir in the yogurt. Season with pepper to taste.

Chicken Soong

This popular Cantonese dish is eaten much like Moo Shu Pork, using a lettuce leaf, instead of a pancake, as a wrapper for the filling.

6 SERVINGS

½ **pound skinless, boneless chicken breast, partially frozen**
1 **egg white**
2 **tablespoons medium-dry sherry**
1½ **teaspoons water chestnut powder* or cornstarch**
½ **ounce dried Chinese mushrooms* (about 4)**
2 **tablespoons hoisin sauce***
1 **tablespoon dark soy sauce***
¼ **teaspoon freshly ground pepper**
2 **cups peanut oil**
⅓ **cup minced shallots**
¼ **cup diced (¼-inch) carrots**
1 **medium garlic clove, minced**
1 **teaspoon minced fresh gingerroot**
¼ **cup diced (¼-inch) red bell pepper**
½ **cup diced (¼-inch) water chestnuts, preferably fresh***
½ **cup diced (¼-inch) snow peas (strings removed)**
1 **teaspoon Oriental sesame oil**
¼ **cup pine nuts (pignoli), lightly toasted**
1 **head of iceberg lettuce—cored and cut in half, with individual leaves loosened**

*Available at Oriental groceries

1. Cut the chicken into small dice.

2. In a medium bowl, combine the chicken with the egg white, ½ tablespoon of the sherry and the water chestnut powder. Stir to coat. Cover and refrigerate for at least 1 hour, or up to 12 hours.

3. Rinse the mushrooms under cold running water. Put them in a bowl and cover them with 2 cups of cold water. Soak until soft, about 1 hour. Squeeze the excess moisture out of the mushrooms. Remove the stems and discard. Cut the mushroom caps into ¼-inch dice.

4. In a small bowl, combine the remaining 1½ tablespoons sherry, the hoisin sauce, soy sauce and pepper. Blend well.

5. Place a wok over high heat for about 1½ minutes. Pour in the oil and heat to 325°. Stir the marinated chicken and carefully add it to the hot oil. Cook, stirring constantly, until the chicken turns opaque, about 1 minute. Turn off the heat. Pour the chicken and the oil into a colander set over a large bowl. Shake to drain off as much oil as possible. Reserve 1 tablespoon of the oil. If desired, the remaining oil can be strained and reserved for other frying.

6. Put the wok over moderate heat and add the 1 tablespoon reserved oil along with the shallots, carrots and mushrooms. Stir-fry for 1 minute. Add the garlic and ginger and stir-fry for 1 minute longer.

7. Increase the heat to high and add the bell pepper, water chestnuts and snow peas. Stir-fry for 1 minute and then remove the vegetables from the wok.

8. Return the wok to high heat. Stir the seasoning sauce and add it to the wok. Cook, stirring, for 30 seconds.

9. Return the cooked chicken to the wok. Stir-fry for about 30 seconds. Add the cooked vegetable mixture to the wok and stir-fry for 30 seconds longer, until all the ingredients are heated through.

10. Turn off the heat and add the sesame oil. Stir to blend. Transfer the mixture to a heated platter. Sprinkle the pine nuts on top. Serve hot, with the leaves of lettuce.

Chicken Curry Calcutta Style

Tomato Chutney (p. 223) makes a fine accompaniment to this tasty sweet-sour curry. The chicken can easily be made ahead and reheated.

F&W Beverage Suggestion:
Chilled lager beer

4 SERVINGS

1 **chicken (about 3½ pounds)**
1 **tablespoon corn or peanut oil**
½ **medium onion, coarsely chopped**
2 **medium garlic cloves, minced**
1 **teaspoon minced fresh gingerroot**
2 **teaspoons curry powder**
½ **teaspoon crushed hot red pepper**
½ **cup coarsely chopped tomato, fresh or canned**
1 **tablespoon cider vinegar**
2 **teaspoons dark brown sugar**
½ **teaspoon salt**
1 **medium red potato, peeled and cut into ½-inch cubes**

1. Pull off and discard all excess fat and as much skin as possible from the chicken. Cut the chicken into 8 or 10 serving pieces.

2. In a large deep skillet or flameproof casserole, heat the oil. Add the onion, garlic and ginger and fry over moderate heat, stirring, until the onion is softened and translucent, about 2 minutes.

3. Add the curry powder and hot pepper and stir over the heat for a few seconds.

4. Add the chicken pieces and fry, turning once, until golden, about 2 minutes on each side.

5. Add ¾ cup of water, the tomatoes, vinegar, brown sugar, salt and potato. Simmer, uncovered, turning the chicken occasionally, until the meat is tender, 30 to 35 minutes.

Baked Acorn Squash Stuffed with Curried Chicken

This recipe calls for no curry powder but for plenty of its component spices. Also, both butternut and acorn squash are used. There's a good reason for this: the butternut squash meat adds color to the curry, and the acorn squash, when halved, makes a perfect receptacle for baking the curry. If you prefer to make this recipe in stages, the chicken curry can be prepared and the squash baked ahead.

6 SERVINGS

4 tablespoons clarified unsalted butter
4 large skinless, boneless chicken breast halves, cut into 1½-by-¼-inch strips
1 large Spanish onion, coarsely chopped
1 small red bell pepper, cut into ¼-inch-wide strips
1 large garlic clove, crushed
½ teaspoon turmeric
¼ teaspoon cinnamon
¼ teaspoon ground cardamom
¼ teaspoon ground cumin
¼ teaspoon ground coriander
¼ teaspoon hot red pepper flakes
Pinch of ground cloves
½ cup canned chicken broth
½ cup apple juice or cider
1 tablespoon tomato paste
3 small acorn squash (about ¾ pound each)
1 small butternut squash (about 1 pound)
½ cup heavy cream
½ teaspoon salt
Freshly ground black pepper

1. Preheat the oven to 350°. In a large heavy skillet, heat 2 tablespoons of the clarified butter. Add the chicken and stir-fry over high heat until golden brown, 3 to 5 minutes. Remove to a bowl with a slotted spoon and reserve.

2. Add another tablespoon clarified butter to the skillet and reduce the heat to moderate. Add the onion, red bell pepper and garlic and stir-fry until the onion is softened and translucent, about 5 min-

utes. Blend in the turmeric, cinnamon, cardamom, cumin, coriander, hot pepper flakes and cloves and cook, stirring, over moderate heat until fragrant, about 2 minutes. Stir in the chicken broth, apple juice and tomato paste. Return the chicken to the skillet and adjust the heat so that the liquid barely bubbles. Cover and cook for 45 minutes.

3. Meanwhile, place the acorn and butternut squashes in a baking dish and bake for 20 minutes. Turn and cook for 20 to 25 minutes longer, or until they feel fairly soft to the touch. Remove from the oven and let stand until cool enough to handle. Leave the oven on.

4. Halve the butternut squash and scoop out the seeds and strings; peel and cut the flesh into ¾-inch cubes. Add the butternut squash and cream to the curried chicken. Season with the salt and pepper to taste.

5. Halve each acorn squash and scoop out all the seeds and stringy portions; brush the cut surfaces with the remaining 1 tablespoon butter. Place the acorn squash, cut-sides up, in a large shallow baking pan. Mound the hollows with the curried chicken. Cover loosely with foil and bake for 30 minutes, or until the acorn squash is tender.

Chicken and Sausage Stew with Parsley and Lemon

This is a crowd-pleasing stew, full of hearty flavors and textures. It can be prepared completely in advance and will probably be the better for it. It is generously liquid by intent. Serve with lots of crusty semolina bread for mopping up the sauce.

F&W Beverage Suggestion:
Simi Rosé of Cabernet Sauvignon

6 SERVINGS

8 tablespoons olive oil
1 pound sweet Italian-style sausages, pricked all over
2½- to 3-pound chicken, cut into serving pieces, giblets reserved
1 teaspoon salt
½ teaspoon freshly ground pepper
2 medium onions, finely chopped
3 celery ribs, including leafy tops, cut on the diagonal into 1-inch pieces
4 large garlic cloves, minced
1½ teaspoons oregano
1 teaspoon thyme
1 bay leaf
3 tablespoons all-purpose flour
1 cup dry white wine
2 cups chicken stock or canned broth
1 can (28 ounces) Italian peeled tomatoes, with their juice
1 pound medium mushrooms, stemmed
1 cup Calamata olives
½ cup chopped Italian flat-leaf parsley
1 tablespoon finely julienned lemon zest

1. In a large, noncorrodible, deep skillet or flameproof casserole, warm 2 tablespoons of the oil over moderate heat. Add the sausages and the chicken giblets and cook, turning occasionally, until well browned, about 10 minutes. Transfer the sausages to a bowl; leave the giblets in the skillet.

2. Add the chicken pieces, skin-side down, and season with ½ teaspoon of the salt and ¼ teaspoon of the pepper. Cook until golden brown, about 5 minutes. Turn, season with the remaining ½ teaspoon salt and ¼ teaspoon pepper and brown on the other side, about 5 minutes longer. Transfer to the bowl with the sausages. Discard the giblets and pour off any oil from the pan.

3. Return the pan to moderate heat. Add 3 tablespoons of the oil, the onions, celery, garlic, oregano, thyme and bay leaf. Reduce the heat to moderately low, cover and cook, stirring occasionally, until the onions are soft and golden, 15 minutes. Uncover, sprinkle the vegetables with the flour and cook over very low heat, stirring, for 5 minutes without allowing the flour to color to make a roux.

4. Gradually whisk in the wine. Add the stock and the tomatoes (crushing them with your fingers) and their juice. Bring to a boil over moderately high heat, stirring; reduce the heat to a simmer, partially cover and cook until the liquid is slightly thickened, about 30 minutes.

5. Cut the reserved sausages on the diagonal into 1-inch pieces. Add the sausages and chicken to the pan. Simmer uncovered until the chicken is very tender, about 30 minutes.

6. Meanwhile, in a large skillet, heat the remaining 3 tablespoons oil. Add the mushrooms and sauté over moderately high heat, until the mushrooms begin to yield their juice, about 5 minutes. Season with salt and pepper to taste and remove from the heat.

7. When the chicken is tender, transfer it with a slotted spoon to a serving bowl; cover to keep warm. Add the mushrooms, their juices and the olives to the sauce. Simmer for 5 minutes. (**The stew may be prepared to this point a day ahead.** Pour the sauce over the chicken, let cool to room temperature, then cover and refrigerate. Reheat the stew gently, stirring, until hot.)

8. Skim off any fat. Stir the parsley into the sauce and pour it over the chicken. Sprinkle the lemon zest on top.

Indonesian Braised Chicken Livers with Watercress

F&W Beverage Suggestion: Alsace Gewürztraminer, such as Hugel, or California Gewürztraminer, such as Rutherford Hill

2 TO 3 SERVINGS

1 tablespoon corn or peanut oil
1 small onion, thinly sliced
1 garlic clove, thinly sliced
1 large plum tomato—peeled, seeded and coarsely chopped
½ teaspoon minced fresh hot red pepper or ¼ teaspoon crushed dried
¾ pound chicken livers, trimmed and cut in half
2 bunches of watercress, tough stems removed
2 teaspoons soy sauce
1 teaspoon sugar
½ teaspoon salt

1. In a large skillet or wok, heat the oil. Add the onion, garlic, tomato and hot pepper. Stir-fry over moderate heat until the onion is softened but not browned, about 2 minutes.

2. Add the chicken livers and stir-fry for 2 minutes. Add the watercress, soy sauce, sugar, salt and 1 tablespoon of water. Cover and cook until the watercress wilts, about 3 minutes.

3. Uncover, increase the heat to high and stir-fry for about 2 minutes to reduce the sauce slightly. Serve hot.

Chicken and Dumplings

F&W Beverage Suggestion: California Zinfandel, such as Ridge

4 SERVINGS

3-pound chicken, cut into 8 pieces, giblets reserved
1 teaspoon salt
½ teaspoon freshly ground pepper
2 medium carrots, thinly sliced
2 medium onions, thinly sliced
2 celery ribs, thinly sliced
3 garlic cloves, crushed through a press
2 cups sifted all-purpose flour
1 tablespoon baking powder
1 teaspoon salt
2 eggs, lightly beaten
⅔ cup milk
½ cup chopped parsley

1. Place the chicken pieces and giblets in a large flameproof casserole. Season with the salt and pepper. Add the carrots, onions, celery, 2 of the garlic cloves and water to cover. Bring to a boil over high heat. Reduce the heat to moderately low and simmer for about 1 hour, or until the chicken is very tender. With a slotted spoon, remove the chicken pieces to a deep platter and cover with foil to keep warm.

2. In a medium mixing bowl, combine the flour, baking powder and salt. Add the eggs, milk, parsley and the remaining clove of garlic and stir to blend well.

3. Over moderately high heat, return the chicken stock to a boil. Drop the batter by rounded teaspoons into the broth. Cover the casserole and cook for 15 minutes.

4. To serve, place the dumplings on the platter around the chicken and pour on the cooking liquid and vegetables.

Chicken Livers with Sautéed Sherry Onions

These sautéed onions are equally deli-cious served over slices of steak or a hamburger.

F&W Beverage Suggestion:
Hearty red, such as Côtes-du-Rhône or California Zinfandel

4 SERVINGS

About 4 tablespoons bacon fat, olive oil or butter
3 medium onions, sliced crosswise into thin rounds
⅓ cup dry sherry
1 pound chicken livers, trimmed and halved if large
½ teaspoon salt
¼ teaspoon freshly ground pepper

1. In a heavy medium skillet, melt 2 tablespoons of the fat over moderate heat. Add the onions and sauté, separat-ing the rounds into rings, until soft and golden brown, about 15 minutes. If nec-essary to prevent sticking, add 1 or 2 teaspoons additional fat or oil and re-duce the heat slightly. Add the sherry and simmer for 1 minute, scraping up any browned bits from the bottom of the skillet; remove from the heat and set aside.

2. In a large heavy skillet, melt the re-maining 2 tablespoons fat over moderate heat. Add the chicken livers in a single layer and cook without turning for 3 minutes. Turn the livers over and cook for 2 to 3 minutes longer. Add the re-served onion mixture to the skillet and season with the salt and pepper. Stir gently over moderate heat for 1 to 2 minutes, until the onions are heated through.

Turkey Galantine

This recipe must be begun at least 2 days ahead of time, so plan accordingly.

F&W Beverage Suggestion:
California Merlot, such as Mondavi

18 TO 20 SERVINGS

One turkey (10 to 12 pounds), boned (see Note)
3 ounces smoked tongue, cut into ½-inch cubes
3 ounces lean ham, cut into ½-inch cubes
2 pounds pork fat, ground, plus 3 ounces cut into ½-inch cubes
½ cup Cognac
¾ cup shelled and skinned pistachios (about ½ pound)
1 cup Madeira, preferably Boal
2 tablespoons salt
1 tablespoon freshly ground pepper
2 teaspoons allspice
2 teaspoons thyme
1 teaspoon nutmeg
1 jar (1 ounce) truffles, quartered
1 turkey liver, cut into thick strips
4 quarts Rich Turkey Stock (p. 219)
8 egg whites
1 pound skinless, boneless chicken breast, ground
1 medium tomato, diced
2 medium leeks, coarsely chopped
Blanched leek greens and tomato, carrot or pimiento slices, for garnish

1. Separate the meat from the skin of the turkey by pulling gently with your hands and severing the connective tis-sues with the tip of a knife, being careful not to pierce the skin. Remove each breast in a single piece. Set one aside. Cut the remaining flesh into 1- to 2-inch chunks. Place the cut meat in the freezer for about 45 minutes (the meat will be easier to grind when partially frozen).

2. Meanwhile, cut the reserved turkey breast into ½-inch cubes and place in a medium bowl. Add the tongue, ham, cubed pork fat and Cognac and toss. Marinate at room temperature, tossing once or twice, for 1 hour.

3. Coarsely grind the partially frozen chunks of turkey in a food processor (in

batches) or in a meat grinder. Place in a large bowl. Add the ground pork fat and blend well with your hands. Add the cubed turkey and other meats (plus the Cognac), the pistachios, ½ cup of the Madeira, the salt, pepper, allspice, thyme and nutmeg; blend well. To check the seasoning, sauté 1 tablespoon of this forcemeat filling in a small skillet over moderate heat, turning once, until cooked through, about 2 minutes on each side. Taste and adjust the season-ings if necessary. Remember, the galan-tine will be served cold, so season gen-erously; flavors are muted by chilling.

4. Preheat the oven to 325°. Lay the tur-key skin, outer-side down, on a large, triple-layered rectangle of dampened cheesecloth. Pull the skin of the wings and legs inside out and press flat to form a rough rectangle of skin. Remove any excess fat from around the neck and tail. Spread the forcemeat in a thick rectangle over the center of the turkey skin, leav-ing a 3½-inch margin all around. Place a row of truffles lengthwise down the cen-ter of the forcemeat. Arrange the strips of liver on both sides of the truffles.

5. Fold up the neck and tail skin. Gently and evenly, using the cheesecloth to help, pull the skin from the long sides up and around the forcemeat. Wrap firm-ly to shape the meat into a thick log; be sure the ends overlap to completely en-close the forcemeat.

6. Wrap the cheesecloth tightly around the galantine. Tie the two ends with heavy kitchen string. Wrap the cheese-cloth-covered galantine in a damp kitch-en towel and tie the two ends. Tie the galantine at 1-inch intervals to form a round sausagelike shape about 15 inches long and 4½ to 5 inches in diameter. Secure the galantine lengthwise with 3 or 4 ties.

7. In a large saucepan, bring the stock to

a boil. Place the wrapped galantine, seam-side down, in a turkey roaster or other large deep roasting pan. Pour the hot stock over the galantine to no higher than 1 inch from the top of the pan. Cover and bake for 1 hour. Turn the galantine over, cover and bake for 1 hour longer, or until the internal temperature reaches 140° to 150°. Remove from the oven, uncover and let the galantine cool in the stock for 2 hours.

8. Remove the galantine from the stock; reserve the stock. Cut the strings and remove the towel. Leave the cheesecloth in place. Retie the galantine in a clean, damp towel the same way as before, at 1-inch intervals with several lengthwise wraps. Place in a shallow pan and weigh down with about 3 pounds of weight (a heavy cutting board works well, or a baking sheet with several cans on top). Refrigerate overnight. Let the stock cool to room temperature, cover and refrigerate until chilled. Remove the congealed fat from the surface of the stock. Let return to room temperature before proceeding.

9. Clarify the stock to make a clear aspic: In a stockpot, mix the egg whites thoroughly with the chicken, tomato and leeks. Slowly whisk in the stock. Place the pot over moderate heat and bring almost to a boil. Immediately reduce the heat to maintain a gentle simmer. Carefully adjust the pan off-center so that it bubbles on one side. Simmer without stirring at all, gently rotating the pot quarter-turns every 10 minutes, for 40 minutes. Turn off the heat.

10. Make an opening in the cooked egg white mixture on top of the stock. Gently ladle out the clear stock and strain through a sieve lined with several layers of dampened cheesecloth into a large saucepan.

11. Bring the clarified stock to a boil over high heat and continue to cook, skimming lightly with a paper towel if you see any scum, until the liquid is reduced by half to about 6 cups, 40 to 50 minutes. Stir in the remaining ½ cup Madeira and salt to taste.

12. To decorate the galantine classically, undo all the wrappings. If any of it sticks to the skin, loosen with a bit of hot water. With a very sharp slicing knife, cut about half of the galantine into ⅜-inch slices. Arrange the slices and the unsliced portion of the galantine on a rack set over a shallow pan. Return to the refrigerator to chill thoroughly.

13. Pour the clarified stock into a medium bowl set over a larger bowl of ice and water. Stir slowly, to avoid any bubbles, until the aspic begins to thicken and set; remove from the ice. Remove the galantine from the refrigerator. Immediately ladle the aspic over the galantine and the slices and return to the refrigerator until set. Repeat until the meat is covered evenly with a shiny layer of aspic. Cut the leek greens into thin strips. Cut the tomato, carrot or pimiento into small flowerlike shapes. Dip the decorations into the aspic and arrange on top of the galantine half. Refrigerate until set. After decorating, coat the galantine with 2 more layers of aspic.

14. Coat the bottom of a large oval platter with a thin layer of aspic. Refrigerate until set. Pour the remaining aspic into a shallow baking pan. Refrigerate until firmly set; then chop.

15. As final assembly, set the galantine half on one end of the aspic-coated platter. Arrange the slices in front. Spoon the chopped aspic around the galantine. Refrigerate until serving time.

NOTE: Reserve the carcass, giblets and trimmings to make the Rich Turkey Stock, but reserve the liver for the galantine itself.

Apple and Prune Stuffing with Almonds

MAKES 6 CUPS OF STUFFING, ENOUGH FOR A 12- TO-16-POUND TURKEY

1 cup cider vinegar
½ cup sugar
2 cups pitted prunes (12 ounces)
1 cup slivered almonds (4 ounces)
1¾ pounds Granny Smith apples— peeled, cored, cut into 8 wedges and halved crosswise
1 teaspoon crumbled sage
1 teaspoon salt
1 teaspoon freshly ground pepper

1. In a small noncorrodible saucepan, bring the vinegar and sugar to a boil over moderately high heat, stirring to dissolve the sugar. Remove from the heat, add the prunes and set aside to let cool, turning occasionally.

2. Meanwhile, preheat the oven to 350°. Spread the almonds in a baking dish and toast in the oven, shaking the pan once or twice, until golden, 8 to 10 minutes.

3. In a medium bowl, combine the prunes and their liquid, the apples, almonds, sage, salt and pepper; toss well. Drain off the vinegar syrup before using.

EGGS, CHEESE & SANDWICHES

Eggs with Sour Cream-Dill Sauce

Dressed in a tangy, herb-flecked cold sauce, these hard-cooked eggs are an ideal dish for a buffet or a picnic. Both the eggs and the sauce may be prepared one day ahead and assembled at the last minute.

8 TO 10 SERVINGS

1 raw egg
½ cup sour cream
1 tablespoon plus 1 teaspoon fresh lime juice
1 tablespoon minced scallion (white and tender green)
¼ teaspoon salt
¼ teaspoon freshly ground pepper
¼ teaspoon sugar
2 tablespoons chopped fresh dill or 2 teaspoons dried dillweed
10 hard-cooked eggs

1. In a medium bowl, beat the raw egg until frothy. Whisk in the sour cream until blended. Whisk in the lime juice, scallion, salt, pepper, sugar and dill until blended. Cover and refrigerate the dressing until chilled, 30 minutes to 1 hour. (**The recipe can be prepared a day ahead to this point.**)

2. Shortly before serving, cut the hard-cooked eggs in half lengthwise. Arrange them, rounded-side up, on a large serving platter. Drizzle the sour cream-dill dressing over the eggs in an attractive pattern.

Soft Scrambled Eggs with Herbed Cheese

The secret of making this delicious breakfast dish is to cook the eggs slowly over very low heat; the total cooking time should be about 20 minutes. Properly prepared, the texture of the eggs is similar to a soft, stirred custard. Serve spooned over or alongside toasted English muffins.

4 SERVINGS

8 eggs
½ cup heavy cream

2½ ounces herbed fresh cream cheese, such as Alouette, cut into small pieces
3 tablespoons chopped parsley
Salt and freshly ground pepper

1. In a large heavy skillet, place the eggs and cream over very low heat. Stir gently to break the egg yolks and to combine with the cream. Cook, scraping the bottom of the skillet frequently, until about half the eggs form soft curds, about 10 minutes.

2. Add the cheese and parsley to the eggs. Continue to cook, stirring frequently, until the eggs form large soft curds, 8 to 10 minutes. Remove from the heat and season with salt and pepper to taste.

Poached Egg on Grilled Tomato with Fines Herbes

4 SERVINGS

4 medium tomatoes
Salt and freshly ground pepper
1 tablespoon olive oil
¾ pound fresh mushrooms, coarsely chopped
3 medium garlic cloves, minced
2 large shallots, minced
1 tablespoon chopped fresh chervil or Italian flat-leaf parsley
2 tablespoons distilled white vinegar
4 eggs
8 large spinach leaves, briefly blanched in boiling water
Lightened Béarnaise Sauce (p. 222)

1. Preheat the oven to 400°. Slice off the top of each tomato and set the tops aside. Scoop out the tomato, discarding the seeds and pulp. Season the inside of each with a pinch of salt and pepper; place in a baking dish.

2. In a medium skillet, heat the oil. Add the mushrooms, garlic, shallots, ¼ teaspoon salt and ⅛ teaspoon pepper and sauté over moderate heat until the mush-

rooms are soft and lightly colored, about 5 minutes. Remove from the heat and stir in the chervil.

3. Spoon the mushroom stuffing into the tomatoes. Cover each tomato with a reserved top. Bake for 10 minutes, until warmed through.

4. Meanwhile, in a large noncorrodible saucepan or deep skillet, bring 2 quarts of water with the vinegar to a simmer. Break each egg into a saucer and then slip the egg into the water. Poach, until just set, 3 to 4 minutes. Remove, trim off any ragged edges and keep warm in hot water until the tomatoes are cooked.

5. To serve, place 2 spinach leaves on each of 4 plates. Place a tomato on each plate, remove the top and set alongside. Drain the eggs on paper towels and set one on top of each tomato. Coat each egg with Lightened Béarnaise Sauce.

Shirred Eggs with Basil and Parmesan Cheese

This makes a light and savory brunch dish.

4 SERVINGS

8 eggs
4 teaspoons Basil Preserved in Oil (p. 224)
4 scant tablespoons heavy cream
2 teaspoons freshly grated Parmesan cheese
Salt and freshly ground pepper

1. Preheat the oven to 300°. Lightly butter four ½-cup ovenproof ramekins or custard cups. Break 2 eggs into each ramekin. Sprinkle 1 teaspoon of the basil, 1 tablespoon of the cream, ½ teaspoon of the Parmesan and a light seasoning of salt and pepper over each.

2. Place the ramekins in a larger baking dish and pour in enough hot water to reach halfway up the sides of the ramekins. Bake until the eggs are set, 18 to 20 minutes.

Right, Egg and Onion Pie (p. 116) and Onion Squash Soup (p. 43).

Above, Tibetan Spice Omelet (p. 114) with Tibetan Cauliflower in Sesame Sauce (p. 124). Right, top, a serving of Crown Roast of Lamb (p. 65) with Vegetable Mélange (p. 66). Right, bottom, Creole Leeks Vinaigrette (p. 125).

111

Papa's Chili-Cheese Omelet

A splendidly simple and attractive open-faced omelet.

2 SERVINGS

4 eggs
⅛ teaspoon hot pepper sauce
⅛ teaspoon salt
¼ teaspoon freshly ground black pepper
1 tablespoon unsalted butter
½ teaspoon minced fresh or canned hot green chilies
½ cup grated Monterey Jack cheese
½ cup grated Cheddar cheese

1. Preheat the broiler. In a medium bowl, beat the eggs with the hot pepper sauce, salt, black pepper and 1 tablespoon of cold water until just blended.

2. In a medium ovenproof omelet pan or skillet, preferably nonstick, melt the butter over moderate heat. Pour in the egg mixture and let the pan sit over the heat for 3 to 5 seconds, until the edges begin to set. Then swirl the pan firmly over the heat until the eggs begin to pull away from the sides of the pan, 20 to 25 seconds. Tilt the pan occasionally to let some of the uncooked egg flow underneath. While the center of the omelet is still liquid, sprinkle the green chilies and grated cheeses evenly over the surface.

3. Broil the omelet 4 inches from the heat until the cheese is melted and the edges are slightly puffed and very lightly browned, 30 seconds to 1 minute. To serve, cut the omelet into wedges.

Left, Mini-Yorkshire Puddings (p. 137) and Roast Potatoes and Shallots (p. 128).

Basic Omelet

1 SERVING

3 large eggs, at room temperature
1 tablespoon water
¼ teaspoon salt
⅛ teaspoon freshly ground pepper
1 tablespoon plus 1 teaspoon unsalted butter

1. Combine the eggs, water, salt and pepper in a medium bowl. Beat lightly with a fork until the eggs are mostly blended but small amounts of white are still visible.

2. Heat a 10-inch omelet pan (7 to 7½ inches across the bottom), preferably nonstick. Add 1 tablespoon of butter and melt over high heat until the foam subsides and the butter just starts to turn golden. Quickly tilt the pan to coat the bottom and sides with the butter.

3. Pour in the eggs and let the pan sit over the heat for 2 to 3 seconds, until the edges begin to set. Then swirl the skillet firmly over the heat in a counter-clockwise direction (clockwise, if you're left-handed) until the eggs begin to mass away from the sides of the pan, about 20 seconds. Remove from the heat and give the pan a few more swirls. The top of the eggs will still be slightly liquidy; the omelet finishes cooking as it is filled and rolled. If you are using a filling, sprinkle about ¼ cup over the surface of the omelet.

4. Tilt the pan and fold over one-third of the omelet onto itself. Roll out the omelet onto a warm plate, flipping it over on itself, so that both ends are tucked neatly underneath. Rub 1 teaspoon of butter over the top and serve.

Cheese Omelet: Follow the directions for Basic Omelet (above), but sprinkle ¼ cup coarsely grated Cheddar, Gorgonzola, Fontina and/or Parmesan over the eggs at the end of Step 3.

Watercress and Brie Omelet: Follow the directions for Basic Omelet (above), but sprinkle ½ ounce Brie, cut into small pieces, and ¼ cup chopped watercress over the eggs at the end of Step 3.

Fresh Herb Omelet: Follow the directions for Basic Omelet (above), but beat 1 tablespoon plus 2 teaspoons chopped fresh parsley, chervil, tarragon, thyme, basil and/or chives into the eggs in Step 1.

Omelet with Chicken Liver and Chive Filling

MAKES 2 OMELETS

¼ pound chicken livers—rinsed, trimmed and cut into ½-inch pieces
1 tablespoon unsalted butter
1 tablespoon red wine vinegar
¼ cup heavy cream
⅛ teaspoon coarsely ground black pepper
½ teaspoon lemon juice
1 tablespoon minced chives
Salt
2 recipes of Basic Omelet (at left)

1. Pat the livers dry. In a medium non-corrodible skillet, melt the butter over moderately high heat. When the foam subsides, add the livers and cook, stirring several times until browned, about 2 minutes. Remove the livers with a slotted spoon.

2. Return the skillet to moderately high heat. Add the vinegar and boil for about 30 seconds until almost dry, scraping up any browned bits from the bottom of the pan. Add the cream and boil for 2 minutes. Add the livers with any juices that have collected and cook until the sauce thickens, about 1 minute longer. Add the pepper, lemon juice, chives and salt to taste.

3. Make a Basic Omelet and add half of this filling at the end of Step 3. Repeat for the second omelet and remaining filling.

Omelet with Potato-Bacon Filling

MAKES 2 OMELETS

1 medium potato, peeled and cut
  into ¼-inch dice
4 slices of bacon
¼ cup coarsely chopped onion
Salt and freshly ground pepper
2 recipes of Basic Omelet (p. 113)

1. In a medium saucepan of boiling salted water, cook the potato until tender, 5 to 10 minutes. Drain well.

2. In a medium skillet, cook the bacon over moderate heat until browned and crisp, 5 to 10 minutes. Drain on paper towels, then crumble. Pour off all but 1½ tablespoons of the bacon drippings.

3. Add the potato to the skillet and cook in the bacon drippings over moderate heat until browned and crisp, about 15 minutes. Add the onion and cook until just softened, about 2 minutes longer. Add the bacon and toss. Season with salt and pepper to taste.

4. Make a Basic Omelet and add half of this filling at the end of Step 3. Repeat for the second omelet and remaining filling.

Tibetan Spice Omelet

1 SERVING

2 eggs
¼ teaspoon salt
⅛ teaspoon freshly ground pepper
⅛ teaspoon cinnamon
⅛ teaspoon ground cloves
1 tablespoon sour cream
1 teaspoon freshly grated Parmesan
  cheese
1 tablespoon peanut or corn oil
1 small tomato, thinly sliced

1. Beat the eggs with the salt, pepper, cinnamon, cloves, sour cream and Parmesan cheese until blended.

2. In a small skillet, heat the oil over high heat until almost smoking. Pour in

the egg mixture, cook for 15 to 30 seconds to set the bottom, then reduce the heat to moderate.

3. Cover the omelet with the tomato slices and continue cooking until the eggs are set, about 2 minutes. Slide the omelet onto a plate and then invert back into the pan, tomato-side down. Cook for 1 minute; then invert onto a plate, tomato-side on top. Serve hot.

Omelet with Crab and Dill Filling

MAKES 2 OMELETS

1 tablespoon unsalted butter
¼ cup small (¼-inch) bread cubes,
  made from stale Italian or French
  bread
2 ounces lump crabmeat
2 teaspoons chopped fresh dill
Pinch of salt and freshly ground
  pepper
2 recipes of Basic Omelet (p. 113)

1. In a small skillet, melt the butter over moderately high heat. As soon as the foam subsides, add the bread cubes and sauté, tossing for 1 minute. Reduce the heat to low and cook, tossing frequently, until the croutons are golden brown and crisp, about 10 minutes. Add the crabmeat, dill, salt and pepper; toss lightly to mix.

2. Make a Basic Omelet and add half of this filling at the end of Step 3. Repeat for the second omelet and remaining filling.

Pipérade

An omelet, but not quite, this *pipérade* comes from the Basque country in the Pyrenees.

4 TO 6 SERVINGS

4 eggs
½ cup olive oil
2 medium green bell peppers, cut
  into julienne strips about 3 by ¼
  inch
2 medium leeks (white part only),
  thinly sliced
1 medium onion, coarsely chopped
2 garlic cloves, minced
2 firm, ripe tomatoes—peeled,
  seeded and cut into ¼-inch dice
½ pound smoked ham, cut into ½-
  inch dice (about 1 cup)
½ teaspoon sugar
½ teaspoon salt
⅛ teaspoon freshly ground black
  pepper
¼ cup minced fresh parsley

1. In a small bowl, beat the eggs and set aside while you prepare the vegetables.

2. In a large heavy (preferably nonstick) skillet, heat the oil. Add the green peppers, leeks, onion and garlic and sauté over moderate heat, stirring occasionally, until tender but not browned, 8 to 10 minutes. Add the tomatoes and ham and cook, stirring, for 5 minutes, or until the mixture forms a thick sauce. Season with the sugar, salt and black pepper.

3. Gently stir the eggs and parsley into the vegetables. Cook the mixture, carefully lifting and turning with a spatula to let the uncooked portion run underneath, until set but not dry, 2 to 3 minutes. Do not mash or stir. Serve hot.

Giant Frittata

12 SERVINGS

2 ounces dried mushrooms
2 cups boiling water
2 ounces sun-dried tomatoes*
¼ cup plus 2 tablespoons olive oil
1 pound baking potatoes, peeled
    and cut into ½-inch cubes
½ cup dry white wine
2½ teaspoons salt
6 tablespoons unsalted butter
3 bunches of scallions (white and 2
    inches of the green), thinly
    sliced
2 medium garlic cloves, minced
½ cup pine nuts (pignoli)
½ pound boiled ham, cut into 1½-
    by-⅛-inch julienne strips
½ pound sharp Cheddar cheese,
    shredded
24 eggs
½ teaspoon freshly ground pepper
1 tablespoon oregano
½ cup freshly grated Parmesan
    cheese
½ cup minced fresh parsley
Pimientos and black olives, for
    garnish
*Available at specialty food shops

1. Soak the dried mushrooms in the boiling water until softened, about 1 hour. Drain the mushrooms, squeeze dry and chop coarsely.

2. Meanwhile, soak the sun-dried tomatoes in ¼ cup of the olive oil for 1 hour. Reserving the oil, drain the tomatoes and chop coarsely.

3. In a large saucepan of boiling salted water, cook the potatoes until just tender, 8 to 10 minutes; do not overcook. Drain well and transfer to a large bowl. While still hot, toss with the wine and ½ teaspoon of the salt.

4. In a 12-inch ovenproof skillet, melt 4 tablespoons of the butter in 1 tablespoon oil over moderate heat. Add the scallions and garlic and sauté until softened, about 7 minutes.

5. Add the pine nuts and sauté until lightly browned, about 5 minutes. Add the ham strips and cook for 5 minutes

longer. Add this mixture to the bowl of potatoes; set the skillet aside.

6. Add the Cheddar cheese, chopped mushrooms and tomatoes with their reserved tomato oil to the potato mixture; toss well. Set this filling aside.

7. Preheat the oven to 450°. In a large bowl, beat 12 of the eggs with 1 teaspoon of the salt, ¼ teaspoon of the pepper and ½ tablespoon of the oregano. Using the reserved skillet, melt the remaining 2 tablespoons butter in the remaining 1 tablespoon oil over high heat. When the foam subsides, add the egg mixture. Cook until the omelet begins to set at the edges. Lift one side slightly and tilt the pan so that the uncooked egg runs underneath. Continue to cook, repeating this process, until most of the egg is set. Remove the skillet from the heat.

8. Spread the reserved filling evenly over the omelet. In a bowl, beat the remaining 12 eggs with the remaining 1 teaspoon salt, ¼ teaspoon pepper and ½ tablespoon oregano. Pour the egg mixture over the filling. Place the skillet in the top third of the oven and bake until the top layer of egg is set, 20 to 30 minutes.

9. Invert the frittata onto a large heated platter. Sprinkle on the Parmesan cheese and parsley. Garnish with pimientos and olives.

Asparagus Pancake with Mozzarella

For serving, treat this vegetable pancake as you would an omelet. It makes a fine brunch or light lunch dish.

1 OR 2 SERVINGS

10 to 12 large asparagus spears,
    trimmed and peeled
1 egg, beaten
¼ teaspoon salt
Pinch of freshly ground pepper
2 teaspoons olive oil
2 thin slices of mozzarella cheese

1. In a large pot of boiling salted water, cook the asparagus until tender but still bright green, about 3 minutes. Drain and rinse under cold running water; drain well.

2. Reserve 2 asparagus tips for garnish and coarsely chop the remainder. Place the pieces in a clean towel and press out the moisture. Stir the asparagus into the egg. Add the salt and pepper.

3. Warm a large seasoned skillet over moderately high heat for 1 minute. Add the olive oil and let heat for 30 seconds. Scrape in the asparagus mixture and press it into an even layer. Reduce the heat to low and cook until the pancake is almost set, about 5 minutes.

4. Slide the pancake onto a plate. Cover the plate with the skillet and invert so that the pancake slides back into the pan, uncooked-side down. Place the mozzarella on top of the pancake, cover the skillet and cook until the cheese melts, about 1 minute. Slide the pancake onto a serving plate. Garnish with the asparagus tips.

Egg and Onion Pie

This tart can be prepared ahead of time. After baking, let cool, wrap in foil and refrigerate. To serve, unwrap and reheat on a baking sheet in a 300° oven for 25 minutes.

6 TO 8 SERVINGS

Pastry:
1 cup (2 sticks) cold unsalted butter, cut into bits
3⅓ cups all-purpose flour
½ teaspoon salt
2 egg yolks
2 tablespoons cream cheese, chilled
5 to 6 tablespoons ice water

Filling:
4 tablespoons unsalted butter
1 tablespoon olive oil
2 medium onions, thinly sliced into rings
2 medium garlic cloves, minced
1½ pounds bulk pork sausage
2 tablespoons all-purpose flour
1 cup buttermilk
3 whole eggs
2 tablespoons strong Dijon-style mustard
1 teaspoon ground cumin
½ teaspoon freshly grated nutmeg
1 teaspoon salt
½ teaspoon freshly ground pepper
8 hard-cooked eggs, sliced

1. Make the pastry: In the bowl of a food processor, combine the chilled butter, flour, salt, egg yolks and cream cheese. (Depending on the size of your work bowl, you might want to divide the ingredients in half.) Process for 10 seconds, or until the mixture resembles oatmeal. Add the ice water, 1 tablespoon at a time, and process just until the dough forms a ball. Divide the pastry in half and press into 2 equal disks. Flour them lightly, wrap in plastic and refrigerate for at least 2 hours.

2. Meanwhile, make the filling: In a large skillet, melt 2 tablespoons of the butter in the oil over low heat. Add the onions and garlic and sauté, stirring occasionally, until softened but not

browned, about 10 minutes. Add the sausage and cook until lightly browned, 15 minutes longer. Set aside.

3. Meanwhile, in a small saucepan, melt the remaining 2 tablespoons butter over moderate heat. Add the flour and cook, stirring constantly, until the mixture turns golden, about 3 minutes. Immediately remove from the heat and whisk in the buttermilk. Return to moderate heat and cook, stirring constantly, until the sauce is thick and smooth, about 5 minutes. Add 2 of the whole eggs and beat rapidly until blended. Add the mustard, cumin, nutmeg and salt and pepper and cook for 3 minutes.

4. Transfer the sauce to a large bowl. Add the reserved onion and sausage mixture and the hard-cooked eggs. Fold gently to mix. Set the filling aside to cool.

5. Preheat the oven to 350°. Roll out one of the pastry disks. Arrange the pastry in a 9-inch tart pan with a removable bottom. Trim the edges, to a ½-inch overhang. Spoon the filling into the pastry.

6. Roll out the remaining pastry disk. Using a pastry brush, moisten the overhanging ½-inch bottom edge with water. Drape the top crust over a rolling pin and unroll it over the filling. Seal the two crusts together by pressing down with your fingertips. Trim away the excess dough and crimp the edges with the tines of a fork. (Make sure the top crust does not extend beyond the circumference of the tart pan.) Reserve any scraps of dough.

7. Beat the remaining whole egg. Brush lightly over the top crust. Cut a steam vent in the top of the pastry. If desired, cut leaf shapes from the reserved scraps and use to decorate the pie. Brush the leaves with more of the beaten egg.

8. Place the tart pan on a cookie sheet and bake for 30 minutes. Let rest on a rack for 15 minutes before loosening and removing the rim. Serve hot or at room temperature.

Egg Charlotte

8 TO 10 SERVINGS

1½ cups (3 sticks) unsalted butter, clarified
16 slices firm-textured white bread
18 eggs
1½ teaspoons dried dillweed
2 teaspoons salt
¾ teaspoon freshly ground pepper
1 small onion, minced
¾ pound smoked fish (such as trout or whitefish)—skinned, boned and flaked
1 package (10 ounces) frozen spinach—cooked, squeezed dry and coarsely chopped
2 tablespoons fresh lemon juice
2 tablespoons olive oil
4 large tomatoes—peeled, seeded and coarsely chopped
Pinch of sugar
1 package (8 ounces) cream cheese, cut into bits
Tomato-Horseradish Sauce (p. 223)

1. Preheat the oven to 400°. Butter the bottom of a 9-inch springform pan. Line it with an 11-inch circle of aluminum foil to reach about 1 inch up the sides of the pan. Butter the foil.

2. Brush clarified butter on both sides of the bread slices. Line the sides of the pan with slightly overlapping slices of bread. Cut triangles of bread and line the bottom of the pan, overlapping as necessary. Reserve any remaining slices and scraps of the bread.

3. Place the pan in the oven and bake for 20 minutes, until the bread is lightly toasted. (If any of the slices collapse toward the center, reposition after baking.)

4. In a medium bowl, beat together 5 of the eggs with ½ teaspoon of the dill, ½ teaspoon of the salt and ¼ teaspoon of the pepper.

5. In a medium skillet, warm 2 tablespoons of the clarified butter over moderately high heat. Pour in the egg mixture and cook, stirring, until scrambled but still quite custardy. Remove from the heat and spread the scrambled eggs in an even layer over the bottom of the bread-lined pan.

6. In a large skillet, warm 2 tablespoons of the clarified butter over moderate heat. Add the onion and sauté until it is translucent but still somewhat firm, about 5 minutes. Add the smoked fish, spinach and lemon juice and cook, stirring constantly, for 5 minutes. Remove from the heat, add 1 of the remaining eggs and beat until blended. Distribute this mixture evenly over the layer of eggs in the cake pan.

7. Repeat Steps 4 and 5, using 6 eggs and spreading the scrambled eggs on top of the fish layer.

8. In a large skillet, warm the oil over moderate heat. Add the tomatoes to the skillet. Cook slowly for 15 minutes. Add the sugar and ½ teaspoon of the salt. Increase the heat to high and cook, stirring constantly, for 5 minutes, until thick. Stir in the cream cheese. Pour the mixture on top of the eggs.

9. Repeat Steps 4 and 5, using the remaining 6 eggs and spreading the scrambled eggs on top of the tomatoes.

10. Cover the top of the eggs with the reserved bread slices. Drizzle any remaining butter over the bread. Bake for 30 minutes.

11. Remove the charlotte to a rack and let stand for 15 minutes. Invert onto a large round platter and gently remove the springform. Peel off the foil. **(The recipe can be prepared up to 2 hours ahead. Reheat in a 350° oven for 10 to 15 minutes before serving.)**

12. The charlotte can be eaten hot, warm or at room temperature. To serve, cut into wedges. Pass the Tomato-Horseradish Sauce separately.

Fromage Blanc

MAKES ABOUT 1¾ CUPS

1 container (15 ounces) part-skim ricotta cheese
¼ cup plain yogurt
¼ teaspoon salt

Combine the ricotta, yogurt and salt in a blender. Blend until very smooth with no trace of graininess. Scrape into a container, cover tightly and refrigerate until ready to use. (If allowed to ripen for 12 hours, the flavor will become fuller and more balanced.)

Onion and Cheese Quiche

🍷 **F&W Beverage Suggestion:** 1983 Beaujolais-Villages

8 SERVINGS

Pastry Shell:
1½ cups all-purpose flour
¼ teaspoon salt
1 stick (¼ pound) cold unsalted butter, cut into small bits
1 egg yolk
4 tablespoons ice water

Filling:
2 to 3 tablespoons unsalted butter
1 pound onions, thinly sliced
4 ounces Gruyère or Swiss cheese, finely grated (about 1¼ cups)
3 egg yolks
2 teaspoons Dijon-style mustard
¼ teaspoon salt
Pinch of white pepper
1 cup heavy cream

1. Make the pastry shell: In a medium bowl, combine the flour and salt. Cut in the butter until the mixture resembles coarse meal. Mix together the egg yolk and ice water. Sprinkle over the flour mixture, tossing with a fork to moisten all the flour. Gather the dough loosely into a ball. If there are dry bits that do not adhere easily, sprinkle with a few extra drops of water. Turn out the dough onto a lightly floured surface and knead gently for about 30 seconds to complete the blending. Pat the dough into a 6-inch disk, wrap tightly in plastic wrap and refrigerate for at least 1 hour, or overnight.

2. On a lightly floured surface, roll out the dough into a large circle at least 12 inches in diameter and about ⅛ inch thick. Transfer the pastry to a 9-inch tart pan, about 1 inch high, with a removable bottom. Ease the pastry into the pan, fitting it against the bottom and sides without stretching the dough. Trim the edges to form an even ½-inch overhang.

Fold down this extra dough, pressing it into the sides with your finger.

3. Preheat the oven to 375°. Prick the pastry all over with a fork. Line the shell with a sheet of parchment paper or aluminum foil and fill with dried beans or pie weights. Bake the pastry shell in the middle of the oven for about 15 minutes, until the liner peels away easily and the dough has lost its moist appearance. Remove the liner and weights. Return the pastry shell to the oven and bake for about 20 minutes longer, until the pastry is golden and completely cooked. **(The recipe can be prepared ahead to this point.)**

4. Meanwhile, prepare the filling: In a large heavy skillet, melt 2 tablespoons butter. Add the onions, cover and cook over moderately low heat, stirring occasionally, for 40 minutes; if the onions begin to stick, add another tablespoon of butter. Uncover the skillet and continue to cook, stirring frequently, until the onions are a deep brown but still moist, 15 to 20 minutes. **(The filling can be prepared ahead to this point.)**

5. Assemble and bake the quiche: Preheat the oven to 325°. Sprinkle the bottom of the pastry with ¾ cup of the grated cheese. In a small bowl, whisk together the egg yolks, mustard, salt and pepper until blended. Whisk in the cream. Pour half of this mixture over the cheese in the pastry shell. Cover evenly with the browned onions. Sprinkle on the remaining cheese and pour the remaining custard evenly over the surface.

6. Place the tart on a baking sheet and bake in the middle of the oven for about 30 minutes, until the filling is bubbling and golden brown. Serve warm or at room temperature.

Montrachet Cheesecake

Serve this mild, elegant goat cheese pie as part of the buffet or as a separate cheese course. Sliced papaya or other sweet fruit is an excellent accompaniment.

16 TO 20 SERVINGS

1½ cups all-purpose flour
⅛ teaspoon salt
⅛ teaspoon sugar
6 tablespoons unsalted butter
2 tablespoons solid vegetable shortening
2 to 3 tablespoons cold water
1 log (11 ounces) Montrachet blanc goat cheese, at room temperature
2 packages (8 ounces each) cream cheese, at room temperature
3 eggs
½ teaspoon chopped fresh rosemary or ⅛ teaspoon dried, crumbled
¾ cup (¼ pound) pine nuts, lightly toasted

1. In a large bowl, combine the flour, salt and sugar. Cut in the butter and shortening until the mixture is the consistency of coarse meal. Add 2 tablespoons of the cold water and toss to moisten the flour. Gather the pastry into a ball. If any flour doesn't adhere, sprinkle with up to 1 tablespoon more water. Flatten into a 6-inch disk, wrap well and refrigerate for at least 1 hour, or overnight.

2. Roll out the pastry to a thin round 14 inches in diameter. Place it in an 11- to 12-inch tart pan with a removable bottom, fitting the pastry against the sides and trimming any overhanging edges. Refrigerate the pastry-lined pan for at least 30 minutes. Preheat the oven to 350°.

3. Cover the pastry with parchment paper or foil and fill with pie weights or dried beans. Bake in a 350° oven for 30 minutes, or until golden around the sides. Remove the weights and liner and

bake for about 5 minutes longer, until the center is dry.

4. Meanwhile, prepare the pie filling. Beat together the Montrachet and cream cheeses until light and fluffy. Beat in the eggs, one at a time; then blend in the rosemary.

5. Fill the warm pie shell with the cheese mixture. Sprinkle the pine nuts over the top. Return the pie to the 350° oven and bake for 25 minutes, until set. Let cool to room temperature. Cut into thin wedges to serve.

Feta Cheese Tart

Thinly sliced, this flavorful cheese pie is good served as an appetizer with ripe olives. Cut into more generous wedges, it works well as a light entrée accompanied with a hearty green salad.

MAKES ONE 9-INCH PIE

3 tablespoons unsalted butter
3 tablespoons sesame seeds
½ cup plus 1 tablespoon finely crushed rye cracker crumbs, made from all-rye crackers, such as Finn Crisp
6 ounces (1 cup lightly packed) feta cheese, patted dry and crumbled
6 ounces cream cheese, at room temperature, cut into small pieces
2 eggs, at room temperature
1 tablespoon minced fresh basil or 1½ teaspoons dried
2 teaspoons minced fresh rosemary or ¾ teaspoon dried
½ teaspoon freshly ground pepper
½ cup sour cream

1. Preheat the oven to 325°. In a small heavy saucepan, melt the butter over low heat. Add the sesame seeds and sauté, stirring, until lightly browned, about 2 minutes. Remove from the heat and stir in the rye crumbs.

2. Pat the crumbs into a 9-inch pie pan. Place another 9-inch pie pan on top of the crumbs and press down to pack into a firm crust.

3. In a mixer bowl, beat the feta cheese and cream cheese until smooth and light. Beat in the eggs, one at a time. Beat

in the basil, rosemary, pepper and sour cream until blended. Pour into the pie crust and smooth the top.

4. Make a water bath by placing the pie pan inside a larger pan and pouring in enough water to reach halfway up the sides of the pie pan. Bake for 1 hour, until a knife inserted near the center emerges clean. Serve warm or at room temperature.

Melted Cheddar on Basil Toast

This quick open-faced sandwich lends itself to many variations. Try adding a slice of shredded boiled ham to the cheese or place thin slices of tomato on the toast and spread the cheese on top.

1 SERVING

1 medium garlic clove, cut in half
2 large slices coarse peasant bread, toasted
2 teaspoons Basil Preserved in Oil (p. 224)
2 ounces Cheddar cheese, grated or thinly sliced (about ½ cup)
¼ teaspoon coarsely ground pepper

1. Rub the garlic over 1 side of each toast slice. Spread 1 teaspoon of the basil over each slice.

2. In a small skillet or saucepan, preferably nonstick, melt the cheese over very low heat until just creamy, about 2 minutes (do not raise the heat or the cheese will become oily and tough). Spread the cheese evenly over the toast slices. Sprinkle with the pepper and serve hot.

Open-Faced Zucchini Sandwiches

These delicious, savory vegetable sandwiches are quick and easy to make. They're just right for a light lunch or a hearty snack.

2 TO 4 SERVINGS

2 individual hero rolls (about 6 ounces each), split and hollowed out
6 tablespoons fruity olive oil
½ teaspoon freshly ground pepper
¾ teaspoon thyme
2 medium zucchini (about 1 pound), thinly sliced
2 medium tomatoes—peeled, seeded and chopped—or ¾ cup drained chopped canned tomatoes (16-ounce can)
2 garlic cloves, minced
¼ teaspoon salt
1 tablespoon fresh lemon juice
1 tablespoon unsalted butter
2 tablespoons freshly grated Parmesan cheese

1. Preheat the oven to 400°. Place the roll halves, cut-side up, on a baking sheet. Brush each half with 1 tablespoon of the olive oil and sprinkle with the pepper and thyme. Bake for 5 to 6 minutes until lightly toasted. Leave the oven on.

2. Meanwhile, in a large heavy skillet, heat the remaining 2 tablespoons oil. Add the zucchini and sauté, stirring, for 2 minutes. Add the tomatoes, garlic and salt and sauté for 2 minutes longer. With a slotted spoon, transfer the mixture to a bowl.

3. Add the lemon juice to the juices remaining in the skillet and boil over high heat until reduced to 2 tablespoons, about 2 minutes. Remove from the heat and swirl in the butter.

4. Brush the cut sides of the toasted rolls with the sauce. Mound the zucchini-tomato mixture on each roll. Sprinkle with the Parmesan and bake until the cheese melts, 3 to 4 minutes. Serve warm.

Chicken Salad Sandwiches with Anchovies and Eggs

10 SMALL SANDWICHES

1 cup finely chopped cooked chicken (about ½ pound)
4 hard-cooked eggs, finely chopped
1 can (2 ounces) flat anchovy fillets in olive oil, drained and chopped
1 small onion, grated
¼ teaspoon freshly ground pepper
⅓ cup mayonnaise, preferably homemade (p. 221)
Salt
20 thin slices of firm white or whole wheat sandwich bread, crusts removed
7 tablespoons unsalted butter, at room temperature
¼ cup minced fresh parsley

1. In a medium bowl, combine the chicken, eggs, anchovies, onion and pepper. Mix in the mayonnaise. Taste for salt and add if necessary, though the saltiness of the anchovies should be enough.

2. Spread each slice of the bread with about 1 teaspoon of the butter. Then spread 3 tablespoons of the chicken filling evenly over 10 slices of the bread. Mound about 1 teaspoon of the parsley over the center of the chicken filling. Place the remaining 10 bread slices, buttered-side down, over the filling and cut the sandwiches diagonally in half.

3. Dip a clean kitchen towel or several layers of paper towels in cold water and wring out. Stack the sandwiches and wrap them tightly in the damp cloth. Refrigerate until serving time and serve cold. (**These can be made up to 6 hours ahead of time and kept this way.** If making further ahead, wrap the sandwiches in plastic wrap.)

Sausage and Red Pepper Sandwiches

4 SANDWICHES

2 tablespoons olive oil
1 large onion, halved lengthwise and cut into thin slivers
1 large red or green bell pepper, cut into ¼-inch strips
4 sweet Italian sausages with fennel seeds (about 1 pound)
½ teaspoon oregano, crumbled
½ teaspoon salt
4 hero rolls, 5 to 6 inches long, or a loaf of Italian bread, cut into 5-inch lengths and split

1. In a large heavy skillet, warm the olive oil over moderate heat. Add the onion and pepper and sauté until soft and lightly browned, about 10 minutes. Remove with a slotted spoon and set aside; reduce the heat to low.

2. Prick the sausages all over with a fork. Place the sausages in the skillet and cook, turning frequently, until they are well browned, about 10 minutes. Tilt the pan and pour off the fat.

3. Return the onion and pepper to the skillet and add the oregano, salt and 1 tablespoon of water. Cover and simmer over low heat, until the sausages are cooked through, about 10 minutes.

4. Meanwhile, preheat the oven to 350°. Place the rolls on a baking sheet and warm until hot throughout, 3 to 5 minutes.

5. Remove the sausages with tongs and cut each one lengthwise into 6 long thin slices. Arrange over the bottom of each roll and top with one-quarter of the pepper and onion mixture. Add the tops; cut in half on the diagonal and serve hot.

Zucchini Frittata Sandwiches

A tasty zucchini frittata (open-faced omelet) is wedged between slices of garlic toast to make a comforting sandwich for lunch or brunch.

4 SANDWICHES

3 tablespoons olive oil
1 medium onion, coarsely chopped
2 garlic cloves
2 small zucchini (about 6 inches long), cut into ¼-inch slices
½ teaspoon basil
¼ teaspoon oregano
¼ teaspoon salt
¼ teaspoon freshly ground pepper
3 eggs
½ cup freshly grated Parmesan cheese
4 hero rolls, 5 to 6 inches long, or a loaf of Italian bread, cut into 5-inch lengths and split
4 tablespoons unsalted butter, at room temperature

1. In a medium (8-inch) ovenproof skillet, warm the oil over moderate heat. Add the onion and sauté until soft and lightly colored, 5 to 7 minutes. Finely mince one of the garlic cloves and add it to the skillet along with the zucchini, basil, oregano, salt and pepper. Sauté until the zucchini is just tender, about 5 minutes; if the onions begin to brown too much, reduce the heat to low as the zucchini cooks.

2. Preheat the oven to 350°. In a medium bowl, whisk the eggs until evenly blended. Whisk in the Parmesan cheese. Add the egg mixture to the skillet and reduce the heat to very low. Without stirring, cook until the omelet is set but the top is still runny, about 15 minutes. Place in the oven and bake until completely set, 8 to 10 minutes.

3. Meanwhile, spread each roll with 1 tablespoon of the butter using half for each cut side of bread. Place the halves on a baking sheet and lightly toast in the upper portion of the oven, about 5 minutes. Cut the remaining garlic clove in half and rub the cut side of each toasted roll with the pieces.

4. Slide the frittata onto a plate. Slicing from the top to the bottom of the round,
cut about ⅓ of the left side of the omelet away. Turn the plate so that the straight edge is at the top, and slice the remaining portion into 3 equal pieces. Place the 4 frittata pieces on the rolls (trim to evenly distribute as needed) and top with the corresponding tops. Cut in half lengthwise on the diagonal to make 2 long wedges and serve hot.

Mushroom and Mozzarella Sandwiches

These meltingly tender sandwiches can be served open-face style, if you wish, by eliminating the top portion of each roll. To simulate the creamy texture of the southern Italian buffalo-milk mozzarella cheese, domestic mozzarella is marinated in olive oil before cooking.

4 SANDWICHES

1 cup (4 ounces) coarsely shredded whole-milk mozzarella cheese
1 tablespoon olive oil
4 round sandwich rolls (4- to 4½-inch diameter), split
3 tablespoons unsalted butter
8 large mushrooms, cut into ¼-inch slices
½ teaspoon salt
¼ teaspoon freshly ground pepper

1. Toss the cheese and olive oil together in a small bowl and let the cheese marinate for 15 minutes.

2. Preheat the oven to 400°. Place the rolls, cut-side up, on a baking sheet. Set aside.

3. In a medium skillet, melt the butter over moderate heat. Add the mushroom slices, increase the heat to moderately high and sauté until just cooked through, about 2 minutes.

4. Arrange one-quarter of the mushrooms over each of the four bottom portions of the rolls. Top each with one-quarter of the cheese. Season with the salt and pepper. Bake in the upper third of the oven until the sandwiches are hot and the cheese has melted, about 7 minutes. Add the toasted tops, if you are using them, and serve hot.

Grilled Cheese and Green Olive Sandwiches

Although these are best when made with Italian Fontina cheese, any good melting cheese such as Port Salut, Muenster or Monterey Jack will work very well. In Italy these sandwiches are grilled with a decorative iron, which leaves a geometric design on the bread. Here, you can use an inexpensive metal skewer.

4 SANDWICHES

8 thin slices firm white or whole wheat sandwich bread, crusts removed
8 teaspoons mayonnaise, preferably homemade (p. 221)
1 cup (4 ounces) coarsely shredded Fontina or other melting cheese
8 to 10 Italian green brine-cured olives, pitted and chopped
8 teaspoons unsalted butter

1. Spread each slice of bread with 1 teaspoon of the mayonnaise.

2. Top each of 4 slices of the bread with one-quarter of the cheese. Mound one-quarter of the chopped olives onto the center over the cheese and top with the remaining bread, mayonnaise-side down.

3. In a heavy medium skillet, melt 2 teaspoons of the butter over moderately low heat. Place two sandwiches in the pan and cook until light golden brown, 2 to 3 minutes. Add 2 more teaspoons of butter to the pan, turn the sandwiches with a spatula and cook until golden brown, 2 to 3 minutes. Transfer to a platter. Repeat with the 2 remaining sandwiches.

VEGETABLES

Dilled Beets and Cucumbers

8 SERVINGS

4 bunches of small beets (about 20), with their leafy tops
4 cucumbers—peeled, halved lengthwise and seeded
4 tablespoons unsalted butter
2 tablespoons white wine vinegar
2 tablespoons minced fresh dill or 2 teaspoons dried dill weed
½ teaspoon salt
¼ teaspoon freshly ground pepper

1. Preheat the oven to 350°. Cut off the leafy beet tops (reserving the greens), leaving about 2 inches of the stem intact. Wrap the beets in aluminum foil and bake for about 25 minutes, or until the beets are tender when pierced with a knife. Unwrap and let stand until cool enough to handle. Peel off the skins. Quarter the beets.

2. Pick out about 12 unblemished beet leaves and wash and dry them; discard the remainder or reserve for another use. Working from the outside edge in, arrange the leaves on a large serving platter.

3. Cut the cucumbers crosswise in half. Trim the corners to form long ovals.

4. In a large heavy skillet, melt 2 tablespoons of the butter over moderately high heat until sizzling. Add the beets and cook until they are heated through, 2 to 3 minutes. Add 1 tablespoon of the vinegar, 1 tablespoon of the dill, ¼ teaspoon of the salt and ⅛ teaspoon of the pepper and toss until coated. Mound the beets in the center of the platter.

5. In another large skillet, melt the remaining 2 tablespoons butter over moderately high heat. Add the cucumbers and cook until heated through, 2 to 3 minutes. Add the remaining 1 tablespoon vinegar, 1 tablespoon dill, ¼ teaspoon salt and ⅛ teaspoon pepper and toss until coated. Arrange the cucumbers around the beets. Serve warm.

Black-Eyed Peas with Sausage

It is a tradition among many families to eat stewed black-eyed peas on New Year's Day for good luck.

6 SERVINGS

¼ pound sweet Italian sausage, cut into ½-inch rounds
¼ pound hot Italian sausage, cut into ½-inch rounds
2 cans (16 ounces each) black-eyed peas, drained and rinsed
¼ cup fresh lemon juice
5 tablespoons tomato paste (see Note)
¼ cup minced celery
¼ cup minced fresh parsley
2 tablespoons minced onion

1. In a large heavy skillet, cook the sweet sausage and hot sausage over moderate heat, stirring occasionally, until well browned, about 10 minutes. Drain on paper towels.

2. In a large noncorrodible saucepan, combine the black-eyed peas, lemon juice and tomato paste with 1¼ cups of water. Bring to a boil over moderately high heat. Add the sausages and return to a boil.

3. Before serving, stir in the celery, parsley and onion. (If the consistency is too thick, add more water.) Serve hot in soup plates, alone or over cooked rice.

NOTE: For a special taste treat, substitute ⅔ cup (¼ pound) finely chopped sun-dried tomatoes for the tomato paste.

Broccoli Spears with Lemon-Butter Sauce

8 SERVINGS

2 bunches of broccoli
4 tablespoons unsalted butter
1 tablespoon fresh lemon juice
½ teaspoon salt
¼ teaspoon freshly ground pepper

1. Separate the broccoli into spears. Cut off the bottom inch or so and peel the stalks.

2. Steam the broccoli until crisp-tender, 8 to 10 minutes.

3. Meanwhile, in a small saucepan, warm the butter, lemon juice, salt and pepper over moderate heat, stirring, until the butter melts. Transfer the broccoli to a serving bowl and pour the hot sauce over the broccoli.

Cassis-Glazed Carrots

For this recipe, the carrots may be cooked several hours ahead. Bring them to room temperature before glazing and broiling. The cassis syrup may also be prepared ahead and stored, covered, in the refrigerator.

8 SERVINGS

16 medium carrots, peeled
3 tablespoons plus a pinch of sugar
¾ cup crème de cassis
3 tablespoons red wine vinegar
4 scallions, cut into 1½-inch-long julienne strips

1. In a large heavy saucepan of boiling salted water, cook the whole carrots with the pinch of sugar until tender but still firm, about 20 minutes. Immediately drain and rinse under cold running water until cool. Halve the carrots lengthwise and arrange flat-side up on a broiler pan.

2. Preheat the broiler. In a medium, noncorrodible saucepan, combine the 3 tablespoons of sugar, the cassis and the vinegar. Bring to a boil over high heat, stirring to dissolve the sugar. Boil until thick and syrupy, 3 to 5 minutes.

3. Brush the carrots heavily with the cassis syrup. Broil 4 inches from the heat, until caramelized and brown, 4 to 5 minutes. Transfer the carrots to a platter and sprinkle the scallions on top. Serve hot or at room temperature.

Carrots Glazed with Lime Butter

This simple recipe yields a refreshing vegetable side dish because the lime perfumes the sweetness of the carrots.

4 SERVINGS

1 pound carrots (about 8 medium)
2 tablespoons sugar
½ teaspoon salt
3 tablespoons unsalted butter, sliced
2 tablespoons fresh lime juice

1. Cut the carrots crosswise on the diagonal into ¼-inch slices. In a medium saucepan, bring the carrots and 4 cups of cold water to a boil over high heat and boil for 3 minutes; drain.

2. Return the carrot slices to the dry pan. Add 1 cup of water, the sugar and the salt. Bring to a boil over moderate heat and cook until the carrots are just tender and the liquid has reduced to 1 to 2 tablespoons, about 8 minutes. Stir in the butter and lime juice and serve hot.

Ginger-Glazed Carrots and Turnips

This pretty, orange and white vegetable side dish goes well with robust meat, poultry and fish entrées.

2 SERVINGS

1 white turnip, peeled and cut into 2-inch julienne strips
2 carrots, peeled and cut into 2-inch julienne strips
1½ tablespoons unsalted butter
1 small garlic clove, minced

1 teaspoon minced fresh gingerroot
1 teaspoon brown sugar
Salt and freshly ground white pepper
2 teaspoons minced fresh parsley, for garnish

1. Bring a medium saucepan of salted water to a boil over high heat. Add the turnip and cook for 2 minutes. Add the carrots and continue cooking until the vegetables are cooked but still firm to the bite, about 2½ minutes longer. Drain, rinse under cold running water until cool and drain again.

2. In a large heavy skillet, melt the butter over moderately high heat. Add the garlic and ginger and cook, stirring, for 30 seconds. Add the turnip and carrots and cook until heated through, 1 to 2 minutes. Sprinkle with the brown sugar and stir until the vegetables are lightly glazed. Season with salt and pepper to taste. Sprinkle with the parsley and serve.

Carrot and Cauliflower Loaf

Inspired by a vegetable pâté at a two-star restaurant in Lyons, Léon de Lyon, this makes a lovely room temperature appetizer, but an equally lovely side vegetable with roasted meat.

6 TO 8 SERVINGS

1 head of cauliflower (about 2 pounds), broken into 1-inch florets
1½ pounds carrots, cut into ¼-inch slices
4 eggs
⅔ cup heavy cream, preferably not ultrapasteurized
½ teaspoon salt
2 pinches of cayenne pepper
2 pinches of freshly ground white pepper

1. In a kettle, bring 6 quarts of salted water to a boil.

2. Add the cauliflower and cook until very tender, 15 to 20 minutes. Remove

with a slotted spoon and transfer to a sieve. Let drain for at least 10 minutes.

3. Meanwhile, return the water to a boil and add the carrots. Boil until tender, about 15 minutes. Drain them in a separate sieve.

4. Puree each vegetable separately in a food processor or food mill; then pass each through a fine-mesh sieve. Let the vegetables drain again in separate sieves for about 15 minutes.

5. With an electric mixer, beat 2 eggs, ⅓ cup cream, ¼ teaspoon salt and a pinch of cayenne and white pepper into each puree.

6. Preheat the oven to 400°. Butter a 4- to 6-cup loaf pan. First pour in the carrot puree, then the cauliflower.

7. Place the loaf pan in a larger pan filled with hot water that reaches about halfway up the sides of the pan. Bake in the middle of the oven for 1 hour, or until a cake tester comes out clean.

8. Remove the loaf pan from the water bath and let rest for about 1 hour, until lukewarm, before unmolding onto a platter. (Water may ooze out; just wipe dry with paper towels.)

9. Gently cut into ½-inch slices and serve lukewarm or at room temperature.

Tibetan Cauliflower in Sesame Sauce

4 SERVINGS

1 tablespoon tahini (sesame paste)*
1 teaspoon soy sauce
½ teaspoon salt
¼ teaspoon freshly ground pepper
1 tablespoon corn or peanut oil
1 small onion, thinly sliced
½ large head of cauliflower, cut into 1-inch florets
*Available at health food stores and Oriental markets

1. In a small bowl, stir together the tahini, soy sauce, salt and pepper until well blended. Set the sauce aside.

2. In a large skillet, heat the oil. Add the onion and sauté over moderate heat, stirring occasionally, until it begins to brown, about 3 minutes.

3. Add the cauliflower and stir-fry for 3 minutes. Add the tahini sauce and toss to coat.

4. Reduce the heat to low, cover and cook until the cauliflower is tender but still slightly resistant to the bite, about 10 minutes.

Justine's Celery Root and Pear Puree

This dish would make a delightful accompaniment to a pork roast or braised meat.

8 SERVINGS

2 lemons
2 pounds celery root (celeriac)
½ teaspoon sugar
2 ripe pears
12 tablespoons (1½ sticks) unsalted butter, softened
½ cup minced shallots
3 to 5 tablespoons heavy cream
½ teaspoon salt
¼ teaspoon freshly ground white pepper
Pinch of nutmeg

1. Fill a medium bowl with cold water. Add the juice from the lemons. Peel the celery root and cut into ½-inch dice. Immediately place in the acidulated water to prevent discoloration.

2. Bring a large pot of salted water to a boil and add the sugar. With a slotted spoon, remove the celery root from the acidulated water and add to the boiling water (reserve the acidulated water). Cover partially and cook over moderately high heat until tender but not mushy, 5 to 8 minutes. Drain and set aside.

3. Meanwhile, peel and core the pears. Cut into ½-inch dice and hold in the reserved acidulated water until ready to use them.

4. In a medium skillet, melt 2 tablespoons of the butter over low heat. Add the shallots and cook, covered, until translucent, about 5 minutes.

5. Place the celery root in a food processor or blender and puree briefly. Drain the pears and add to the celery root. Scrape in the shallots with their butter and puree until smooth.

6. In a small heavy saucepan, cook 6 tablespoons of the butter over moderate heat until golden brown and faintly nut-scented, about 3 minutes. (Be careful not to burn the butter.) Immediately add to the puree and blend well. Pass through a fine-mesh sieve for finer texture.

7. In a large heavy saucepan, combine the puree and 3 tablespoons of the cream. Cook, stirring, over low heat, until warm. Season with the salt, pepper and nutmeg. Stir in the remaining 4 tablespoons of butter, 1 tablespoon at a time. If not serving immediately, hold in the top of a double boiler for up to 1 hour. Add the additional 2 tablespoons heavy cream as needed if the puree thickens too much.

Gratin of Eggplant Caviar

In Provence, a poor man's caviar is a puree of eggplants, beaten with egg yolks and thickened with olive oil as for a mayonnnaise. The "caviar" cooked with Gruyère and Parmesan cheeses makes a delicious gratin and goes well with poached fish or a broiled steak. This can be prepared a day ahead of time.

6 SERVINGS

3½ to 4 pounds medium eggplants (about 3), unpeeled
2 large garlic cloves, cut in slivers
½ teaspoon thyme
3 egg yolks
⅓ cup plus 1 teaspoon light-scented olive oil
⅓ cup freshly grated Gruyère cheese (1½ ounces)
½ teaspoon salt
Pinch of cayenne pepper
2 tablespoons freshly grated Parmesan cheese

1. Preheat the oven to 400°. Cut several incisions in each eggplant. Dip the garlic slivers in the thyme and bury the garlic slivers in the eggplant cuts.

2. Place the eggplants on a jelly roll pan and bake in the middle of the oven, turning 2 or 3 times, until the eggplants are soft to the touch, 30 to 60 minutes, depending on the thickness of the eggplants.

3. Peel the cooked eggplants, discarding the stems and peels. Puree the eggplant in a food processor for 1 minute or pass through the fine disk of a food mill.

4. Force the puree through a fine-mesh sieve to discard the seeds (if you have a food mill with a very fine blade, this step may not be necessary).

5. Transfer the puree to a large mixer bowl. Beat in the egg yolks at medium speed. Slowly drizzle in ⅓ cup of the olive oil. Stir in the Gruyère, salt and cayenne.

6. Pour the eggplant mixture into a lightly buttered 1½-quart baking dish.

Sprinkle ½ teaspoon oil over the surface to prevent it from drying out.

7. Bake for 20 minutes. Sprinkle the Parmesan cheese and remaining ½ teaspoon oil over the top. Continue to bake for 10 to 15 minutes, until lightly browned. (**The recipe can be made ahead of time and reheated in a 350° oven for 10 to 15 minutes.**)

Roasted Eggplant with Basil

Try this recipe with baby or Oriental eggplant if you can get it, for it tends to be less bitter than ordinary eggplant. You will need four for this recipe.

4 SERVINGS

1 medium eggplant
1 tablespoon plus ½ teaspoon coarse (kosher) salt
2 tablespoons basil oil, drained from Basil Preserved in Oil
1 tablespoon Basil Preserved in Oil (p. 224)
¼ teaspoon freshly ground pepper

1. Cut the eggplant into lengthwise slices about ½ inch thick and score with a small sharp knife in a crosshatch pattern. Sprinkle the slices with 1 tablespoon of the salt, then drain on a rack or in a large colander for 20 minutes.

2. Rinse the eggplant; pat dry. Heat a heavy, well-seasoned skillet, preferably cast iron, over high heat until a drop of water in the pan evaporates on contact. Lightly brush the eggplant on both sides with 4 teaspoons of the oil. Place in the skillet and cook until slightly charred, 4 to 5 minutes; turn over and cook until the eggplant is soft, 2 to 3 minutes. Remove to a serving plate.

3. Combine the remaining 2 teaspoons oil with the basil, the remaining ½ teaspoon salt and the pepper. Brush over the cut sides of the eggplant. Serve warm or at room temperature.

Fall Kale with Pork Stock and Red Onion

4 SERVINGS

¾ pound "streak of lean" or slab bacon in one piece, rinsed
3 pounds kale, washed and picked over, stems removed
Salt and freshly ground pepper
1 medium red onion, thinly sliced

1. Slice into the bacon at 1-inch intervals without cutting all the way through. Put the bacon in a 2-quart saucepan filled three-quarters of the way with cold water. Cook, covered, over moderate heat for 1 hour. Discard the bacon; reserve the stock.

2. Add the kale to the hot stock, packing it in tightly; it will shrink considerably. Cook uncovered over moderately high heat until tender, about 20 minutes; drain. Season with salt and pepper to taste. Serve the kale garnished with the onion slices.

Creole Leeks Vinaigrette

4 SERVINGS

8 medium leeks (white and tender green)
3 tablespoons white wine vinegar
1 teaspoon Creole or Dijon-style mustard
1 teaspoon munced fresh dill or ½ teaspoon dried dillweed
½ teaspoon paprika
¼ teaspoon sugar
1 cup plus 2 tablespoons olive oil or a combination of olive and other vegetable oil
¼ to ½ teaspoon cayenne pepper, or more to taste
Salt and coarsely ground black pepper

1. Split the leeks in half lengthwise. Soak and rinse well under cold running water to remove all grit.

2. Heat a deep skillet or large shallow saucepan of water to boiling. Blanch the leeks for 1 minute; remove and plunge them into a bowl of cold water to set the green color. Return the leeks to the boiling water and cook about 1½ minutes, until the base is barely tender when tested with the tip of a knife. Rinse under cold water, drain well and pat dry. Arrange the leeks in a serving dish.

3. In a small bowl, mix the vinegar, mustard, dill, paprika and sugar until blended. Gradually, whisk in the oil about ½ tablespoon at a time. Season with the cayenne and salt and black pepper to taste. Drizzle the vinaigrette over the leeks and serve at room temperature or slightly chilled.

Green Lentils

Be sure to use a very flavorful chicken stock when cooking these lentils. Use any leftovers the next day in a salad, dressed lightly with wine vinegar.

6 VERY GENEROUS SERVINGS

1 pound lentils, rinsed and picked over to remove any grit
Boiling water
1 medium onion, coarsely chopped
2 large shallots, coarsely chopped
About 4 cups boiling, homemade, extra-strength chicken stock
Salt and freshly ground pepper
2 tablespoons chopped fresh parsley, for garnish

1. Place the lentils in a large heatproof bowl. Add boiling water to cover by about 1 inch and set aside to soak for 1½ hours.

2. Drain the lentils and transfer them to a heavy medium saucepan. Add the onion, shallots and enough boiling chicken stock just to cover. Simmer over moderately low heat for 20 minutes, until almost all of the liquid has been absorbed. Check after about 15 minutes and add more stock if the lentils are drying out. Season with salt and pepper to taste and serve warm, garnished with the parsley.

Onions Stuffed with Mushrooms and Spinach

4 SERVINGS

4 large onions (about 2 pounds)
4 tablespoons olive oil
6 ounces fresh mushrooms, cut into ¼-inch dice (about 2 cups)
½ teaspoon basil
1 package (10 ounces) frozen chopped spinach, defrosted and squeezed dry
⅓ cup plus 1 tablespoon bread crumbs
¼ cup chopped parsley
¼ cup heavy cream
¼ cup plus 1 tablespoon dry white wine
¼ teaspoon salt
¼ teaspoon pepper
¾ cup vegetable broth, chicken stock or water
2 tablespoons thinly sliced scallions or chopped parsley, for garnish

1. Trim off the root end from each onion. Remove the peel and cut away about ½ inch from the stem end. Using a teaspoon or melon baller, scoop out and reserve the center portion of each onion, leaving a shell about ¼ inch thick (depending on the thickness of the onion layers, the shells will be 2 to 3 layers thick). Finely chop enough of the center portions to yield ½ cup; discard the remainder or reserve for another use.

2. Bring a large pot of water to a boil over high heat. Add the onion shells; when the water returns to a boil, cook for 5 minutes. Drain the onions upside down.

3. Preheat the oven to 350°. In a medium skillet over moderate heat, warm 3 tablespoons of the olive oil. Add the ½ cup chopped onion and sauté until softened and translucent, about 5 minutes. Add the mushrooms and basil and cook, stirring frequently, until the mushrooms

are soft, about 3 minutes. Remove from the heat and stir in the spinach, ⅓ cup of the bread crumbs, the parsley, cream, 1 tablespoon of the wine and the salt and pepper.

4. Place the onion shells, upright, in a shallow casserole or baking dish just large enough to hold them. Lightly stuff the onions with the spinach-mushroom mixture, mounding it slightly. Pour the broth and the remaining ¼ cup wine into the casserole. Cover loosely with foil and bake in the top third of the oven for 1 hour.

5. Increase the oven temperature to 400°. Uncover the casserole, sprinkle the remaining 1 tablespoon bread crumbs evenly over the tops of the onions and drizzle with the remaining 1 tablespoon oil. Return to the oven and bake until the tops are brown, about 15 minutes.

6. Transfer the onions to a serving plate. Pour the cooking liquid from the casserole into a small saucepan and boil over high heat until reduced to ⅓ cup, about 3 minutes. Pour over the onions and sprinkle the tops with the scallions. Serve hot or at room temperature.

Crispy Onion Rings

The delicate, crunchy coating on these tasty onion rings is created by adding cornstarch to the batter. Prepare the batter at least 1 hour before you plan to fry the onion rings.

4 SERVINGS

⅔ cup all-purpose flour
⅓ cup cornstarch
¼ teaspoon salt
1 cup ice water
Vegetable oil, for deep-frying
½ teaspoon baking soda
2 medium onions, sliced crosswise into ¼-inch-thick rounds and separated into rings

1. Sift the flour and cornstarch into a medium bowl. Add the salt and ice water

and whisk rapidly to form a smooth batter; cover and refrigerate for at least 1 hour.

2. Preheat the oven to 250°. In a wok, deep-fryer or heavy saucepan, heat about 2½ inches of oil to 375°.

3. Remove the batter from the refrigerator and whisk in the baking soda. Coat a few of the onion rings in the batter at one time and drop them, one by one, into the hot oil. Fry until crisp and golden brown, about 1 minute. Remove with tongs or a slotted spoon and drain on paper towels. Lightly sprinkle with salt. Keep warm in the oven while remaining onion rings are fried; serve hot.

Stir-Fried Onions with Pork Sauce

This unusual side dish goes well with a simple steak or egg noodles. It also complements Chinese dishes such as stir-fried shrimp or beef and broccoli. Be sure to start with fresh, firm onions and have all of the ingredients ready before beginning to cook.

4 TO 6 SERVINGS

½ cup chicken stock or canned broth
1 tablespoon cornstarch
½ teaspoon sugar
2 tablespoons soy sauce
2 tablespoons dry sherry
4 tablespoons vegetable oil, preferably peanut
2 jumbo Spanish onions (about 2 pounds), cut lengthwise in half and sliced lengthwise
2 garlic cloves, minced
1 tablespoon minced peeled fresh ginger
½ pound lean pork, ground or finely minced
6 scallions, thinly sliced
2 eggs, at room temperature
2 teaspoons Oriental sesame oil

1. In a small bowl, combine the stock, cornstarch, sugar, soy sauce and sherry. Stir to dissolve the cornstarch and set aside.

2. In a large heavy wok, warm 3 tablespoons of the vegetable oil over moderately high heat. Add the onions and stir-fry until softened and beginning to brown, about 8 minutes. Reduce the heat slightly, if necessary, to prevent burning. Remove the onions and cover loosely to keep warm. Wipe out the wok with paper towels.

3. Heat the remaining 1 tablespoon vegetable oil in the wok over moderate heat. Add the garlic and ginger and stir-fry until fragrant, about 30 seconds. Crumble the pork into the wok. Increase the heat to moderately high and stir-fry until the pork is cooked through with no trace of pink, 3 to 5 minutes.

4. Stir the reserved stock mixture and pour it over the pork. Add three-fourths of the scallions and stir-fry until the sauce thickens and boils, about 1 minute. Lightly beat the eggs and stir into the sauce. Immediately remove from the heat and stir in the sesame oil. Pour the sauce over the onions and sprinkle with the remaining scallions. Serve hot.

Roasted Onions with Chopped Red Onion

If you can find them, use sweet onions for this recipe, such as Vidalia, Walla Walla or Maui. If they are not available, plain yellow onions will do nicely.

6 SERVINGS

6 medium yellow onions, in their skins
Unsalted butter
2 to 3 tablespoons finely chopped red onion

1. Preheat the oven to 375°. Place the onions (in their skins) in a foil-lined pie tin and bake for 1½ hours. Turn off the oven and leave the onions inside for another 1½ hours.

2. To serve, peel the onions and halve or quarter them. Butter them generously and return to the still-warm oven until serving time. Just before serving; sprinkle the red onions on top.

Puree of Apples and Onions with Calvados

This sweet-savory puree goes beautifully with pork chops, ham, duck or goose.

4 SERVINGS

3 tablespoons unsalted butter
1 large sweet onion, thinly sliced
3 tart apples, preferably Granny Smith, cored and sliced
1 cup dry white wine
½ cup Calvados
½ cup heavy cream
½ teaspoon salt
¼ teaspoon white pepper

1. In a large noncorrodible skillet, combine 2 tablespoons of the butter, the onion, apples, wine and ¼ cup of the Calvados. Cover and simmer over moderately low heat until the onions are very soft and the apples are falling apart but not brown, about 40 minutes.

2. Pass the mixture through a food mill fitted with a fine blade or puree in a blender or food processor.

3. In a medium, noncorrodible saucepan, bring the apple-onion mixture and the cream to a gentle boil over moderately high heat and continue to cook until thickened but not browned, 6 to 8 minutes.

4. Pass the puree through a fine mesh sieve. Return to the saucepan, add the remaining ¼ cup Calvados and bring to a boil over moderately high heat. Remove from the heat and stir in the remaining 1 tablespoon butter. Season with the salt and pepper.

Ragout of Winter Vegetables

4 SERVINGS

¼ pound green beans, as small as possible
2 medium carrots
1 medium turnip
1 medium celery root
1 medium beet
8 tablespoons (1 stick) unsalted butter
¼ cup Rich Duck Stock (p. 219) or chicken stock
¼ teaspoon salt
⅛ teaspoon freshly ground pepper

1. Trim the ends off the green beans. Peel the carrots, turnip, celery root and beet; cut into 2-by-¼-inch sticks.

2. In a large pot of boiling salted water, blanch the beans for 2 to 3 minutes, until just tender. Drain and rinse them under cold running water.

3. In a large skillet, melt 7 tablespoons of the butter over moderately high heat. Add the carrots, turnip and celery root; toss to coat with butter. Add the stock and cook, tossing occasionally, until the vegetables are tender and the liquid has reduced to a glaze, about 5 minutes.

4. Meanwhile, in a small skillet, sauté the beet in the remaining 1 tablespoon butter over moderate heat until crisp-tender, 3 to 5 minutes.

5. Add the beet and the green beans to the other cooked vegetables. Season with the salt and pepper and cook, tossing, until heated through.

Roast Potatoes and Shallots

8 SERVINGS

4 large baking potatoes, peeled and halved crosswise
1½ teaspoons salt
16 unpeeled shallots (about 1¼ pounds)
⅓ cup rendered lamb or beef fat (see Note)
½ teaspoon freshly ground pepper

1. Place the potatoes in a medium saucepan with 1 teaspoon of the salt and 1 quart of water, or more, to cover by 1 inch. Bring to a boil, reduce the heat and simmer, covered, for 15 minutes (they will finish cooking in the oven). Drain.

2. When the potatoes are cool enough to handle, cut them in half lengthwise to yield 16 wedges.

3. Place the potatoes in a single layer in a 13-by-9-inch baking dish. Pick off any loose, broken shallot skin and add the unpeeled shallots to the baking dish. **(The recipe may be prepared ahead to this point.)** Preheat the oven to 350°.

4. Drizzle the rendered fat over the potatoes; turn to coat the potatoes. Sprinkle with the remaining ½ teaspoon salt and the pepper. Bake for 35 minutes.

5. Increase the oven temperature to 400°. Remove the baking dish from the oven, and transfer the shallots, which should be tender, to a plate; cover and keep warm until serving time. Turn the potatoes and return them to the oven. Cook for 25 to 30 minutes, until brown and crisp.

NOTE: If you are making roast beef or lamb to go with this, use the pan drippings. Otherwise, ask your butcher for beef suet and render it to yield ⅓ cup.

Swedish Potatoes with Fresh Dill

To facilitate cutting the potatoes into accordion slices (Step 2), place two chopsticks (or even two long clean pencils) on either side of a potato and hold them together with a rubber band at either end. Now you can slice the potato without cutting through completely.

8 SERVINGS

6 tablespoons unsalted butter, melted
1 teaspoon salt
½ teaspoon freshly ground pepper
2 tablespoons chopped fresh dill
8 medium boiling potatoes, unpeeled

1. Light the charcoal or preheat the broiler. In a small bowl, combine the butter, salt, pepper and dill.

2. Cut a thin slice from one side of each potato so that the potato will have a firm base. With a sharp knife make a series of parallel vertical cuts ⅛ inch apart and to within ¼ inch of the base. Be careful not to cut through the base completely.

3. Cut two squares of heavy foil large enough to hold 4 potatoes each. Brush the center of the foil with the dill butter. Place 4 potatoes on each square. Spread the potato slices gently and brush generously with the butter.

4. Seal each packet with double folds around the edges. Grill 4 to 6 inches from the heat, turning frequently to avoid charring, until a skewer poked gently into the top of a packet slides easily into a potato, about 45 minutes. Pass any leftover melted dill-butter if desired.

Potatoes and Ham au Gratin

6 SERVINGS

3 tablespoons unsalted butter
2 medium onions, thinly sliced
1½ pounds baking potatoes
Freshly ground pepper
½ pound sliced smoked country ham
1¼ cups heavy cream

1. Preheat the oven to 325°. In a medium skillet, melt 2 tablespoons of the butter over moderate heat. Add the onions and sauté until translucent but not browned, about 8 minutes; set aside.

2. Peel and thinly slice the potatoes, rinse in cold water; pat dry with paper towels.

3. Grease a 2-quart gratin dish with the remaining 1 tablespoon butter. Evenly layer half of the potato slices in the dish and sprinkle lightly with pepper. Evenly layer all of the onions over the potatoes. Cover the onions with the ham slices and then the remaining potatoes. Pour the cream over the potatoes, making sure all of the slices are moistened. Sprinkle with additional pepper.

4. Bake for about 1½ hours, basting the top layer with the cream in the dish once or twice, until most of the cream is absorbed and the potatoes are tender and golden brown on top.

Rösti

♟ **F&W Beverage Suggestion:** Cold hard cider, such as Purpom, or beer

MAKES 4 PANCAKES

4 medium baking potatoes
½ cup lard
About 2 tablespoons unsalted butter
Salt and freshly ground pepper

1. In a large saucepan of boiling salted water, cook the whole, unpeeled potatoes over moderate heat for about 15 minutes, until a skewer or knife point easily pierces the outer ½ inch of potato but meets resistance in the center (the potatoes will finish cooking later). Drain the potatoes and rinse under cold running water. Refrigerate uncovered until well chilled, 3 to 4 hours or overnight.

2. Peel the potatoes. In a food processor fitted with a shredding blade or on the large holes of a hand grater, shred the potatoes lengthwise to make long, even shreds.

3. In a heavy 8-inch skillet with sloping sides or in an omelet pan, melt 2 tablespoons of the lard over high heat until the lard begins to smoke.

4. Sprinkle one quarter (about ¾ cup) of the shredded potato into the skillet. Season lightly with salt and pepper. Quickly push any stray shreds in from the outer rim of the pan to form an even round pancake. Lightly tamp down the top of the *rösti*.

5. Reduce the heat to moderately high, and cook the *rösti*, shaking and rotating the pan occasionally to loosen the potatoes, until well browned on the bottom, about 3 minutes. (If the potatoes stick, remove the pan from the flame and rap it sharply on a hard surface, such as a cutting board, to loosen them.)

6. Add ½ tablespoon butter to the edge of the pan. Rotate quickly to melt and distribute the butter. Flip the *rösti* like a flapjack or turn over with a wide spatula.

7. Season lightly again with salt and pepper. Continue cooking over moderately high heat, adding additional butter if the pan becomes dry, until browned on the second side, about 3 minutes longer. Keep warm in a low oven while you make the other three *rösti* with the remaining ingredients.

Cheese Rösti:

Prepare as for the master *rösti* recipe (above) through Step 6. After turning the *rösti*, sprinkle 2 tablespoons of shredded Gruyère cheese over the top. The cheese will melt as the second side browns.

Onion Rösti:

Prepare as for the master *rösti* recipe (at left), but toss the shredded potatoes with 2 medium onions, thinly sliced, before cooking.

Bacon (or Ham) Rösti:

Prepare as for the master *rösti* recipe (at left), but toss the potatoes with 1 pound of bacon—cooked, drained and crumbled—or finely diced ham before cooking.

Shepherd's Rösti:

Prepare bacon *rösti* as directed above. Then after turning in Step 6, top each *rösti* with 2 tablespoons of shredded Gruyère cheese. Top each *rösti* with a fried egg before serving.

Bacon-Onion Rösti:

This is a favorite in the Swiss capital of Bern. Prepare as for the master *rösti* recipe (at left), but toss the potatoes with 1 pound of bacon—cooked, drained and crumbled—and 2 medium onions, thinly sliced, before cooking.

Giant Rösti (4 servings):

Prepare one large *rösti* in a 12-inch skillet using the same technique as above with 2 large baking potatoes, ¼ cup lard, 1 tablespoon butter and salt and pepper to taste. Turn by inverting onto a plate and sliding back into the pan. To serve, cut into 4 wedges.

Sautéed Herbed Tomatoes with Bacon

Sliced, seasoned and sautéed, firm winter tomatoes take on a new flavor dimension—they become tender and sweet.

4 SERVINGS

6 strips of bacon
¼ cup all-purpose flour
2 tablespoons sugar
1 teaspoon salt
½ teaspoon oregano
¼ teaspoon freshly ground pepper
3 large firm tomatoes (about 1 pound), cored and cut into ½-inch slices

1. In a large heavy skillet, cook the bacon over moderately high heat, turning once, until browned and crisp, about 5 minutes. Drain on paper towels; crumble and set aside. Pour off the bacon fat

into a small bowl and reserve; set the skillet aside.

2. In a small bowl, stir together the flour, sugar, salt, oregano and pepper until well mixed. Lightly dredge the tomato slices in the seasoned flour.

3. Warm 2 tablespoons of the bacon fat in the skillet over moderately high heat until sizzling. Add half of the tomato slices in a single layer and sauté until lightly browned on the bottom, about 3 minutes. Add 1 more tablespoon of bacon fat to the skillet and turn the slices over. Sauté until lightly browned on the second side, about 3 minutes longer. Transfer the cooked slices to a warm serving platter. Repeat with the remaining tomato slices.

4. Sprinkle the crumbled bacon over the tomatoes and serve warm.

Stir-Fried Watercress

You will seem to have an enormous amount of watercress for this dish, but, like other greens, it will reduce considerably during cooking.

6 SERVINGS

6 large bunches of watercress, as young as possible, large stems removed
1 tablespoon rice vinegar
1 teaspoon salt
1 tablespoon peanut oil
2 large garlic cloves, finely chopped

1. Wash the watercress and dry well. Combine the vinegar and salt in a small bowl and set aside.

2. Place the oil in a large wok over high heat. When the oil begins to smoke, add the garlic and stir-fry for 10 seconds. Add the watercress and cook, tossing, until the greens start to wilt. Continue tossing for 15 to 30 seconds longer.

3. Drizzle the vinegar and salt over the watercress and toss to distribute evenly. Serve at once.

Spinach Ring Filled with Creamed Chestnuts

For most recipes fresh spinach is preferable to frozen, but not when it comes to preparing this recipe, which would require eight pounds of fresh spinach and endless preparation.

6 TO 8 SERVINGS

Creamed Chestnuts:

1 pound frozen shelled and peeled Italian chestnuts* or 1 can (1 pound) whole unsweetened chestnuts
2 cups heavy cream
½ teaspoon salt
⅛ teaspoon freshly ground pepper

Spinach Ring:

8 packages (10 ounces each) frozen chopped spinach
1½ teaspoons salt
⅛ teaspoon freshly ground pepper
¼ teaspoon freshly grated nutmeg
1 cup heavy cream
Paprika, for garnish
*Available at specialty food shops

1. Make the creamed chestnuts: If using the frozen chestnuts, place them in a large heavy saucepan with 3 cups of water. Bring to a simmer over moderate heat, cover, reduce the heat to low and simmer until tender, 8 to 10 minutes. Drain well. If using canned, simply drain.

2. Place 10 whole chestnuts in a food processor and process to a fine powder. Empty the chestnut powder into a heavy medium saucepan. Add the cream, salt and pepper and boil, uncovered, until reduced to 1¾ cups, 20 to 30 minutes.

3. Halve or quarter the remaining chestnuts, depending on their size, and add to the chestnut cream. Set aside off heat while you prepare the spinach ring. **(The creamed chestnuts can be made ahead to this point.** Cover and refrigerate, then bring to room temperature while you cook the spinach.)

4. Meanwhile, prepare the spinach ring: Place the frozen spinach in a large heavy kettle; add the salt but no water.

Cover and simmer over moderate heat, stirring occasionally to break up any large frozen clumps, until the spinach is thawed and heated through, about 30 minutes. If it threatens to boil dry at any time, reduce the heat and add a little water.

5. As soon as the spinach is steaming hot, dump into a very large fine sieve and press to extract as much liquid as possible. When the spinach is very dry, return it to the kettle. Add the pepper, nutmeg and cream. Cook over moderate heat, stirring, for 3 to 4 minutes, until heated through. Reheat the creamed chestnuts.

6. Just before serving, pack the hot spinach mixture into a lavishly buttered 6-cup ring mold.

7. To serve, loosen the spinach ring around the edges with a thin-bladed spatula and invert onto a heated round plate (see Note). Fill the center of the spinach ring with the creamed chestnuts, ladling a little of the sauce over the ring at intervals and arranging a few chestnuts about the base. For a holiday touch, add a blush of paprika.

NOTE: If any bits of spinach should cling to the ring mold, no harm done. Simply lift them out and replace on the spinach ring, smoothing the surface as needed with a spatula.

Vegetable Kebabs Monaco

The marinade for this recipe must mellow for two hours before being used, then the vegetables must marinate for at least one hour. Place the bamboo skewers in water to soak when you start the marinade.

8 SERVINGS

⅓ cup dry white wine
¼ cup vegetable oil
¼ cup fresh lime juice
¼ cup fresh lemon juice
1 teaspoon salt
¼ teaspoon freshly ground pepper
1 teaspoon tarragon
¼ teaspoon rosemary
1 garlic clove, finely chopped
2 green bell peppers, cut into 1-inch squares

1 large onion, cut into 8 wedges
2 small zucchini, cut into 1-inch chunks
32 medium mushrooms (about 1½ pounds)
32 cherry tomatoes

1. In a large bowl, stir together the wine, oil, lime juice, lemon juice, salt, pepper, tarragon, rosemary and garlic to make a marinade. Cover and set aside for 2 hours before using. Meanwhile, soak 20 bamboo skewers in water.

2. Add the peppers, onion, zucchini and mushrooms to the marinade and toss to coat. Marinate at room temperature, tossing occasionally, for 1 to 2 hours.

3. Light the charcoal or preheat the broiler. Thread the tomatoes together on 4 skewers. Thread the green peppers, onion, zucchini and mushrooms on the remaining 16 skewers, alternating the ingredients and pushing them close together.

4. Pour the marinade into a saucepan. Gently warm the marinade on a corner of the grill or over low heat on the stove.

5. Grill the vegetables 4 to 6 inches from the heat, turning frequently and basting occasionally with the warm marinade, until still crisp outside but tender inside, about 10 minutes. Grill the tomatoes separately, turning and basting frequently, until warmed through, about 3 minutes.

6. To serve, remove the tomatoes from the skewers and place in a warmed serving dish. Serve 2 skewers of mixed vegetables to each person and pass the tomatoes separately.

PASTA, RICE & BREADSTUFFS

Summer Pasta with Basil, Tomatoes and Cheese

F&W Beverage Suggestion: California Zinfandel, such as Simi

6 TO 8 SERVINGS

4 medium tomatoes—peeled, seeded and coarsely chopped
4 garlic cloves, minced
½ cup chopped fresh basil
1 tablespoon chopped fresh mint
1 teaspoon salt
½ teaspoon freshly ground black pepper
¼ teaspoon hot pepper flakes
½ cup olive oil, preferably extra-virgin
1 pound small macaroni shells
½ cup freshly grated Parmesan cheese
½ pound Italian Fontina cheese, finely diced (about 2 cups)

1. In a medium bowl, toss together the tomatoes, garlic, basil, mint, salt, black pepper, hot pepper flakes and olive oil. Let stand at room temperature, tossing occasionally, for 2 to 3 hours.

2. In a large pot of boiling salted water, cook the macaroni until tender but still firm to the bite, 8 to 10 minutes. Drain and transfer to a large serving bowl. Spoon off ¼ cup of liquid from the tomatoes and toss with the macaroni to coat.

3. While the macaroni is still warm, add the Parmesan and Fontina cheeses and toss until the cheeses begin to melt. Add the tomatoes with their liquid and toss until mixed. Serve warm or at room temperature.

Pasta with Grilled Scallops in Chardonnay Cream Sauce

Beverage Suggestion: California Chardonnay, such as Chalone

4 FIRST-COURSE SERVINGS

Chardonnay Fish Stock (recipe follows)
1 cup heavy cream
4 teaspoons minced fresh chives
20 small sea scallops (in the shell with their coral, if available)
½ pound linguine, preferably fresh
2 ounces black sturgeon caviar
2 ounces golden whitefish caviar
1 tablespoon finely diced red bell pepper
4 sprigs of basil

1. In a heavy medium saucepan, boil the fish stock over moderately high heat until reduced to about 2 tablespoons of glaze, 15 to 20 minutes. Add the cream and all but 1 teaspoon of the chives (which are reserved for garnish) to the reduced stock. Simmer for 3 minutes. Remove from the heat.

2. Meanwhile, bring a large pot of salted water to a boil.

3. If you have whole scallops in the shell, grill them over hot coals until they open, 1 to 2 minutes. Remove from the grill and when cool enough to handle, cut the scallops with their coral from the shell. Carefully cut away everything but the soft, white muscle and the coral.

4. Lightly oil the grill. Put the scallops on it (whether they are from the shell with coral attached or loose, fresh from the market). Cook, turning occasionally, for 3 to 4 minutes, until browned. (If you do not have a grill, the scallops may be cooked in 1 teaspoon of oil in a very hot skillet, preferably nonstick, over high heat, turning once, until firm and well browned on the outside, about 1 minute.)

5. Cook the pasta in the boiling water until just tender, 1 to 2 minutes if fresh; 6 to 8 if dried. Drain well.

6. Rewarm the cream sauce if necessary. Pour into a large, warmed bowl. Add the cooked pasta and toss until coated. Divide the pasta among four dinner plates, mounding it in the center. Spoon one-fourth of the black caviar and one-fourth of the golden onto each portion of pasta. Arrange 5 grilled scallops around the pasta. Sprinkle each plate with a pinch of minced chives and a pinch of diced red pepper. Garnish with a sprig of basil.

Chardonnay Fish Stock

For a special and rich stock, use ½ pound sea scallops instead of the fish bones and simmer them for 15 minutes.

MAKES ABOUT 2 CUPS

2 teaspoons extra-virgin olive oil
1 medium onion, thinly sliced
3 pounds of non-oily fish bones and heads (such as flounder or sole)
2 cups California Chardonnay
Bouquet garni: 10 parsley stems, 2 sprigs of thyme, 2 crushed garlic cloves, ¼ teaspoon tarragon, 5 black peppercorns tied in a double thickness of cheesecloth

In a large noncorrodible saucepan, heat the olive oil. Add the onion and sauté over moderate heat until softened and translucent, 3 to 4 minutes. Add the fish bones, wine and bouquet garni. Simmer for 25 minutes. Strain through a sieve lined with a triple layer of dampened cheesecloth.

Spaghetti with Trout Marinara

F&W Beverage Suggestion:
California Fumé Blanc

8 TO 10 SERVINGS

¼ cup plus 2 tablespoons olive oil
1 garlic clove, finely chopped
1 medium onion, coarsely chopped
½ pound mushrooms, sliced
4 12-inch trout—filleted, skinned and cut crosswise into 1-inch-wide strips (2¾ pounds meat)
3 cups tomato sauce, preferably homemade
½ teaspoon minced fresh oregano or a pinch of dried
½ teaspoon minced fresh basil or a pinch of dried
1½ teaspoons salt
¾ teaspoon freshly ground pepper
2 pounds spaghetti
2 tablespoons unsalted butter
2 tablespoons chopped parsley, for garnish

1. In a large heavy pot or flameproof casserole, heat ¼ cup of the oil over moderate heat. Add the garlic, onion and mushrooms and sauté until the onions have softened, about 5 minutes.

2. Add the trout strips, tomato sauce, oregano, basil, 1 teaspoon of the salt and ½ teaspoon of the pepper. Simmer gently over low heat, stirring occasionally, until the trout is just opaque, about 10 minutes. Turn off the heat and let the sauce sit until the pasta is ready.

3. In a large pot of boiling salted water, cook the spaghetti until tender but still firm, 8 to 10 minutes. Drain well. Toss with the butter, the remaining 2 tablespoons oil and the remaining salt and pepper.

4. Place the pasta on a warm serving platter and top with the sauce. Sprinkle with the chopped parsley.

Parioli Romanissimo's Fedelini with Smoked Salmon

F&W Beverage Suggestion:
A light, dry fruity Italian wine with just a touch of brio, such as Gavi dei Gavi, La Scolca (black label)

4 TO 6 SERVINGS

3 imported bay leaves, broken into small pieces
2 large shallots, coarsely chopped
Pinch of salt
Pinch of white pepper
5 ounces fresh salmon steak
1 teaspoon tomato paste
3 cups heavy cream
2 teaspoons green peppercorns, rinsed and drained
1 pound fedelini No. 10 or vermicelli or spaghettini
5 ounces Norwegian smoked salmon, sliced and cut into ½-inch squares

1. In a small noncorrodible saucepan, combine the bay leaves, shallots, salt, pepper and 1 cup of water. Bring to a boil over moderately high heat. Add the salmon steak, reduce the heat and simmer, turning once, until the salmon is barely translucent in the center, about 5 minutes.

2. Remove the salmon and strain the poaching liquid into a bowl. Return the liquid to the pan and boil until reduced to ½ cup. Skin and bone the salmon.

3. In a blender or food processor, combine the reduced poaching liquid, tomato paste and poached salmon. Puree until smooth.

4. In a large saucepan, boil the cream over moderately high heat until reduced by half to 1½ cups, about 25 minutes. Reduce the heat to moderately low. Add the pureed salmon mixture and simmer for 2 minutes to blend the flavors. Add the green peppercorns and season with additional salt and pepper to taste.

5. In a large pot of boiling salted water, cook the pasta until tender but still firm, about 5 minutes. Drain well and toss with the creamy salmon sauce.

6. To serve, divide the sauced pasta among warmed plates. Arrange the smoked salmon on top.

Linguine with Aparagus and Mustard

F&W Beverage Suggestion:
California Sauvignon Blanc, such as Preston

4 SERVINGS

2 pounds thin asparagus, trimmed and cut on the diagonal into 1-inch pieces
3 tablespoons grainy mustard
3 tablespoons olive oil, preferably extra-virgin
2 large shallots, thinly sliced
1 small garlic clove, minced
1½ teaspoons anchovy paste
Pinch of thyme
2 tablespoons minced fresh parsley
1 pound linguine
Salt and freshly ground pepper

1. In a large pot of boiling salted water, cook the asparagus until tender but still bright green, about 3 minutes. Drain and rinse under cold running water; drain well and set aside.

2. In a small bowl, combine the mustard, olive oil, shallots, garlic, anchovy paste, thyme and parsley. Mix well and set aside.

3. In a large pot of boiling salted water, cook the linguine until tender but still firm to the bite, 7 to 10 minutes. Drain well.

4. In a serving bowl, toss the linguine with the dressing and the asparagus. Season with salt and pepper to taste. Serve warm or at room temperature. **(This dish can be made 1 hour before serving.)**

Linguine with Bacon and Onion Sauce

The natural sweetness of cooked onions dominates this earthy pasta dish. The onions tint the linguine a beautiful golden straw color, while the bacon and Romano complement the sweetness of the onions.

F&W Beverage Suggestion:
Full-flavored beer, such as Ballantine India Pale Ale

4 TO 6 SERVINGS

¼ pound lean slab bacon, sliced ¼ inch thick and cut into ¼-inch dice
¼ cup olive oil
8 medium onions, coarsely chopped
4 garlic cloves, minced
1 cup chicken stock or canned broth
¼ cup dry white wine
½ teaspoon freshly ground pepper
2½ teaspoons salt
¾ pound linguine
¼ cup minced fresh parsley
1 cup freshly grated Romano cheese

1. In a large heavy skillet, cook the bacon over moderate heat, stirring frequently, until crisp and golden brown, about 5 minutes. Remove from the heat; pour off and discard all but 2 tablespoons of the bacon drippings. Add the oil, onions and garlic to the pan. Cook, stirring frequently, over moderate heat for about 2 minutes to coat the onions with oil. Cover the pan, reduce the heat to very low and cook, stirring 2 or 3 times, for 1 hour.

2. Uncover the skillet and increase the heat to moderate. Cook, stirring frequently, until all the liquid has evaporated. Continue to cook until the onions are golden, about 20 minutes.

3. Add the stock, wine, pepper and ½ teaspoon of the salt. Increase the heat to moderately high and boil until the liquid is evaporated and the consistency of the sauce resembles the consistency of ap-

plesauce, about 5 minutes. **(The recipe can be made ahead to this point.)**

4. Bring a large pot of water to a boil and add the remaining 2 teaspoons salt. Add the linguine and cook until tender but still firm, 9 to 10 minutes; drain.

5. Transfer the onion sauce to the pasta pot and bring it just to the boiling point over high heat. Remove from the heat, add the pasta and toss well. Stir in the parsley and ½ cup of the Romano cheese; toss well. Serve immediately. Pass the remaining cheese in a small bowl.

Fettuccine with Smoked Salmon and Whiskey

You may want to buy less costly smoked salmon tails and scraps for this recipe.

F&W Beverage Suggestion:
Italian white, such as Orvieto Secco

4 FIRST-COURSE SERVINGS

1 cup heavy cream
¼ cup Irish whiskey
½ pound fettuccine, preferably fresh
½ pound smoked salmon, shredded or cut into julienne strips
3 tablespoons unsalted butter, at room temperature
2 ounces red lumpfish caviar or American golden caviar
¼ teaspoon freshly ground pepper
Salt

1. In a large saucepan, boil the cream over moderately high heat until reduced by about half, 8 to 10 minutes.

2. Add the whiskey and continue boiling for 15 seconds longer. Remove from the heat.

3. In a large pot of boiling lightly salted water, cook the fettuccine until tender but still firm, 2 to 3 minutes for fresh or 8 to 10 minutes for dried. Drain well.

4. Add the salmon and butter to the whiskey-cream mixture. Stir over moder-

ately low heat until the salmon is heated through and the butter is melted. Add half of the caviar.

5. Pour the sauce into a warmed serving dish. Add the pepper and salt to taste. Add the fettuccine and toss to coat.

6. To serve, divide the fettuccine among four warmed shallow bowls. Top each serving with one-fourth of the remaining caviar and serve with additional freshly ground pepper.

Chicken Lasagna

F&W Beverage Suggestion:
Light Italian white, such as Galestro, or Italian red, such as Dolcetto or Bardolino

12 SERVINGS

10 tablespoons unsalted butter
4 tablespoons olive oil
3 medium onions, minced
2 small garlic cloves, finely chopped
½ cup plus 2 tablespoons all-purpose flour
2½ cups hot milk
2½ cups hot chicken stock or canned broth
1 tablespoon dried tarragon
1½ teaspoons salt
½ teaspoon white pepper
½ teaspoon freshly grated nutmeg
4 eggs
2½ to 3 pounds tomatoes—peeled, seeded and chopped
2 tablespoons tomato paste
½ cup dry red wine
1 tablespoon dried basil
½ teaspoon sugar
½ teaspoon red wine vinegar
8 skinless, boneless chicken breast halves (about 2 pounds total)
1½ pounds chicken livers, trimmed
1 tablespoon dried oregano
1 package (16 ounces) lasagna noodles
2 cups freshly grated Parmesan cheese (about 8 ounces)

1. In a large saucepan, melt 5 tablespoons of the butter in 1 tablespoon of the oil over moderate heat. Add the onions and garlic and sauté until softened and translucent, about 5 minutes.

2. Stir in the flour. Reduce the heat to low and cook, stirring, for 3 minutes without coloring to make a roux. Off the heat, gradually whisk in the hot milk and hot stock. Return to moderate heat, bring to a boil and cook, stirring, for 5 minutes.

3. Add the tarragon, 1 teaspoon of the salt, the pepper and the nutmeg. Remove from the heat and, one at a time, briskly whisk in the eggs. Cover partially and set the béchamel sauce aside.

4. In a large noncorrodible skillet, combine the tomatoes with the tomato paste, red wine, basil, sugar, vinegar and the remaining ½ teaspoon salt. Cook, stirring frequently, over moderate heat until thick, about 15 minutes. Remove from the heat and set aside.

5. In a large skillet, melt the remaining 5 tablespoons butter in 1 tablespoon of the oil over moderate heat. Add the chicken, cover and cook, turning once, for 5 minutes on each side. Remove with tongs, leaving any fat in the pan. Let the chicken cool, then cut crosswise into ½-inch slices.

6. Add the chicken livers to the same skillet and sauté over moderately high heat, tossing, until nicely browned on the outside, 3 to 4 minutes. Add the oregano and let cool slightly. Mince the livers fine.

7. Bring a large pot of water to a boil and add the remaining 2 tablespoons oil. Cook the lasagna noodles until tender but still slightly firm, about 12 minutes. Drain and return the pasta to the pot; add warm water to cover (it will keep the noodles soft to facilitate handling).

8. Preheat the oven to 375°. Picking the noodles out of the water, arrange one layer in a well-buttered large, shallow baking dish. Cover the pasta with about 1¼ cups of the béchamel sauce. Top with half of the sliced chicken and then with ⅓ cup of the Parmesan cheese. Add another layer of pasta, all of the tomato sauce and ⅓ cup of the cheese. Add another layer of pasta, spread all of the chicken livers over the pasta and cover with 1¼ cups of the béchamel and then ⅓ cup of the cheese. Form another layer of pasta, then 1¼ cups béchamel, the

remaining chicken and ⅓ cup cheese. Top with a final layer of pasta, the remaining béchamel and the remaining cheese. (**The lasagna can be assembled to this point ahead of time.** Cover with plastic wrap and refrigerate overnight. Let return to room temperature before proceeding.)

9. Bake for 45 minutes to 1 hour, until the top is golden brown and somewhat crusty. Let stand for 15 minutes before serving. (If preparing the lasagna ahead of time, bake and set aside to cool completely. Cover with plastic wrap and refrigerate overnight. Next day, let return to room temperature and reheat at 300° for 30 mintues. Let stand for 15 minutes before serving.)

Macaroni and Cheese

6 SERVINGS

½ **pound elbow macaroni**
7½ **tablespoons unsalted butter**
1 **cup fresh bread crumbs**
1½ **cups shredded sharp Cheddar cheese (about 6 ounces)**
½ **teaspoon salt**
¼ **teaspoon freshly ground white pepper**
¾ **cup milk**

1. Preheat the oven to 350°. In a large pot of boiling salted water, cook the macaroni, stirring occasionally, until barely tender, 6 to 8 minutes. Drain and rinse under cold running water; drain well.

2. In a medium skillet, melt 3 tablespoons of the butter over moderate heat. When the foam subsides, add the bread

crumbs and sauté, tossing frequently, until golden brown, 3 to 4 minutes.

3. Sprinkle a layer of the browned bread crumbs in a buttered 2-quart casserole.

4. Layer about one-third of the macaroni in the casserole. Sprinkle with one-third of the grated cheese and season with about one-third of the salt and pepper. Dot with 1½ tablespoons of the butter and one-third of the remaining bread crumbs. Repeat this layering one more time. Then add a layer of the remaining macaroni and season with the remaining salt and pepper.

5. Gently pour in the milk. Add a final layer of the remaining cheese and top with the remaining bread crumbs. Dot with the remaining 1½ tablespoons of butter.

6. Place in the lower third of the oven and bake for about 40 minutes. Remove from the oven and wait 10 minutes before serving.

Noodles with Gorgonzola Sauce

4 SERVINGS

1 **cup heavy cream**
6 **ounces imported ripe Gorgonzola cheese, rind removed**
1 **pound egg noodles, preferably fresh**
⅓ **cup freshly grated Parmesan cheese**
Freshly ground pepper

1. In a small saucepan, combine the cream and Gorgonzola. Bring to a boil, stirring, over moderate heat. Boil for 30 seconds. Remove from the heat and allow the sauce to rest while the pasta cooks.

2. In a large pot of boiling, lightly salted water, cook the noodles until they are just tender but still slightly firm, about 2 minutes for fresh, 7 minutes for dried. Drain well and turn into a large warmed serving bowl. Add the sauce and Parmesan and toss gently until the noodles are coated. Season with pepper to taste.

Gorgonzola-Stuffed Pasta Shells

6 SERVINGS

Gorgonzola Filling:
½ **pound unaged Gorgonzola (dolcelatte) cheese, at room temperature**
½ **pound ricotta cheese, drained of excess liquid**
½ **cup grated mozzarella cheese**
¼ **cup freshly grated Parmesan cheese**
2 **teaspoons minced fresh parsley**
1 **egg**
½ **teaspoon salt**
1 **teaspoon freshly ground pepper**
Pinch of freshly grated nutmeg

Assembly:
½ **pound jumbo pasta shells (#95)**
2¼ **cups Italian Tomato Sauce (p. 222)**
2½ **tablespoons freshly grated Parmesan cheese**
3 **tablespoons grated mozzarella cheese**
1 **tablespoon olive oil**

1. Make the filling: In a large bowl, mash together the Gorgonzola and ricotta cheeses. Add the mozzarella, Parmesan, parsley, egg, salt, pepper and nutmeg; mix until well blended. (**The filling can be prepared up to 8 hours in advance; cover and refrigerate. Return to room temperature before using.**)

2. Assemble the dish: In 4 quarts of boiling salted water, cook the shells, stirring occasionally, until the pasta is just tender but still slightly firm, about 16

minutes. Drain in a colander and rinse briefly under cold water. Drain well.

3. Preheat the oven to 350°. Spread ¾ cup of tomato sauce in the bottom of a 13-by-9-by-2-inch baking dish. Fill each shell with about 1 tablespoon of the filling. Arrange the shells, open-side up, in a single layer in the dish. Pour the remaining 1½ cups tomato sauce evenly over the shells. Sprinkle the top with the Parmesan and mozzarella cheeses. Drizzle with the olive oil.

4. Bake for 30 minutes, or until the cheeses have melted and the sauce is hot and bubbling. Remove from the oven and let rest for about 2 minutes before serving.

Baked Wild Rice with Carrots and Mushrooms

You will probably not need to add any salt to this recipe because of the saltiness of the stock and the bacon.

6 TO 8 SERVINGS

2½ **cups Savory Duck Stock (p. 220) or chicken broth**
1 **cup wild rice, rinsed well in cool water**
6 **slices lean double-smoked bacon, cut crosswise into julienne strips**
1 **medium onion, coarsely chopped**
2 **small carrots, cut into ¼-inch dice**
¼ **pound mushrooms, finely diced**
½ **teaspoon thyme**
½ **teaspoon marjoram**
⅛ **teaspoon freshly ground pepper**
1½ **tablespoons unsalted butter**

1. In a heavy medium saucepan, bring the stock to a boil. Add the wild rice and when the stock returns to a boil, reduce the heat to low, cover and simmer *just* until tender (the rice will cook further in the oven), 35 to 40 minutes. Remove from the heat and reserve; do not drain.

2. In a large heavy skillet, fry the bacon over moderate heat until crisp and brown, 5 to 8 minutes. Remove the bacon and drain on paper towels.

3. Pour off all but 3 tablespoons of the bacon drippings from the skillet (if your bacon is exceptionally lean and there is

not enough fat in the skillet, add enough butter to equal 3 tablespoons). Add the onion and carrots and sauté, stirring, over moderate heat until the carrots are crisp-tender, 3 to 4 minutes. Add the mushrooms, thyme, marjoram and pepper and cook for 2 minutes longer.

4. Dump the rice and any remaining cooking liquid into the skillet; add the reserved bacon and toss lightly to mix. (**The rice can be prepared ahead to this point.** Cover and refrigerate; return to room temperature before proceeding.)

5. Preheat the oven to 350°. Transfer the rice mixture to a generously buttered 2-quart casserole. Cover and bake for 25 to 30 minutes, or until the rice is tender. Dot the surface of the rice with the 1½ tablespoons butter and toss lightly. Serve at table from the casserole.

Shrimp Fried Rice

The secret for making perfectly cooked fried rice is to use rice that has been cooked and cooled a day in advance.

6 SERVINGS

½ **pound raw shrimp—shelled, deveined and cut into ½-inch dice**
1 **teaspoon medium-dry sherry**
½ **teaspoon salt**
1 **teaspoon water chestnut powder* or cornstarch**
1 **tablespoon dark soy sauce***
1 **tablespoon oyster sauce***
½ **teaspoon sugar**
5 **tablespoons peanut oil**
2 **eggs, lightly beaten**
1 **cup mung bean sprouts**
⅓ **cup sliced scallions**
½ **cup diced (¼-inch) red bell pepper**
½ **cup diced (¼-inch) zucchini**
3 **cups cooked white rice, cooled**
*****Available at Oriental groceries**

1. In a medium bowl, combine the shrimp, sherry, salt and water chestnut powder. Toss to coat. Refrigerate, covered, for at least 30 minutes, or up to 12 hours.

2. In a small bowl, combine the soy sauce, oyster sauce and sugar. Set aside.

3. In a large heavy skillet, heat 1 tablespoon of the oil over high heat. Pour in the beaten eggs, rotating the skillet to coat the bottom evenly. Cook the egg crêpe without turning until set, about 1 minute. Remove from the skillet and let cool; then shred into 3-by-¼-inch strips.

4. Place a large wok over high heat for about 2 minutes. Add the bean sprouts to the dry wok and cook, tossing once, until scorched, about 3 minutes. Remove from the wok.

5. Return the wok to high heat. Add 1 tablespoon of the oil and heat to just below the smoking point. Stir the shrimp and add to the wok. Stir-fry until they start to turn pink but are not completely curled, about 30 seconds. Remove from the wok.

6. Return the wok to high heat. Add 1 tablespoon of oil. Add the scallions, red pepper and zucchini and stir-fry for 1 minute. Remove the vegetables from the wok.

7. Return the wok to high heat, add the remaining 2 tablespoons oil and heat to just below the smoking point. Add the rice and stir-fry until heated through, about 2 minutes. Add the shredded egg crêpe, bean sprouts, shrimp and vegetables. Add the seasoning sauce and stir-fry for 30 seconds longer.

NOTE: If necessary, the fried rice can be kept warm in a preheated oven for 10 minutes. Do not cover.

Lemon-Dill Rice

This simple treatment of rice contributes a light and refreshing flavor to balance most meats, vegetables and seafood. Lemon slices are cooked on top of the rice for added flavor.

8 SERVINGS

3 tablespoons olive oil or flavorless vegetable oil
1 cup long-grain white rice
1 cup finely diced celery (2 to 3 inside ribs)
1 cup finely diced onion (1 large)
1 large garlic clove, minced
1¾ cups chicken stock or canned broth
2 tablespoons fresh lemon juice
2 tablespoons unsalted butter
¼ cup minced fresh dill
1 tablespoon sugar
½ teaspoon salt
¼ teaspoon freshly ground pepper
5 lemon slices
1 sprig of fresh dill, for garnish

1. In a medium flameproof casserole, combine the oil and rice. Cook over moderate heat, stirring frequently, until the grains are light golden brown, about 5 minutes.

2. Add the celery and onion and cook, stirring frequently, until the vegetables are slightly softened, about 3 minutes. Add the garlic and cook for 1 minute. Add the chicken stock, lemon juice, butter, minced dill, sugar, salt and pepper. Bring to a boil, reduce the heat to low and arrange the lemon slices on top of the rice.

3. Cover tightly and cook at a bare simmer until the rice is tender and the liquid absorbed, 18 to 20 minutes. Let stand, covered, for 10 minutes. Serve with the lemon slices on top, garnished with a sprig of dill.

Mini-Yorkshire Puddings

The batter in this recipe can be baked in a 9-inch square pan, but it will take 35 to 40 minutes to cook.

MAKES 12 SMALL PUDDINGS

¾ cup all-purpose flour
½ teaspoon salt
2 eggs
¾ cup plus 2 tablespoons milk
¼ cup rendered beef fat (see Note)

1. Place the flour and salt in a medium bowl. Add the eggs and pour in half of the milk. Beat well with a wooden spoon until fairly smooth, about 1 minute.

2. Add the remaining milk and beat for 2 minutes. The batter need not be perfectly smooth. Cover and set aside for 30 minutes to 1 hour.

3. Spoon 1 teaspoon of the rendered fat into each of twelve 3-inch muffin tins. Place the muffin tin in the hot oven and heat until the fat is sizzling and slightly smoking, about 3 minutes.

4. Stir the batter, then ladle about ¼ cup into each muffin cup to fill halfway. Promptly return to the top third of the 400° oven and bake until the puddings are puffed, golden brown and crisp, about 20 to 25 minutes. Serve warm.

NOTE: If you are making the Yorkshire puddings to accompany a beef roast, use the pan drippings from the roasting pan. Otherwise, ask your butcher for beef suet and render it to yield ¼ cup.

Squash Pancakes with Brown Squash Gravy

These pancakes are *savory,* not sweet, perfect for a light brunch or lunch. Ideal accompaniments would be steamed asparagus, broccoli or even a crisp green salad. The pancake batter, by the way, can be made as much as 24 hours ahead of time and kept in the refrigerator. The gravy can be made ahead, too, then brought to serving temperature.

MAKES 3 DOZEN 3-INCH PANCAKES

Pancakes:

2 cups coarsely shredded winter squash, such as butternut, buttercup, turban or pumpkin (about 1 pound)
1 medium onion, coarsely chopped
4 tablespoons unsalted butter, melted
⅛ teaspoon thyme
⅛ teaspoon marjoram
⅛ teaspoon ground mace
¼ teaspoon freshly ground pepper
1 cup sifted all-purpose flour
1 tablespoon sugar
½ teaspoon baking powder
1 teaspoon salt
3 large eggs, lightly beaten
1 cup milk

Gravy:

2 large shallots, minced
2 tablespoons unsalted butter
Pinch of ground mace or nutmeg
Pinch of thyme
Pinch of marjoram
2 tablespoons all-purpose flour
1 cup canned beef consommé
1¼ to 1½ pounds winter squash, cooked and pureed (to yield 1 cup firmly packed)
⅓ cup heavy cream
¼ teaspoon freshly ground pepper
Salt
2 tablespoons minced fresh chives or parsley

1. Make the pancakes: In a heavy medium skillet, sauté the shredded squash and onion in 1 tablespoon of the melted butter over moderate heat, stirring often, for 2 minutes. Add the thyme, marjoram, mace and pepper and sauté 2 minutes longer. Remove from the heat and let cool to room temperature.

2. In a large bowl, combine the flour, sugar, baking powder and salt and make a well in the center of the mixture. Put the eggs, milk and remaining 3 tablespoons melted butter into the well; stir just enough to moisten the dry ingredients (the batter should be lumpy). Stir in the reserved squash-onion mixture. Cover the bowl of batter and set in the refrigerator while you prepare the gravy.

3. Make the gravy: In a heavy medium skillet, sauté the shallots in the butter over moderate heat until soft, about 3 minutes. Stir in the mace, thyme and marjoram and cook over moderate heat for 2 minutes; add the flour and continue to cook, stirring, 2 to 3 minutes longer. Gradually whisk in the consommé and cook about 3 minutes, until the mixture is thickened. Blend in the pureed squash, cream, pepper and salt to taste; keep warm over low heat while you cook the pancakes.

4. Cook the pancakes: Lightly oil a large heavy skillet or griddle and set it over moderately high heat. When hot enough to sizzle a drop of water, drop on heaping tablespoons of the pancake batter, spacing them about 2 inches apart and flattening the surface of each slightly with the back of the spoon. Cook until the bubbles on the surface of the pancake break, 2 to 3 minutes, then turn and brown the other side about 2 minutes longer. Transfer the cooked pancakes to a hot platter or plate and keep warm while you cook the balance.

5. To serve, overlap 4 pancakes on individual plates. Ladle the gravy on top. Sprinkle with chives; serve immediately.

Southern Biscuits

Since the buttermilk activates the baking powder, waste no time in rolling out these biscuits and getting them into the oven after the liquid has been added.

MAKES 10 TO 12

2 cups all-purpose flour
2 teaspoons baking powder
½ teaspoon salt
4 tablespoons unsalted butter, cut into small pieces
¾ cup buttermilk

1. Arrange the oven rack to an upper middle position and preheat the oven to 450°.

2. In a large bowl, sift together the flour, baking powder and salt. Cut in the butter until no small lumps are visible.

3. Add the buttermilk and stir it quickly into the flour. Gather the dough into a ball and pat it into a smooth disk.

4. On a lightly floured surface, roll the dough into an 8-inch circle about ½ inch thick. Using a 2-inch floured cutter or a glass, cut out 8 biscuits. Gather the scraps together and roll into a 4-inch square; cut out 3 or 4 more biscuits.

5. Place the biscuits 1 inch apart on a greased baking sheet and bake for 10 to 12 minutes, until well risen and lightly golden on top. Serve hot.

Farmhouse Biscuits

Having the oven really hot and getting the biscuits into it as quickly as possible after preparing the batter will give you a reputation for "best biscuit maker."

MAKES 8 BISCUITS

¾ cup milk
1 tablespoon white wine vinegar
2 cups all-purpose flour
2 teaspoons baking powder
1 teaspoon baking soda
½ teaspoon salt
5 tablespoons unsalted butter

1. In a small bowl, combine the milk and vinegar. Set aside for about 30 minutes, until it forms clots and becomes soured. Stir. **(The sour milk may be prepared one day ahead.** Refrigerate, but bring it to room temperature before proceeding.) Meanwhile, butter a baking sheet, arrange an oven rack in the top third of the oven and preheat the oven to 450°.

2. Sift the flour, baking powder, baking soda and salt into a medium bowl.

3. Cut the butter into small pieces and cut or rub it into the flour mixture until it resembles bread crumbs.

4. Pour in the sour milk and stir quickly just until the dough masses together. It will be a little sticky. Working quickly, turn the dough out onto a lightly floured surface and pat with floured fingers into an 8-inch circle.

5. Cut the dough into 8 wedges with a floured knife. Using a floured spatula, transfer the wedges to the prepared tray and immediately place it in the oven.

6. Bake for about 12 minutes, or until light brown and crusty. Cool on a rack for 5 minutes. Serve as soon as possible with butter or jam and whipped cream. Also good with butter and Cheddar cheese or chutney.

Rye Muffins

MAKES 12 SMALL MUFFINS

½ cup rye flour
⅓ cup unbleached all-purpose flour
¾ teaspoon baking powder
¼ teaspoon baking soda
¼ teaspoon salt
¼ teaspoon caraway seeds
¼ teaspoon poppy seeds (optional)
3 tablespoons chopped walnuts
½ cup buttermilk
1 egg
1 tablespoon walnut or peanut oil
1 tablespoon honey

1. Lightly grease the bottoms of 12 miniature muffin cups. Preheat the oven to 400°.

2. In a mixing bowl, blend together the rye flour, all-purpose flour, baking powder, baking soda, salt, caraway seeds, poppy seeds and walnuts. Mix to combine the ingredients thoroughly.

3. In another bowl, whisk together the buttermilk, egg, oil and honey until well blended. Pour this into the dry ingredients and mix with a fork to just blend; do not mix until smooth.

4. Divide the batter among the cups. Bake in the upper middle level of the oven for about 15 minutes, until browned. Let stand on a rack to cool for 2 to 3 minutes. Turn out into a basket and serve.

Sally Lunn Corn Bread

MAKES 1 DOZEN ROLLS

⅓ cup lukewarm water (105° to 115°)
2 envelopes (¼ ounce each) active dry yeast
¼ teaspoon granulated sugar
⅔ cup milk
½ cup (1 stick) unsalted butter, at room temperature
¼ cup firmly packed light brown sugar or ⅓ cup granulated maple sugar*
4 eggs, at room temperature

1 teaspoon salt
3 cups sifted all-purpose flour
1¼ cups sifted stone-ground yellow cornmeal

*Available at specialty food shops

1. Place the water in a small bowl, sprinkle on the yeast and granulated sugar and stir well. Let stand until bubbly.

2. Meanwhile, scald the milk; let cool to lukewarm (105° to 115°). Combine the milk with the yeast mixture. Set aside.

3. Cream the butter until light. Add the brown sugar and beat until fluffy. Add the eggs, one at a time, beating well after each addition. Mix in the salt.

4. Combine the flour and cornmeal and add alternately with the yeast mixture to the butter mixture, beginning and ending with the dry ingredients. Beat until smooth and elastic. (If you use a food processor, do not beat longer than 60 seconds or the dough will overheat and kill the yeast.)

5. Scrape the dough into a well-buttered bowl, cover with a dry kitchen towel and set to rise in a warm draft-free spot until doubled in bulk, about 1 hour.

6. Stir the dough down, then beat hard with a wooden spoon, about 100 strokes. (Because the dough is too sticky to knead, you must beat the very daylights out of it to develop the gluten.)

7. Divide the dough equally among 12 well-buttered 2-inch muffin-tin cups. Cover with a cloth and again let rise until doubled in bulk, 25 to 30 minutes.

8. About 10 minutes before the end of the rising period, preheat the oven to 350°. Bake the Sally Lunn 15 to 20 minutes, until the rolls are nicely browned and sound hollow when thumped.

9. Cool the rolls in their pans on a wire rack for 5 minutes. Turn out and serve hot with plenty of butter.

NOTE: The rolls can also be made ahead of time and frozen. To reheat, wrap the rolls in foil and set in a 350° oven for 10 to 15 minutes.

Cold Water Corn Bread

This corn bread resembles a pancake, and that's exactly what it is—a flat cake, cooked in a pan. The consistency of the batter is the key here. It should be thin enough to run quickly out toward the edge of the skillet, leaving a few holes around the edge as it does. This will give the cake a crunchy texture. Since cornmeals vary widely, so will the quantity of water.

MAKES ABOUT 1 DOZEN 7-INCH ROUNDS

1½ cups yellow cornmeal
1 cup all-purpose flour
¾ teaspoon baking soda
¾ teaspoon salt
¾ to 1 cup peanut oil, for frying

1. Preheat the oven to 225°. In a medium bowl, combine the cornmeal, flour, baking soda and salt. Cover a baking sheet with paper towels.

2. Pour ½ cup of the oil into a heavy 9-inch skillet, preferably cast iron, and set over high heat. Meanwhile, stir 2½ cups of cold water into the cornmeal mixture until blended. Add up to 1 cup more water, as necessary, to make a very thin batter.

3. When the oil begins to smoke, pour about ¼ cup of the batter into the center of the pan; it will form a thin layer over the bottom. Cook for 3 to 4 minutes, until browned; turn over and cook until browned on the other side, about 30 seconds to 1 minute. (Since each round almost fills the pan, turning can be a bit awkward. Use a turner and a small spatula to slide it over.) Drain on the paper towels and keep warm in the oven. Continue making rounds, replenishing the oil as necessary, until all of the batter is used; you may have to add 1 or 2 tablespoons more water if the batter becomes too thick.

Herb Bread

This bread has a lovely crust when baked in a big, stoneware, cloche-type bread baker (a domed cover that fits over a round baking dish). If you don't own one, don't fret. It's equally chewy and good when made on a baking sheet.

MAKES 1 LARGE LOAF

1 envelope (¼ ounce) active dry yeast
1 teaspoon sugar
2 cups lukewarm water (105° to 115°)
5 to 6 cups unbleached all-purpose flour
1 tablespoon salt
1 garlic clove, finely minced
3 tablespoons minced fresh parsley
2 tablespoons minced onion
1 tablespoon olive oil
Cornmeal

1. In a small bowl, combine the yeast and sugar in ¼ cup of the water and let stand until the yeast dissolves and the mixture is bubbly.

2. In a large bowl, combine 4½ cups of the flour with the salt. Add the yeast mixture, the remaining 1¾ cups water, the garlic, parsley, onion and oil. Stir until the mixture forms a soft dough.

3. Turn out onto a floured board and knead until smooth and elastic, 8 to 10 minutes, adding more flour as needed to make a firm dough. Place in a clean oiled bowl and turn to coat lightly with oil. Cover with plastic wrap and a towel and let rise in a warm draft-free place until doubled in bulk, 1 to 1½ hours.

4. Sprinkle the bottom of a stoneware cloche or a baking sheet with coarse cornmeal. Turn out the dough onto a floured surface, punch down, fold over twice and form into a tight smooth ball. Place on the cloche bottom or baking sheet, cover with the cloche lid or an

inverted large heatproof bowl and let rise until doubled in bulk, about 1 hour. Meanwhile, preheat the oven to 375°.

5. Bake the bread covered if using the cloche, uncovered if using just a baking sheet, for 45 to 60 minutes, until brown and crusty. Remove the cover, turn off the heat and let rest 15 minutes with the oven door slightly ajar. The bread is done when the bottom sounds hollow when tapped.

Onion-Rosemary Bread

This savory, pizzalike flatbread is fortified with Parmesan cheese and topped with a scattering of onion rings, olive oil and rosemary. It's best right out of the oven.

4 TO 6 SERVINGS

1 cup lukewarm water (105° to 115°)
1 envelope (¼ ounce) active dry yeast
½ teaspoon sugar
About 3¼ cups all-purpose flour
½ cup freshly grated Parmesan cheese
5 tablespoons olive oil
1 medium onion, sliced crosswise into paper-thin rounds
1½ teaspoons rosemary
1 teaspoon coarse (kosher) salt

1. Place ¼ cup of the warm water in a small bowl and sprinkle the yeast and sugar over the top. Stir until thoroughly dissolved and let the yeast proof until foamy and doubled in bulk, about 5 minutes.

2. In a large bowl or in a food processor, place 3 cups of the flour, the Parmesan cheese and 3 tablespoons of the oil. Add the proofed yeast and remaining ¾ cup warm water. Mix or process, adding enough of the remaining flour to make a soft dough. Turn out onto a lightly floured surface and knead until smooth and elastic—by hand for 10 minutes or in a food processor for 3 to 5 minutes.

3. Rub 1 teaspoon of the remaining oil over the bottom of a medium bowl. Add the dough, turn it to oil the top, cover and let rise in a warm, draft-free place until doubled in bulk, about 1½ hours.

4. Using 1 teaspoon of the remaining oil, lightly coat a 12-by-16-inch baking sheet. Punch down the dough and knead it on a lightly floured surface for 1 minute. Place the dough on the sheet and pat it out into a 10-by-14-inch rectangle. Using your fingertips, make indentations all over the surface of the dough, pressing about halfway into the dough. Brush the dough with 2 teaspoons of the remaining oil. Separate the onion slices into rings and scatter them all over the dough, lightly pressing the onions onto the surface of the dough. Cover with plastic wrap and let rise in a warm, draft-free place until doubled in bulk, about 45 minutes. After 15 minutes, adjust one oven shelf to the lower third of the oven and another to the upper third of the oven; preheat the oven to 400°.

5. Drizzle the remaining 2 teaspoons oil over the onions and sprinkle with the rosemary and salt. Bake the bread in the lower third of the oven for 20 minutes. Transfer to the upper third and bake until the onion rings are deep golden brown and the bread is golden brown, 10 to 15 minutes. Serve hot.

Squash Crescents with Hazelnuts

These are the loveliest dinner rolls imaginable—feather light and butter rich. If you have a food processor, you can mix and knead them in about five minutes flat. If not, you'll find the unrisen dough so tender and soft that it's easier to beat than to knead. Feel free to substitute any pureed winter squash for the acorn squash as long as the consistency is slightly thicker than applesauce.

MAKES ABOUT 2½ DOZEN

2 envelopes (¼ ounce each) active dry yeast
4 tablespoons sugar
¼ cup lukewarm water (105° to 115°)
5½ cups sifted all-purpose flour
1 teaspoon salt
½ cup (1 stick) unsalted butter
½ cup lukewarm milk (105° to 115°)
1 large egg, lightly beaten
1 pound acorn squash or other winter squash, cooked and pureed (to yield ¾ cup firmly packed)
1 cup toasted hazelnuts, finely ground

1. Dissolve the yeast and 1 tablespoon of the sugar in the lukewarm water; set aside.

2. Place the remaining 3 tablespoons sugar, the flour and salt in a large bowl. Cut in 4 tablespoons of the butter until the mixture resembles coarse meal. Stir in the yeast mixture until blended. Add the milk, egg and squash puree and continue to stir until all the ingredients are incorporated.

3. Empty the dough into a well-buttered bowl. Turn the dough so that it is buttered all over and smooth the surface as much as possible with your hands. Cover the bowl with a towel, set in a warm, draft-free place and let the dough rise until doubled in bulk, about 1½ hours.

4. Punch the dough down, turn it out onto a well-floured work surface and

knead vigorously until smooth, 3 to 5 minutes. Divide the dough in half. Roll one-half into a circle about 14 inches in diameter and ⅜ inch thick. Melt the remaining 4 tablespoons butter and brush the dough with half of it. Sprinkle half the hazelnuts evenly over the dough. With a floured sharp knife, cut the dough circle into quarters, then eighths, then sixteenths.

5. Starting at the wide base of each triangle, roll up the dough toward the point. Ease it onto an ungreased baking sheet and then curve the ends of each roll to form a crescent. Do not crowd the rolls on the baking sheet, because they will double in size as they rise. Roll and shape the remaining dough the same way. Cover the rolls with a kitchen towel, set in a warm, draft-free place and let rise until doubled in bulk, about 1 hour.

6. Toward the end of the rising period, preheat the oven to 425°. As soon as the rolls have doubled in bulk, bake for 10 to 12 minutes, until lightly browned.

Apple Puff

This fragrant breakfast treat combines sautéed apples with a baked puff, much like a Yorkshire pudding.

4 TO 6 SERVINGS

½ cup plus 2 tablespoons all-purpose flour
3 eggs
¾ cup milk
¼ teaspoon salt
5½ tablespoons unsalted butter
3 large tart apples, such as Granny Smith, thinly sliced
2 tablespoons sugar
Cinnamon and freshly grated nutmeg

1. Preheat the oven to 400°. Place the flour in a large bowl.

2. In a medium bowl, beat together the eggs and milk until blended. Pour into the center of the flour and stir until smooth. Stir in the salt.

3. In a large, heavy, ovenproof skillet, melt 1½ tablespoons of the butter over low heat; remove from the heat. Pour the batter into the skillet and place in the oven. Bake for 20 minutes. Reduce the oven temperature to 350° and continue to bake for 10 minutes, until the edges are puffed and slightly brown.

4. Meanwhile, in a medium skillet, melt the remaining 4 tablespoons butter over moderately high heat. Add the apples and sugar and cook, stirring, until the apples are slightly softened but still crisp, 3 to 4 minutes. Remove from the heat.

5. To assemble, scrape the apple mixture into the center of the cooked puff, spreading the slices evenly. Sprinkle lightly with cinnamon and nutmeg. Serve hot, cut into wedges.

Pineapple Pan Stuffing

This fruity stuffing is baked in a shallow pan and served, cut into squares, as an accompaniment to roast meat. It is excellent with ham, beef, turkey, chicken or pork.

6 SERVINGS

½ cup (1 stick) unsalted butter, at room temperature
½ cup sugar
3 eggs
1 can (20 ounces) pineapple chunks in syrup, well drained
6 slices firm-textured white bread, cut into ½-inch cubes

1. Preheat the oven to 350°. Lightly grease an 8½- or 9-inch square baking pan.

2. In a medium bowl, cream the butter and sugar until light and fluffy. Add the eggs one at a time, beating until well blended.

3. Stir in the pineapple. Fold in the bread cubes. Turn the stuffing into the pan and spread evenly.

4. Bake uncovered for 1 hour, until the top is brown and crusty. Serve hot or warm.

Funnel Cakes

Essentially a light, simple and very tasty doughnut with an intriguing appearance, funnel cakes are a favorite among the Pennsylvania Dutch. Traditionally, the batter is poured into the hot oil through a large funnel, but we found pouring from a pitcher worked perfectly well.

MAKES ABOUT 12 CAKES

3 eggs
2 cups milk
¼ cup sugar
2¾ cups all-purpose flour
1 cup yellow cornmeal
2½ teaspoons baking powder
½ teaspoon salt
3 cups vegetable oil, for frying
Cinnamon sugar

1. In a medium bowl, whisk the eggs, milk and sugar until the sugar dissolves.

2. In a large bowl, stir together the flour, cornmeal, baking powder and salt. Pour the egg mixture into the flour mixture, stirring to make a thick, smooth batter. Fill a pitcher with the batter.

3. In a large heavy skillet, warm the oil over moderately high heat until a drop of batter rises immediately to the surface and sizzles. Pouring from the outside edge of the skillet and working toward the center, quickly drizzle some batter in a wavy spiral to form a lacy-patterned cake. Cook the funnel cake until golden brown on the bottom, about 2 minutes. Using two spatulas, turn and cook until golden brown on the second side, 1 to 2 minutes. Drain briefly on paper towels and serve warm, dusted with cinnamon sugar.

SALADS:
SIDE-DISH

Winter Squash, Snow Pea and Endive Salad with Ginger-Sesame Dressing

Here is an unusual, nutritious salad. You can use the butternut squash raw if you like (it has a faintly nutty flavor), but blanching it briefly in lightly salted boiling water will remove the raw edge to its taste.

8 SERVINGS

Salad:

1 small butternut squash (¾ to 1 pound)
½ pound snow peas, strings removed, cut lengthwise into ¼-inch strips
3 large Belgian endives, halved crosswise, then cut lengthwise into ¼-inch strips
6 large radishes, trimmed and cut into ¼-inch matchsticks
¼ teaspoon salt
⅛ teaspoon freshly ground pepper

Dressing:

1 small garlic clove, crushed
1½ teaspoons crushed, peeled fresh gingerroot
¼ teaspoon finely grated orange zest
1 tablespoon honey
2 tablespoons soy sauce
3 tablespoons Oriental sesame oil
1 tablespoon peanut oil
3 tablespoons fresh lemon juice

1. Prepare the salad: Halve the butternut squash lengthwise, scoop out all seeds and stringy portions, then cut crosswise in half. Peel the squash and cut into matchstick strips, about 1½ by ¼ inch.

2. Place the squash in a strainer and dip into a large pot of boiling salted water. Blanch the squash until crisp-tender, 10 to 20 seconds. Remove and rinse under cold running water; drain well.

3. In the same water, blanch the snow peas until bright green but still crisp, about 5 seconds; rinse under cold running water and let drain well.

4. In a large serving bowl, combine the squash, snow peas, endives and radishes. Season with the salt and pepper.

5. Make the dressing: In a small bowl, whisk together the garlic, ginger, orange zest, honey, soy sauce and sesame and peanut oils; let stand at room temperature for 20 minutes to allow the flavors to blend.

6. To assemble, drizzle the dressing over the salad and toss lightly to mix. Let stand at room temperature for 10 minutes. Then add the lemon juice, toss again and serve.

Parsley Salad

This marinated vegetable salad is deliciously pungent; the large amount of parsley balances the anchovies and garlic. Serve at room temperature as an hors d'oeuvre with thin slices of French bread.

10 TO 12 SERVINGS

8 cups loosely packed, coarsely chopped parsley (about 10 bunches)
1 small onion, halved and cut lengthwise into thin slices
1 pound carrots, peeled and grated
2 medium red bell peppers, cut into thin julienne strips
10 garlic cloves, minced
2 cans (1.7 ounces each) flat anchovy fillets, drained and coarsely chopped
½ cup red wine vinegar
¾ cup corn or peanut oil
¾ cup olive oil
2 teaspoons salt
½ teaspoon freshly ground black pepper
½ teaspoon crushed hot pepper

1. In a large serving bowl, combine the parsley, onion, carrots, bell peppers and garlic.

2. In a medium bowl, whisk together the anchovies, vinegar, corn oil, olive oil, salt, black pepper and hot pepper until creamy. Pour the vinaigrette over the salad ingredients and toss until thoroughly coated. Refrigerate, covered, for several hours or overnight before serving.

Port and Stilton Salad

8 SERVINGS

1½ tablespoons unsalted butter
2 teaspoons safflower oil
1 garlic clove, unpeeled but bruised
¾ cup walnuts
1 large head of red leaf lettuce, separated into leaves and tough ends removed
2 small heads of Bibb lettuce, separated into leaves
Port Dressing (p. 225)
2 Belgian endives, thinly julienned
½ pound Stilton cheese, coarsely chopped

1. In a medium skillet, melt the butter in the oil over moderate heat. When the foam subsides, add the garlic and cook for 2 minutes. Discard the garlic.

2. Add the walnuts and cook, shaking the pan frequently, until toasted to a dark golden color. Drain the nuts on paper towels.

3. In one bowl, toss the lettuce leaves with ⅔ cup of the Port Dressing. In another bowl, gently toss the julienned endives with the remaining dressing.

4. On each of 8 chilled salad plates, place 1 large leaf of red lettuce. Arrange 3 Bibb lettuce leaves in a cloverleaf shape on top. Neatly bunch the endive julienne in a fringe below the Bibb.

5. Place a heaping spoonful of the Stilton in the middle of each salad and top each with 1½ tablespoons of the toasted walnuts.

A buffet of plenty: Chicken Lasagna (p. 134), Tortellini Salad with Chestnuts (p. 167) and a Granita di Limone (p. 194) with frozen grapes.

Clockwise from left, Spicy Southeast Asian Shrimp Salad (p. 166), Sardinian Roasted Pepper Salad (p. 156) and Veal Tonnato Salad (p. 158).

*Salad of Grilled Chicken Stuffed with California Goat Cheese
with a Tomato Vinaigrette (p. 159).*

Top, Fedelini with Smoked Salmon (p. 133). Bottom, Hot Chicken Salad with Walnut Oil Dressing (p. 160).

Left, Smoked Pork and Cabbage Soup (p. 42) with Rye Muffins (p. 139) and a Compote of Prunes and Oranges (p. 184). Top, Pasta with Grilled Scallops in Chardonnay Cream Sauce (p. 132). Bottom, Lemon-Dill Rice (p. 137).

Lettuce-Walnut Salad with Goat Cheese

6 SERVINGS

3 medium heads of limestone
   lettuce
¼ cup walnut pieces
3 to 4 ounces goat cheese,
   preferably caprini di capra from
   Italy
¼ cup olive oil
1 tablespoon white wine vinegar
⅛ teaspoon salt
¼ teaspoon pepper

1. Trim off and discard any brown outer lettuce leaves and separate the leaves from the head; wash well and dry. Arrange the leaves on a platter with the darker, larger leaves on the outside and the lighter yellow leaves in the center, to resemble a split head of lettuce.

2. Sprinkle the walnut pieces over the lettuce. Crumble the goat cheese or cut it into small bits if it is creamy and sprinkle it over the salad.

3. In a small bowl, whisk together the oil, vinegar, salt and pepper and drizzle over the salad. Serve immediately with crusty bread and more of the goat cheese if you wish.

Spinach and Sprout Salad with Peanuts

2 SERVINGS

½ pound fresh spinach
1½ to 2 tablespoons fresh lime
   juice, to taste
1½ teaspoons finely grated fresh
   peeled gingerroot
1 teaspoon soy sauce
1 teaspoon brown sugar
⅛ teaspoon minced garlic
Pepper
1½ tablespoons peanut oil
1½ cups (about 5 ounces) mung
   bean sprouts, drained
2 tablespoons roasted, unsalted
   peanuts, coarsely chopped

---

*Fresh and summery Corn and To-
mato Salad (p. 154) made with Basil
Preserved in Oil (p. 224).*

1. Stem the spinach. Wash the leaves well, drain, then dry thoroughly. Cut into bite-size pieces and place in a serving bowl in the refrigerator.

2. Combine the lime juice, ginger, soy sauce, brown sugar, garlic and pepper to taste in a small jar; shake to blend. Add the oil and shake again.

3. Add the sprouts to the spinach. Pour on the dressing and toss to coat. Sprinkle the peanuts on top.

Spinach Salad with Warm Balsamic Dressing

The balanced, mellow flavor of balsamic vinegar makes possible a one-to-one, vinegar to oil ratio. The warm dressing softens the spinach slightly without wilting it, and the sliced toasted almonds are deliciously crunchy.

6 SERVINGS

½ pound fresh spinach, torn into
   bite-size pieces
1 large red bell pepper, cut into
   thin strips
¼ cup balsamic vinegar
¼ cup fruity olive oil
2 garlic cloves, minced
¼ teaspoon freshly ground black
   pepper
½ cup sliced toasted almonds

1. In a medium bowl, combine the spinach and bell pepper.

2. In a small heavy saucepan, whisk the vinegar and oil until well blended. Whisk in the garlic and black pepper.

3. Warm the dressing over low heat, stirring, until heated through, about 1 minute. Pour the warm dressing over the spinach and red pepper and toss until coated. Just before serving, add the almonds and toss to mix.

Snow Pea Salad with Walnut Vinaigrette

This crisp vegetable salad is best eaten as a separate course.

4 SERVINGS

1 pound fresh snow peas, strings
   removed
1½ tablespoons fresh lime juice
2 teaspoons low-salt tamari or soy
   sauce
⅓ cup walnut oil
3 thin scallions, thinly sliced on
   the diagonal
2 teaspoons minced fresh
   gingerroot

1. In a large pot of boiling water, blanch the snow peas until bright green and beginning to puff, 45 to 60 seconds. Drain and rinse under cold running water; drain well and pat dry. Place in a serving bowl.

2. In a small bowl, whisk the lime juice and tamari until blended. Whisk in the walnut oil. Stir in the scallions and ginger. Pour the vinaigrette over the snow peas and toss until well coated.

Winter Salad

4 SERVINGS

1 small bunch of arugula
1 head of radicchio
1 Belgian endive
1 small head of red leaf lettuce
4 ounces *mâche* (lamb's lettuce)
1 tablespoon sherry vinegar
1½ teaspoons minced shallots
¼ teaspoon salt
⅛ teaspoon freshly ground pepper
¼ cup extra-virgin olive oil
½ tablespoon hazelnut oil
1 tablespoon walnut oil

1. Carefully wash the salad greens, drain and pat dry. Tear into bite-size pieces and place in a large bowl.

2. In a small bowl, use a whisk to blend the vinegar, shallots, salt and pepper. Gradually whisk in the oils, from the heaviest to the lightest: first, the olive oil, then hazelnut and finally the walnut. Drizzle the dressing over the greens, toss and serve.

Beet, Leek and Zucchini Salad with Radicchio and Romaine

To prepare this salad ahead of time, cook all of the vegetables; cool and wrap individually, then refrigerate. Cut into matchstick strips when you're ready to assemble the salad, not before. Make the dressing several hours ahead of time (or the day before) so that its flavors have a chance to mingle and mellow.

6 TO 8 SERVINGS

6 medium beets, with root ends and 1 inch of the tops left on
4 medium leeks (white and light green)
4 medium zucchini
1 small head of romaine lettuce, washed and patted very dry
1 medium head of radicchio, washed and patted very dry
Lemon-Dill Dressing (p. 225)

1. In a heavy medium saucepan, cook the beets in boiling water to cover over moderate heat until fork-tender, 30 to 45 minutes. Drain, let cool to room temperature, then peel and cut into matchstick strips; set aside.

2. Quarter each leek lengthwise, cutting to within 1½ inches of the base. Fan out, plunge into tepid water and slosh gently up and down to remove all grit and sand. Lay the leeks flat in a heavy medium skillet and add water to cover. Simmer, covered, until tender, 10 to 15 minutes. Drain and let cool to room temperature; cut into matchstick strips.

3. In a covered medium saucepan, cook the whole zucchini in boiling water to cover until crisp-tender, about 10 minutes. Drain and let cool to room temperature; cut into matchstick strips.

4. To assemble the salad, wreathe the romaine and radicchio leaves around the edge of a round plate; place additional leaves in the center. Arrange clusters of the beets, leeks and zucchini strips on top. Shake the dressing well, then drizzle evenly over the salad. Let marinate at room temperature for about 30 minutes before serving.

Corn and Tomato Salad with Basil

4 SERVINGS

3 large (or 4 medium) ears of corn (see Note)
2 large tomatoes—peeled, seeded, coarsely chopped and drained
1 tablespoon plus 1 teaspoon Basil Preserved in Oil (p. 224)
1 tablespoon basil oil, drained from Basil Preserved in Oil
½ teaspoon salt
½ teaspoon freshly ground pepper

1. In a large pot of boiling water, cook the corn until just tender, about 5 minutes. Drain and rinse under cold running water until cool; drain well. Using a sharp knife, scrape the kernels off the ears.

2. In a large serving bowl, combine the corn with the tomatoes, basil, oil, salt and pepper; toss to mix. Serve at room temperature.

NOTE: If fresh corn is not available, substitute 1 package (10 ounces) frozen corn, thawed to room temperature.

Orange-Basil Salad with Pine Nuts

6 SERVINGS

4 navel oranges, peeled and sliced
½ teaspoon coarsely ground pepper
⅓ cup pine nuts (pignoli), toasted (see Note)
1 tablespoon Basil Preserved in Oil (p. 224)
2 tablespoons orange juice, preferably fresh
1½ tablespoons basil oil, drained from Basil Preserved in Oil
¼ teaspoon salt

1. Arrange the orange slices on a serving platter and sprinkle with the pepper.

2. Reserve 2 tablespoons of the pine nuts; coarsely chop the remainder. Toss with the basil, orange juice, oil and salt.

3. Spoon the basil-nut mixture onto the center of each orange slice. Sprinkle the reserved whole nuts on top.

NOTE: To toast pine nuts, preheat the oven to 375°. Place the pine nuts in a baking pan and roast for about 10 minutes, shaking occasionally, until golden.

Asparagus and Beet Salad with Tarragon

4 SERVINGS

2 medium beets, with root ends and 1 inch of the tops left on
8 large asparagus spears, trimmed
2 teaspoons finely chopped fresh tarragon or ½ teaspoon dried
2 tablespoons olive oil
2 teaspoons fresh lemon juice
Salt and freshly ground pepper

1. In a small heavy saucepan, cook the beets in boiling water to cover until fork-tender, 30 to 45 minutes. Drain, let cool to room temperature, then peel and cut into 2-inch julienne strips.

2. In a large pot of boiling salted water, cook the asparagus until tender but still bright green, 3 to 4 minutes. Drain and rinse under cold running water; drain well. Cut the spears into 2-inch lengths; then quarter lengthwise.

3. Toss the beets and asparagus with the tarragon, olive oil and lemon juice. Season with salt and pepper to taste. Marinate for at least 30 minutes at room temperature to let the flavors develop before serving.

Leek Salad

This unusual dish comes from a very old "salet" recipe, which in the Middle Ages would have been marigold blossoms. Use only the tender and delicate part of the leek; if the green is too strong (try a nibble), use only the white.

6 SERVINGS

1 cup thinly sliced leek, tender part only (white and mild green)
1 cup chopped celery (2 medium ribs)
1 cup (5 ounces) frozen peas, thawed
1 tablespoon finely chopped fresh mint or fennel leaves
Small bunch of chicory, torn into bite-size pieces (about ½ pound)
4 or 5 thin rounds of red onion, separated into rings
1 small navel orange, peeled and cut into thin rounds
6 tablespoons vegetable oil
2 tablespoons cider vinegar
1 teaspoon Dijon-style mustard
1 teaspoon minced fresh dill or ½ teaspoon dried dillweed
¼ teaspoon sugar
¼ teaspoon paprika
¼ teaspoon salt
⅛ teaspoon freshly ground pepper

1. Place the sliced leek in a colander; pour 2 cups of boiling water over it. Rinse under cold water and drain well.

2. In a medium bowl, combine the leek, celery, peas and mint. Toss together and place on a bed of chicory. Arrange the onion rings and orange slices on top.

3. In a small bowl, whisk the oil, vinegar, mustard, dill, sugar, paprika, salt and pepper until blended (or place in a small jar, cover and shake well). Drizzle the dressing over the salad.

Marinated Gazpacho Salad

This salad tastes best if made a day ahead. Serve slightly chilled.

6 TO 8 SERVINGS

1¼ pounds ripe tomatoes—peeled, seeded and chopped
2 medium cucumbers—peeled, seeded and chopped
2 green bell peppers, chopped
½ Bermuda or Spanish onion, chopped
½ cup oil- or brine-cured black olives, pitted and cut into slivers
½ cup chopped fresh parsley
¼ cup chopped fresh mint
⅔ cup olive oil
⅓ cup red wine vinegar, preferably balsamic
2 garlic cloves, minced
½ teaspoon salt
½ teaspoon freshly ground black pepper
¼ teaspoon ground cumin

1. In a large bowl, combine the chopped tomatoes, cucumbers, green peppers, onion, olives, parsley and mint.

2. In a small bowl, whisk the olive oil, vinegar, garlic, salt, black pepper and cumin until blended. Pour the dressing over the vegetables and toss until mixed. Refrigerate, covered, for several hours or overnight. Stir before serving.

Creamy Tomato-Zucchini Salad

6 SERVINGS

3 small zucchini, thinly sliced
2 scallions, minced
½ teaspoon salt
⅔ cup (6 ounces) custard-style or whole-milk plain yogurt
1 very small garlic clove, minced
2 tablespoons chopped parsley
¼ teaspoon ground cumin
Freshly ground pepper
2 cups (1 pint) cherry tomatoes, quartered

1. Place the zucchini, scallions and salt in a medium bowl and toss until mixed. Let sit for about 10 minutes; drain off any liquid.

2. Meanwhile, place the yogurt, garlic, parsley and cumin in a small bowl and mix until smooth. Season with pepper to taste.

3. Add the cherry tomatoes and the yogurt dressing to the zucchini and toss again to combine. Serve chilled.

Orange-Jicama Salad

Jicama is a crunchy root vegetable, which here adds a crisp note to a marvelously refreshing salad. Serve as a salad or as a first course.

8 SERVINGS

2 heads of butter lettuce or romaine, cut into long shreds
¼ of a large jicama,* peeled and cut into ⅛-inch julienne strips
4 large navel oranges, peeled and sectioned
1 medium red onion, chopped
8 radishes, cut into roses or sliced
6 tablespoons vegetable oil
2 tablespoons fresh orange juice
½ teaspoon chili powder
1 teaspoon distilled white vinegar
¼ teaspoon salt
⅛ teaspoon freshly ground pepper
*Available in Latin American markets and in some supermarkets

1. On 8 individual salad plates, arrange a bed of shredded lettuce. Sprinkle the jicama on top. Arrange about 5 orange sections in a flower pattern on top of each. Sprinkle with the chopped red onion. Put a radish in the center of each salad.

2. In a small, tightly lidded jar, combine the oil, orange juice, chili powder, vinegar, salt and pepper. Shake to blend well. Sprinkle about 1 tablespoon over each salad just before serving.

Guatemalan Radish and Carrot Salad

4 SERVINGS

2 medium carrots, cut into 1½-by-¼-inch julienne strips
12 large radishes, thinly sliced
1 small onion, thinly sliced and separated into rings
2 tablespoons olive oil
3 tablespoons fresh lemon juice
½ teaspoon sugar
½ teaspoon salt
Romaine lettuce leaves, for garnish

1. In a medium bowl, combine the carrots, radishes and onion.

2. In a small bowl, combine the olive oil, lemon juice, sugar and salt. Stir to dissolve the sugar and salt. Pour the dressing over the vegetables and toss.

3. Cover and refrigerate until chilled, at least 1 hour, or overnight if desired. To serve, mound the salad in the lettuce leaves.

Sardinian Roasted Pepper Salad

Charring peppers on an outdoor grill gives them great flavor. This savory yet fruity salad goes well with grilled lamb or chicken. It keeps for about a week in the refrigerator.

6 SERVINGS

6 medium bell peppers, preferably 2 red, 2 green and 2 yellow
2 tablespoons balsamic or red wine vinegar
½ cup raisins
1 small fresh hot red pepper, seeded and minced (about 1 teaspoon) or ½ teaspoon dried hot red pepper flakes
1 small garlic clove, minced
6 ripe plum tomatoes (about 1 pound)—peeled, seeded and coarsely chopped—or 1 can (20 ounces) Italian peeled tomatoes, drained and coarsely chopped
6 tablespoons olive oil, preferably extra-virgin
¼ teaspoon oregano
½ teaspoon salt

¼ teaspoon freshly ground black pepper

1. Light the charcoal or preheat the broiler. Grill or broil the bell peppers 3 to 4 inches from the heat, turning, until completely charred, 10 to 20 minutes. Let cool for 1 minute, then seal in a brown paper bag and let steam for 10 minutes.

2. Remove the peppers from the bag and scrape off the charred skin. Halve the peppers and remove the stems, seeds and ribs. Cut the peppers into ¼-inch strips. (**The recipe may be prepared a day ahead to this point.** Wrap and refrigerate the peppers overnight. Let return to room temperature before continuing.)

3. In a small noncorrodible saucepan, bring the vinegar to a boil. Reduce the heat to moderately low, add the raisins and simmer, covered, for 15 minutes.

4. In a large bowl, place the roasted bell peppers, the hot pepper, garlic, tomatoes, oil, oregano, salt and black pepper. Add the raisins, toss and let marinate at room temperature for at least 30 minutes before serving.

Gyttosasouao (Black-Eyed Peas in Olive Oil and Lemon)

8 TO 12 SERVINGS

1 pound dried black-eyed peas, rinsed and picked over
1 medium onion
6 whole peppercorns
1 bay leaf
1 teaspoon salt
¼ cup fresh lemon juice
½ cup olive oil
4 garlic cloves, crushed
¼ teaspoon oregano
Freshly ground pepper

1. In a large heavy saucepan or flameproof casserole, combine the dried peas with 6 cups of cold water. Bring to a boil, cover and remove from the heat. Let stand for 1 hour; drain well.

2. Return the black-eyed peas to the

saucepan. Add 6 cups of fresh cold water. Tie the onion, whole peppercorns and bay leaf in a double thickness of cheesecloth. Add to the saucepan and bring to a boil over high heat. Reduce the heat to low and simmer, uncovered, until the peas are soft but still firm, 25 to 30 minutes. Add the salt.

3. Drain the peas, discarding the cheesecloth bag, and place in a large serving bowl.

4. In a small bowl, whisk the lemon juice, olive oil, garlic and oregano until blended. Pour the dressing over the peas and toss until evenly coated. Season with salt and pepper to taste. Serve at room temperature, or cover and refrigerate until shortly before serving.

Grandma Linahan's Macaroni Salad

6 TO 8 SERVINGS

⅓ cup minced green bell pepper
⅔ cup minced onion
⅓ cup minced celery
2 cups uncooked macaroni
½ cup mayonnaise
½ teaspoon powdered mustard or more to taste
1 tablespoon sugar
2 tablespoons distilled white vinegar
½ cup milk
¾ teaspoon salt
½ teaspoon black pepper
Pinch of cayenne pepper
2 tablespoons butter, melted and still warm
¼ cup thinly sliced scallions, for garnish

1. Prepare the green pepper, onion and celery while cooking the macaroni according to package directions.

2. Drain the macaroni but don't rinse. In a small bowl, blend the mayonnaise, mustard, sugar, vinegar, salt, black pepper and cayenne. Slowly blend in the milk.

3. Stir in the butter and toss the dressing with the still warm macaroni. Add the vegetables, toss thoroughly, correct the seasoning, cover and refrigerate for 3 hours or overnight. Before serving, sprinkle with the scallions.

SALADS: MAIN-COURSE

Veal Tonnato Salad

Serve this zesty salad with plenty of warm, crusty Italian bread. The grilled veal scallops may be served warm or at room temperature.

F&W Beverage Suggestion:
Orvieto, such as Antinori

6 SERVINGS

2 tablespoons Dijon-style mustard
¼ cup fresh lemon juice
2 tablespoons minced red onion plus 1 small red onion, thinly sliced and separated into rings
2 tablespoons drained capers
1 tablespoon minced fresh parsley
¾ teaspoon salt
1 cup plus 2 tablespoons olive oil, preferably extra-virgin
1 can (3½ ounces) tuna packed in olive oil, drained and finely chopped
¼ teaspoon freshly ground pepper
6 large veal scallops (about 1½ pounds), pounded ⅛ inch thick
1½ teaspoons minced fresh thyme or ½ teaspoon dried
1 head of romaine lettuce
1 lemon, thinly sliced
3 hard-cooked eggs, sliced
6 flat anchovy fillets (optional)

1. In a small mixing bowl, combine the mustard, lemon juice, minced onion, capers, parsley and ¼ teaspoon of the salt. Gradually whisk in 1 cup of the oil in a steady stream. Stir in the tuna and set aside.

2. Light the charcoal. Brush the veal scallops on both sides with the remaining 2 tablespoons olive oil. Combine the remaining ½ teaspoon salt, the pepper and thyme and sprinkle over both sides of the scallops.

3. Grill the veal scallops as close to the hot coals as possible until they just lose their pink color, 1½ to 2 minutes on each side. If no grill is available, sauté the veal in a heavy skillet over moderately high heat for about 2 minutes on each side.

4. Place the veal scallops in a large shallow bowl and add half the tuna dressing, turning the veal to coat well. Set the remaining dressing aside. (**The recipe may be prepared ahead to this point.** Let the veal cool to room temperature, cover and refrigerate overnight. Let return to room temperature before continuing.)

5. To serve, place the romaine leaves on a large serving platter and arrange the veal on top. Garnish with the onion rings, lemon slices, eggs and anchovies. Pour the reserved dressing over the veal or serve on the side.

Kentucky Pork Salad

This hearty dish is beautiful to behold as well as exceedingly tasty. Serve it with biscuits hot from the oven. For authentic regional flavor, add applewood or hickory chips to the coals before grilling. A grill with a cover allows the cook more heat control and helps capture the smoky taste imparted by the wood chips.

F&W Beverage Suggestion:
Chilled lager beer

6 SERVINGS

5 tablespoons Dijon-style mustard
6 tablespoons unsulphured molasses
5 tablespoons bourbon
¼ teaspoon hot pepper sauce
6 loin pork chops, cut 1 inch thick (2½ to 3 pounds)
¾ pound yams (about 3), peeled and cut into ¼-inch slices
½ cup fresh lime juice
3 tablespoons minced shallots
1 tablespoon minced fresh parsley
¾ teaspoon salt
½ teaspoon coarsely cracked black pepper
⅔ cup peanut oil
1 head of chicory, torn into bite-size pieces
1 small red cabbage (about 1 pound), shredded
2 tart apples, such as Granny Smith, cored and cut into wedges

1. In a large baking dish, combine 2 tablespoons of the mustard, 3 tablespoons of the molasses, 2 tablespoons of the bourbon and ⅛ teaspoon of the hot sauce. Add the pork chops and sliced yams and turn to coat. Cover and let marinate at room temperature for at least 30 minutes or up to 4 hours.

2. Light the charcoal or preheat the broiler. Remove the pork chops and yams from the marinade, scraping off most of it. Grill the chops, covered with a tent of aluminum foil, or broil about 3 to 4 inches from the heat, turning once, until glazed and browned but white and moist throughout, about 6 minutes on each side. Grill the yam slices for 8 to 10 minutes on each side, until soft and browned. (**The recipe may be prepared a day ahead to this point.** Let the meat and yams cool to room temperature. Wrap and refrigerate overnight. Let return to room temperature before continuing.)

3. In a medium bowl, combine the remaining 3 tablespoons mustard, molasses and bourbon and ⅛ teaspoon hot sauce with the lime juice, shallots, parsley, salt and pepper. Gradually whisk in the oil in a steady stream to make a dressing.

4. Bone the pork chops and cut the meat into ½-inch cubes. Place the pork in a shallow bowl, add the yams and half the dressing. Toss to coat well.

5. Line a platter with the chicory tossed with a little dressing. Add the shredded cabbage, also tossed with dressing, in a ring on the platter. Toss the apple wedges in dressing and arrange in spokes around the platter, then mound the dressed pork and sweet potato slices in the center. (Or if you prefer, toss all the ingredients with the remaining dressing at one time.)

Roast Pork and Vegetable Salad

We've given directions for cooking a pork loin here, but this recipe was actually designed as a perfect salad for leftover roast pork. If you have any on hand, begin with Step 2.

F&W Beverage Suggestion:
Alsatian Gewürztraminer, such as Château de Mittelwihr

8 SERVINGS

1 pound pork loin, rolled and tied
½ pound sunchokes (Jerusalem artichokes), peeled

1 small red cabbage (1½ pounds),
  shredded
1 pound medium turnips, peeled
  and sliced into thin rounds
¼ pound snow peas, strings
  removed
¾ cup safflower oil
4 teaspoons fresh lime juice
2 egg yolks
1 tablespoon Dijon-style mustard
½ teaspoon anchovy paste
2 tablespoons tarragon vinegar
½ teaspoon ground cumin
¼ teaspoon salt
⅛ teaspoon freshly ground black
  pepper
½ cup olive oil
Pinch of sugar
¼ cup dry white wine
2 tablespoons minced fresh parsley
2 tablespoons finely minced fresh
  hot red pepper

1. Preheat the oven to 375°. In a shallow roasting pan, roast the pork loin for 45 to 60 minutes, or until the internal temperature measures 145° to 150° on an instant-reading thermometer. Remove and let cool to room temperature.

2. Meanwhile, separately steam the vegetables until crisp-tender: about 20 minutes for the sunchokes, about 15 minutes for the cabbage, about 10 minutes for the turnips and about 5 minutes for the snow peas. Drain and rinse under cold running water; pat dry. **(The recipe may be prepared a day ahead to this point.** Wrap and refrigerate the pork and vegetables. Let stand at room temperature for 1 hour before continuing.)

3. In a small bowl or glass jar, mix ¼ cup of the safflower oil with 1 teaspoon of the lime juice. In separate bowls, toss each of the cooked vegetables with 1 tablespoon of this oil and lime mixture.

4. Meanwhile, make the mayonnaise dressing: In a food processor or blender, combine the egg yolks, mustard, anchovy paste, remaining 3 teaspoons lime juice, vinegar, cumin, salt and black pepper. Process until blended.

5. With the machine on, gradually pour in the remaining ½ cup safflower oil in a thin stream. Gradually pour in the olive

oil. Add the sugar. Gradually add the white wine to thin the mayonnaise. Stir in the parsley.

6. Slice the pork ⅛ inch thick. On a large serving platter, arrange the vegetables in decorative concentric circles, starting with the cabbage and ending with the pork slices in the center. Pour ¾ cup of the mayonnaise onto the pork; garnish with the hot red pepper. Pass the remaining mayonnaise separately.

Michael's Salad of Grilled Chicken Stuffed with California Goat Cheese with a Tomato Vinaigrette

This salad can be served warm or at room temperature.

F&W Beverage Suggestion: California Fumé Blanc, such as Chateau St. Jean

4 SERVINGS

2 whole chicken breasts, with
  wings attached
4 ounces fresh, mild goat cheese, at
  room temperature
1½ tablespoons unsalted butter, at
  room temperature
¼ teaspoon thyme
Salt and freshly ground pepper
10 large basil leaves, finely
  chopped
10 sprigs of fresh coriander, finely
  chopped, plus the leaves from 2
  sprigs
2 tablespoons finely chopped
  chives
8 tablespoons olive oil, preferably
  extra-virgin
1 small shallot, minced
1 small garlic clove, minced
1 jalapeño pepper—roasted, peeled,
  seeded and minced
2 tablespoons champagne vinegar
  or white wine vinegar
2 large tomatoes—peeled, seeded
  and coarsely chopped
About 4 cups mixed salad greens
  (see Note), torn into pieces
1 red bell pepper, cut into julienne
  strips

1 yellow bell pepper, cut into
  julienne strips

1. Preheat the oven to 350°. Carefully bone the chicken breasts, leaving the wing bone and skin attached.

2. In a small bowl, blend the goat cheese, 1 tablespoon of the butter, the thyme, a pinch of salt and pepper and all but a pinch of the basil, chopped coriander and chives. Reserve the pinches of chopped herbs for the vinaigrette.

3. Using your finger, carefully make a pocket between the skin and the meat of each chicken breast with as small an opening to the outside as possible. Stuff the herbed cheese mixture in a thin layer under the skin.

4. In a large skillet, warm 2 tablespoons of the oil and the remaining ½ tablespoon of butter over moderately high heat. When the foam subsides, add the chicken breasts, skin-side down, and sauté, turning once, until well browned, 6 to 8 minutes.

5. Transfer the chicken to a baking pan and roast in the oven for about 5 minutes. Remove from the oven and let rest for about 10 minutes.

6. Meanwhile, make the tomato vinaigrette. In a bowl, whisk the remaining 6 tablespoons olive oil, the shallot, garlic, jalapeño pepper, vinegar, ¼ teaspoon salt and ¼ teaspoon pepper. Stir in the tomatoes. Just before serving, add the reserved herbs and the whole coriander leaves.

7. Arrange the greens on 4 large plates. Slice the chicken breasts on the diagonal, leaving the wing on, and fan out the slices in the middle of the plate. Arrange the bell peppers around the edge of the greens. Dot the plate with the vinaigrette, spooning some around the chicken for color contrast.

NOTE: Use a combination of sweet and bitter salad greens, such as Boston, Bibb or limestone lettuce with arugula, chicory or radicchio.

The Ginger Man's Chicken Breast with Mustard and Sesame Sauce

In this chicken salad, the pungency of ginger and scallions infuses the chicken as it poaches. Mustard dressing is mellowed with sherry and sesame oil and the earthy taste of fresh coriander. The flavor, at once French and Chinese, is so intense that it belies the ease with which the dish is made.

F&W Beverage Suggestion:
White Châteauneuf-du-Pape, such as Château de Beaucastel

4 SERVINGS

2 whole chicken breasts (about 3 pounds)
4 scallions, cut into 4-inch lengths
5 quarter-size slices of peeled fresh ginger
½ cup Dijon-style mustard
½ cup vegetable oil
1 tablespoon Oriental sesame oil
1½ teaspoons dry sherry
4 leaves of crisp lettuce, such as romaine or iceberg, cut into julienne strips
Fresh coriander leaves, for garnish

1. Place the chicken breasts, skin-side down, in a pot just large enough to hold them in a single layer.

2. In a blender or food processor, puree the scallions and ginger with 1 cup of water and add to the pot. Add cold water to cover the chicken by 1 inch. Bring to a boil over high heat. Reduce the heat to low and simmer until just cooked through, about 20 minutes. Plunge the chicken into a large bowl of ice water to cool it quickly to room temperature. Remove the breast meat in 4 intact halves, discarding the skin and bones. Cut each breast crosswise on the diagonal into ½-inch slices. Arrange one breast on each of four plates.

3. In a medium bowl, whisk together the mustard, vegetable oil, sesame oil and sherry. Spoon about 3 tablespoons of the dressing over each serving of chicken and serve the remainder in a sauceboat.

4. Garnish each plate with one-fourth of the lettuce and fresh coriander leaves.

Maxwell's Plum Hot Chicken Salad

This hot chicken salad is an exuberant expression of summer. Lettuces are shredded and mounded high, with a fan of sautéed chicken flowing down from the top. A dressing of nuts and herbs is spiked with the sharpness of good wine vinegar. This recipe takes only minutes to prepare.

F&W Beverage Suggestion:
Italian white, such as Gavi

4 SERVINGS

4 skinless, boneless chicken breast halves (about 2 pounds)
8 cups shredded mixed greens, such as Bibb, romaine, red leaf lettuce and watercress
2 tomatoes, cut into julienne strips
Salt and freshly ground pepper
3 tablespoons vegetable oil
2 teaspoons coarsely chopped fresh tarragon or dill
2 teaspoons coarsely chopped fresh parsley
2 teaspoons coarsely chopped chives
¼ cup thinly sliced scallion greens
1 tablespoon plus 1 teaspoon red wine vinegar
2 tablespoons pine nuts (pignoli)
Walnut Oil Dressing (recipe follows)

1. Cut each chicken breast lengthwise into ½-inch slices, keeping the shape of the breast. Place each breast between two layers of waxed paper and pound until ½ to ¾ inch thick.

2. Arrange the greens and tomatoes in a mound in the center of each of four plates.

3. Season the chicken with salt and pepper. In a large noncorrodible skillet, heat the oil over moderately high heat. Add the chicken and sauté, turning once, until lightly browned outside and opaque throughout, about 1½ minutes on each side. Fan out each breast half on top of the greens on each plate.

4. Add the tarragon, parsley, chives, scallions, vinegar and pine nuts to the skillet and reduce the heat. Cook, stirring, for 1 minute. Drizzle over the chicken. Serve with Walnut Oil Dressing on the side.

Maxwell's Plum Walnut Oil Dressing

MAKES ABOUT ½ CUP

1 teaspoon minced garlic
2 tablespoons Dijon-style mustard
2 tablespoons plus 2 teaspoons red wine vinegar
½ teaspoon salt
¼ teaspoon freshly ground white pepper
¼ cup walnut oil

In a medium bowl, mix the garlic, mustard, vinegar, salt and white pepper. Gradually whisk in the oil until well blended.

One Fifth's Smoked Chicken with Apples and Arugula

Fragrant wood smoke, the tart snap of a crisp apple and the play of walnuts and walnut oil against the pungent flavor of arugula produce a richly flavorful combination in this chicken salad.

F&W Beverage Suggestion:
Gewürztraminer, such as DeLoach Vineyards

4 SERVINGS

⅓ cup coarsely chopped walnuts
Juice of 1 lemon
2 Red Delicious or other crisp apples
4 skinless, boneless smoked chicken breast halves (about 1 pound)
6 cups arugula, stems removed
Walnut Vinaigrette (recipe follows)

1. Preheat the oven to 300°. In a shallow pan, bake the walnuts in the oven, shaking the pan occasionally, until toasted, 25 to 30 minutes. Set aside to cool. Reserve 1 tablespoon of the nuts for the Walnut Vinaigrette.

2. In a small bowl, combine the lemon juice with 1 cup of cold water. Core, peel and thinly slice the apples and dip the slices into the mixture to prevent discoloration; drain.

3. Cut the chicken crosswise on the diagonal into thin slices. Arrange the chicken and apple slices on one side of each of four plates, alternating and overlapping the slices. Arrange the arugula on the other half of the plates. Spoon 1½ tablespoons of Walnut Vinaigrette over each serving of arugula, and drizzle 1 tablespoon of the vinaigrette over the chicken. Garnish each serving of chicken with about 1 tablespoon of the toasted walnuts. Pass the remaining vinaigrette in a sauceboat.

One Fifth's Walnut Vinaigrette

MAKES ABOUT 1½ CUPS

1 egg yolk
2 tablespoons Dijon-style mustard
¼ cup white wine vinegar
1 teaspoon salt
¼ teaspoon freshly ground pepper
1 cup walnut oil
1 tablespoon chopped toasted walnuts (see Note)

In a medium bowl, whisk together the egg yolk and mustard. Mix in the vinegar, salt and pepper. Gradually whisk in the oil. Add the walnuts and serve at room temperature.

NOTE: Use the walnuts reserved from Step 1 of Smoked Chickens with Apples and Arugula (above).

Windows on the World's Chicken Salad with Crème Fraîche

In this variation on the classic chicken salad, the crème fraîche binds the ingredients and marries their flavors. A confetti of red and green bell peppers and a bed of radicchio leaves provide the crunch.

🍷 **F&W Beverage Suggestion:**
Alsace Riesling, such as Trimbach

4 SERVINGS

1 whole chicken (about 3 pounds)
Salt and freshly ground black pepper
3 tablespoons vegetable oil
⅔ cup crème fraîche

⅓ cup diced (½-inch) red bell pepper
1 cup diced (½-inch) green bell pepper
2 tablespoons minced fresh coriander
1 head of Bibb lettuce
2 heads of radicchio (about ½ pound) or an equal quantity of tender red cabbage leaves

1. Preheat the oven to 375°. Season the chicken inside and out with salt and pepper.

2. In a roasting pan just large enough to hold the chicken, warm the oil over moderate heat. Place the chicken on its side in the pan and roast for 20 minutes. Turn onto the other side and roast for 20 minutes. Turn onto its back and roast, basting often with the pan juices, for 20 to 25 minutes longer, until the juices run clear when the thigh is pierced with a fork. Remove the chicken from the pan, let cool to room temperature and refrigerate, covered, until chilled.

3. Remove the meat from the carcass, discarding the skin and bones. Cut the meat into ½-inch chunks.

4. In a medium bowl, combine the chicken, crème fraîche, red and green peppers, coriander, ½ teaspoon salt and ¼ teaspoon pepper. Toss well to coat. Refrigerate, covered, until ready to serve.

5. Arrange the lettuce leaves on each of four plates. Arrange the radicchio leaves in a circle within the lettuce. Mound the chilled chicken mixture in the center of the lettuces and serve.

"21" Chicken Salad

At the venerable "21" in New York, chilled chicken is mixed with shredded lettuce and cabbage and tossed with a combination of watercress, chili sauce and a thick French dressing.

🍷 **F&W Beverage Suggestion:**
Spanish Rioja, such as Domecq Privilegio

4 SERVINGS

2 whole chicken breasts (about 3 pounds)
½ cup chili sauce
½ cup coarsely chopped watercress
½ cup "21" French Dressing (recipe follows)
1 small head of crisp lettuce, such as romaine or iceberg, finely shredded (about 4 cups)
1 small head (1 pound) of green cabbage, finely shredded (about 4 cups)
Capers, for garnish

1. Place the chicken breasts skin-side down in a pot just large enough to hold them with cold water to cover by 1 inch. Bring to a boil over high heat. Reduce the heat to low and simmer until just cooked through and no longer pink in the center, about 20 minutes. Remove from the pot and set the chicken aside to cool to room temperature; cover and refrigerate until chilled. Discard the skin and bones and cut the meat into julienne strips.

2. In a small bowl, mix the chili sauce and watercress with the ½ cup "21" French Dressing.

3. In a large salad bowl, combine the chicken with the lettuce and cabbage. Add the dressing and toss well. Serve chilled, with capers passed separately.

"21" French Dressing

<u>MAKES ABOUT 1 CUP</u>

1 egg yolk
4 tablespoons cider vinegar
1 teaspoon Worcestershire sauce
1 teaspoon salt
¼ teaspoon paprika
¼ teaspoon powdered mustard
¼ teaspoon freshly ground pepper
⅔ cup olive oil

1. Beat the egg yolk with 3 tablespoons of the vinegar, the Worcestershire sauce, salt, paprika, mustard and pepper.

2. Slowly beat in the oil drop by drop until the mixture begins to thicken. Continue to beat in the oil in a thin stream.

3. Add the remaining 1 tablespoon vinegar and blend well. Cover and refrigerate for up to 5 days, until needed.

Auntie Yuan's Ma La Chicken

A Chinese version of chicken salad includes shredded chicken and strips of scallion green atop a bed of slivered aromatic vegetables. A dressing of soy, sesame oil and hot oil comes next, and the ground red Szechuan peppercorns that blanket the top are just hot enough to make your tongue tingle.

<u>4 SERVINGS</u>

1 whole chicken (about 3 pounds)
1 large cucumber
¼ cup Szechuan peppercorns*
½ carrot, cut into 3-by-⅛-inch julienne strips
3 celery ribs, cut into 3-by-⅛-inch julienne strips
¼ teaspoon salt
2½ tablespoons soy sauce, preferably dark*
1 tablespoon Oriental sesame oil
1½ teaspoons Chinese hot oil*
½ teaspoon vinegar
½ teaspoon sugar
⅛ teaspoon freshly ground white pepper
4 scallions (green part only), cut into 3-by-⅛-inch julienne strips

1 tablespoon minced garlic
***Available in Oriental groceries**

1. Place the whole chicken in a pot just large enough to hold it with water to cover by 1 inch. Bring to a boil over high heat. Reduce the heat to low and simmer until cooked through and no longer pink near the bone, 30 to 35 minutes. Remove the chicken from the pot and let stand until cool enough to handle. Remove the meat from the carcass, discarding the skin and bones. Tear the meat into ¼- to ½-inch-thick shreds. Cover and keep warm.

2. Meanwhile, peel the cucumber and halve it lengthwise. Remove the seeds with a spoon. Cut into 3-by-⅛-inch julienne strips; drain on paper towels.

3. In a small dry skillet, toast the peppercorns over high heat until they begin to smoke. Remove from the heat and grind to a powder in a coffee mill, blender or food processor.

4. In a bowl, combine the carrot, celery and cucumber. Toss with the salt and mound in the center of a serving dish. Arrange the shredded chicken over the vegetables.

5. In a small bowl, whisk together the soy sauce, sesame oil, hot oil, vinegar, sugar and white pepper. Pour over the chicken.

6. Garnish the chicken with the scallion greens. Pass the ground Szechuan pepper and minced garlic separately.

Grilled Chicken Balsamico

<u>6 SERVINGS</u>

1½ pounds boneless chicken breasts or thighs
⅓ cup fresh lemon juice
½ cup plus 3 tablespoons olive oil, preferably extra-virgin
2 teaspoons coarsely cracked black pepper
¾ teaspoon salt
¼ teaspoon hot pepper sauce
3 tablespoons balsamic or red wine vinegar
1 tablespoon Dijon-style mustard
1½ teaspoons minced fresh thyme or ½ teaspoon dried
2 tablespoons minced Italian flat-leaf parsley
¾ pound green beans, cut into 2-inch pieces
2 Belgian endives, trimmed and separated into leaves
1 head of romaine lettuce
2 large red bell peppers, cut into 2-by-¼-inch strips
3 firm ripe tomatoes, cut into wedges
3 scallions, thinly sliced

1. Place the chicken in a shallow bowl. Combine the lemon juice, 3 tablespoons of the olive oil, the black pepper, ½ teaspoon of the salt and the hot sauce. Pour over the chicken and marinate at room temperature, turning occasionally, for 1 hour.

2. Light the charcoal or preheat the broiler. Grill or broil the chicken 3 to 4 inches from the heat, turning once, until the skin is crisp and the meat is no longer pink, about 12 minutes for the breasts and 5 minutes longer for the thighs. (**The recipe may be prepared ahead to this point.** Let the chicken cool to room temperature, wrap and refrigerate overnight. Let return to room temperature before continuing.)

3. In a large bowl, combine the vinegar, mustard, thyme, parsley and the remaining ¼ teaspoon salt. Gradually whisk in the remaining ½ cup olive oil.

4. Cut the chicken into bite-size pieces (keep the skin on for its flavor unless you are watching your calorie intake) and toss to coat well with half of the dressing.

5. Bring a large saucepan of salted water to a boil. Add the green beans and cook until crisp-tender, about 3 minutes. Drain and rinse under cold water; drain well.

6. On a large serving platter, arrange some of the endive and romaine leaves; tear the rest into bite-size pieces. Just before serving, combine the torn lettuce with the green beans, peppers, tomatoes, scallions and chicken. Add the remaining dressing and toss until coated. Serve on the bed of endive and romaine leaves.

The Lark's Curried Duck Salad

F&W Beverage Suggestion: Chenin Blanc, such as Simi

8 FIRST-COURSE SERVINGS

2 ducks (5 pounds each)
⅔ cup sweet mango chutney
1 cup mayonnaise, preferably homemade
2 tablespoons plus 2 teaspoons curry powder
2½ teaspoons fresh lemon juice
½ teaspoon salt
¼ teaspoon freshly ground pepper
2 large celery ribs, peeled and cut crosswise on the diagonal into ¼-inch slices
1 small onion, quartered and thinly sliced
½ cup canned lichee nuts, quartered (optional)
¼ cup toasted sliced almonds

1. Preheat the oven to 350°. Rinse and dry the ducks thoroughly. Prick all over with a fork. Place on a rack in a large roasting pan and roast, breast-side down, for 30 minutes. Turn the birds onto one side and roast for 30 minutes; turn onto the other side and roast for 30 minutes

longer. Turn the birds breast-side up, prick all over again and roast for an additional 30 minutes, until the joints move easily.

2. Remove the ducks from the oven and let rest until cool enough to handle. Remove all the meat from the bones. Remove the skin and discard or reserve for another use. Tear the meat into 2-inch strips. (**The recipe may be prepared up to this point a day ahead.** Wrap the duck well and refrigerate.)

3. In a food processor or blender, puree the chutney until smooth. Add the mayonnaise, curry powder, lemon juice, salt and pepper and blend well.

4. In a large bowl, toss the duck with the celery, onion and lichees. Add the chutney dressing and toss to coat. Cover and refrigerate until well chilled, at least 2 hours. Serve on a platter, garnished with the toasted almonds.

Smoked Turkey Salad

For this meaty, delicious salad, strips of smoked turkey and sliced scallions are sautéed and then mounded on a bed of lettuce; a fresh tomato vinaigrette is spooned over, and the salad is sprinkled with parsley and toasted sesame seeds.

4 SERVINGS

½ head of Boston lettuce
½ head of red leaf lettuce
1 bunch of scallions, sliced diagonally into 1-inch lengths
6 tablespoons olive oil
¾ pound thinly sliced smoked turkey, cut into 3-by-1-inch strips
¾ pound plum tomatoes, seeded and minced
3 tablespoons red wine vinegar
Salt and freshly ground pepper
Chopped fresh parsley and toasted sesame seeds, for garnish

1. Arrange the Boston and red leaf lettuces on a platter. Reserve about 10 pieces of scallion for garnishing.

2. In a large skillet, heat 4 tablespoons of the oil until shimmering. Add the turkey and scallions and cook over moder-

ately high heat, stirring, until warmed through, about 3 minutes. Remove from the heat and mound in the center of the platter.

3. Warm the remaining 2 tablespoons oil in the skillet over high heat. Add the tomatoes and vinegar. Cook until the liquid is evaporated, about 2 minutes. Season with salt and pepper to taste. Spoon the sauce over the turkey and sprinkle with the reserved scallions, the parsley and toasted sesame seeds. Serve warm or at room temperature.

Poached Salmon Salad

2 SERVINGS

⅓ pound spinach—stemmed and shredded
½ pound poached salmon, broken into large chunks
2 small celery ribs, peeled and cut on the diagonal into ¼-inch slices
½ cup cooked wild rice
1 hard-cooked egg, thinly sliced
2 tablespoons walnut oil
2 tablespoons dry white wine
1 tablespoon white wine vinegar
¼ teaspoon salt
½ teaspoon freshly ground pepper
1 tablespoon finely grated lemon zest
2 tablespoons finely diced onion
2 tablespoons minced fresh parsley

1. Line 2 plates with the shredded spinach. Arrange rows of salmon, celery, rice and egg slices decoratively on top.

2. Whisk together the walnut oil, wine, vinegar, salt and a pinch of pepper. Drizzle over the salad.

3. In a small bowl, toss together the lemon zest, onion, parsley and the remaining pepper. Sprinkle a little on the egg slices; pass the remainder separately.

Sautéed Fresh Tuna Salad

Mixing bitter and delicate greens produces a lovely backdrop for this simple composed salad. If radicchio and mâche are not available, increase the amount of red leaf lettuce and substitute watercress for the mâche.

4 SERVINGS

2 tablespoons drained capers
1 tablespoon caper vinegar
(drained from the jar of capers)
1 tablespoon fresh lemon juice
8 tablespoons extra-virgin olive oil
Salt and freshly ground pepper
1 small head of radicchio
2 ounces of mâche (lamb's lettuce)
4 leaves of red leaf lettuce
1 medium head of Boston lettuce
1 Belgian endive, cut into julienne
strips
1 pound fresh tuna steak, cut into
2-by-1-inch pieces

1. In a small bowl, crush 1 tablespoon of the capers. Mix in the caper vinegar and lemon juice. Slowly whisk in 6 tablespoons of the olive oil. Season the dressing with a generous pinch each of salt and pepper.

2. In a large bowl, toss the radicchio, mâche, red leaf and Boston lettuces with

about ¼ cup of the dressing. Divide the salad greens among 4 large plates.

3. In a small bowl, toss the endive with 1 tablespoon of the dressing. Arrange about one-fourth of the endive in a crescent around one side of each plate of greens.

4. Season the tuna with salt and pepper. In a heavy medium skillet, bring 1 tablespoon of oil almost to the smoking point over high heat. Add half the tuna and sauté quickly, tossing frequently, for about 2 minutes, until browned on the outside but still rare inside. Transfer to a bowl. Wipe out the pan and sauté the remaining tuna in the last tablespoon of oil.

5. Toss the cooked tuna with the remaining vinaigrette.

6. Pile about one-fourth of the tuna chunks in the center of each plate. Garnish each serving with about ½ teaspoon of whole capers. Serve the salad warm or at room temperature.

Grilled Swordfish and Avocado Salad Baja-Style

Warm flour tortillas and sweet butter go well with this easy summertime salad.

F&W Beverage Suggestion:
Simple California white, such as The Monterey Vineyard Classic California Dry White

6 SERVINGS

1½ pounds swordfish steak, cut
about 1 inch thick
6 tablespoons fresh lemon juice
2 tablespoons fresh lime juice
1 tablespoon distilled white vinegar
2 tablespoons hot red or green
chili salsa

2 tablespoons minced onion
1 tablespoon minced fresh
coriander
½ teaspoon salt
½ cup plus 2 tablespoons olive oil,
preferably extra-virgin
¾ pound tomatoes (about 5
plum)—peeled, seeded and
coarsely chopped
1½ cups cooked corn kernels, fresh
or frozen
3 large ripe avocados
1 head of romaine lettuce
Sprigs of coriander, for garnish

1. Place the fish in a shallow bowl. Sprinkle with 3 tablespoons of the lemon juice, the lime juice, vinegar, chile salsa, onion, minced coriander and salt. Let marinate at room temperature, turning occasionally, for 30 minutes.

2. Light the charcoal or preheat the broiler. Remove the steaks, reserving the marinade. Brush both sides of the fish liberally with about 2 tablespoons of the olive oil. Grill or broil 3 to 4 inches from the heat for 8 to 10 minutes on the first side and 4 to 8 minutes on the second, or until just opaque throughout. (**The recipe may be prepared ahead to this point.** Let the swordfish cool to room temperature, wrap and refrigerate overnight. Let return to room temperature before continuing.)

3. Gradually whisk the remaining ½ cup oil into the reserved marinade to make a dressing. Cut the cooked fish into 1-inch cubes and toss with half of the dressing. Let marinate at room temperature for 30 minutes.

4. To serve, toss the fish with the tomatoes, corn and remaining dressing. Halve, pit and peel the avocados. Paint the avocado halves with the remaining 3 tablespoons of lemon juice. On a large serving platter, arrange the romaine leaves and top with the avocado halves. Spoon the swordfish salad in and around the avocados. Garnish with the coriander sprigs.

Dijon Mussel Salad

6 SERVINGS

Mussels:

6 pounds mussels, scrubbed and debearded
5 cups dry white wine
2 medium onions, coarsely chopped (about 2 cups)
4 large garlic cloves, crushed
4 bay leaves
1 medium bunch of parsley stems, tied in a bundle
1 tablespoon olive oil

Sauce:

3 egg yolks
2 tablespoons fresh lemon juice
2 tablespoons Dijon-style mustard
1 cup vegetable oil
2 teaspoons tarragon
Salt and freshly ground pepper
¼ cup minced fresh parsley, for garnish

1. Prepare the mussels: In a large noncorrodible kettle with a cover, combine the mussels, wine, onions, garlic, bay leaves and parsley stems over moderate heat. Bring to a boil, cover, reduce the heat to low and simmer until the mussels open, 5 to 7 minutes. Discard any that do not open. With a slotted spoon, remove the mussels to a bowl and reserve.

2. Increase the heat under the mussel liquid and cook rapidly until the liquid has reduced to about 1 cup, 20 to 30 minutes. Strain through a fine sieve and reserve.

3. Meanwhile, remove the mussels from their shells and toss with the 1 tablespoon olive oil; reserve.

4. Make the sauce: In a food processor or blender, combine the egg yolks, lemon juice and mustard. Add the oil in droplets until the mayonnaise begins to thicken, then add the remaining oil in a steady stream. Continue blending until thick.

5. In a bowl, combine the mayonnaise with the reserved mussel liquid, the tarragon and salt and pepper to taste.

6. Assemble the dish: Place the mussels on a platter or in a bowl. Pour the sauce over them and toss well. Cover and refrigerate for at least 2 hours, until well chilled. To serve, garnish with the parsley.

Scandinavian Herring Salad

4 SERVINGS

1 teaspoon Dijon-style mustard
¼ teaspoon sugar
Pinch of salt
⅓ cup vegetable oil
4 teaspoons fresh lemon juice
1 teaspoon minced fresh dill
2 medium cucumbers
2 pickled herrings (about 10 ounces each)
3 tart apples, such as Granny Smith
6 beets (about 1½ pounds), cooked and cut into ¼-inch dice
2 small red onions, thinly sliced and separated into rings
1 bunch of watercress
Sprigs of fresh dill, for garnish

1. In a medium bowl, whisk together the mustard, sugar and salt. Gradually whisk in the vegetable oil, lemon juice and dill. Set the dressing aside.

2. Peel the cucumbers, halve lengthwise and scoop out the seeds. Cut each half crosswise into ¼-inch crescents.

3. With a sharp knife, cut the herring fillets away from the backbone. Cut the fish into 1¼-inch squares.

4. Quarter, peel and core the apples. Cut each quarter lengthwise into thin slices. Toss with 1 tablespoon of the dressing to prevent discoloration.

5. On a large platter, arrange separate rows of the beets, onions, apples, cucumbers, herrings and watercress in an attractive pattern.

6. Whisk the dressing and drizzle it over the vegetables. Garnish the platter with sprigs of dill.

Hambleton Hall's Warm Salad of Oysters with Champagne Sabayon

4 SERVINGS

Salad:

1 medium head of radicchio, torn into bite-size pieces
½ medium head of chicory, torn into bite-size pieces
1 bunch of mâche (lamb's lettuce) or Bibb lettuce torn into bite-size pieces
3 tablespoons walnut oil
1½ teaspoons sherry vinegar
1½ teaspoons fresh lemon juice
¼ teaspoon grainy mustard
¼ teaspoon salt
¼ teaspoon freshly ground black pepper

Champagne Sabayon:

2 tablespoons minced shallots
1 cup brut champagne
2 egg yolks
2 tablespoons unsalted butter
¼ teaspoon salt
⅛ teaspoon white pepper

Oysters and Assembly:

12 fresh oysters, on the half shell
2 tablespoons chopped chervil, if available
2 tablespoons chopped chives

1. Prepare the salad: Place the radicchio, chicory and mâche in a large bowl. In a small bowl, whisk together the oil, vinegar, lemon juice, mustard, salt and black pepper.

2. Make the champagne sabayon: In a small noncorrodible saucepan, combine the shallots and champagne. Cook over moderately high heat until reduced by half, 3 to 4 minutes. Reduce the heat to low. Quickly whisk in the egg yolks, one at a time. Continue to cook, whisking constantly, until the sabayon is light and foamy. Remove from the heat and stir in the butter, salt and white pepper.

3. Cook the oysters: Preheat the broiler. In a shallow ovenproof dish, arrange the oysters in a single layer. Spoon the champagne sabayon over the oysters and broil 4 inches from the heat until the sauce is lightly browned, 45 to 60 seconds.

4. Assemble the dish: Pour the dressing over the salad greens and toss to coat. Arrange the greens in the center of 4 individual salad plates. Place three hot glazed oysters around the edge of each plate and garnish with the chopped chervil and chives.

Spicy Southeast Asian Shrimp Salad

6 SERVINGS

2 tablespoons fresh lemon juice
1 large garlic clove, crushed
1 teaspoon salt
¼ cup peanut oil
½ teaspoon Oriental sesame oil
¼ teaspoon Chinese hot oil or cayenne pepper
1½ pounds medium shrimp, shelled and deveined (about 24)
½ cup plus 1 tablespoon rice vinegar or distilled white vinegar
2 tablespoons honey
3 tablespoons finely chopped unsalted dry-roasted peanuts
3 heads of Boston lettuce, separated into leaves
4 carrots, shredded (about 2 cups)
1 small cucumber, seeded and thinly sliced
12 radishes, thinly sliced
¼ cup coarsely chopped fresh mint
⅓ cup chopped fresh coriander or Italian flat-leaf parsley
4 scallions, thinly sliced

1. In a medium bowl, combine the lemon juice, garlic, salt, peanut oil, sesame oil and hot oil. Add the shrimp and toss to coat. Let marinate at room temperature, tossing occasionally, for at least 30

minutes or up to 1 hour. Meanwhile, soak about 1 dozen 6-inch bamboo skewers in water.

2. Light the charcoal or preheat the broiler. Thread the shrimp onto the skewers. Grill or broil about 4 inches from the heat for 1½ to 2 minutes on each side, or until loosely curled and just opaque throughout. (**The recipe may be prepared a day ahead to this point.** Remove the shrimp from the skewers and let cool to room temperature. Wrap and refrigerate overnight. Let return to room temperature before continuing.)

3. In a small bowl, make a dressing by mixing together the vinegar and honey until blended. Stir in the peanuts.

4. Cover a large serving platter with some of the lettuce leaves. Arrange the shrimp, bunches of the remaining lettuce and mounds of the carrots, cucumber, radishes, mint, coriander and scallions on top. To serve, drizzle with some of the dressing and serve the rest on the side, or suggest that guests make a package of a lettuce leaf filled with shrimp, vegetables, a sprinkle of herbs and a drizzle of the dressing.

Pasta Salad with Sweet Red Peppers and Pecans

The colorful ingredients in this appealing, robust salad make it an attractive dish to serve as part of a buffet meal. For fullest flavor, let the salad marinate for several hours.

6 TO 8 SERVINGS

¼ cup red wine vinegar
1 teaspoon anchovy paste
1 teaspoon salt
½ teaspoon freshly ground black pepper
¾ cup olive oil, preferably extra-virgin
1 pound fresh spinach fettuccine or ½ pound dried
⅓ pound sliced salami, casing removed and cut into ¼-inch strips
2 small red bell peppers, cut into thin slices
½ cup pitted black olives, cut into thin slivers
½ cup minced scallions
1 cup pecan halves (4 ounces), halved lengthwise

1. In a medium bowl, whisk the vinegar, anchovy paste, salt and pepper until mixed. Gradually whisk in the oil until smooth and creamy.

2. In a large pot of boiling salted water, cook the pasta until tender but still firm, 3 to 5 minutes for fresh, 10 to 12 minutes for dried. Drain and rinse briefly under cold water; drain well.

3. Place in a very large serving bowl and toss, while still warm, with the vinaigrette until well coated. Add the salami, red peppers, olives and scallions and toss well to mix. Cover and refrigerate until chilled, several hours or overnight. Before serving, add the pecans and season with additional salt and black pepper to taste.

Tortellini Salad with Chestnuts

<u>10 SERVINGS</u>

1 cup olive oil
½ cup balsamic vinegar
2 tablespoons Dijon-style mustard
2 garlic cloves, crushed through a
  press
2 tablespoons fresh lemon juice
¼ teaspoon salt
¼ teaspoon freshly ground pepper
2 packages (15 ounces each) white
  tortellini
1 package (15 ounces) green
  tortellini
1 pound green beans, cut into 1-
  inch lengths
1 package (12 to 16 ounces) frozen
  chestnuts, cooked according to
  package directions, or 1 jar (16
  ounces) roasted chestnuts,
  quartered
2 red bell peppers, cut into ¼-inch
  dice
2 bunches of scallions (white and
  tender green), thinly sliced
1 cup finely chopped basil leaves

1. In a large bowl, whisk together the oil, vinegar, mustard, garlic, lemon juice, salt and pepper.

2. In a large pot of boiling salted water, cook the tortellini until tender, 10 to 12 minutes; drain. Add to the dressing and toss while the pasta is still hot.

3. In a large saucepan of boiling salted water, cook the green beans until crisp-tender, 5 to 7 minutes. Drain and rinse under cold running water; drain well.

4. Add the chestnuts, red peppers, scallions and green beans to the tortellini; toss well and let cool to room temperature. **(If making this dish ahead of time, cover and refrigerate at this point.** Let return to room temperature for 1 hour before serving.)

5. Just before serving, add the basil and toss; serve at room temperature.

Basil Potato Salad with Smoked Chub

Smoked chub, a small fatty fish, is readily available at delicatessens or the appetizer counters of many supermarkets. If you cannot find it, any medium-oily variety of smoked fish may be substituted.

<u>4 TO 6 SERVINGS</u>

3 large red potatoes, sliced
1 pound smoked chub—skinned,
  boned and flaked
2 tablespoons basil oil, drained
  from Basil Preserved in Oil
1 tablespoon Basil Preserved in Oil
  (p. 224)
½ teaspoon salt
¼ teaspoon freshly ground pepper
1 small red onion, diced

1. Place the sliced potatoes in a large pot of cold salted water. Bring to a boil and cook until almost tender, 8 to 10 minutes. Drain well.

2. While still warm, toss the potatoes with the chub, oil, basil, salt and pepper. Let cool to room temperature, about 1 hour, tossing occasionally. Add the onions and toss to incorporate.

L'Orangerie's Warm Chicory and Endive Salad with Poached Eggs and Bacon

The type of bacon used will affect the saltiness of this recipe, so be sure to taste for seasoning before adding additional salt.

<u>2 SERVINGS</u>

1 small head of chicory
2 Belgian endives
¼ cup white wine vinegar
4 medium eggs
¼ pound slab bacon, thickly sliced
  and cut crosswise into ¼-inch
  strips
2 tablespoons red wine vinegar
Freshly ground black pepper
Salt
1 teaspoon minced chives

1. Tear the chicory and endive into bite-size pieces and place in a bowl; set aside.

2. In a large, shallow, noncorrodible saucepan, bring 3 to 4 quarts of water and the white wine vinegar to a boil. Slip the eggs into the water, reduce the heat to maintain a gentle simmer and poach the eggs, until barely firm, 2 to 3 minutes. Remove with a slotted spoon, trim any ragged edges and keep warm in a bowl of hot water.

3. Meanwhile, in a skillet, over moderately high heat, cook the bacon until browned and crisp, about 5 minutes. Drain the bacon, reserving 2 tablespoons of the bacon grease.

4. Toss the greens with the red wine vinegar and a few grinds of the pepper. Add the bacon and the reserved bacon fat and toss again. Taste and correct the seasoning, adding salt to taste.

5. Arrange the greens on 2 large plates. Drain the poached eggs and place 2 on each portion. Garnish each with ½ teaspoon chives.

Grilled Vegetable Salad

4 SERVINGS

4 large mushrooms
¼ cup cubed (¼ inch) mozzarella cheese
2 tablespoons tarragon vinegar
About 8 tablespoons olive oil
¾ teaspoon salt
½ teaspoon freshly ground black pepper
½ teaspoon tarragon, crumbled
2 medium zucchini, cut lengthwise into 4 slices
1 small eggplant, cut lengthwise into 4 slices, ½ inch thick
4 leeks—trimmed to 6 inches, halved lengthwise and well cleaned
2 medium red bell peppers
1 egg
1 garlic clove, mashed
⅓ cup finely chopped parsley
1 teaspoon Dijon-style mustard
1 tablespoon dry vermouth
½ cup safflower oil
1 small head of chicory, separated into leaves

1. Remove the mushroom stems and trim their ends; cut the stems into ¼-inch dice. In a small bowl, combine the diced stems, whole caps, mozzarella, 1 tablespoon of the vinegar, 2 tablespoons of the olive oil, ¼ teaspoon of the salt, ¼ teaspoon of the black pepper, and the tarragon; toss to mix. Set aside.

2. Place a heavy skillet, preferably cast iron, over high heat. Brush the zucchini on both sides with olive oil, then arrange in the hot skillet in a single layer (in batches if necessary); if the skillet is hot enough, the zucchini will sizzle. Grill, turning once, until lightly browned, about 1 minute on each side. Hold the zucchini (and all the grilled vegetables) at room temperature until time to assemble the salad.

3. Brush the eggplant slices with oil and grill in the hot skillet, turning once, until lightly browned, 2 to 3 minutes on each side. (Reduce the heat slightly if necessary to prevent scorching.)

4. Brush the leeks with oil and grill for 3 to 4 minutes per side, until browned and slightly translucent.

5. Roast the red peppers over an open flame or under a hot broiler, turning, until charred all over. Seal in a bag and let steam for 5 minutes. Scrape off the charred skin and remove the stem, seeds and membranes. Cut the peppers lengthwise into ¼-inch-wide strips.

6. Make the dressing by beating the egg with the garlic, parsley, mustard, vermouth and remaining 1 tablespoon vinegar, ½ teaspoon salt and ¼ teaspoon black pepper. Slowly whisk in 4 tablespoons of olive oil and the safflower oil.

7. To assemble the salad, line 4 large plates or a platter with chicory leaves. Pick the whole mushroom caps out of the reserved mushroom-cheese mixture and fill them with the diced stems and cheese. Arrange the filled mushroom caps, grilled vegetables and red pepper strips in a decorative pattern on top of the chicory. Drizzle about one-fourth of the dressing over the salad and pass the remainder on the side.

DESSERTS

Reine de Saba

Except for melting the butter and chocolate, this fabulously rich version of a French dessert classic created by Paris chef Jacques Cagna involves no cooking. And like most chocolate desserts, it is best made a day or two ahead.

12 TO 16 SERVINGS

1 cup coarsely chopped walnuts
12 ounces semisweet or bittersweet chocolate, broken into pieces
1½ sticks unsalted butter
¼ cup sugar
6 eggs, separated, at room temperature
Candied violets, whipped cream or walnut halves, for garnish

1. Line the bottom and short ends of a 1-quart loaf pan or rectangular mold with a strip of heavy duty aluminum foil long enough to overhang both ends of the pan by at least 1½ inches. Sprinkle half the walnuts over the bottom; set aside.

2. In a small heavy saucepan, melt the chocolate with the butter over very low heat. Add the sugar and mix well. Scrape into a large bowl and let cool to room temperature.

3. One at a time, beat the egg yolks into the chocolate mixture. Stir in the remaining walnuts.

4. Beat the egg whites until stiff but not dry. Fold one-quarter of the egg whites into the chocolate to lighten the mixture. Fold in the remaining whites just until no streaks of white remain.

5. Spoon the mixture into the prepared pan. Cover and refrigerate for at least 4 hours, or overnight, until firm.

6. Unmold, pulling gently on the ends of the foil if necessary. Decorate with candied violets, whipped cream rosettes and/or walnut halves.

Chocolate Truffle Torte

16 TO 20 SERVINGS

1½ pounds dark sweetened chocolate (preferably Lindt or Tobler semisweet or bittersweet), broken into small pieces
3 sticks (¾ pound) unsalted butter
8 eggs
Dutch-process unsweetened cocoa powder, for dredging the truffles
1 cup heavy cream
1 tablespoon superfine sugar
½ teaspoon vanilla extract
Raspberry Sauce (p. 225)

1. Preheat the oven to 425°. Butter a 9-inch springform pan. Line the bottom with a round of parchment or waxed paper and butter the paper. Dust the entire pan with flour; tap out any excess.

2. Melt the chocolate and butter in a double boiler over hot—not simmering—water, stirring occasionally. Remove from the heat and let cool slightly while you beat the eggs.

3. In a large bowl set over a pan of simmering water, whisk the eggs until warm to the touch. Remove from the heat and beat with an electric beater until the eggs are cooled and tripled in volume, about 5 minutes. Gently pour about half of the chocolate down the side of the bowl and fold until partially blended. Add the remaining chocolate mixture and fold until almost blended. Some streaks may remain; do not overmix or the batter will deflate.

4. Pour ¾ of the batter into the springform pan and ¼ (for the truffles) into a 6-cup loaf pan. Place the loaf pan in a larger pan and pour in enough hot water to reach halfway up the sides of the loaf pan. Cover the loaf pan with a piece of buttered aluminum foil.

5. Bake both cakes for 15 minutes, covering the springform pan loosely with buttered foil after 10 minutes.

6. Remove both cakes from the oven; remove the loaf pan from the water bath. Let cool on a rack, still covered, for 45 minutes. Refrigerate both cakes, covered, for 3 hours until chilled and very firm, or overnight. Run a metal spatula around sides of the springform pan. Invert onto a plate, remove the bottom of the springform and peel off the paper; invert again right-side up onto a serving platter. Refrigerate until 1 hour before serving.

7. Shape the truffle mixture in the loaf pan into balls about 1 inch in diameter by rolling between the palms of your hands. Dredge the truffles in cocoa, and toss them lightly to coat. Store in the refrigerator for up to 3 weeks or freeze for up to 3 months.

8. Whip the heavy cream until it forms soft peaks. Beat in the sugar and vanilla just until stiff. Refrigerate, covered, until serving time. If the cream becomes watery, beat lightly to restore consistency.

9. Remove the cake from the refrigerator at least 1 hour before serving to allow the texture to lighten. To assemble, arrange the truffles on top of the cake (there will probably be some extra to serve on the side or on another occasion with coffee). Garnish with the whipped cream and Raspberry Sauce.

Simone Beck's Le Diabolo

6 SERVINGS

Cake:
¾ cup sugar
4 eggs, separated
6 ounces German's sweet chocolate, broken into pieces
¾ cup unsalted butter (1½ sticks)
4 tablespoons cake flour
2 tablespoons pulverized blanched almonds
Pinch of salt

Chocolate Buttercream Glaze:

3½ ounces German's sweet chocolate, broken into small pieces
2 to 3 tablespoons coffee or water

3 tablespoons unsalted butter
Toasted slivered almonds, for
decoration

1. Make the cake: Preheat the oven to 375°. Cut a round of waxed paper to fit the bottom of an 8-inch round cake pan, 1¾ inches deep. Butter the sides of the pan and one side of the paper. Lay the paper butter-side up in the pan and flour the paper and the sides of the pan. Set aside.

2. Beat the sugar with the 4 egg yolks until they are a creamy yellow. Put the chocolate and the butter in an enamel saucepan over simmering water, and stir until the chocolate is smooth. Add the egg and sugar mixture, and continue stirring over low heat until well blended.

3. Stir in the flour and the pulverized almonds.

4. Beat the 4 egg whites with a pinch of salt until stiff but not dry. Stir one-quarter of the egg whites into the chocolate mixture to lighten it; then fold all back into the remaining egg whites.

5. Fill the cake pan three-fourths full and tap it gently on the table to distribute the mixture evenly. Bake in the preheated oven for 25 to 30 minutes, watching carefully, until the outside is solid and the center still creamy (not runny and not dry) when tested with a sharp knife. Let the cake cool before unmolding.

6. Make the glaze: Melt the chocolate with the coffee or the water until smooth. Remove from the heat and stir in the butter.

7. Glaze and decorate the cake: Pour the warm chocolate buttercream on top of the cake. Using a metal spatula (moistened in hot water and dried), spread over the top and sides of the cake. Decorate as desired with the almonds. Refrigerate before serving.

Marjolaine

This spectacular creation of the late chef Fernand Point needs to be refrigerated overnight, so plan accordingly.

20 SERVINGS

1⅓ cups whole hazelnuts
1¼ cups whole blanched almonds
1½ cups sugar
¼ cup all-purpose flour
8 egg whites
½ teaspoon lemon juice
15 ounces semisweet chocolate, broken into small pieces
10 ounces crème fraîche (1 cup plus 2 tablespoons)
Meringue Vanilla Buttercream (recipe follows)
Chocolate curls, for garnish

1. Preheat the oven to 350°. Butter the bottom of a 15½-by-10½-by-1-inch jelly roll pan. Line the bottom with parchment paper; butter and flour the paper and sides of the pan. Tap to remove excess flour.

2. On two separate baking sheets, roast the hazelnuts and almonds for about 10 minutes, until the nuts are lightly browned. Rub the hazelnuts in a towel to remove as much of the brown skin as possible. Reduce the oven temperature to 300°.

3. Combine 1 cup plus 1½ tablespoons of the hazelnuts, the almonds, 1¼ cups of the sugar and the flour. Using a blender or food processor and working in batches, grind to a powder, 15 to 20 seconds for each batch. Set aside in a medium bowl.

4. In a large bowl, beat the egg whites until stiff. Gradually fold the nut mixture into the whites, one-fourth at a time.

5. Pour the batter into the pan and spread evenly with a spatula. Bake for 45 minutes, or until the top is light golden and slightly crisp. Loosen the edges with a knife, invert onto a cooling rack and peel off the paper. Let cool thoroughly.

6. Butter a small metal cake or pie pan and set aside. In a small heavy saucepan,

combine the remaining ¼ cup sugar and the lemon juice. Cook over moderate heat without stirring until the sugar dissolves and the syrup is golden. Pour in the remaining hazelnuts and stir with a wooden spoon to coat the nuts. Immediately pour into the buttered pan. Let cool to room temperature. When thoroughly cooled, break the praline into pieces and grind to a powder in a blender.

7. In a double boiler or a bowl over hot water, melt the chocolate. Remove from the heat and stir in the crème fraîche. Scrape the chocolate cream into a bowl and set aside to cool.

8. To assemble, place the cake on a flat surface and, with a large serrated knife, cut crosswise into four equal strips (about 10½ by 3½ inches). Line them up, side by side. Measure out 1 cup of the chocolate cream and spread it evenly onto one of the strips; reserve the remaining cream for coating.

9. Spread 1 cup of the Meringue Vanilla Buttercream onto the second strip of cake.

10. Combine the remaining buttercream with the praline powder and spread 1 cup of it onto the third strip of cake. (You may have a little left over.)

11. Place the chocolate-covered layer on a serving platter, top with the plain buttercream layer and then the praline buttercream layer. Top with the fourth cake strip and press lightly.

12. Spread the reserved chocolate cream in a thin layer over the top and sides of the cake. Comb the sides with a fork to decorate. With a vegetable peeler, shave curls of chocolate directly onto the top of the cake. Refrigerate overnight before slicing.

Meringue Vanilla Buttercream

This lighter version of traditional butter-cream is made with the whites instead of the yolks.

MAKES ABOUT 2 CUPS

3 egg whites, at room temperature
Pinch of cream of tartar
½ cup sugar
¾ cup unsalted butter, at room
  temperature
1½ teaspoons vanilla extract

1. In a large mixer bowl, beat the egg whites and cream of tartar until soft peaks form.

2. In a small saucepan, combine the sugar with ¼ cup of water. Bring to a boil over high heat and cook until the syrup reaches the soft-ball stage, 240° on a candy thermometer.

3. Immediately remove the syrup from the heat and, at high speed, beat it into the egg whites in a thin steady stream. Continue to beat the mixture until tepid, about 8 minutes.

4. Gradually beat in the butter, 2 tablespoons at a time. Beat in the vanilla. Refrigerate, covered, until ready to use.

Vacherin

🍷 **F&W Beverage Suggestion:**
Sweet Asti Spumante

ABOUT 10 SERVINGS

1½ recipes (6 cups) plus 1 recipe
  (4 cups) Swiss Meringue (recipe
  follows)
2 quarts ice cream, softened
1 cup heavy cream, chilled
¼ cup confectioners' sugar
1 teaspoon vanilla extract
1 pint strawberries, for garnish

1. To make the base and sides of the *vacherin*, preheat the oven to 250°; space the racks evenly, not too close to the heat. Butter and flour four small baking sheets (see Note) or line them with parchment. Trace four 10-inch circles onto the sheets. Make the 1½ recipes of meringue.

2. Fill a pastry bag fitted with a ½-inch (#5) plain tip with the meringue, and starting in the center of one of the circles, pipe, spiraling outward, a solid 10-inch circular base. Continue to use the bag to pipe out three 10-inch rings.

3. Bake for about 1½ hours, checking occasionally to see that they are cooking evenly, until the meringues are crisp but not colored. Turn off the heat and leave the meringues in the closed oven to dry out completely; this can take from 2 to 8 hours, depending on the humidity (they may be left overnight).

4. When the base and rings are completely dry, carefully remove them from the baking sheets. Place on a rack to cool if necessary. **(The base and rings can be made up to 3 days ahead and stored in a dry place.)**

5. To assemble the *vacherin* case, make the additional 1 recipe of meringue. Place the cooked meringue base on a buttered and floured or parchment-lined baking sheet. Pipe a border of uncooked meringue around the edge to act as mortar and stick a ring on top. Stack the second and third rings in the same way.

6. Holding the top ring gently and working with a delicate bottom-to-top motion, frost the outside of the *vacherin* case with a thin layer of meringue. Using a narrow metal spatula, dipping it in warm water and wiping it dry between strokes, smooth the meringue. Cover and level the top edge.

7. Use the remaining meringue to decorate the *vacherin* as desired. Return to a 250° oven for about 1½ hours to dry out the uncooked meringue. **(The completed *vacherin* case can be stored in a dry place for up to 3 days.)**

8. Fill the *vacherin* case with the softened ice cream. If desired, cover and freeze until about 20 minutes before serving.

9. In a medium bowl, beat the cream until it forms soft peaks. Beat in the sugar and the vanilla; continue beating until stiff peaks form (do not overbeat). Shortly before serving, cover the top of the *vacherin* with the sweetened whipped cream and garnish with the strawberries. Use any remaining whipped cream to pipe out more decorations if desired. Serve immediately.

NOTE: You can use inverted cake pans if you don't have enough baking sheets.

Swiss Meringue

MAKES ABOUT 4 CUPS

4 egg whites, at room temperature
Pinch of cream of tartar
1 cup sugar

1. In a mixer bowl, beat the egg whites and cream of tartar at low speed. When the whites begin to foam, increase the speed to high and beat until soft peaks form.

2. Continuing to beat on high speed, gradually add ½ cup of the sugar 1 or 2 tablespoons at a time, beating briefly between each addition to be sure the sugar dissolves. When the ½ cup of sugar is incorporated, turn off the mixer. The whites will be glossy and dense and will form stiff peaks at this point.

3. Sprinkle the remaining ½ cup sugar over the beaten egg whites. Using a spatula, gently fold the sugar into the whites until thoroughly blended.

Croquembouche

This dramatic pyramid of caramel-dipped cream puffs is traditional at French weddings. It makes a spectacular centerpiece for any buffet table. Though the final assembly should be done as close to serving time as possible, the cream puff shells can be made well ahead of time and refrigerated or even frozen.

16 TO 20 SERVINGS

Cream Puff Shells (recipe follows)
Vanilla Pastry Cream (recipe follows)
3 cups sugar
Candied violets, for garnish

1. Make 2 recipes of the Cream Puff Shells. Do not try to make a double recipe at one time.

2. Make the Vanilla Pastry Cream.

3. Fill the shells with the cream: place the pastry cream in a pastry bag fitted with a narrow plain tip. Insert the tip into the small hole in each puff and squeeze to fill.

4. Make the caramel: in a heavy medium saucepan, combine the sugar with 1 cup of water. Bring to a boil over high heat, stirring to dissolve the sugar. Cook without stirring until the syrup caramelizes to a light golden brown, 350° on a candy thermometer, 8 to 10 minutes. During the cooking process, wash any grains of sugar from the sides of the pan with a small pastry brush dipped in cold water to prevent crystallization. Remove from the heat and place in a container of simmering water to keep the caramel at a working consistency.

5. Assemble the *croquembouche*: one by one, pick up the filled cream puff shells with tongs and dip the tops about halfway into the hot caramel; try to keep the tongs clean. As they are dipped, arrange a single layer of puffs in an 8-inch circle on a flat platter. Then build up a pyramid of the filled puffs, indenting each succeeding layer slightly and angling the outside puffs top-side out. The finished croquembouche should be 12 to 14 inches high. (An oiled *croquembouche* mold facilitates this task, but it is not necessary.) Decorate with candied violets if desired.

NOTE: There will be extra caramel. To make an attractive spun-sugar garnish, bring the caramel to 210° to 220° on a candy thermometer—cooling or heating gently, as necessary. Dip a fork into the caramel and, using a smooth back-and-forth motion, drizzle over the *croquembouche* in fine threads. This decorative element is best applied in cool, dry weather; it will dissipate quickly if the air is hot and humid.

Cream Puff Shells

MAKES ABOUT 3 DOZEN SMALL PUFFS

½ cup (1 stick) unsalted butter
¼ teaspoon salt
1 cup all-purpose flour
5 eggs

1. Preheat the oven to 400°. Lightly butter and flour two heavy baking sheets.

2. In a medium saucepan, combine the butter and 1 cup of water. Cook over moderate heat until the butter melts. Increase the heat to moderately high and bring to a boil. Immediately add the salt and flour all at once and cook, stirring constantly with a wooden spoon, until the dough masses together and a crust forms on the inside of the pan, 2 to 3 minutes.

3. Off the heat, add 4 of the eggs, 1 at a time, beating well with a wooden spoon until smooth and glossy between each addition.

4. Spoon the mixture into a pastry bag fitted with a ½-inch (#6) plain tip. Pipe 1½-inch mounds of the batter onto the prepared baking sheets, spacing them about 2 inches apart.

5. In a small bowl, beat the remaining egg with 1 tablespoon of water to make an egg wash. With a small pastry brush dipped in the egg wash, gently smooth the top of each pastry mound, flattening any peaks that stick up and evenly coating the top of each one. Avoid letting the egg wash drip down the sides onto the baking sheet; it will retard rising.

6. Bake for 35 minutes, or until golden. Remove from the oven. As soon as the puffs are cool enough to handle, punch a small hole in the bottom of each with a narrow pastry tip or small knife. Return the puffs to the baking sheet punctured-sides up. Return to the still-warm oven, with the heat off, and let them dry out for 1 hour. Let cool completely before filling.

Vanilla Pastry Cream

MAKES ABOUT 3¾ CUPS

3 cups milk
1 vanilla bean, split
9 egg yolks, at room temperature
1 cup sugar
6 tablespoons all-purpose flour

1. In a saucepan, bring the milk and vanilla bean to the boiling point. Remove from the heat. Remove the vanilla bean and cover the surface with buttered waxed paper to prevent a skin from forming.

2. In a large bowl, beat the egg yolks and sugar until pale and thick. Gradually beat in the flour, 1 tablespoon at a time.

3. Gradually whisk the hot milk into the egg yolk mixture. Pour into a clean heavy saucepan and bring to a boil over moderately low heat, whisking constantly. Reduce the heat to low and cook, stirring, for 3 to 5 minutes, or until the custard is thick enough to coat a spoon heavily and has completely lost any raw flour taste.

4. Scrape the custard into a bowl and cover the surface with buttered waxed paper to prevent a skin from forming. Let cool, then refrigerate, covered, for up to 3 days before using.

Babas au Rhum

MAKES ABOUT 6 BABAS

1 envelope (¼ ounce) active dry
   yeast
¾ cup plus ¼ teaspoon sugar
¼ cup lukewarm milk (105° to
   115°)
1 cup all-purpose flour
2 eggs, at room temperature
5 tablespoons unsalted butter, at
   room temperature
3 tablespoons currants
½ cup dark rum
1 tablespoon fresh lemon juice
½ cup sieved apricot jam, for
   garnish

1. Butter and flour six ½-cup baba
molds or 2-inch muffin tins about 2 inches deep.

2. In a small bowl, combine the yeast, ¼
teaspoon of the sugar and the milk. Place
the flour in a medium bowl. Make a well
in the center and pour in the yeast mixture. Cover and set in a warm place for
30 minutes.

3. Stir the yeast mixture to blend in the
flour. Beat in the eggs, one at a time,
with a wooden spoon. Gradually beat in
the butter until blended. Mix in the currants.

4. Drop about ¼ cup of the mixture into
each prepared mold, filling them up
halfway. Set aside in a warm place until
doubled in bulk, 45 to 60 minutes. After
about 30 minutes, preheat the oven to
400°.

5. Bake the babas in the middle of the
oven for 20 minutes, or until golden and
springy when touched. Invert onto a
wire rack with a shallow dish or tray set
underneath.

6. In a small heavy saucepan, combine
the remaining ¾ cup sugar with 2 cups
of water; boil over moderate heat for 7

minutes to make a light syrup. Remove
from the heat and stir in the rum and
lemon juice.

7. Spoon the warm syrup over the babas
until they are saturated and ooze syrup
when pressed with the back of a spoon.
Reuse the syrup that collects underneath
the rack.

8. Melt the jam in a small heavy saucepan over low heat. Brush lightly over the
babas.

Ilona Torte

Although this cake is at its best the day it
is baked, it will keep in the refrigerator
for up to two days. This modern classic
was devised by George Lang for his *Cuisine of Hungary* and is named for his
mother and daughter.

14 TO 16 SERVINGS

1 cup sugar
5 ounces semisweet chocolate, cut
   into small pieces
6 tablespoons unsalted butter, at
   room temperature
8 eggs, separated
1¾ cups plus ⅓ cup coarsely
   ground walnuts
2 tablespoons fresh bread crumbs
Pinch of salt
Mocha Buttercream (recipe
   follows)
Walnut halves, for garnish

1. Preheat the oven to 375°. Butter a 10-
inch round, 2½-inch-deep springform
pan. Line with a round of waxed paper.
Butter and flour the paper and the sides
of the pan; tap out any excess.

2. In a saucepan, combine the sugar and
¼ cup of water and cook over moderate
heat, stirring occasionally, until the sugar
dissolves, about 5 minutes.

3. Add the chocolate, remove from the
heat and stir until the chocolate is melted. Let the syrup cool for 15 minutes.

4. In a medium mixer bowl, beat the
butter at medium speed until light. Beat
in the egg yolks, one at a time, beating
until each is incorporated before adding
another. On low speed, add half the
chocolate syrup, then 1¾ cups of the
ground walnuts, then the remaining syr-

up and the bread crumbs, mixing just
enough to blend after each addition.

5. In a large bowl, beat the egg whites
with the salt until stiff peaks form. Stir
one-third of the whites into the choco-
late-nut mixture to lighten it, then pour
the chocolate mixture into the egg
whites, letting it run down one side of
the bowl. Fold the two together until
thoroughly blended; do not overmix.
Pour the batter gently into the prepared
pan.

6. Bake in the center of the oven for 35
to 40 minutes, or until the center feels
set when pressed.

7. Let the torte cool in the pan for 15
minutes. Release the sides of the springform and invert the torte onto a rack
covered with a paper towel. Remove the
pan bottom and the waxed paper, and let
the torte cool completely, for at least 2
hours, before frosting.

8. Split the torte in half horizontally.
Place the top half, top-side down, on a
round platter. Reserve 1 cup of the buttercream for decoration. Cover the cake
with ¾ cup of the remaining buttercream (see Note).

9. Place the second layer on top of the
filling, smooth-side up. Frost the top and
sides of the cake with the remaining buttercream, using a thin, flexible spatula.

10. Press the remaining ⅓ cup nuts into
the frosting on the sides of the cake.
Using a pastry bag with a star or shell tip,
decorate the top edges and the base of
the cake with the reserved 1 cup buttercream. Garnish the top with walnut
halves. Refrigerate until serving time.

NOTE: If you prefer not to decorate the
cake with a pastry bag, use 1¾ cups of
the buttercream to fill the cake and the
remainder to frost it.

Mocha Buttercream

MAKES ABOUT 3 CUPS

6 ounces semisweet chocolate, cut
  into small pieces
2 teaspoons instant espresso
  powder
1 cup (2 sticks) plus 2 tablespoons
  unsalted butter, at room
  temperature
3 egg yolks
⅔ cup confectioners' sugar

1. In a heavy saucepan, combine the chocolate, ⅓ cup of water and the instant espresso. Stir over low heat until the chocolate is completely melted. Scrape into a bowl and cool completely.

2. Using an electric mixer, cream the butter until light and fluffy. Beat in the egg yolks one at a time, beating until each is incorporated before adding another. Gradually add the confectioners' sugar. Scrape in the cooled chocolate mixture and blend thoroughly.

Sicilian Cassata

12 SERVINGS

2 cups heavy cream
1⅓ cups (about 12 ounces) whole-
  milk ricotta cheese
3 tablespoons plus 2 teaspoons
  sugar
4 tablespoons (about 2 ounces)
  finely chopped citron or candied
  orange peel
3 tablespoons coarsely chopped
  semisweet chocolate
1 teaspoon finely grated orange
  zest

¼ cup plus 1 teaspoon orange
  liqueur, such as Strega, or
  brandy
1 pound cake, about 9 by 3½
  inches

1. Beat ½ cup of the cream until soft peaks form. In a medium bowl, mix the ricotta cheese and 3 tablespoons of the sugar. Fold in the whipped cream, 3 tablespoons of the citron, the chocolate, orange zest and ¼ cup of the liqueur.

2. Cut the cake crosswise into ⅜-inch slices. Line the bottom and sides of a 1½-quart bowl with a layer of cake slices, trimming or shaping as necessary.

3. Spoon a layer of the ricotta filling about ¾ inch deep over the bottom. Cover with a layer of cake slices. Repeat with two more layers of filling and cake, trimming the cake slices as necessary. Press gently to level the top slices with the sides, cover and refrigerate for 4 hours, or preferably overnight, until firm.

4. To unmold, invert the cake onto a platter. Beat the remaining 1½ cups cream, 2 teaspoons sugar and 1 teaspoon liqueur until stiff peaks form. Cover the cake with the whipped cream, using a spatula or a pastry bag with a star tip. Stud the sides with the remaining citron. The *cassata* may be refrigerated for several hours before serving if desired.

Cold Lemon Soufflé

F&W Beverage Suggestion:
Sauternes, such as Château Climens

8 TO 10 SERVINGS

2 envelopes unflavored gelatin
6 eggs, separated
1½ cups sugar
3 tablespoons grated lemon zest
  (from about 4 medium lemons)
¾ cup fresh lemon juice (from
  about 4 medium lemons)
1 cup heavy cream
2 tablespoons finely chopped
  pistachio nuts
Candied Lemon Peel, for garnish
  (p. 205)
Whipped cream (optional)

1. Wrap a 5-cup soufflé mold with a folded strip of heavy-duty aluminum foil

or parchment paper to form a collar. Arrange the collar to extend about 3 inches above the rim of the dish and secure it with string.

2. Sprinkle the gelatin over ⅓ cup of water in a small saucepan.

3. In a large bowl, beat the egg yolks with 1 cup of the sugar, the lemon zest and lemon juice until well blended. Place the bowl over a pan of gently simmering water and continue beating until the mixture is thick and creamy, about 15 minutes. Remove from the heat.

4. Warm the gelatin over low heat, stirring, until melted. Stir into the hot lemon mixture. Continue beating until cool.

5. In a large bowl, beat the egg whites until soft peaks form. Add the remaining ½ cup sugar and continue beating until stiff and glossy.

6. Beat the cream until it forms stiff peaks.

7. Place the lemon-egg yolk mixture over a bowl of ice and water and stir until it begins to thicken and set. Gently fold in the whipped cream. Then fold in the beaten egg whites. Pour the mixture into the prepared soufflé dish. Smooth the top with a spatula.

8. Refrigerate for at least 3 hours, or until set. **(The soufflé can be made to this point a day ahead, but the gelatin may toughen a bit under extended refrigeration.)**

9. Before serving, remove the collar from the soufflé. Gently press the chopped pistachios onto the sides of the soufflé that rise above the dish. Arrange the candied lemon peel garnish on top and decorate with whipped cream.

Cold Banana Soufflé with Burnt Orange Sauce

8 SERVINGS

1 tablespoon plus 2 teaspoons gelatin (about 1⅔ envelopes)
2½ cups milk
¼ teaspoon freshly grated nutmeg
5 eggs, separated
¾ cup sugar
1 cup pureed ripe bananas (2 large or 3 medium)
1 tablespoon fresh lemon juice, or more to taste
Pinch of salt
1 cup heavy cream
Sifted confectioners' sugar, for garnish
Burnt Orange Sauce (recipe follows)

1. Fold a length of parchment paper or aluminum foil in half lengthwise and wrap around a 6-cup soufflé dish to form a collar that extends about 2½ inches above the dish. Secure well with tape. Make sure the extended edges are standing straight up with no wrinkles. Set aside.

2. Place a large metal bowl in a sink. Fill the sink with enough cold water to reach halfway up the sides of the bowl. Or place the bowl in a larger bowl half-filled with ice and water.

3. Pour ⅓ cup water into a small saucepan. Slowly sprinkle the gelatin over the water, swirling to separate the lumps. Let stand to soften.

4. In a heavy medium saucepan, heat the milk and nutmeg over moderate heat until just simmering, about 4 minutes.

5. Meanwhile, in a medium bowl, using a wooden spoon, beat the egg yolks with the sugar until the mixture thickens and begins to lighten in color, about 2 minutes.

6. Gradually pour the hot milk into the egg yolk mixture in a slow steady stream, beating all the time with a wooden spoon and scraping down the sides of the bowl with a rubber spatula. Pour the custard base back into the saucepan. Cook, stirring constantly, over moderately low heat until the custard thickens enough to coat the back of the spoon, 3 to 4 minutes. The mixture will register about 180° on a candy thermometer and will be very hot to the touch; do not let simmer, or the eggs will curdle. Immediately strain the custard through a medium wire sieve into the metal bowl in the sink to stop the cooking. If the custard is cooked enough to thicken properly, you will probably find a few grains of curdled egg mixture left in the strainer.

7. Warm the softened gelatin over low heat, swirling until the gelatin is completely dissolved and the mixture is hot to the touch, about 1 minute. Immediately pour the hot gelatin into the hot custard mixture. Stir well until blended.

8. Place the pureed bananas in a bowl and slowly stir 1 cup of the custard base into the bananas to lighten the mixture. Then pour the banana mixture back into the remaining custard. Stir until the bananas are blended and the custard is just barely warm; replace the water in the sink several times with cold water, if necessary, to cool. Add 1 tablespoon of lemon juice to the custard base. If the bananas are very sweet, add up to 1 teaspoon more, to taste.

9. Replace the water in the sink with 3 inches of cold water and add 2 trays of ice cubes. Using a rubber spatula, stir the custard base, continuously scraping across the bottom and sides of the bowl with the spatula. When the custard begins to feel cool to the touch, remove the pan momentarily from the ice water.

10. Beat the egg whites with the salt until they are stiff but not dry. When you pick up a dollop of the egg white on a beater, the egg white should cling to it but the tail on the top will still fall over slightly. Set the egg whites aside.

11. Beat the heavy cream until soft peaks form.

12. Return the container of custard to the ice water and continue scraping the bottom and sides of the bowl with the rubber spatula. When the mixture is almost on the point of setting, you will be able to see the bottom of the bowl when you draw the rubber spatula down the center, and the custard will begin to mound.

13. Immediately remove the pan from the ice water and stir in ⅓ of the lightly whipped cream until well blended. Fold in the remaining cream. Fold in the beaten egg whites until no streaks of white remain.

14. Pour the soufflé mixture into the prepared soufflé dish. Refrigerate until firm, about 5 hours, or overnight.

15. To serve, remove the soufflé from the refrigerator and cut the tape that holds the collar together. Pressing a knife gently against the soufflé mixture, carefully peel the collar away, rotating the knife around the soufflé as the collar is pulled away. If desired, dust the top of the soufflé with sifted confectioners' sugar. Serve Burnt Orange Sauce on the side.

Burnt Orange Sauce

MAKES ABOUT 2 CUPS

6 tablespoons confectioners' sugar
6 tablespoons unsalted butter
1½ cups strained orange juice
1 teaspoon cornstarch
1 teaspoon grated orange zest
3 tablespoons fresh lemon juice

1. In a heavy, medium, noncorrodible saucepan, combine the confectioners' sugar and 3 tablespoons of the butter. Cook over moderately high heat, stirring constantly, until the mixture turns a caramel color. Remove from the heat and immediately pour in 1¼ cups of the orange juice. Return to the heat and cook, scraping the bottom of the pan, until the caramel and orange juice are combined. Remove from the heat.

2. In a small bowl, slowly beat the remaining ¼ cup orange juice into the cornstarch. Scrape the cornstarch mixture into the caramelized orange juice. Add the grated orange zest. Cook over high heat, stirring, until the sauce comes to a boil. Boil, stirring occasionally, for 2 minutes.

3. Add the lemon juice. Cut the remaining 3 tablespoons butter into 4 or 5 pieces. Gradually whisk the butter into the boiling sauce, one piece at a time, adding each piece as soon as the previous piece has just dissolved. Remove the sauce from the heat. Cover with waxed paper to prevent a skin from forming and set aside to cool. Serve at room temperature. (**This sauce can be made ahead and refrigerated.** To bring back to room temperature, place it in a double boiler over hot water and stir with a whisk until it has thinned slightly.)

Gravetye Manor's Chocolate Mousse with Coffee Sauce

This mousse must be refrigerated overnight, so plan accordingly.

6 SERVINGS

6 ounces good quality bittersweet or semisweet chocolate
1 whole egg plus 1 egg yolk
1 cup heavy cream
1½ tablespoons crème de cacao
1 tablespoon brandy
Coffee Sauce (recipe follows)
Chocolate curls (see Note) and confectioners' sugar, for garnish

1. In a small bowl over hot—not simmering—water, melt the chocolate.

2. In a double boiler over barely simmering water, whisk the whole egg and egg yolk until thickened, 4 to 5 minutes. Remove from the heat and let cool slightly. When the chocolate and the eggs are about the same temperature, fold them together until blended.

3. In a medium bowl, beat the cream, crème de cacao and brandy until soft peaks form. Stir one-quarter of the whipped cream into the chocolate to lighten the mixture. Fold in the remaining cream until blended.

4. Pour into a medium bowl, cover and refrigerate overnight.

5. To serve, coat 6 chilled dessert plates with Coffee Sauce. Using 2 cold serving spoons dipped in water, scoop 2 egg-shaped ovals of mousse onto each plate. Decorate with chocolate curls dusted with confectioners' sugar.

NOTE: To make chocolate curls, bring a block of dark chocolate to room temperature in a warm place. When just pliable, shave off curls with a swivel-bladed vegetable peeler.

Coffee Sauce

MAKES ABOUT 1½ CUPS

1½ cups milk
2 teaspoons instant coffee
1 tablespoon coffee liqueur, such as Tia Maria or Kahlua
4 egg yolks
2 tablespoons sugar
2 tablespoons heavy cream, lightly whipped

1. In a medium saucepan, scald the milk over moderately high heat. Cover and set aside.

2. In a small bowl, combine the instant coffee and the liqueur and stir until the coffee is dissolved.

3. In a medium bowl, whisk together the egg yolks, sugar and coffee mixture until thickened. Gradually whisk in the hot milk. Place the bowl over barely simmering water and cook, stirring, until the sauce is thickened, about 15 minutes; do not allow it to simmer. Remove from the heat and let cool to room temperature.

4. Stir in the cream. Cover and chill until ready to serve.

Lemon Butter Mousse

This fluffy, creamy, buttery mousse is very simple to make. It is a refreshing dessert.

🍷 **F&W Beverage Suggestion:** Sauternes, such as Château Rieussec

10 TO 12 SERVINGS

⅓ cup plus 3 tablespoons fresh lemon juice
1 teaspoon finely grated lemon zest
1 envelope (¼ ounce) unflavored gelatin
1 cup heavy cream
6 eggs, separated, at room temperature
¼ teaspoon salt
3 cups sifted confectioners' sugar
1 stick (¼ pound) unsalted butter, at room temperature

1. In a small bowl, stir together the ⅓ cup lemon juice and the lemon zest. Sprinkle on the gelatin and set aside to soften for 10 minutes. Set the bowl in a larger saucepan of hot water over low heat and stir to dissolve the gelatin. Remove from the heat and let cool to room temperature.

2. In a large bowl, whip the cream until just stiff. Cover and refrigerate until needed.

3. In a large bowl, combine the egg whites with the salt. Beat until soft peaks form. Gradually add 1 cup of the confectioners' sugar and beat until stiff peaks form.

4. In another large bowl, beat the butter until soft and fluffy. Add 1 cup of confectioners' sugar and beat until smooth. Add the egg yolks, one at a time, alternating them with the dissolved gelatin and the remaining 1 cup confectioners' sugar. Continue to beat until smooth. Fold in one-third of the egg whites. Quickly but gently fold in the remaining egg whites. Beat the remaining 3 tablespoons lemon juice into the whipped cream and fold into the mousse. Turn into a serving dish, cover and refrigerate until chilled and set, about 3 hours.

Easy Chocolate Mousse

This incredibly simple, velvety mousse can be made in 15 minutes. The better the quality of the chocolate used, the better the mousse.

2 SERVINGS

2½ ounces semisweet chocolate
1 cup heavy cream, chilled
½ teaspoon brandy, or more to taste
Unsweetened powdered cocoa, for garnish

1. In the top of a double boiler or in a small heavy saucepan, melt the chocolate over very low heat. Transfer to a medium bowl set in a larger bowl half filled with ice cubes.

2. Gradually pour in the cream, whisking constantly, until the mixture is thick and firm, about 10 minutes. Add the brandy and whisk until just blended. Spoon into two large parfait glasses. Just before serving, sieve a little cocoa on top.

Uncle Jim's New York-Style Cheesecake

At its best, cheesecake is so tender and moist that it quivers like custard when you slice and serve it. This recipe is baked very slowly in a water bath for a smooth, creamy texture.

12 SERVINGS

5 eggs, at room temperature
2 cups (1 pint) sour cream, at room temperature
4 packages (8 ounces each) cream cheese, at room temperature
1 stick (¼ pound) unsalted butter, at room temperature
1½ cups sugar
2 tablespoons cornstarch
1½ teaspoons vanilla extract
1 teaspoon grated lemon zest
1 teaspoon fresh lemon juice

1. Preheat the oven to 300°. Generously butter a 10-inch springform pan. Wrap a double layer of heavy-duty aluminum foil tightly around the bottom and sides of the pan, crimping and pleating the foil so that it conforms to the shape of the pan. Fold the top edge of the foil down so that it is even with the top edge of the pan.

2. Bring a large pot of water (about 4 quarts) to a boil.

3. Meanwhile, in a large mixer bowl, beat the eggs with the sour cream until well blended.

4. In a medium bowl, beat the cream cheese with the butter until creamy, smooth and slightly fluffy. Scrape into the egg-sour cream mixture and beat, starting on low speed and gradually increasing to high, until smooth.

5. Add the sugar, cornstarch, vanilla, lemon zest and lemon juice; beat on high speed until well blended and very smooth, 2 minutes.

6. Pour the cheese mixture into the prepared springform pan. Place in a roasting pan large enough to hold the springform without touching the sides and place in the oven. Carefully pour in enough boiling water to reach halfway up the sides of the springform pan.

7. Bake for 2 hours and 15 minutes, or until the cake is very lightly colored and a knife inserted in the center emerges clean; the cheesecake will have risen only slightly. Remove from the water bath and peel off the foil from around the pan. Let stand at room temperature until completely cool, about 4 hours. Refrigerate, covered, until ready to serve.

Crème Brûlée

8 SERVINGS

1 quart heavy cream
10 egg yolks
3 tablespoons granulated sugar
2 teaspoons vanilla extract
⅓ cup superfine sugar

1. Preheat the oven to 325°. In a medium saucepan, scald the cream over moderate heat. While the cream is heating, combine the egg yolks, granulated sugar and vanilla in a large bowl and beat with a wooden spoon for 1 minute. Beating constantly, slowly pour the hot cream into the egg mixture.

2. Pour the custard into a 6-cup soufflé dish. Place the dish in a roasting pan set in the middle of the oven. Pour enough hot water into the roasting pan to reach halfway up the sides of the soufflé dish.

3. Bake until the custard sets, 55 to 60 minutes. Remove the custard from the water bath. Let cool to room temperature. Cover and refrigerate until thoroughly chilled, at least 4 hours or overnight.

4. Adjust the rack of your broiler so that the top of the soufflé dish will be about 2 inches from the heating element. If necessary, place a rimmed baking sheet or a shallow container upside down on the rack to elevate the container to the proper height. Preheat the broiler for 15 minutes.

5. Sprinkle the superfine sugar evenly over the surface of the custard to cover completely without building up a thick layer. Place under the preheated broiler until the sugar caramelizes, 3 to 5 minutes. Watch carefully: once the sugar begins to caramelize, it may be necessary to rotate the dish once or twice if the broiler element is uneven so that the top will brown evenly. Adjust the rack if necessary to keep the sugar from burning.

6. Refrigerate uncovered for at least 1 hour or chill in a bowl of ice before serving.

Mocha Pots de Crème

Open a fresh jar of coffee to be sure of capturing the best flavor for this simple, delicious dessert.

6 SERVINGS

6 egg yolks
½ cup sugar
1½ cups heavy cream
½ cup milk
2 tablespoons instant coffee granules
Whipped cream (optional)

1. Preheat the oven to 325°. In a medium bowl, lightly whisk the egg yolks and ¼ cup of the sugar until smooth but not thick or frothy.

2. In a medium saucepan, combine the remaining ¼ cup sugar, the cream and milk. Bring to a boil over moderate heat. Immediately remove from the heat and stir in the coffee until dissolved.

3. Gradually stir the coffee mixture into the beaten egg yolks in a thin stream. Strain into a bowl. Skim off any surface bubbles.

4. Gently ladle the custard into six ½-cup pots de crème or small ramekins. Place in a baking dish, cover the individual dishes with lids, or loosely with a sheet of aluminum foil, and pour 1 inch of warm water into the baking dish.

5. Bake for 25 minutes, or until the custards are firm around the edges but still wobbly in the center (they will set when cool). Remove the dishes from the water bath and let cool to room temperature. Cover and refrigerate for 6 hours or overnight. Decorate with whipped cream if desired.

Raspberry Bavarian

10 SERVINGS

2 packages (10 ounces each) frozen raspberries in syrup, defrosted
2 envelopes unflavored gelatin
5 egg yolks
⅓ cup sugar
1½ cups milk
1 teaspoon vanilla extract
1 cup heavy cream, chilled
Raspberry Sauce (optional; p. 225)

1. In a blender or food processor, puree the raspberries and their syrup for 30 seconds. Press through a strainer to remove the seeds. There will be about 2 cups of puree.

2. Pour ½ cup of the puree into a small bowl. Sprinkle the gelatin over the top and set aside to soften.

3. Meanwhile, in a medium bowl, whisk together the egg yolks and sugar until they are thick and form a ribbon when the whisk is lifted, about 3 minutes.

4. In a heavy medium saucepan, scald the milk with the vanilla. Gradually whisk into the beaten eggs in a thin stream to form a custard.

5. Set a bowl of ice and water next to the stove. Pour the custard into a clean heavy saucepan. Cook over low heat, stir-ring constantly, until the custard is thick enough to coat the back of the spoon, 5 to 8 minutes; do not allow the custard to boil. Immediately place the saucepan in the ice water to prevent overcooking and stir for 1 minute. Remove from the ice water.

6. Add the softened gelatin to the warm custard, whisking until completely dissolved. Pour into a large bowl, preferably metal. Blend in the remaining raspberry puree.

7. Beat the cream until it doubles in volume and forms soft peaks.

8. Place the bowl of raspberry custard in the bowl of ice and water and fold with a rubber spatula, scraping in the chilled outer edges, until the mixture begins to thicken. Remove from the ice and fold in the cream. Rinse a 6-cup mold with cold water and shake out the excess. Turn the Bavarian into the rinsed mold, cover and refrigerate until set, 4 hours or overnight.

9. To unmold, tilt the mold and gently pull the edge of the custard with your fingers to break the vacuum. Plunge the mold almost to the top in a bowl of hot water for 1 to 3 seconds. Place a platter over the mold and invert; shake smartly several times to release. Serve with Raspberry Sauce if desired.

Steamed Pumpkin-Pecan Pudding with Ginger Sabayon

6 TO 8 SERVINGS

2 cups sifted all-purpose flour
1½ teaspoons baking soda
1 teaspoon salt
1½ teaspoons cinnamon
¾ teaspoon ground ginger
½ teaspoon freshly grated nutmeg
¼ teaspoon ground cloves
1 cup finely ground pecans (4 ounces)
3 eggs
1 cup firmly packed light brown sugar

¼ cup molasses

1½ cups unsweetened, solid-pack canned pumpkin

3 tablespoons unsalted butter, melted

Ginger Sabayon (recipe follows)

1. Sift the flour, baking soda, salt, cinnamon, ginger, nutmeg and cloves together into a large bowl; stir in the pecans.

2. In a mixer bowl, beat the eggs and brown sugar until thick and light, about 3 minutes at high speed. Slowly beat in the molasses and pumpkin.

3. Make a well in the center of the dry ingredients; dump in the pumpkin mixture and stir lightly just until combined (there will be some lumps but this is how it should be). Drizzle in the melted butter and stir lightly just to mix.

4. Pour the batter into a lavishly buttered 2-quart steamed pudding mold (preferably a fluted one) and snap the lid on tight (the inside of the lid should be well buttered, too). Lower the mold onto a rack or a folded towel in a kettle containing enough boiling water to reach about one-quarter of the way up the pudding mold.

5. Cover the kettle and steam the pudding for 2 hours, adding more boiling water, if necessary, to keep the level of the water from reducing too drastically. Keep the water at a good boil as the pudding steams.

6. When the pudding has steamed for 2 hours, transfer it to a wire rack and let stand upright, covered, for 15 minutes.

7. To serve, remove the lid from the pudding mold and invert the pudding onto a dessert platter. Decorate with sugar-frosted grapes or sprigs of holly, if desired. Whisk the sabayon for 5 to 10 seconds. Pour into a large heated sauceboat and pass separately.

Ginger Sabayon

MAKES ABOUT 2 CUPS

4 egg yolks

1 whole egg

½ cup sugar

½ cup fresh orange juice

2 tablespoons orange liqueur such as Grand Marnier

1 tablespoon finely minced preserved stem ginger* (see Note)

1 tablespoon preserved stem ginger liquid

*Available at specialty food shops

In the top of a large double boiler, place all of the ingredients and whisk slowly to combine. Set over simmering water and whisk slowly until the mixture begins to thicken and mount in volume. Continue to cook, whisking briskly, until the mixture is about the consistency of boiled icing and nearly fills the double boiler top, about 10 minutes. Remove from the heat and let the sabayon rest over the hot water 1 minute before serving.

NOTE: If the stem ginger is unavailable, use 1½ tablespoons finely minced crystallized ginger and omit the ginger liquid.

Chutney Steamed Pudding with Rum-Butter Sauce

6 SERVINGS

1 cup all-purpose flour

½ teaspoon baking soda

½ cup (1 stick) unsalted butter, cut into small pieces, at room temperature

½ cup firmly packed dark brown sugar

2 eggs, at room temperature

⅓ cup fruit chutney (see Note)

⅓ cup chopped walnuts

Confectioners' sugar, for garnish

Rum-Butter Sauce (recipe follows)

1. Generously butter and flour a 1-quart steamed pudding or kugelhopf mold; set aside. Choose a deep pot, large enough to afford good circulation around the mold, with a tight-fitting lid. Place a trivet or rack in the bottom of the pot; set aside. Put a kettle of water on to boil.

2. Sift the flour and baking soda onto a plate or a sheet of waxed paper; set aside.

3. In a medium bowl, cream the butter and sugar together with a wooden spoon until light and fluffy.

4. Place the eggs, chutney and walnuts in a food processor and process for 2 to 3 seconds just to mix; do not overmix or the nuts will be too fine. Gradually stir this mixture into the butter mixture. Gradually add the flour mixture about a third at a time, mixing after each addition.

5. Pour the batter into the prepared mold and tap the mold on the table a few times to settle the mixture. The mold will be only two-thirds full. Cover the mold with a fitted lid or a sheet of buttered waxed paper and a sheet of aluminum foil. Twist and crimp the foil tightly around the rim to seal. Place the pudding on the rack and add boiling water to reach halfway up the sides of the mold.

6. Cover the pot with a sheet of aluminum foil and the lid; steam over moderate heat for 1½ hours, replenishing the boiling water as needed about every 30 minutes. Insert a skewer into the center; it should come out almost clean. If wet batter clings to it, re-cover and steam the pudding a bit longer. Remove the pudding mold from the pot and let cool on a rack for 15 minutes. Invert onto a serving plate and tap lightly to loosen the pudding; let rest with the mold over it to keep warm until serving time. Sprinkle the pudding with confectioners' sugar and accompany with Rum-Butter Sauce.

NOTE: This pudding tastes best when made with a thick homemade peach, pear or gooseberry chutney. If none is available, use a commercially prepared one.

Rum-Butter Sauce

MAKES ABOUT 1 CUP

½ cup (1 stick) unsalted butter, at
  room temperature
¾ cup sifted confectioners' sugar
2 tablespoons dark rum
1 tablespoon grated orange zest
½ teaspoon freshly grated nutmeg

1. In a medium bowl, cream the butter and sugar together until light and fluffy. Gradually beat in the rum. Stir in the zest and nutmeg.

2. Transfer the mixture to a small serving crock and let stand in a cool place, covered with waxed paper, or refrigerate for longer storage. Let stand at room temperature until it's of a soft and spreadable consistency.

French Bread and Peanut Butter Pudding

Peanut butter fans will find this creamy, custardy pudding irresistible. Serve it warm with a dusting of confectioners' sugar, or pair it with vanilla ice cream for a delicious warm/cold combination.

12 SERVINGS

1 quart milk
2 cups heavy cream
2 tablespoons unsalted butter,
  softened
16 slices of French bread, cut ½ to
  ¾ inch thick, crusts removed
1 cup crunchy peanut butter
5 whole eggs
4 egg yolks
1 cup sugar
⅛ teaspoon salt
2 tablespoons vanilla extract

1. Preheat the oven to 350°. Lightly grease a deep 4-quart casserole.

2. In a large heavy saucepan, scald the milk and cream over moderate heat. Remove from the heat and set aside.

3. Meanwhile, lightly butter one side of the bread. Thickly spread the peanut butter over the butter. Arrange in the casserole, peanut butter side up, overlapping the slices slightly if necessary.

4. In a large bowl, beat the whole eggs, egg yolks, sugar and salt until well blended. Gradually whisk in the milk-cream mixture in a thin stream until well mixed. Whisk in the vanilla. Slowly pour the custard mixture evenly over the bread slices, which will float to the top.

5. Place the casserole in a roasting pan and center in the oven. Pour boiling water into the roasting pan until it reaches halfway up the sides of the casserole. Bake for 60 minutes, or until the pudding is not quite set in the center.

6. Transfer to a wire rack and let cool for at least 30 minutes before serving.

Palaçinke (Sweet Crêpes)

These orange- and lemon-flecked crêpes can be served warm for dessert, sprinkled with sugar and orange liqueur. They may also be spread with marmalade, jam or melted chocolate and eaten for breakfast or as a snack.

MAKES ABOUT 2 DOZEN 7-INCH CRÊPES

2 eggs, beaten
2½ cups milk
About 10 tablespoons sugar
½ teaspoon salt
1 tablespoon dark rum
1 teaspoon vanilla extract
Grated zest of 1 orange
Grated zest of 1 lemon
2 cups all-purpose flour
½ cup (1 stick) plus 4 tablespoons
  unsalted butter, melted
Vegetable oil
About ½ cup orange liqueur, such
  as Grand Marnier

1. In a large bowl, combine the eggs, milk, 6 tablespoons of the sugar, the salt,

rum, vanilla, and the orange and lemon zests; beat until blended.

2. Slowly add the flour. Stir in the melted butter and mix until the batter is smooth.

3. Brush a 7-inch crêpe pan or skillet with vegetable oil and place over moderate heat. When the pan is hot, pour in ¼ cup of batter; tilt and swirl to coat the bottom of the pan evenly; pour back any excess. Cook until the crêpe is light brown around the edges and on the bottom, about 2 minutes. Turn and cook until spotted brown on the second side, about 1 minute. Repeat with the remaining batter.

4. To serve, sprinkle each crêpe with about 1 teaspoon orange liqueur and ½ teaspoon sugar. Roll or fold into quarters; serve warm.

Fresh Berry and Toasted Oat Dessert (Cranachan)

This authentic Scottish recipe comes from a little town on the shores of Loch Lomond.

3 SERVINGS

1 cup rolled oats
1 cup heavy cream, chilled
1 tablespoon sugar
2 teaspoons Scotch whisky
1 pint fresh strawberries,
  quartered, or whole raspberries
  or blackberries

1. Preheat the oven to 400°. Spread the oats on an ungreased baking sheet. Bake for 10 to 12 minutes, shaking occasionally, until toasted and golden. Pour onto a plate and let cool.

2. Beat the cream until soft peaks form. Add the sugar and Scotch and continue beating until stiff peaks form. Fold in the toasted oats.

3. Layer the cream and berries into large wine glasses, beginning with a layer of cream and ending with a layer of berries on top. Serve immediately.

Strawberry Shortbread

The combination of fresh sliced strawberries, whipped cream and buttery shortbread is one that appeals to nearly everyone. The crisp, wedge-shaped servings here are generous. The two circular shortbread layers may be baked a day ahead. The strawberries may be sliced and sugared and the cream whipped several hours ahead. Once assembled, the shortbread should be eaten promptly, or the bottom crust will become soft.

8 SERVINGS

2 sticks (½ pound) unsalted butter, softened
½ teaspoon vanilla extract
¾ cup sugar
3 cups all-purpose flour
2½ pints fresh strawberries, sliced
2 cups (1 pint) heavy cream, chilled
2 teaspoons orange liqueur, such as Grand Marnier, Cointreau or Triple Sec
Confectioners' sugar, for garnish

1. In a mixer bowl, beat the butter with the vanilla until creamy and light. Gradually add ½ cup plus 1 tablespoon of the sugar and beat until the sugar dissolves, about 4 minutes. Slowly add the flour ¼ cup at a time, beating until smooth.

2. Turn the dough out onto a lightly floured surface and knead for 1 minute, until a smooth ball forms. Divide the dough in half. Shape the halves into 6-inch disks; wrap and refrigerate at least 30 minutes. (**The dough can be made up to 2 days ahead.**)

3. Preheat the oven to 350°. Line two large cookie sheets with aluminum foil.

4. To form each shortbread layer, place a disk of dough between 2 sheets of waxed paper. Roll out into a circle about 12 inches in diameter and ⅛ inch thick. Remove the top sheet of paper and center an 11-inch pie pan on the dough. Run the tip of a paring knife around the pan's edge to cut the dough. Lift the pan off and discard the trimmings.

5. Invert one circle of dough onto one of the cookie sheets and peel off the waxed paper. Invert the second disk of dough onto the other cookie sheet. Prick both of the circles all over with a fork. Lightly score 1 of the circles into 8 equal wedges, cutting only about halfway through the dough.

6. Bake for 15 minutes, until the circles are pale golden. Remove from the oven and let cool for 10 minutes, then transfer with two large spatulas to a wire rack.

7. Set aside 1 cup of the prettiest strawberry slices for garnish. Place the remaining berries in a medium bowl. Toss with 2 tablespoons of the remaining sugar.

8. Whip the cream until soft peaks form. Add the remaining 1 tablespoon sugar and the orange liqueur and beat until stiff peaks form.

9. To assemble the dessert, place the unmarked shortbread circle bottom-side up on a large platter. Using a slotted spoon, spread the sugared berries in an even layer over the shortbread. Reserve 1½ cups of the whipped cream. Spread the rest of the whipped cream evenly over the berries. Carefully center the marked shortbread circle, bottom-side down, on top of the whipped cream. Arrange the remaining strawberries on top of the shortbread. Dust the top with confectioners' sugar.

10. With a pastry bag fitted with a star tip, use the remaining whipped cream to pipe stars around the edge of the shortbread between the top and bottom crusts, or place in a bowl and pass separately. Use a serrated cake knife to slice the shortbread wedges.

Poires Belle Hélène

4 SERVINGS

3 cups plus 1 tablespoon sugar
2 teaspoons vanilla extract
4 Bartlett or Bosc pears, peeled
4 ounces dark chocolate (semisweet, bittersweet or sweet), coarsely chopped
3 tablespoons unsalted butter
¾ cup heavy cream
1 pint vanilla ice cream, slightly softened
Candied violets, for decoration

1. In a medium saucepan, cook 3 cups of the sugar and 3 cups of water over moderate heat, stirring until the sugar dissolves. Increase the heat to high and boil for 2 minutes. Reduce the heat to moderately low. Add 1 teaspoon of the vanilla and the pears. Cover and poach for 20 to 30 minutes, until the pears are tender but still slightly resistant to a fork.

2. Remove the pears from the syrup and let cool to room temperature. Refrigerate the syrup until chilled.

3. Remove the cores from the cooled pears from the bottom, leaving the tops intact. Return to the syrup and refrigerate, covered, until ready to use.

4. In a small heavy saucepan, combine the chocolate, butter, ¼ cup of the cream, the remaining 1 tablespoon sugar and ¼ cup of water. Bring to a boil over low heat. Simmer until the sauce is thick and smooth, about 5 minutes. Add the remaining 1 teaspoon vanilla and remove from the heat.

5. To assemble, divide the ice cream among 4 chilled dessert dishes. Place the pears on top of the ice cream (hold in the freezer up to 15 minutes at this point if necessary).

6. Beat the remaining ½ cup cream until stiff peaks form. Using a pastry bag with a star tip, pipe the whipped cream around the base of the pears. Decorate with candied violets.

7. Rewarm the chocolate sauce slightly if it has cooled and pass separately or drizzle over the pears just before serving.

Poached Pears in Orange Sauce

6 SERVINGS

2 tablespoons fresh lemon juice
6 large ripe Bosc or Bartlett pears
4 cups orange juice
¼ cup liquid fructose*
1 cinnamon stick
1 teaspoon vanilla extract
¾ cup orange liqueur, such as Cointeau or Grand Marnier
½ cup Cognac or brandy
Zest of 1 orange, cut into thin julienne strips
Fresh mint leaves, for garnish
*Available at health food stores

1. Fill a large bowl with cold water and stir in the lemon juice. Peel the pears and drop into the acidulated water to prevent discoloration

2. In a large saucepan, combine the orange juice, fructose, cinnamon stick, vanilla, ½ cup of the orange liqueur and the brandy. Bring to a simmer over moderately low heat

3. Drain the pears and add them to the saucepan. Simmer until the pears are tender when pierced with a sharp knife, 25 minutes to 1 hour, depending on the type of pear and degree of ripeness. Remove the pears with a slotted spoon, cover loosely and let cool.

4. Meanwhile, boil the poaching liquid until reduced to about 1½ cups of syrup.

5. In a small heavy saucepan, bring the remaining ¼ cup orange liqueur to a boil. Add the orange zest and reduce the heat to moderately low. Cover and simmer until the zest is soft, about 15 minutes. Add to the reduced syrup.

6. To serve, spoon 4 tablespoons of syrup over each pear and garnish with a fresh mint leaf at the stem.

Poached Bartlett Pears with Vanilla Custard Sauce

4 SERVINGS

Poached Pears:
4 cups sugar
½ vanilla bean
4 ripe Bartlett pears

Custard Sauce:
2 cups milk
4 egg yolks
⅓ cup sugar
¼ teaspoon salt
1 teaspoon vanilla extract

1. Poach the pears: In a large saucepan, combine the sugar and vanilla bean with 2 quarts of water. Simmer over moderate heat to make a light syrup while preparing the pears.

2. One at a time, peel the pears, leaving them whole with the stems intact. As they are peeled, add to the simmering syrup and cover the saucepan. Repeat until all the pears have been peeled and put into the syrup. Simmer, covered, until the pears are soft, but still hold their shape, about 25 minutes. Remove the pan from the heat and let the pears cool in the syrup while you make the custard sauce.

3. Make the sauce: Scald the milk in a heavy 2-quart saucepan.

4. In a medium bowl, lightly beat the

egg yolks with the sugar and salt until blended. Slowly stir in the scalded milk. Return the mixture to the saucepan and cook over low heat, stirring constantly, until the custard is thick enough to coat the spoon heavily, 7 to 10 minutes.

5. Immediately place the saucepan in a bowl of cold water and stir for about 2 minutes to stop the cooking. Stir in the vanilla and let cool to room temperature. Pour into a serving bowl and pass with the pears.

Blueberry Kissel

Kissel is a tart pureed fruit dessert from Russia, which is generally made with berries and has a thickish consistency in between pudding and gelatin. Prepare this winy-dark sweet only when blueberries are at their flavorful peak—during late June, July and August.

6 SERVINGS

2 pints blueberries
4 to 6 tablespoons sugar
2 tablespoons plus 2 teaspoons cornstarch
3 to 4 tablespoons orange liqueur, such as Grand Marnier
⅓ cup sour cream

1. Set aside a few berries for each dessert glass as a garnish. In a blender or food processor, puree the remaining berries to a fine consistency.

2. Press the blueberry puree through a fine sieve into a noncorrodible saucepan and stir in 4 tablespoons of sugar. Blend the cornstarch with ½ cup of water and add it to the puree. Stir over low heat until the sugar dissolves. Taste and add up to 2 tablespoons more sugar, to taste (remember that the orange liqueur will add a bit of sweetness).

3. Continue stirring over low heat until the mixture comes to a full boil. Remove from the heat and stir in the liqueur to taste, adding a tiny bit more than tastes right, as the flavor is dulled by chilling.

4. Spoon the mixture into 6 stemmed dessert or wine glasses. Cool to room temperature, cover and chill for at least 3 hours.

5. To serve, spoon the sour cream over the desserts and top with the reserved blueberries.

Baked Apples with Raspberry Vinegar

The raspberry vinegar is a sprightly addition to these homey baked apples.

6 SERVINGS

3 large, firm baking apples, such as Rome Beauty or Pippin
2 tablespoons light brown sugar
1 tablespoon raspberry vinegar
2 tablespoons unsalted butter, melted

1. Preheat the oven to 375°. Wash and dry the apples. Cut in half crosswise and scoop out the seeds with a melon baller or teaspoon; do not dig through the apple. Place the apple halves, cut-side up, in a baking dish. Take care that they do not tip; trim a slice from the bottoms if necessary.

2. Fill each cavity with 1 teaspoon of the sugar and ½ teaspoon of the vinegar. Brush the cut surfaces with the melted butter.

3. Pour ½ cup of hot water into the bottom of the baking dish and bake for 30 to 45 minutes, until tender. Add additional water if water evaporates during baking.

4. Let cool until just warm and serve with whipped cream or a custard sauce.

Ginger-Glazed Oranges

For this light dessert, the bright color of thinly sliced orange rounds is enhanced with a marmalade glaze, spiced with the tang of ground ginger. Fresh mint, scattered on top, is a pretty contrast.

6 SERVINGS

5 large navel oranges
½ cup bitter orange marmalade
1¼ teaspoons ground ginger
3 tablespoons chopped fresh mint
Mint sprigs, for garnish

1. Cut the peel and underlying mem-
brane off the oranges in lengthwise strips, following the shape of the fruit. Slice the peeled oranges crosswise into thin rounds and arrange, overlapping, on a small serving platter.

2. In a small heavy saucepan, combine the marmalade with ¼ cup of water. Melt, stirring occasionally, over low heat. Stir in the ginger and bring the glaze to a boil. Remove from the heat and press through a sieve.

3. Brush the glaze over the sliced oranges. Scatter the chopped mint over the top and decorate with sprigs of mint.

Compote of Prunes and Oranges

4 SERVINGS

¾ cup pitted prunes
¾ cup fresh orange juice
3 small navel oranges
¼ cup amber or dark rum
1 tablespoon light molasses
½ cup plain yogurt

1. In a noncorrodible medium saucepan, combine the prunes and orange juice. Strip off the zest from about half of one of the oranges and add this to the saucepan along with the rum and molasses. Bring the mixture to a simmer, stirring constantly.

2. Cover and simmer over moderately low heat until the prunes are soft, but not falling apart, about 20 minutes. Scrape into a serving dish, remove the orange strips and refrigerate until serving time.

3. At serving time, peel all of the oranges. Halve the oranges lengthwise, then cut across into thin semicircles. Add to the prunes. Serve the yogurt on the side.

Prunes in Red Wine and Armagnac

The prunes must steep for two days, so plan accordingly.

10 SERVINGS

2 tablespoons plus 1 teaspoon dried lemon verbena*
2 cups strong red wine (see Note)
Zest of ½ orange, cut into julienne strips
Zest of ½ lemon, cut into julienne strips
¼ cup fresh orange juice
1½ tablespoons fresh lemon juice
2 tablespoons sugar
1 vanilla bean, split lengthwise
1½ pounds moist pitted prunes
¾ cup Armagnac or other brandy

*Available in specialty food stores

1. In a small bowl, pour 1 cup of boiling water over 2 tablespoons of the verbena. Cover and let infuse for at least 15 minutes.

2. Meanwhile, in a medium noncorrodible saucepan, bring the wine to a boil over high heat. Ignite with a match and let the alcohol burn off, gently shaking the pan over the heat. Add the orange and lemon zests and juices and boil for 5 minutes.

3. Add the sugar, vanilla bean and the remaining teaspoon of dried verbena. Strain the verbena infusion into the red wine mixture. Stir in the prunes. Return to the boil and cook for 5 minutes. Remove from the heat and let cool to room temperature.

4. Stir in the Armagnac. Cover loosely and let steep in a cool place for 2 days. The prunes are then ready to serve (½ cup per person) or will keep sealed and refrigerated for at least a month.

NOTE: In order to flame the wine in Step 2, it should be at least 14 percent alcohol. Use a good strong wine such as a Côtes-du-Rhône, California Petite Sirah or Barolo.

A tart and lemony slice of Uncle Jim's Lemon Meringue Pie (p. 198).

A tempting assortment of old-fashioned desserts: Angel Food Cake with Orange-Almond Cream (p. 209), Strawberry Shortbread (p. 182), Lemon Chiffon Pie with Almond Praline (p. 199), Uncle Jim's New York-Style Cheesecake (p. 178) and American Chocolate Cake with Fudge Frosting (p. 208).

ANGEL FOOD CAKE
with
ORANGE-ALMOND CREAM

LEMON CHIFFON PIE
with
ALMOND PRALINE

UNCLE JIM'S
NEW YORK-STYLE
CHEESECAKE

STRAWBERRY
SHORTBREAD

LEMON CHIFFON PIE
with
ALMOND PRALINE

AMERICAN
CHOCOLATE CAKE
with
FUDGE FROSTING

*Left, Filbert-Ginger Ring Torte with Fresh Fruit
(p. 213). Above, Strawberry Cake (p. 205).*

Left, Lemon Celebration Cake (p. 203).
Above, top, Vacherin (p. 172);
bottom, Poires Belle Hélène (p. 182).